Dog-Friendly
NEW ENGLAND
A Traveler's Companion

Dog-Friendly NEW ENGLAND

A Traveler's Companion

Trisha Blanchet

The Countryman Press
Woodstock, Vermont

Library of Congress Cataloging-in-Publication Data
Blanchet, Trisha
     Dog-friendly New England : a traveler's companion / Trisha
     Blanchet.—1st ed.
          p. cm.
     ISBN 0-88150-569-2
     1. Travel with dogs—New England—Guidebooks. 2. Hotels—Pet
accommodations—New England—Directories. 3. Motels—Pet accommodations—New England—Directories. 4. New England—Guidebooks. I. Title.

SF427.4574.N427 B63 2003
917.4'044—dc21

2002192506

Book design, maps, and composition by Hespenheide Design
Maps © 2003 The Countryman Press
Cover photo © Kindra Clineff
All interior photographs by the author

Published by The Countryman Press,
P.O. Box 748, Woodstock, Vermont 05091

Distributed by W. W. Norton & Company, Inc.,
500 Fifth Avenue, New York, NY 10110

Printed in the United States of America

10 9 8 7 6 5 4 3

For Duncan and Oly

Heartfelt thanks

to Scott, Mom, Dad, and Tricia
for your help and company
on the road

CONTENTS

Introduction

Admit it—you throw birthday parties for your dog. You have a picture of him in your wallet and another one, framed, on your desk. You say the words *shmoopy, woopy,* or *poopie* at least once a day (and don't mind). Maybe it's a poodle that you pine for, or a bloodhound, or a mutt. The breed doesn't really matter. The truth is, you're a dog lover. And the dog you love the most is your own.

But you're also a normal, social human being, one who wouldn't mind getting away once in a while to see new places, meet new people, and escape the daily grind. So you try to make vacation plans, and quickly learn a hard truth: There are some people in the world, in fact many people, who don't enjoy the company of a 75-pound shedding, drooling canine. These people may say they would rather you *didn't* bring Fido to their hotel, B&B, campground, or cottage. They may be very adamant on that point. You make call after call, continue to come into contact with this strange breed of humans, and finally come to the conclusion that you've got two choices: You can give in to those chocolate-brown, sad eyes and skip the vacation altogether, or you can hit the road and leave your furry friend in a (gulp) kennel. For a whole week. Alone.

Luckily for us, it doesn't have to come to that. From the Green Mountains of Vermont to the posh digs of Boston, there are many small and large, inexpensive and extravagant accommodations in New England that allow and even welcome animals. There are also bookstores, outdoor restaurants, tour boats, and countless other businesses that cater to furry, scaled, or feathered clientele. The only problem is that many don't advertise their pet-friendly status, so they have, in the past, been difficult to find. But not anymore.

Dog-Friendly New England is designed to take you on a four-legged tour of every region of Connecticut, Maine, Massachusetts, New Hampshire, Rhode Island, and Vermont. Within each region, you'll find pet-friendly overnight accommodations in every style and price range, restaurants that offer outdoor seating or take-out service, parks and historic sites where animals are allowed, and even doggie day-care centers, groomers, and pet shops. From here on in, your family vacations can include *every* member of the family—

even the one that likes to stick his head out the window on the
way there.

ACCOMMODATIONS

Few things can make or break a vacation like the roof over your
head. Each of us has a different expectation of the "perfect" accommodation: Some prefer to be left on their own, cook their own
meals, and bask in a rustic, unadorned atmosphere; others want
pampering, personal attention, gourmet breakfasts, and a concierge.
Or maybe you're searching for something in between.

Bringing an animal along changes the equation a bit, but it shouldn't
alter your plans and hopes for a great trip. The bad news is, roughly
85 to 90 percent of New England accommodations *don't* allow dogs.
The good news is that our beautiful region has a lot of accommodations to start with, so the 10 or 15 percent that do accept pets
offer plenty of wonderful choices. This book divides them into the
following categories:

MANY INNKEEPERS HAVE RESIDENT DOGS THAT WELCOME CANINE GUESTS.

Hotels, Motels, Inns, and Bed & Breakfasts

This is the largest group and includes everything from luxury and chain hotels to the tiniest B&Bs with one or two guest rooms. In general, inns are more intimate than standard hotels but don't include breakfast in the rates (though some do). Rates are comparable at all three types, depending on the location. Hotels typically appeal to those who prefer to know in advance precisely what they're getting and enjoy their privacy and anonymity; with a B&B or inn, you can expect to get to know the hosts, share a main entrance and living areas, and perhaps sit down to breakfast with other guests. Motels, motor inns, efficiencies, and "housekeeping cottages" (meaning that you do your own cleaning) are the most affordable accommodations in each region—and you'll notice that some regions have more to offer than others. The efficiencies and cottages are usually rented by the week, though you can also sometimes rent them by the night upon request.

Campgrounds

Always a popular standby with pet owners, New England campgrounds offer a surprisingly diverse range of experiences. Some simply provide a place to park your RV; others are full-fledged "resorts" with daily scheduled activities, recreation halls, hot showers, and heated swimming pools. The privately owned facilities tend to cater to families; the state-run campgrounds have fewer amenities and usually appeal to those seeking a more secluded, quiet escape.

Sport Camps

Sport camps differ drastically from traditional campgrounds in that they're designed specifically with hunters and fishermen in mind. The accommodations, usually cabins, are simple and rustic; guests typically purchase a meal plan and dine together in a common hall or room. Hunting and fishing guides are often available to lead groups onto the water or into the wilderness. In New England, the camps are found almost exclusively in northern Maine and New Hampshire.

Homes, Cottages, and Cabins for Rent

If you're seeking a getaway of a week or longer, renting a private home, cottage, cabin, or apartment can be a convenient and comfortable alternative to a hotel. In most cases, the renter will have to contact the homeowner directly to check on availability and may have to answer a few questions about the number of people in the party and the personality and type of pet that's coming along. Most owners require a standard security deposit; many ask for an additional deposit against pet damage.

Rental Agencies

Perhaps you have special requests or requirements or are just having trouble locating the type of lodging you want: In either case, rental agencies can often help. Some are simply listing services; others are traditional real estate agencies that also dabble in vacation rentals. Costs vary from nothing at all to a hefty finder's fee—make sure you're clear on the charges before starting the search process.

IN THE DOGHOUSE

So why do so few hotel/motel/B&B owners allow pets? The majority cite "guests' allergies" as the most common reason for their humans-only policies. But many also point to factors that have nothing to do with physical health and everything to do with quality of life. Among those who used to permit pets but stopped, those who allow pets now but are considering changing that policy, and even those who happily allow pets, there are several common complaints that come up again and again when discussing the issue of traveling animals. These mistakes lead to anger on the part of innkeepers and frustration on the part of conscientious pet owners, who are left to bear the brunt of others' irresponsibility. There are other concerns, of course, but these rank as the top five:

1. **Not cleaning up after your animal.** Few things are more disconcerting or disgusting than stumbling across a little

A Note about the Pet-Friendly Ratings

Each region has been given a pet-friendly rating that ranges from one to five biscuits. The rating is not simply a reflection of the number of pet-friendly accommodations in that region (though a high number certainly helps); instead, it is intended to give pet owners a feel for the overall experience they might enjoy while visiting. For example, will you have a wide selection of types of accommodations, or will you be stuck in a campground when you wanted an inn? Will you have to avoid the region's most popular attractions, or will you be able to participate fully in the vacation experience of that area? The ratings are not intended to disparage or tout any particular areas, but merely to point out that some regions offer a more well-rounded, comfortable, and relaxing experience for pet owners.

"present" left by an animal—especially when you're in your own yard, driveway, or walking path and you don't own a pet. This is far and away the greatest complaint that lodging owners and the general public have with pets in their communities. There's a simple solution, of course; nevertheless, some pet owners still refuse to carry pooper-scooper bags and dispose of the mess. We've all seen it happen, even on trails with posted fines where scooper bags are provided.

2. **Leaving your pet alone in the room or at the campsite.** "My dog doesn't bark." "My cat would never claw at the furniture." Uh huh. We'd all like to think that—and maybe it's true, when we're around. But who knows what our pets do when they're alone in a strange place? Lodging owners say *they* know, and they've learned the hard way. This is one of the most common reasons lodging managers give for changing their pet-friendly policies: No one wants to pay $150 per night to listen to someone else's dog whine, whimper, and bark for hours on end.

3. **Letting your animal sleep or sit on the furniture.** For many of us, it is perfectly acceptable and natural to let our dog curl up next to us on the couch or sleep at the end of the bed. But for innkeepers trying to control dander and allergens, pet hair and upholstery usually don't mix. (Many maintain hardwood floors in designated pet rooms specifically for this

reason.) In addition, many B&Bs and hotels pride themselves on providing a decor filled with fine furnishings and price-less antiques—most likely, they didn't intend for them to be used as doggie beds or kitty scratching posts. If you antici-pate a problem in this area, bring along your own bedspread and towels to cover and protect your host's furniture.

4. **Not adhering to leash requirements.** Most innkeepers who require dogs to be on a leash on their property have a good reason: Maybe they have cats. Maybe the home has residents or visitors who are afraid of animals. Maybe they have a prized flower garden to protect. In any case, letting your pooch have free rein isn't likely to endear you to the owners. Some innkeepers, on the other hand, don't mind; but be sure to ask before setting Fluffy free.

5. **Leaving the place in a shambles.** At best, this can result in disarray. At worst, total destruction. One B&B owner described a situation in which a guest's large dog knocked over a TV set, smashing it, and left mud caked all over the furniture. The guest then checked out and drove away quickly before the owner could discover the damage. A manager of a large chain hotel described a guest who washed his dog in the tub and clogged the drain with hair, and the bathwater flooded the floor. Another innkeeper said he was shocked to discover that two dogs staying with him had never been treated with flea and tick preventative medication; he spent hundreds of dollars ridding his home of fleas after they left.

A Note about Rates and Pet-Friendly Policies

Few things change more quickly in the tourism industry than rates. Often, they vary from season to season and year to year. Pet-friend-ly (or -unfriendly) policies also undergo subtle or dramatic changes: An innkeeper may have a bad experience with a four-legged guest and abruptly reverse his animal-friendly rules. One hotel owner might decide to raise her fees for pet guests, while another might choose to do away with pet fees altogether. It is always a good idea to ask directly about fees and policies before making a reservation; it also never hurts to ask if the owners have any specific requests or requirements for their animal guests.

Of course, these strange cases are the exceptions to the rule. But we can all do little things to make cleanup easier on our hosts—and make them more likely to continue inviting animals into their homes, hotels, and campgrounds.

If enough of us avoid these common mistakes, hopefully the list of pet-friendly accommodations choices will grow as we change naysayers' minds about the joys—and feasibility—of traveling with a furry friend in tow.

OUT AND ABOUT

You've done it: You've found a great pet-friendly place to stay, unloaded the car, and unpacked your bags. Now what?

Each region of New England is filled with fascinating, fun, and historic things to do and see. Some of them, such as museums, boutiques, and go-cart tracks, are unfortunately off-limits to your pet. But others, including parks, walking tours, and old-fashioned sight-seeing, are not. The "Out and About" section is designed to be a starting point in your animal-friendly explorations of each region; only attractions that allow pets are included. It is not, by any stretch, a complete listing of all there is to explore (we'd need one book per region to cover that). For each attraction, you'll also find a phone number, address, and, in some cases, a web site to visit for more information. These are only the highlights; by starting down the big roads, you'll inevitably stumble upon the quiet corners and fascinating people that make New England such an intriguing place to visit.

QUICK BITES

If you've ever tried to travel with your pet, you may have noticed that one of the most difficult aspects of your trip was eating—or not eating, as the case may be. Unless you've lined up a pet-sitter or kennel, you can pretty much rule out dining in any restaurant that requires you to sit inside and order from a waiter or waitress. And in most cases you can also rule out leaving your favorite pooch in

A Note about Breeds

You may have heard it said that there are no bad breeds, only bad owners. Veterinary professionals and those working in animal welfare—not to mention countless satisfied pit bull owners—tend to agree with that hypothesis. Nevertheless, many campground and hotel owners maintain pet-friendly policies that exclude certain breeds: most commonly pit bulls (Staffordshire bull terriers), rottweilers, and German shepherds. In some cases, the innkeepers are adhering to insurance policy restrictions; in other cases, they chose to initiate the restrictions on their own. Whatever the case, owners of these particular breeds might want to double-check breed-specific policies before arriving with Rover in tow: Fairly or not, it is possible to be turned away at the door. In most cases it is better to be up front with the innkeepers than to have vacation plans ruined at the last minute.

the car. (Heat and cold can reach extremes inside a vehicle and cause severe injury and even death.) Fasting is probably not an option. So where does that leave you? The "Quick Bites" section lists places in each region that offer outdoor seating and take-out: In some cases, that means running inside a restaurant to order sandwiches or pizza; in others, it might mean ordering ice cream or fried clams from a take-out window or sitting at an outdoor café.

Like "Out and About," this section isn't intended to be a complete listing of all dining choices in a region, but simply a place to get started. While some outdoor eateries do offer upscale and even gourmet items, it's important to note that these are, in most cases, truly "quick bites." Also, it's always a good idea to check with the manager or host/hostess before seating yourself and your pet, even in outdoor areas; pet-friendly policies change frequently, and local health codes may prevent the restaurant from serving you and Rover together.

HOT SPOTS FOR SPOT

Like traveling with young children, vacationing with animals comes with a unique set of challenges. Running out of cat food isn't a reason to panic—unless your finicky feline only eats one hard-to-find brand. Or maybe you have your heart set on visiting the renowned art museum at your vacation destination, and pets aren't allowed inside. Or perhaps your cocker spaniel got sprayed by a skunk on one of your hikes at the state park and you're suddenly in need of a groomer. Fast.

You've worked long and hard to save and plan for this vacation, and there's no need to let any of these or similar scenarios ruin your day or your trip. In the "Hot Spots for Spot" section, you'll find specialty pet shops, doggie day-care centers, pet-sitters, groomers, kennels, and other animal-centered businesses in each region. These pet professionals will be happy to keep an eye on your animal or provide much-needed supplies. Pet owners should note, however, that a listing in this book is not tantamount to a recommendation: Whenever possible, take the time to speak with the staff, check out the web site, tour the facilities, and form your own judgments before leaving your animal in the care of others.

IN CASE OF EMERGENCY

You probably, hopefully, won't need them. But in case of an accident or illness, the veterinary hospitals listed in each region should help you locate a nearby veterinarian. Though they represent just a sampling of the total number of animal clinics available, the listings provide a geographically scattered selection—no matter what part of the region you're in, you should find a veterinarian not too far away.

MUST-HAVES

Your animal no doubt has a favorite toy, treat, or blanket that you wouldn't dream of leaving behind. While you're packing it away, stash these ever-important items, too:

- **Vaccination certificates and/or vet records:** Many hotel, campground, and kennel owners require vaccination certificates and/or vet records as a condition of admittance, but not all will

A Note about Motion Sickness

Pets unfortunately can suffer from this dreaded travel affliction as often as people do. If you've never hit the road with your animal before, you might want to speak to your veterinarian beforehand about possible medications and strategies to combat queasiness. In addition, it never hurts to have paper towels and upholstery cleaner somewhere in the car, just in case.

let you know that beforehand. (Strange, but true.) A certificate of rabies vaccination is the most commonly requested, although some lodging and kennel owners also ask to see proof of protection against heartworm and kennel cough. It's almost a sure bet that at least one person will ask to see your pet's vaccination records at some point during your trip. Most pet owners assume that their animal's collar tags will be proof enough of vaccinations, but that's not usually the case. To be on the safe side, have copies of your records made and bring them with you in case the innkeeper is required, by an insurance company for example, to keep the records on file.

- **Crate/kennel:** Even if your dog hasn't stepped foot in a crate since the day she was house-trained, it's always a good idea to have one along. For safety reasons, some innkeepers require that pets be crated when left alone in the room (though most don't allow pets to be left alone at all). As with other policies, you might not learn this one until you arrive at your destination, so having a crate on hand just in case can alleviate a lot of aggravation.

- **Towels, towels, towels:** Simply stated, you can never have enough. Aside from the fact that it's just courteous to wipe your pet's feet before he muddies up your innkeeper's Oriental rugs, some accommodations' owners actually require this. And you'll be happy to have them after Rover finishes up his romp in the pond or his run through dubious puddles on city streets. Some pet owners find it helpful to line their car seats with towels or other coverings before hitting the road—especially if their animal has a tendency to suffer from motion sickness.

- **Water and water bowls:** You can buy fancy water totes and portable bowls at a pet store or simply carry a couple of plastic bottles and a plastic bowl: Either way, make sure to always have an ample supply of H_2O and something for Spot to drink out of. (Water is equally important in the winter as in the summer.) It sounds like common sense, but it can be easy to forget this detail in the flurry of packing and traveling.

- **Pooper-scooper bags:** This is undoubtedly one of life's least-pleasant chores. Still, unless you want to be public enemy number one, make sure to have the necessary picker-upper tools when your pet takes bathroom breaks. Squeamish animal owners can take advantage of the newer bags with wire rims: Your hand never gets too close to the yucky stuff.

- **A spare bag of food:** This can become especially important if you're visiting rural areas, if your travel plans have an indefinite length, or if your pet is a finicky eater. It's better to return home with an unused bag than to be stuck with a hungry pooch in a one-stoplight town.

- **Treats and chew toys:** Traveling brings many lulls, both anticipated and unwelcome. If your dog is used to running around a yard, she might have a hard time being cooped up in a car for hours on end or spending the evening quietly sitting in an antiques-filled guest room. Rawhide bones and other chewy treats may help to keep your pet occupied and happy.

Now that all the details are taken care of, just roll down the window, turn up the radio, and enjoy the New England welcome waggin'. From covered bridges to majestic mountains, seacoast shanties to urban adventures, America's six northeasternmost states are always surprising, always welcoming, and always full of adventure—for any species. After all, dogs love chowdah, too.

Connecticut

Eastern & Central Connecticut

PET-FRIENDLY RATING: 🦴 🦴 🦴 🦴

This multifaceted region offers the best of both worlds for urbanites and solitude seekers: In just a few days you can visit the busy capital city of Hartford, the farms and orchards of the state's northeast Quiet Corner, and the lobster shacks of Mystic and the seacoast—not to mention Connecticut's famous (or infamous?) gambling meccas: Foxwoods and Mohegan Sun.

With the exception of the casinos, where pets are not allowed in any of the hotels or on the property, animal owners will have a fairly easy time getting around and seeing the sights. A good number of chain hotels, motels, and independent B&Bs welcome four-footed travelers, and the area's parks and attractions offer more than enough natural diversions to fill a relaxing and fun vacation. (One of the region's best-known attractions, the Mystic Seaport living-history museum, welcomes companion animals; see "Out and About.") Connecticut isn't traditionally a big tourism draw for New Englanders—Boston-area residents, for example, tend to head north on vacation—but the state's proximity to New York City makes it popular with visitors from the Big Apple, looking for changing leaves, campgrounds, quiet getaways, and colonial charm.

ACCOMMODATIONS

Hotels, Motels, Inns, and Bed & Breakfasts

Berlin

Hawthorne Inn, 2387 Wilbur Cross Highway, Berlin (860-828-4181); $97–101 per night. The Hawthorne Inn's amenities include 70 guest rooms, a swimming pool, a restaurant and lounge, free continental breakfasts daily, a fitness center, computer access, cable TV, and in-room refrigerators, hair dryers, irons, and ironing boards. Well-behaved pets are welcome without extra fees.

Chester

Inn at Chester, 318 West Main Street, Chester (860-526-9541; 1-800-949-7829; innkeeper@innat chester.com; www.innatchester. com); $105–215 per night. In addition to its 42 guest rooms with private baths, this historic inn also provides its visitors with a tavern, a fitness room, tennis courts, a library, antique furnishings, a pool table, darts and board games, and bicycles for borrowing. **Cockaponset State Forest** is next door. Pets are welcome for an additional $25 per stay (not per night).

Dayville

Holiday Inn Express Dayville, 16 Tracy Road, Dayville (860-779-3200; 1-800-HOLIDAY); $59–129 per night. Guest rooms, suites, a restaurant and lounge, cable TV, a fitness center, and an indoor swimming pool are available at this Holiday Inn Express in eastern Connecticut. Pet owners sign a pet-policy form at check-in and pay an additional $10 per night.

East Hartford

Holiday Inn East Hartford, 363 Roberts Street, East Hartford (860-528-9611); $55–139 per night. Guests at this Holiday Inn enjoy air-conditioning, a restaurant and lounge, laundry facilities, in-room coffeemakers and hair dryers, wake-up calls, and photocopying and fax services. Two pets are allowed per room. Pet owners pay a $275 refundable security deposit; animal must be crated if left alone in the room.

East Windsor

Holiday Inn Express Bradley Airport, 260 Main Street, East Windsor (860-627-6585; 1-800-432-0504); $97–115 per night. For an extra $25 per stay (not per night), pets are welcome guests at this 115-room airport hotel. Amenities include a complimentary airport shuttle, a fitness center, air-conditioning, photocopying and fax services, and wake-up calls.

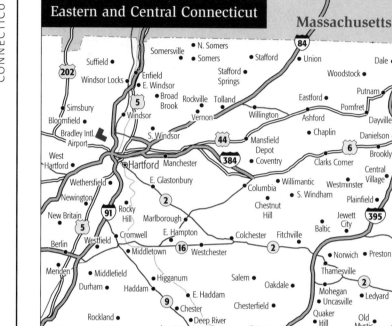

Eastern and Central Connecticut

Massachusetts

Rhode Island

N. Somers
Somersville
Somers
Stafford
Union
Dale
Thompson
Suffield
Woodstock
202
Windsor Locks
Enfield
Stafford
Springs
Eastford
Putnam
Pomfret
E. Windsor
Broad
Brook
Rockville
Tolland
5
Simsbury
Windsor
Vernon
Willington
Ashford
Dayville
East
Killingly
Bloomfield
Chaplin
Danielson
Bradley Intl.
Airport
S. Windsor
44
Mansfield
Depot
Brooklyn
South
Killingly
6
West
Hartford
Manchester
384
Coventry
Clarks Corner
Central
Village
Hartford
Wethersfield
E. Glastonbury
Willimantic
Westminster
Newington
Columbia
S. Windham
Plainfield
Moosup
New Britain
Rocky
Hill
Marlborough
2
Chestnut
Hill
Jewett
City
395
5
Westfield
Cromwell
E. Hampton
Colchester
Fitchville
Baltic
Voluntown
Berlin
Middletown
16
Westchester
2
Meriden
Middlefield
Higganum
Salem
Oakdale
Norwich
Preston
Durham
Haddam
Thamesville
North
Stonington
2
9
E. Haddam
Chesterfield
Mohegan
Ledyard
95
Rockland
Chester
Uncasville
Clintonville
Killingworth
Ivoryton
Deep River
E. Lyme
Quaker
Hill
Old
Mystic
Pawcatuck
N. Madison
Essex
Waterford
Groton
Mystic
Stonington
N. Branford
95
Niantic
New
London
Branford
Guilford
Madison
Clinton
1
Old
Lyme
Old
Saybrook

ATLANTIC
OCEAN

N

0   10
Scale in Miles

©*The Countryman Press*

Enfield

Motel 6, 11 Hazard Avenue, Enfield (860-741-3685). No matter where you travel in the region, you'll find a Motel 6 nearby; the economy motel chain offers amenities such as cable TV with premium movie channels, free coffee and local phone calls, swimming pools at some locations, laundry facilities, and "kids stay free" programs. Your pets are always welcome.

Red Roof Inn, 5 Hazard Avenue, Enfield (860-741-2571). The Red Roof's three locations in central and eastern Connecticut provide lodging near an airport, in a major city, and along the coast.

Guests can enjoy cable TV, free newspapers and local calls, alarm clocks, express checkout services, 24-hour front desks, and smoking and nonsmoking rooms. Pets are welcome.

Super 8 Motel, 1543 King Street, Enfield (860-741-3636; 1-877-466-8358); $59–99 per night. This Super 8, located near Bradley International Airport, has 61 standard guest rooms, three efficiencies, cable TV, a hot tub, free continental breakfasts, and in-room coffeemakers. Pets are welcome guests for an additional $11 per night.

Farmington

Centennial Inn Suites, 5 Spring Lane, Farmington (860-677-4647;

1-800-852-2052); $139–259 per night. Guests choose from one- and two-bedroom suites, some with lofts, at this pet-friendly accommodation designed for long-term stays. The units are grouped together condominium-style and share access to a swimming pool, a hot tub, a fitness center, laundry facilities, free daily newspapers, and a grocery delivery service.

Farmington Inn, 827 Farmington Avenue, Farmington (860-269-2340; 1-800-648-9804; info@ farmingtoninn.com; www. farmingtoninn.com); $129 per night. Located in the historic district of Farmington, this deluxe accommodation has 72 guest rooms and 13 suites, four-poster beds, bathrobes and feather beds in some rooms, cable TV and VCRs, desks, in-room irons and

hair dryers, marble bathrooms, and an on-site café. Pets are welcome in designated rooms.

Homewood Suites by Hilton Farmington, 2 Farm Glen Boulevard, Farmington (860-321-0000); $120–149 per night. This all-suite facility has 121 units with full kitchens, living areas, cable TV, and barbecue grills. Other amenities include a fitness center and an indoor swimming pool. Pets are allowed with prior notice and an additional $150 nonrefundable fee.

Griswold
Homespun Farm Bed & Breakfast, 306 Preston Road (Route 164), Griswold (860-376-5178; 1-888-889-6673; relax@ homespunfarm.com; www.home-spunfarm.com); $95–125 per night. Innkeepers Ron and Kate

DESIGNED FOR LONG-TERM STAYS, THE CENTENNIAL INN SUITES IN FARMINGTON OFFERS CONDOMINIUM-LIKE ACCOMMODATIONS

ABBEY'S LANTERN HILL INN, JUST DOWN THE ROAD FROM FOXWOODS RESORT CASINO, IS CLOSE TO ALL THE MYSTIC-AREA ATTRACTIONS.

Bauer have taken the personal approach to renovating their 1740s farmhouse B&B; Ron handmade all the four-poster beds, and Kate designed the home's interior and gardens. Guests can also wander through the on-site orchard. Well-behaved dogs are welcome as long as owners adhere to the inn's pet policies.

Groton

Bestway Inn, 135 Route 184, Groton (1-800-280-0054); $75–199 per night. Located on Connecticut's eastern shoreline, the Bestway Inn offers rooms and suites, free continental breakfasts, laundry facilities, cable TV, a swimming pool, complimentary newspapers, and in-room alarm clocks and coffeemakers. Pets are allowed in certain rooms for an extra $12–15 per night.

Clarion Inn Groton, 156 Kings Highway, Groton (860-446-0660; 1-800-252-7466); $59–199 per night. Air-conditioning, a restaurant and lounge, an indoor swimming pool, room service, and in-room movies are some of the amenities offered at this coastal Clarion Inn. Guests can also enjoy complimentary breakfasts and newspapers. Dogs (sorry, no cats) weighing less than 30 pounds are allowed for an additional $10 per night.

Guilford

A Victorian Village Inn, 800 Village Walk, Guilford (860-669-4340; www.avictorianvillage.com); $250–650 per week. This unique accommodation consists of separate cottages, which range in style and size from a small studio to a two-bedroom dwelling with a cathedral ceiling and a spiral staircase. All are clustered around a landscaped green and feature Victorian touches and gingerbread detailing. Well-behaved pets are welcome.

Hartford

Crowne Plaza Hotel, 50 Morgan Street, Hartford (860-549-2400); $119–209 per night. This upscale hotel offers room service, a concierge desk, a gift shop and newsstand, a swimming pool, wake-up service, a restaurant, complimentary continental breakfasts, cable TV with premium movie channels, and in-room coffeemakers, hair dryers, irons, and ironing boards. Pets are allowed for an additional $50 charge.

Red Roof Inn, 100 Weston Street, Hartford (860-724-0222). (See listing under Enfield.)

Residence Inn by Marriott, 942 Main Street, Hartford (860-524-5550) The Residence Inn locations in Hartford, Manchester, Mystic, and Windsor offer lodging for long- and short-term stays with studios and one- and two-bedroom suites. Most have amenities such as swimming pools, cable TV, fitness centers, in-room coffeemakers, laundry facilities, and 24-hour front desks. The pet rules and fees vary from site to site; call for details.

Ledyard

Abbey's Lantern Hill Inn, 780 Lantern Hill Road, Ledyard (860-572-0483; info@abbeys lanternhill.com; www.abbeys-lanternhill.com); $79–140 per night. This very pet-friendly B&B has large lawns, picnic areas, and

eight rooms and suites, many of which have decks, private entrances, and private baths. Animal owners will especially appreciate Chateau Eve, a room with hardwood floors and a private fenced-in courtyard. Though the B&B has a quiet countryside setting, Foxwoods Casino is within walking distance, and Mystic is a short drive away.

Manchester

Clarion Suites Inn, 191 Spencer Street, Manchester (860-643-5811; 1-800-992-4004); $115–165 per night. The Clarion Suites hotel was designed for extended stays; guests can choose from 104 studios, as well as one- and two-bedroom suites, and enjoy full breakfasts, a swimming pool, a hot tub, a weight room, a sports court, and conference facilities. Pets are welcome for an additional $10 per night.

Residence Inn by Marriott, 201 Hale Road, **Manchester** (860-432-4242). (See listing under Hartford.)

Meriden

Ramada Plaza Hotel, 275 Research Parkway, Meriden (203-238-2380); $79–139 per night. Guests at this Ramada can take advantage of an indoor swimming pool, a restaurant and lounge, room service, cable TV, laundry facilities, a fitness center, a 24-hour front desk, and in-room coffeemakers. There are no extra fees for pet owners, though they must sign a pet-policy form at check-in.

Mystic

AmeriSuites Mystic, 224 Greenmanville Avenue, Mystic (860-536-9997; 1-800-833-1516);

$89–144 per night. Pets are allowed at this AmeriSuites, but the policy is a bit limiting: Animals weighing less than 15 pounds are allowed in smoking rooms only. The ideally located hotel has suites with living areas, a 24-hour front desk, free shuttles to local attractions, cable TV, a fitness center, laundry facilities, and in-room coffeemakers and alarm clocks.

Old Mystic Motor Lodge, 251 Greenmanville Avenue, Mystic (860-536-9666); call for rate information. This centrally located motel has 25 rooms, an outdoor swimming pool, in-room refrigerators and microwaves, a "kids stay free" program, and complimentary continental breakfasts during the high season. Animal owners pay a $50 refundable security deposit at check-in and are asked to clean up after their pets.

Residence Inn by Marriott, 42 Whitehall Avenue, Mystic (860-536-5150). (See listing under Hartford.)

New Britain

Central Inn, 65 Columbus Boulevard, New Britain (860-224-9161); $39–125 per night. For an extra $10 per night, your pet can join you at this 119-room hotel with cable TV, air-conditioning, complimentary continental breakfasts and newspapers, laundry facilities, a 24-hour front desk, and in-room microwaves, refrigerators, and alarm clocks. Whirlpool tubs are available in some suites.

New London

Red Roof Inn, 707 Colman Street, New London (860-444-

0001); $45–74 per night. (See listing under Enfield.)

Niantic

Motel 6, 269 Flanders Road, Niantic (860-739-6991). (See listing under Enfield.)

North Stonington

John York House Bed & Breakfast, junction of Routes 216 and 49, North Stonington (860-599-3075); $85–165 per night. Leea and David Grote welcome pets and children to their working farm and B&B located near Mystic, beaches, and Foxwoods Casino. Each guest room has a private bath, a fireplace, antiques, and air-conditioning. Full breakfasts are served each morning by candlelight. Pet owners must give prior notice and can't leave pets alone in the rooms.

Simsbury

Ironhorse Inn, 969 Hopmeadow Street (Route 10), Simsbury (860-658-2216; 1-800-245-9938; www.ironhorseofsimsbury.com); $86–160 per night. Guest rooms at the Ironhorse Inn have balconies, voice mail, cable TV, microwaves, refrigerators, and mini-stoves. Guests can also enjoy a picnic area, a swimming pool, a sauna, walking paths, and nearby shops and restaurants in downtown Simsbury. Pets are welcome in designated rooms for an extra $15 per night.

Southington

Another Second Penny Inn, 870 Pequot Trail, Stonington (860-535-1710; innkeepers@ secondpenny.com; www. secondpenny.com); $108–135 per night. Julie the dog will welcome you to Another Second

Penny, a 1710 inn surrounded by 5 acres of forests, fields, and gardens. Five-course breakfasts are served daily. For an extra $25 per stay, pets weighing less than 40 pounds are welcome in the Noyes Room, which has a private bath, garden views, a king-sized bed, a walk-in closet, and a rocking chair.

Motel 6, 625 Queen Street, Southington (860-621-7351). (See listing under Enfield.)

Stonington
Stonington Motel, 901 Stonington Road, Stonington (860-599-2330); $55–80 per night. Located within walking distance of trails, a boat ramp, and scenic coves, the Stonington Motel offers accommodations with cable TV, air-conditioning, and in-room refrigerators and microwaves. "Small- to medium-sized" dogs (call to see if yours qualifies) are welcome, provided they are housebroken, non-destructive, and well behaved.

Voluntown
Tamarack Lodge, 21 Ten Rod Road, Voluntown (860-376-0224); $50–65 per night. This rustic accommodation welcomes families—including well-behaved, house-trained pets—to its 20-acre resort with house-keeping cabins, a private beach, walking paths, a sauna, a swimming pool, and a restaurant and lounge. There are no TVs on-site to disturb the peace and quiet, and there are no extra fees for companion animals.

Waterford
Lamplighter Motel, 211 Parkway North, Waterford (860-442-7227);

$59–119. The Lamplighter, situated on the central Connecticut shore, offers 38 standard guest rooms and efficiencies, an outdoor swimming pool, exercise equipment, and cable TV. "Small-to medium-sized" dogs (call to see if yours qualifies) are allowed with a $100 security deposit and a $10 per dog, per night fee.

Wethersfield
Motel 6, 1341 Silas Deane Highway, Wethersfield (860-563-5900). (See listing under Enfield.)

Windsor
Residence Inn by Marriott, 100 Dunfey Lane, Windsor (860-688-7474); $99–229 per night. (See listing under Hartford.)

Windsor Locks
Homewood Suites by Hilton Hartford/Windsor Locks, 65 Ella Grasso Turnpike, Windsor Locks (860-627-8463); $78–248 per night. Like the Homewood Suites hotel in Farmington, this location offers all-suite lodging along with amenities such as laundry facilities, a gift shop, airport shuttles, complimentary beverages and continental breakfasts, meeting rooms, and a business center. Only pets weighing less than 40 pounds are allowed.

Motel 6, 3 National Drive, Windsor Locks (860-292-6200); $39–59 per night. (See listing under Enfield.)

Sheraton Hotel at Bradley International Airport, 1 Bradley International Airport, Windsor Locks (860-627-5311; 1-877-422-5311); $112–179 per night. The name says it all: Located within the airport itself, this hotel has

237 rooms, a restaurant, a swimming pool and sauna, a fitness center, in-room coffeemakers, and cable TV. Pet owners must agree to abide by the hotel's pet policy, but pay no extra fees.

Woodstock

Elias Child House Bed & Breakfast, 50 Perrin Road, Woodstock (860-974-9836; 1-877-974-9836; tfelice@compuserve. com; www.eliaschildhouse.com); $100–135 per night. Tucked away in Connecticut's Quiet Corner, this 1700s B&B has two guest rooms and one suite, all with private baths and fireplaces. The home itself boasts nine fireplaces in all, cooking hearths, a beehive oven, and antique furnishings; outside, guests can feel free to explore the B&B's 40 acres. Dogs are welcome for an extra $10 per night.

Campgrounds

Baltic

Salt Rock Campground, 120 Scotland Road (Route 97), Baltic (860-822-0884); $25–30 per night. This is one of the few state-owned campgrounds where your pet is allowed: Two animals are permitted per site. The campground offers 71 sites for tents and RVs, access to the Shetucket River, rest rooms with showers, a swimming pool, and 120 acres of land.

Bozrah

Odetah Campground, 38 Bozrah Street Extension, Bozrah (860-889-4144; 1-800-448-1193); $25–35 per night. This large family campground is located

on a 30-acre lake. The facilities include a beach, wooded sites, a swimming pool, tennis courts, a camp store, a snack bar, rest rooms with showers, laundry facilities, a recreation hall, and a pavilion. Well-behaved, quiet dogs are welcome as long as they are leashed and walked off-site.

East Killingly

Stateline Campresort, Route 101, East Killingly (860-774-3016; camplands@aol.com; www. resortcamplands.com); $22–28 per night. Stateline provides campers with a private lake, a swimming pool, a recreation center, a camp store, a teen center and adult clubhouse, a snack bar, a playground, boat rentals, and laundry facilities. A full schedule of planned activities includes barbecues, dances, and softball games. Pets are welcome for an additional $3 per night.

Lebanon

Lake Williams Campground, 1742 Exeter Road (Route 207), Lebanon (860-642-7761; 1-800-972-0020; www.lakewilliams-campground.net); $19–34 per night. Campers choose from sunny, wooded, or waterfront sites at Lake Williams, a campground with a boat launch and boat rentals, a playground, a camp store, a recreation hall, laundry facilities, scheduled family activities, hayrides, and modern rest rooms. One leashed pet per site is allowed, as long as owners clean up after their animals.

Lisbon

Ross Hill Park Family Campground, 170 Ross Hill Road,

Lisbon (860-376-9606; 1-800-308-1089; rosshillpark@snet.net; www.rosshillpark.com); $28–29 per night. The Ross Hill Park facilities include wooded and sunny sites for RVs and tents, rest rooms with showers, three playgrounds, boat rentals, a snack bar, a camp store, weekend breakfasts, laundry facilities, and a pond with a beach. Animal owners are asked to keep their pets on a leash, clean up after them, and not leave them unattended.

North Stonington
Highland Orchards Resort Park, Route 49, North Stonington (860-599-5101; 1-800-624-0829; www.highlandorchards.com); $29–46 per night. Highland Orchards has sites for RVs as well as tents; guests can also rent on-site camping cabins. The campground's amenities include two swimming pools, rest rooms with showers, a miniature golf course, a basketball court, a fishing pond, and a camp store. There is no charge for the first pet; a second pet is allowed for an extra $2 per night.

Stafford Springs
Roaring Brook Campground, 8 South Road, Stafford Springs (860-684-7086; roaringbrook@ snet.net; www.roaringbrook-campground.com); $350 per week or $525 per month. The minimum stay at Roaring Brook is one week. The campground's facilities include a swimming pool, two ponds, a brook, a camp store and restaurant, walking trails, adult and kids' recreation halls, a pavilion, and rest

rooms with showers. Pets are always welcome on a leash.

Voluntown
Pachaug State Forest Campgrounds, Route 49, Voluntown (860-424-3200); $11–13 per night. Though dogs are not allowed in Connecticut's state park campgrounds, they are welcome, on a leash, in a few state forest campgrounds like those at Pachaug. The forest offers two distinct camping areas: **Green Falls,** which has 18 sites and a pond; and **Mount Misery,** which has 22 sites and a stream for fishing. One pet per site is allowed.

Homes, Cottages, and Cabins for Rent

Ashford
Correll Waterfront Cottages, Ashford (860-423-2469; 860-450-1737; jcor0@aol.com); $550–850 per week. Located on a lake in the town of Ashford, these two cottages both have two bedrooms and can accommodate four to six people. The amenities at each include barbecue grills, air-conditioning, cable TV, games, books, linens, and towels; one cottage also has a rowboat and canoe, and picture windows in the living area. Well-behaved, leashed pets are welcome, as long as owners clean up after them.

North Stonington
Stonington Vacation Rental, North Stonington (860-599-9711; kstedman@msn.com); $70–90 per night or $450–610 per week. This three-bedroom rental is located on the second floor of a

Mystic-area vacation home; the lodging can accommodate up to five people with three bedrooms, a private entrance, air-conditioning, a washer and dryer, a microwave, a coffeemaker, and a shared deck, hot tub, and barbecue grill. "I have a lot of pets here already, so you and your pet should feel right at home," says owner Deborah Stedman. There is no extra charge for animals.

OUT AND ABOUT

Bluff Point Coastal Reserve, Depot Road, Groton (860-424-3200). Visitors to Bluff Point can experience salt marsh and forest ecosystems while walking along this rocky shoreline and bluff in Groton. It's a great spot for wildlife watching, hiking, saltwater fishing, cross-country skiing, mountain biking, or just relaxing with an ocean-view picnic. Leashed pets are welcome.

Chatfield Hollow State Park, Route 80, Killingworth (860-424-3200). Have a picnic, hike the trails, swim, fish, skate, ski, or just relax at this 355-acre park centered on man-made Schreeder Pond. Park facilities include a rest room, a concession stand, parking areas, and a picnic shelter. Neighboring **Cockaponset State Forest** provides additional miles of trails. Dogs are welcome on a leash.

Comstock Covered Bridge, Comstock Bridge Road, East Hampton. One of the last remaining covered bridges in the state, this 90-foot span has an original Howe truss; it was first built in 1791 and rehabilitated in 1840. The bridge crosses the Salmon River and carries foot traffic only.

After crossing, you can enjoy a walk and picnic in the nearby state forest.

Day Pond State Park, Route 149, Colchester (860-424-3200). Fully stocked with trout, Day Pond attracts fishing enthusiasts, history buffs, and hikers with 180 acres of land and water. Parking, flush toilets, telephones, and picnic areas are available. Dogs must be leashed.

Fort Saybrook Monument Park, Route 154, Saybrook Point, Old Saybrook (860-395-3123). This scenic 18-acre city park has a boardwalk, views of the Connecticut River, and displays detailing the history of the original Saybrook Colony and the Algonquin Nehantic Native American tribe who once lived here.

Gay City State Park, Route 85, Hebron (860-424-3200). One of Connecticut's most interesting parks, this 1,500-acre gem surrounds an abandoned 18th-century village. You can still see the foundations of the houses and mills as you walk the trails and cross-country ski. Visitors can also swim, fish, and picnic. **Meshomasic State Forest** is right next door. Pets must be leashed.

Haddam Meadows State Park, Route 9A, Higganum (860-424-3200). This is a popular spot from which to access the Connecticut River. The 175-acre property has open spaces for sports, picnic areas, a boat launch, parking areas, walking paths, and an access road for vehicles that winds around the perimeter. Leashed pets are welcome.

Hammonasset Beach State Park, Route 1, Madison (860-424-3200). One of the state's most loved parks, Hammonasset boasts 919 acres, 2 miles of sandy beach, nature trails, an environmental education center, a bike trail, sport fields, saltwater fishing opportunities, picnic areas, rest rooms, a pavilion, and a concession stand. Companion animals must be leashed.

Heritage Trail Vineyards, 291 North Burnham Highway, Lisbon (860-376-0659; vintner@heritage trail.com; www.heritagetrail. com). Stop by this eastern-Connecticut vineyard for a peek at the production of wines made with estate-grown grapes. The scenic property encompasses 38 acres with a pond and deck for relaxing. Leashed dogs are welcome, though Heritage Trail president Diane M. Powell advises caution on the vineyard's busy two-lane road.

Hopeville Pond State Park, Route 201, Griswold (860-424-3200). This 544-acre park provides opportunities for nearly every conceivable recreational activity, including hiking, canoeing, mountain biking, fishing, boating, and picnicking. Visitors can also take advantage of rest rooms, parking areas, a boat launch, and a concession stand. Dogs must be leashed.

James L. Goodwin State Park, Route 6, Hampton (860-424-3200). With more than 2,000 acres, this public park also serves as a forest conservation center, offering educational displays, interpretive trails, hiking and cross-country skiing trails, a nature center, picnic areas, and fishing opportunities. Dogs are welcome on a leash.

Mystic Seaport, 75 Greenman-ville Avenue (Route 27), Mystic (860-572-5315; 1-888-9-SEAPORT; visitor.services@mysticseaport. org; www.mysticseaport.org); $9–17 per person. Sneak a peek at Connecticut's maritime past at this living-history museum with tall ships and a 40-acre re-created village with a one-room school-house, a general store, a chapel, a meetinghouse, a bank, a printing office, a tavern, a ship chandlery, and other relevant buildings. Leashed pets are allowed on the grounds, though not on the ships or in the exhibit buildings and restaurants.

Natchaug State Forest, Route 198, Eastford (860-424-3200). Natchaug is well known among horse lovers, who enjoy riding on the forest's many equestrian trails. But you don't have to have a horse to visit the park, which also provides hiking and cross-country skiing trails, fishing opportunities, and picnic areas. Your dog is welcome on a leash.

Northwest Park, Lang Road, Windsor (860-285-1886; www.northwestpark.org). This town-owned property boasts 473 acres with 12 miles of trails, concerts, nature programs for adults and children, picnic areas, cross-country ski and snowshoe rentals, and community gardens. Pets are welcome on a leash. For more information and a trail map, visit the Friends of Northwest Park web site, listed above.

Old Mistick Village, junction of Route 27 and Coogan Boulevard, Mystic (860-536-4941). This charming outdoor shopping center has tree-lined walking paths, flower gardens, a pond, shady greens, a gazebo, clothing boutiques, toy stores, maritime gift shops, candle makers, a movie theater, bakeries, and restaurants. Several of the shops have animal themes, from wildlife critters to dogs and cats (see **It's Raining Cats and Dogs** under "Hot Spots for Spot").

Pachaug State Forest, Route 49, Voluntown (860-424-3200). Animal lovers will appreciate this preserve's dog-friendly campgrounds, along with its scenic views, picnic areas, and trails for hiking, snowmobiling, and horseback riding. You can also swim, fish, access the on-site boat launch, or explore the park's rhododendron sanctuary. Pets are allowed on a leash.

Penwood State Park, Route 185, Bloomfield (860-424-3200). Penwood offers more than enough activities to keep everyone in the family busy: The 787-park has a bike trail, cross-country skiing and hiking trails, a nature center, scenic views, picnic areas, parking areas, and rest rooms. Pets are welcome on a leash.

Prudence Crandall Museum, Canterbury Green, Canterbury (860-546-9916). Leashed pets are allowed on the grounds (but not in the house) at this notable landmark, the site of one of New England's first academies for women. Local resi-dent Prudence Crandall, who founded the school in 1832, became an outcast and was eventually jailed after admitting young African American women to the school. The museum is a National Historic Landmark and a **Connecticut Freedom Trail** site.

Quaddick State Park, East Putnam Road, Thompson (860-424-3200). This former Native American fishing village has a reservoir, parking areas, public telephones, rest rooms, sports fields, and a boat launch. Popular activities include boating, fishing, swimming, and picnicking. Dogs must be leashed.

Salmon River State Forest, River Road, Colchester (860-424-3200). Your leashed pet is welcome at Salmon River, a popular fly-fishing and hiking spot. Visitors can also access hiking, mountain biking, horseback riding, and cross-country skiing trails, explore remnants of historic buildings, fish, or have a picnic. The preserve adjoins neighboring **Day Pond State Park** (see above).

Shenipsit State Forest, Route 190, Stafford (860-424-3200). The facilities are limited at this 6,100-acre forest—just a parking area and pit toilets—but the property provides ample opportunity for solitude and wildlife-watching. Hike the trails, take in the views, fish, have a picnic, or just enjoy the quiet. Dogs must be leashed.

Stratton Brook State Park, Route 305, Simsbury (860-424-3200). Completely handicapped accessible, Stratton Brook features a railroad-bed-turned-bike path, babbling brooks, swimming and fishing opportunities,

and 148 acres of woods. Cross-country skiing is allowed in the winter; dogs must be on a leash.

Wright's Mill Farm, 63 Creasey Road, Canterbury (860-774-1455; info@wrightsmillfarm.com; www.wrightsmillfarm.com). This Christmas tree farm and popular wedding site welcomes pets on leashes; the farm hosts events and activities throughout the year, including farm tours, hayrides, Oktoberfest, and Father's Day picnics. Visitors are also welcome to visit the on-site 300-year-old mill complex and 20-acre pond.

QUICK BITES

Abbott's Lobster in the Rough, 117 Pearl Street, Noank (860-536-7719). Frequented by locals as well as visitors, Abbott's serves clam chowder, steamed mussels, steamed and stuffed clams, a variety of sandwiches, and of course lobster. Outdoor seating is available at picnic tables.

Giuseppe's Pizza, 129 Church Street, Middletown (860-347-4050). You can order one of Giuseppe's specialty pizzas to go or enjoy your meal out on the patio in the summertime. Other menu items include a variety of hot and cold grinders, soups, salads, and pasta dinners.

Harry's Place, 104 Broadway, Colchester (860-537-2410).

Always busy, this seasonal takeout restaurant isn't fancy: You'll eat your burgers, hot dogs, ice cream, lobster bisque, and fish sandwiches on disposable plates at picnic tables in the parking lot. But no one in the long lines ever seems to mind.

Montana Mills and **Java Joe's Café,** 332 North Main Street, West Hartford (860-761-0330). Fresh-baked breads are the specialty at Montana Mills bakery, along with muffins and other sweet treats. The attached coffee shop, Java Joe's, serves drinks and sandwiches made with their neighbor's still-warm breads. Lunch packs include chips and a cookie.

North End Deli and Catering, 991 Poquonnock Road, Groton

(860-448-0600). Create your own sandwich combination or choose from the North End's specialties. At dinnertime, pasta, chicken, and seafood meals are available for take-out; call ahead and they'll have your order ready when you arrive.

Pump House Grille, 63 Elm Street (Bushnell Park), Hartford (860-728-6730). Open seasonally, this outdoor café is located in Bushnell Park and serves casual fare such as sandwiches, soups, salads, wraps, fruit salads, and burgers. Don't be surprised if you hear live music in the afternoon or evening.

Sea View Snack Bar, Route 27, Mystic (860-572-0096). This decidedly casual spot offers wonderful views of the water, and picnic tables with umbrellas. You can order treats like fried seafood and soft-serve ice cream from the take-out window.

Vanilla Bean Café, 450 Deerfield Road, Pomfret (860-928-1562). This popular café has indoor and outdoor seating, hot and cold sandwiches, soups, baked treats, and cold drinks, including beer and wine. It's located at the junction of Routes 44 and 169.

HOT SPOTS FOR SPOT

Best Friends Pet Resorts and Salons, 60 Harris Road, **Avon** (860-673-0555); 1511 Silas Deane Highway, **Rocky Hill** (860-721-8080). These two Best Friends locations (the Avon site is also known as **Mountain View Kennel**) offer overnight boarding, grooming, and doggie day care, as well as multiple-pet discounts. For cats, rates range $11–13 per night for boarding and $6–10 for day care. Dog owners pay $16–20 for overnight boarding and $11–13 for day care.

Candlewick Kennels, 2811 Hebron Avenue, Glastonbury (860-633-6878; www.candlewickkennels.com). Animal guests at Candlewick can take advantage of grooming services at The Spa, sniff out some new toys in Bartholomew's pet shop, or check in for boarding. Playtime sessions, which can include anything from a brushing to walk in the woods, are available for an extra charge.

Creature Comforts Animal Inn, 454 Providence New London Turnpike (Route 184), North Stonington (860-599-1784; www.creaturecomfortsanimal-inn.com). The "innkeepers" at Creature Comforts strive to make your pet's stay with them fun and stress free: Dogs have access to indoor/outdoor runs and enjoy supervised playtimes in fenced-in areas, while cats relax in 4-by-6-foot kitty condos with skylights and scratching posts.

Cuddly Care Pet Sitting, 6116 Bigelow Commons, Enfield

(860-741-5191; timothyaarons@
msn.com; www.cuddlycarepet-
sitting.com). Pet-sitter Timothy
M. Aarons provides short-term
animal care, dog walks, transportation, and even pet-food
delivery in the towns of **Enfield,
Windsor, Suffield, Somers,
Granby,** and **Windsor Locks.**
Fees vary according to the service provided, but typically range
$15–20 per visit.

DJ's Grooming and Pet Supply,
119 Oakland Street, Manchester
(860-649-0485). DJ's staffers
have been washing, clipping, and
beautifying pets in the Greater
Hartford area for more than 20
years; the shop also sells food
and supplies for companion animals. Reservations are recommended for grooming.

It's Raining Cats and Dogs,
Building One, Old Mistick
Village, Route 27, Mystic (860-
536-CATO). Located within the
popular Old Mistick Village shopping area, this fun shop stocks
everything an animal lover could
want, including breed-specific
gifts, clothing, welcome mats,
mugs, and books. You'll also find
water bowls, key chains, wind
chimes, greeting cards, magnets,
and other items emblazoned with
images of dogs and cats.

Maple Ridge Kennels, 270
Rogers Road, Groton (860-445-
4999; mrkbark@aol.com; www.
mapleridgekennels.com). Maple
Ridge provides grooming and
boarding services for both dogs
and cats: Canine visitors enjoy
heated and air-conditioned
indoor/outdoor runs, while
felines have a separate, quiet
boarding area. Optional dog-
walking services are available
upon request. Reservations are
recommended: Bring vaccination
records with you at check-in.

IN CASE OF EMERGENCY

Clinton Veterinary Hospital,
93 Old Post Road, Clinton (860-669-5721).

Companion Animal Hospital,
801 Poquonnock Road, Groton (860-449-9800).

Connecticut Veterinary Center,
470 Oakwood Avenue, West Hartford (860-233-8564).

Dayville Veterinary Clinic,
21 Putnam Pike, Dayville (860-779-2700).

Norwich Animal Hospital,
439 Salem Turnpike, Bozrah (860-889-1387).

Tolland Veterinary Hospital,
70 Hartford Turnpike, Tolland (860-875-5748).

TWO FRIENDS ENJOY THE VIEW FROM "THE LOOKOUT" AT WEBB MOUNTAIN PARK IN MONROE.

Western Connecticut

PET-FRIENDLY RATING: 🦴 🦴 🦴 🦴

Though geographically small, this region nonetheless seems to have something to please every personality and taste: Drive a half hour in any direction and you'll stumble upon communities that are as different from each other as, well, cats and dogs. Down near New York City, exclusive waterfront towns like Greenwich, Darien, and New Canaan are home to sprawling mansions, gated neighborhoods, and country clubs. Travel north and you'll find lakes, quiet suburbs, and the friendly working-class cities of Danbury and Waterbury. Places like Fairfield and New Haven, meanwhile, provide diverse populations, great restaurants, world-class universities, and lots of green space.

But as lively and interesting as southwestern Connecticut is, its visitors tend to come more for business than for pleasure. If you're looking for a vacation spot, however, the northern reaches of the Housatonic Valley and Litchfield Hills offer your best bet for a quiet getaway. Once you've found a place to stay (note: pets are not allowed in state park campgrounds), you and your pet can set out to explore rivers, covered bridges, downtown shopping areas, town greens, vast natural areas, and state forests and parks. The region provides a unique blend of rural charm and urban sophistication; whether you want to join the crowd or keep to yourself, the sights, sounds, and smells offer a quintessential New England experience.

ACCOMMODATIONS

Hotels, Motels, Inns, and Bed & Breakfasts

Bethel
Microtel Inn and Suites,
80 Benedict Road, Bethel (203-748-8318); $69–119. Choose from standard guest rooms and suites at this recently built Microtel; all rooms have coffeemakers, hair dryers, and cable TV with premium movie channels, while suites also have microwaves, sinks, and refrigerators. Pet owners pay a refundable security deposit of $100.

Branford
Motel 6 New Haven–Branford,
320 East Main Street, Branford (203-483-5828); $39–47 per night. This Motel 6, located about 9 miles from downtown New Haven, offers the economy chain's standard amenities, including cable TV with premium movie channels, free local calls, coffee, a "kids stay free" program, and modem lines. Pets are welcome.

Bridgeport
Holiday Inn Bridgeport,
1070 Main Street, Bridgeport (203-334-1234); $99–139 per night. This high-rise hotel is located near the new baseball and hockey stadiums and offers an indoor swimming pool, room service, free newspapers, a fitness center, alarm clocks, in-room movies, a florist, and a gift shop. Dogs weighing less than 20 pounds are welcome; pet owners paying in cash will be charged a refundable $50 fee.

Brookfield
Twin Tree Inn, 1030 Federal Road (Routes 7/202), Brookfield (203-775-0220; twintreeinn@ msn.com; www.twintreeinn. com); $85–95 per night. Rooms and suites are available at Twin Tree, an economy inn just north of Danbury. The amenities include air-conditioning, Colonial-style furnishings, cable TV, and fax services. Pets are welcome; owners pay a onetime $10 fee.

Cornwall Bridge
Cornwall Inn, 270 Kent Road (Route 7), Cornwall Bridge (860-672-6884; 1-800-786-6884); $79–169 per night. Located in the northwestern Connecticut countryside, the Cornwall Inn is set on 3 acres and provides a swimming pool, six guest rooms in the main inn building, and an

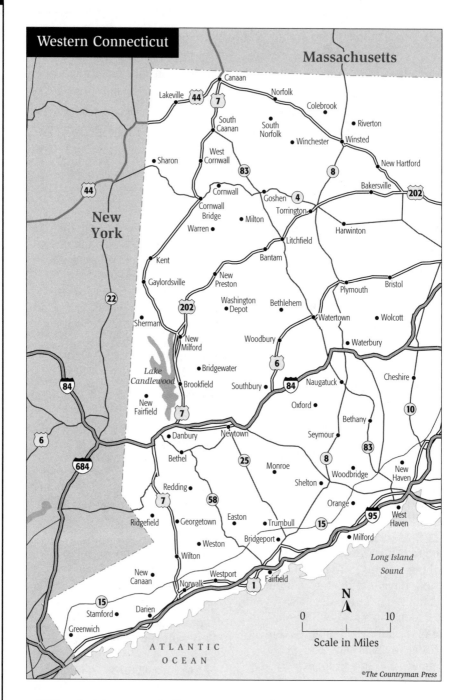

Western Connecticut

Massachusetts

New York

Canaan
Lakeville
44
7
Norfolk
Colebrook
Riverton
South Caanan
South Norfolk
Winchester
Winsted
Sharon
West Cornwall
83
8
New Hartford
Bakersville
202
Cornwall
Goshen
4
Torrington
Cornwall Bridge
Milton
Harwinton
Warren
Litchfield
Kent
Bantam
Gaylordsville
New Preston
Plymouth
Bristol
22
202
Washington Depot
Bethlehem
Sherman
New Milford
Woodbury
Watertown
Waterbury
Wolcott
Lake Candlewood
Bridgewater
Cheshire
84
Brookfield
Southbury
6
84
Naugatuck
New Fairfield
7
Oxford
10
Danbury
Newtown
Bethany
6
Bethel
25
Monroe
Seymour
83
684
Redding
7
58
Shelton
Woodbridge
8
New Haven
Ridgefield
Georgetown
Easton
Trumbull
15
Orange
95
West Haven
Weston
Bridgeport
Milford
Wilton
New Canaan
Westport
Norwalk
Fairfield
1
Long Island Sound
15
Stamford
Darien
Greenwich
ATLANTIC OCEAN

N

0   10

Scale in Miles

©*The Countryman Press*

additional eight rooms in the adjoining country lodge. All rooms have air-conditioning, down comforters, feather beds, and TVs. Pets are welcome in designated rooms.

Danbury
Ramada Inn Danbury,
116 Newtown Road, Danbury (203-792-3800); $77–119 per night. Pets are welcome without

---

extra fees at this Ramada Inn, located at Exit 8 on I-84 near the Danbury–Bethel line. The hotel has an attached steak restaurant, an indoor swimming pool, free passes to a nearby health club, cable TV with premium movie channels, 170 rooms and 10 suites, free morning newspapers, and in-room coffeemakers.

Lakeville

Interlaken Inn Resort and Conference Center, 74 Interlaken Road, Lakeville (860-435-9878; 1-888-222-2909; info@interlaken-inn.com; www.interlakeninn.com); $139–199 per night. This pet-friendly resort has been welcoming guests for more than 200 years with tennis courts, a swimming pool, an adjoining golf course, a fitness center, and 30 acres with two lakes. Animals are welcome in the Woodside Building rooms, which can accommodate up to four people, and in the Town House rooms, which come with fireplaces and kitchens.

Wake Robin Inn, Sharon Road (Route 41), Lakeville (860-435-2515); $139 per night. Surrounded by 12 hilltop acres, this historic inn was once the home of the Taconic School for Young Ladies. Pets weighing less than 40 pounds are allowed in the inn's 15 summer motel units for an additional $10 per stay (not per night). Each motel room has been recently renovated with private baths, cable TV, and private entrances.

Milford

Red Roof Inn, 10 Rowe Avenue, Milford (203-877-6060); $53–69 per night. This Red Roof Inn location has 110 rooms, exterior corridors, laundry facilities, cable TV, a "kids stay free" program, alarm clocks, free local calls, daily newspapers, and express checkout services. One pet per room is welcome without extra charges.

New Haven

Quality Inn Conference Center, 100 Pond Lily Avenue, New Haven (203-387-6651); $79–119 per night. An indoor swimming pool and sauna, cable TV, a restaurant, and free continental breakfasts are some of the amenities available at this Quality Inn. Guests can also take advantage of valet laundry services, free airport shuttles, and baby-sitting services. Well-trained animals, "like show dogs," are welcome without extra fees.

Residence Inn by Marriott New Haven, 3 Long Wharf Drive, New Haven (203-777-5337; 1-800-331-3131); $129–209 per night. A short drive from downtown New Haven and Yale University, this Residence Inn offers suites with kitchens and living areas, a swimming pool, a 24-hour front desk, cable TV, laundry services, and in-room coffeemakers. For stays of one to four days, pet owners pay an additional $150; for each day after that, they pay an extra $15 per night.

North Haven

Holiday Inn North Haven, 201 Washington Avenue, North Haven (203-654-4192); $89–119 per night. This full-service, pet-friendly hotel provides its guests with a restaurant and lounge, an indoor swimming pool, a fitness center, cable TV with premium movie channels, voice mail, and in-room coffeemakers, as well as hair dryers, irons, and ironing boards. Animals are welcome without extra fees, but they cannot be left unattended at any time.

Norwalk

Homestead Studio Suites Norwalk, 400 Main Avenue, Norwalk (203-847-6888); $86 per night. Each suite is equipped with a kitchen, air-conditioning, cable TV, voice mail, a desk, a coffee-maker with complimentary coffee, an iron, and an ironing board. Guests will also find laundry facilities on-site. Pet owners pay an additional $75 nonrefundable fee, regardless of length of stay.

Silvermine Tavern, 194 Perry Avenue, Norwalk (203-847-4558; innkeeper@silverminetavern.com; www.silverminetavern.com); $110–185 per night. This inn and restaurant is a local favorite: Though pets are not allowed in the main building, they are welcome to stay in the rooms just across the street at no extra charge. The restaurant serves hearty New England fare in indoor and outdoor seating areas overlooking a millpond, and the inn's guest rooms are filled with antique furnishings.

Plainville

Ramada Inn Plainville, 400 New Britain Avenue, Plainville (860-747-6876); $74–99 per night. Located midway between Waterbury and Hartford, this Ramada Inn offers 107 rooms

with coffeemakers and cable TV, a swimming pool, a restaurant and lounge, room service, laundry facilities, and fax and photo-copying services. Pet owners using a credit card pay no additional pet fees; those paying with cash must leave a small security deposit.

Salisbury

White Hart Inn, village green, Salisbury (860-435-0030; 1-800-832-0041; www.whitehartinn. com); $109–209 per night. This historic country inn, decked out in floral fabrics, wicker, and chintz, offers a romantic getaway with a large front porch over-looking the green, a gourmet restaurant, gathering rooms with fireplaces, air-conditioning, and 26 guest rooms with private baths. Pets are allowed in designated rooms for an additional $25 per night.

Shelton

Homestead Studio Suites Shelton, 945 Bridgeport Avenue, Shelton (203-926-6868); $86 per night. Designed for long-term stays, these accommodations provide separate living areas and full kitchens in each suite, cable TV, alarm clocks, free local calls, voice mail, business services, and air-conditioning. Pets are welcome for an extra $85 nonrefundable fee, regardless of length of stay.

Torrington

Days Inn Torrington, 395 Winstead Road, Torrington (860-496-8808; 1-800-DAYS-INN); $71–79 per night. This Days Inn offers an indoor swimming pool, a hot tub, a fitness center, a 24-hour front desk, free continental breakfasts daily, and 70 smoking and nonsmoking rooms. Several restaurants are close by. Pets are welcome for an additional $15 per night.

Waterbury
House on the Hill Bed & Breakfast, 92 Woodlawn Terrace, Waterbury (203-757-9901; www.houseonthehill.biz); $125–175 per night. This animal-friendly B&B is listed on the National Register of Historic Places; guests can enjoy full gourmet breakfasts, cable TV, alarm clocks, air-conditioning in some suites, and a hilltop location with more than an acre of gardens and woods. Pet owners are asked to bring along a dog bed and not to leave the animal unattended in the room.

Campgrounds

Barkhamsted
American Legion State Forest Campground, West River Road, Barkhamsted (860-424-3200); $13 per site. Though pets are not allowed in any state park campgrounds, they are allowed, on a leash, in state forest campgrounds. The American Legion property has 30 sites, flush toilets, and trails for hiking and cross-country skiing. One pet is allowed per site. For more park information, see "Out and About."

White Pines Campsites, 232 Old North Road, Barkhamsted (860-379-0124; 1-800-622-6614); $22–32 per night. Campers at

White Pines can enjoy wooded and open sites for tents and RVs, cabin rentals, a swimming pool, a pond, game courts and fields, a camp store, a snack bar, scheduled events and activities, paddleboats, and a game room. Leashed pets are welcome, provided they are walked in the designated area and are not left unattended.

Litchfield
White Memorial Conservation Center Campgrounds, 80 Whitehall Road, Litchfield (860-567-0857; info@white memorialcc.org; www.white-memorialcc.org); call for rate information. The White Memorial Foundation operates three campgrounds at its 4,000-acre conservation area: **Pine Grove Campground** is available for groups only and is free for nonprofit youth groups; the **Windmill Hill Family Campground** has 18 sites; and the **Point Folly Family Campground** at Bantam Lake has 47 sites. Dogs must be on a leash. Call or e-mail for availability and rates.

Homes, Cottages, and Cabins for Rent

Waterfront Farmhouse, Bantam Lake (212-877-2219); $1,800 per week or $3,000–6,000 per month. Surrounded by 40 acres of conservation land, this historic farmhouse has water views, canoes, a boat dock and swim dock with 100 feet of waterfront access, a large yard with two dog runs, hardwood floors, four bedrooms, air-conditioning, a barbecue grill, and cable TV. "The porch is a great place to lounge with your pet," says homeowner Rosemary Stolzenberg.

OUT AND ABOUT

American Legion State Forest, West River Road, Barkhamsted (860-424-3200). This 78-acre park offers hiking, snowshoeing, and cross-country skiing trails, picnic areas, rest rooms, sports fields, a campground (see "Accommodations—Campgrounds"), and access to the Farmington River. The trails provides great views of the valley and the river. The park was named for the organization that donated the original plot of 213 acres.

Ansonia Nature and Recreation Center, 10 Deerfield Road, Ansonia (203-736-1053; www. ansonianaturecenter.org). This former farm is now open free to the public as a 104-acre nature center and park with more than 2 miles of trails, a pond, fields, wetland areas, a butterfly garden, a visitors center, picnic areas, and recreation fields. Dogs are welcome on a leash.

Burr Pond State Park, Route 8, Torrington (860-424-3200). Most visitors to Burr Pond head first to the walking path that surrounds the site's 88-acre pond; other park activities include picnicking, boating, swimming, fishing, and hiking, and ice-skating in the winter. You'll also find rest rooms, a boat launch, and a concession stand. Dogs must be leashed.

Collis P. Huntington State Park, Sunset Hill Road, Redding (860-424-3200). A favorite among mountain bikers, this 878-acre park is also one of the hottest spots around for local dog lovers. The walking paths are wide, flat, and easy to navigate, winding their ways past ponds, small bridges, forests, fields, and a horse farm. Water-loving dogs will enjoy wading into the easy-to-access ponds.

Covered Bridges. Western Connecticut is home to two of these distinctly New England landmarks: **Bulls Bridge,** just off Route 7 in Kent, still carries vehicle traffic to and from New York. The **West Cornwall Bridge** up the road was rehabilitated by the state in 1973 and was originally constructed with a Town lattice truss.

DiGrazia Vineyards, 131 Tower Road, Brookfield (203-775-1616; wine@prodigy.net; www.digrazia. com). The resident cat and dog at DiGrazia hang out in the tasting room of this vineyard and winery where reds, whites, dessert wines, and ports are created. Your dog is also welcome on a leash. Because the vineyard sometimes hosts weddings and other special events, you might want to call ahead.

Haystack Mountain State Park, Route 272, Norfolk (860-424-3200). With 224 acres, this park offers great views for people of all ages and abilities: A paved road leads halfway up the mountain to a parking area. Once you reach the lot, you can stay for a picnic or continue farther up on foot to the summit on a half-mile-long trail. Dogs must be leashed.

Housatonic Meadows State Park, Route 7, Sharon (860-424-3200). Fly-fishermen appreciate the cold, fast waters of Housatonic Meadows; in addition to river access, the 450-acre park provides rest rooms, parking, drinking water, public telephones, picnic areas, sports fields, and boating opportunities.

Kent Falls State Park, Route 7, Kent (860-424-3200). With open fields, picnic areas, streams, trails, and rest rooms, this park is popular with local families as well as visitors. But the highlight of any visit is the waterfall itself: You can follow the cascade all the way to the top via pathways and stairs that allow views along each step of the way. Pets are welcome on a leash.

Kettletown State Park, Route 188, Southbury (860-424-3200). Native Americans traded this 490-acre swath of land to the settlers for one brass kettle: The area was then named Kettletown, and the moniker stuck. The park offers picnic areas, hiking trails, swimming and fishing opportunities on **Lake Zoar,** and sports fields and ice-skating in the winter. Dog must be leashed.

Lake Waramaug, Route 478, Preston (860-424-3200). The main attraction of this 95-acre park is the lake itself. Visitors come to fish, swim, scuba dive, ice-skate, and canoe, and also enjoy land-based activities like picnicking and hiking. Amenities include rest rooms, a concession stand, parking areas, and a picnic shelter. Leashed dogs are allowed.

Mohawk State Park, Route 4, Goshen (860-424-3200). Much of the land for this 3,350-acre park was donated to the state by the White Memorial Foundation (see **White Memorial Conservation Center** below). Hiking and snowmobiling are allowed on the trails, and visitors can also picnic, fish, bird-watch, enjoy scenic views, and wander through an unusual black spruce bog. Dogs must be leashed.

Mount Tom State Park, Route 202, Litchfield (860-424-3200). There's plenty to do at this popular 230-acre park, including fishing, swimming, picnicking, boating, ice-skating, scuba diving, and hiking to the top of the 1,325-foot mountain for which the park is named. Visitors can also take advantage of rest rooms, a concession stand, parking, and public telephones. Leashed dogs are welcome.

New Canaan Nature Center, 144 Oenoke Ridge (Route 124), New Canaan (203-966-9577; www.newcanaannature.org). Leashed pets are welcome at this 40-acre nature center with 2 miles of trails, a wetlands boardwalk, ponds, meadows, and an arboretum and gardens. For a trip map, visit the center's web site, listed above.

New Haven Parks (203-946-8019). The **city's famous green,** surrounded by 17th-century churches, is host to outdoor concerts in the summer and picnickers and walkers year-round; nearby, restaurants, boutiques, and galleries provide opportunities for window-shopping and people-watching. Other parks include **Lighthouse Point** on Townsend Avenue, 426-acre **East Rock Park** on East Rock Road, and **East Shore Park** on Woodward Avenue. Dogs must be leashed.

Peoples State Forest, East River Road, Barkhamsted (860-424-3200). Encompassing nearly 3,000 acres, Peoples State Forest is located just across the road from the **American Legion State Forest** (see above). Visitors to Peoples will find parking, rest rooms, and a picnic shelter; popular activities include fishing, hiking, picnicking beside the Farmington River, cross-country skiing, and snowmobiling. Dogs are allowed, but must be leashed.

Pequonnock River Greenway. Winding through the towns of Newtown, Monroe, and Trumbull, this railroad-line-turned-bike-path will eventually reach all the way down to Bridgeport. It's a quiet, flat, and wide path, frequented by families and dog walkers. One of the most popular stretches runs from Pepper Street in Monroe down to the town's Wolf Park (where pets are not allowed). You can park at the Pepper Street lot to make the hour-long trip up and back.

Puttin' on the Dog, Greenwich. This tail-waggin' annual event, hosted by the nonprofit **Adopt-A-Dog** organization of Greenwich, is typically held in September in Roger Sherman Baldwin Park. Activities include lighthearted dog competitions with celebrity judges, demonstrations, costume contests, pony rides, food, and music. For more information on this year's dates and times, call Adopt-A-Dog at 203-629-9494 or visit www.adopt-a-dog.org.

SoNo Arts Celebration, South Norwalk. Otherwise known as South Norwalk, SoNo is home to an annual arts festival each August in the bustling downtown area. The normally busy streets are roped off to make room for more than 150 exhibits, food carts, and vendors selling everything from sculpture and photographs to clothing and handcrafted furniture. Grab a fresh-squeezed lemonade and wander with Rover—there's always something to see.

Southford Falls State Park, Route 188, Oxford (860-424-3200). Like **Kent Fall State Park** (see above), the big draws here are the waterfalls, which tumble into the Eight Mile River near the south end of the property. Besides "fall-watching," visitors also enjoy fishing, hiking, cross-country skiing, and picnicking. Amenities include rest rooms, parking, and a picnic shelter. Dogs must be leashed.

Webb Mountain Park, Webb Circle, Monroe. It's a bit hard to find, but once you and Spot locate this fairly remote 136-acre park you'll be glad you made the effort. Trails are marked by color: Follow the red blazes to reach the Lookout, a rocky shelf with impressive valley and river views. To reach the park, take East Village Road off Route 111, take a left onto Webb Circle, then turn right at the park entrance sign. Dogs must be leashed.

West Haven Boardwalk, Captain Thomas Boulevard, West Haven. This is a popular spot for local dog owners in warm weather: You'll see almost every breed of dog romping along the beach and the board-walk. A restaurant with picnic tables is across the street (see **Chick's** under "Quick Bites"). Leashed dogs are welcome as long as their owners clean up after them. (The town imposes a heavy fine for violators.)

White Memorial Conservation Center, 80 Whitehall Road, Litchfield (860-567-0857; info@whitememorialcc.org; www.whitememorialcc.org). This environmental education center and museum comprises about 4,000 acres of woodlands, meadows, and riverfront in the northwest region of the state. Visitors can enjoy 35 miles of trails, several picnic areas, activity fields, boat launches, and campgrounds (see "Accommodations—Campgrounds"). Dogs are welcome on a leash.

Winslow Park, North Compo Road, Westport. Winslow Park is the preferred spot for local canine lovers: Dogs are welcome to run off-leash in the northern end of this large grassy park with shady spots and paved walking paths. You'll also find a picnic area, gardens, and a parking lot located at the corner of North Compo Road and Post Road.

QUICK BITES

Chick's, 183 Beach Avenue, West Haven (203-934-4510). Perhaps the best thing about this casual family restaurant—besides the fried seafood, hot dogs, take-out windows, and picnic tables— is its location, right across the street from a boardwalk and beach (see **West Haven Board-walk** under "Out and About"), where dogs are allowed. Make an afternoon of it!

Dr. Mike's Ice Cream, 158 Greenwood Avenue, **Bethel** (203-792-4388); 44 Main Street, **Monroe** (203-452-0499). Renowned locally, Dr. Mike's homemade ice cream shops are busy year-round. The Monroe location has outdoor seating on the porch and a small grassy area; in Bethel, you can enjoy your cone while strolling past the quaint downtown shops.

Downtown Kent. This tiny strip of boutiques, restaurants, and bookstores along Route 7 offers several choices for quick meals. **Stroble Baking Co.** has premade sandwiches, soups, quiche, cookies, and cupcakes; **Kent Market** offers a deli and grocery items; and **Kent Coffee and Chocolate Company** serves . . . well, you can guess. All have outdoor seating in the summer.

Fisherman's Net, 11 Old Kings Highway, Darien (203-655-0561). At Fisherman's Net, you can reel in fast seafood meals like sea scallops, fish-and-chips, fried clams and shrimp, crabcakes, and fish sandwiches, all served with fries and slaw.

Litchfield Gourmet, 33 West Street, Litchfield (860-567-4882). Stop into this casual yet upscale market for wraps, gazpacho, cucumber soup, deli sandwiches, gourmet coffee, and ice cream, then enjoy your treats on the picturesque green across the street.

Meli-Melo, 362 Greenwich Avenue, Greenwich (203-629-6153). Take a moment while you're strolling down tony Greenwich Avenue to stop into this crêperie and juice bar serving sandwiches, salads, crêpes, and freshly blended smoothies made with fruits and vegetables.

Mexicali Rose, 71 South Main Street (Route 25), Newtown (203-270-7003). If you're craving burritos, tacos, black beans, and homemade chips and salsa, this teeny-tiny restaurant is the place. Order your meal to go (most patrons do) and have a picnic at the Newtown green, known as Ram's Pasture, right down the street.

New Haven's Wooster Street. A haven for Italian immigrants since the 1920s, this popular section of New Haven abounds with famous coal-fired-oven pizza shops—most notably **Sally's** (203-624-5271) and **Pepe's** (203-865-5762)—along with several upscale restaurants and bakeries. There's no outdoor seating at the pizza places, but you can pick up a pie to go. Expect a wait, especially on weekends.

Rawley's Hot Dogs, 1886 Post Road, Fairfield (203-259-9023). This roadside stand has been keeping 'em coming for more than 50 years with dogs that are deep fried, then grilled. The cheese and chili dogs are especially popular.

HOT SPOTS FOR SPOT

Best Friends Pet Resort and Salons, 528 Main Avenue, Norwalk (203-849-1010); Route 42, Bethany (203-393-3126). Overnight boarding, doggie day care, and grooming are all available at these two branches of the Best Friends pet-care chain. You can also sign your four-footed friend up for Canine College obedience classes or additional playtimes during boarding. For overnight care, rates range $13–18 per night for cats and $17–27 for dogs. Day-care rates range $10–14 for cats and $13–19 for dogs.

Earth Animal, 606 Post Road East, Westport (203-227-8094; 1-800-622-0260; info@earth animal.com; www.earthanimal. com). This is a fun stop for two- and four-legged customers. Earth Animal stocks holistic supplements and foods, gourmet doggie treats, books, flea and tick remedies, toys, picture frames, and anything else an environmentally conscious pet lover could want. Those who aren't passing through Westport can shop at Earth Animal's online store.

Friends Fur Life, New Milford (860-350-3729; friendsfurlifect@ aol.com). Animal lover Catherine Clark has been providing pet-sitting services for locals and visitors in **Litchfield** and **Fairfield Counties** since 1999. She has walked dogs, cared for cats, and even kept an eye on exotic species and livestock.

IncredaCare, Inc. (203-322-4446; information@incredacare. com; www.incredacare.com). Heading out to dinner? Servicing the **Stamford, Greenwich,** and **Darien** areas, pet-sitter Jennifer Jordan provides short-term care for companion animals; each 30-

to 40-minute visit includes feeding, playing, cuddling, walks, and whatever else your pet might need.

Marta's Vineyard Canine Resort, 519 Federal Road, Brookfield (203-775-4404; martasvineyard@aol.com; www. martasvineyard.abka.com). Owned and operated by veterinarians, Marta's Vineyard offers rooms, luxury suites, junior suites, a "senior center" for geriatric pets, and a "petite center" for especially small canine guests. Each pet is exercised twice a day in fenced-in areas. Grooming services are also available.

Pet Patrol Professional Pet Sitting (203-799-1133; john843@ optonline.net; www.petpatrol. tv). Pet Patrol's service area includes 19 towns in the **Trumbull, Orange,** and **North Haven** areas; owner John Antonucci can provide standard services such as walks and short visits, as well as care for special-needs animals.

Thomaston Feed, 135 East Main Street, Thomaston (1-888-608-PETS; info@thomastonfeed.com; www.thomastonfeed.com). Specializing in companion animal supplies, this family business stocks food, leashes, collars, bowls, pet shampoos, holistic supplements, treats, chew toys, and more for dogs, cats, birds, gerbils, and even horses.

Town House for Dogs and Cats, 1040 Post Road East, Westport (203-227-3276). Town

House provides overnight boarding as well as doggie day care, pickup and delivery services, obedience classes, and grooming. Boarded dogs enjoy large indoor/outdoor runs and outdoor play sessions when the weather permits.

IN CASE OF EMERGENCY

Countryside Veterinary Hospital,
374 Leavenworth Road, Shelton (203-929-0500).

High Ridge Animal Hospital,
868 High Ridge Road, Stamford (203-322-0507).

Litchfield Veterinary Hospital,
286 Torrington Road, Litchfield (860-567-1622).

Mattatuck Animal Hospital,
1095 Chase Parkway, Waterbury (203-754-2105).

Northside Animal Hospital,
21 Padanarum Road, Danbury (203-743-4521).

Pet Shield Veterinary Hospital,
126 East Pearl Street, New Haven (203-776-7799).

Rhode Island

A VISITING GOLDEN RETRIEVER PUPPY CHECKS OUT THE SIGHTS IN DOWNTOWN NEWPORT, RHODE ISLAND.

Rhode Island

PET-FRIENDLY RATING: 🦴 🦴 🦴 🦴

This small state is a big draw for New England visitors. From Providence gondolas to quaint East and West Bay waterfront hamlets and the quieter corners of Blackstone Valley and South County, the area packs agricultural, urban, and small-town attractions into one convenient package. Most Rhode Island tourists head first to Newport, a playground for the country's wealthiest captains of industry that now offers lodgings and fun for everyday folks wanting a peek at the "other half's" lavish lifestyle—past and present. It's a shame that more hotels here don't welcome pets, because Newport is one of the dog-friendliest towns around. From the downtown cobblestone streets and greens to the famed Cliff Walk, massive mansions, and abundant parks, you and Rover will find plenty of playing, hiking, and gawking opportunities. And you won't be alone: Lots of hands are holding leashes in this hopping, upscale spot.

The state's other main tourist attraction is Block Island, a pristine dot in Long Island Sound that offers breathtaking views from all sides and a classic maritime atmosphere. Unfortunately, the islanders seem to have hung a NO DOGS sign at the ferry landing: Pets and their owners have just a few choices for lodging here. But despite the difficulty in finding a place to stay, Block Island still makes for an intriguing doggie day trip from your home-away-from-home base on the mainland. Grab an ice cream, rent a canoe, hike the bluffs, admire the Victorian architecture, and count your blessings that The Nature Conservancy and others are working to preserve the island's natural beauty for future generations.

ACCOMMODATIONS

Hotels, Motels, Inns, and Bed & Breakfasts

Block Island

Blue Dory Inn, Dodge Street, Block Island (401-466-5891; 1-800-992-7290; rundezvous@ aol.com); $65–495 per night. This Victorian-style inn offers a variety of accommodation choices, from traditional guest rooms in the main house to luxury suites and cottages. Guests enjoy views of the ocean and downtown area. Pets are welcome in certain rooms and cottages for an additional $25 per stay,though they cannot be left unattended at any time.

Eastgate Hill, P.O. Box 332, Block Island (401-466-2164; www.eastgatehill.com); $300–400 per night. Set on a 3-acre property with a pond and rolling lawns, Eastgate Hill has a large deck with patio furniture, a dining area, ocean views, and a living room with a fireplace. Pets are welcome with prior approval in the suite, which can accommodate four people and has a private entrance.

Gothic Inn, P.O. Box 537, Block Island (401-466-2918; 1-800-944-8991; bennetbirx@cs.com; www.blockisland.com/gothic); $85–295 per night. Well-behaved dogs and cats are allowed in the two-bedroom apartments and one large guest room at the Gothic Inn, a cheery accommodation located in Block Island's historic district. Each room has a private entrance, making dog walks convenient. Continental breakfasts are served each morning in the sitting rooms.

Island Home, Beach Avenue, Block Island (401-466-5944; 1-888-261-6118; innkeeper@theisland-home.com; www.theislandhome.com); $95–295 per night. This hilltop inn has guest rooms in the main house and the carriage house, country furnishings, porches, large lawns and views of the harbor, rolling hills, and Block Island's famous Great Salt Pond. Breakfast and afternoon tea are included in the rates; pets are welcome in certain rooms for an extra $25 per stay (not per night).

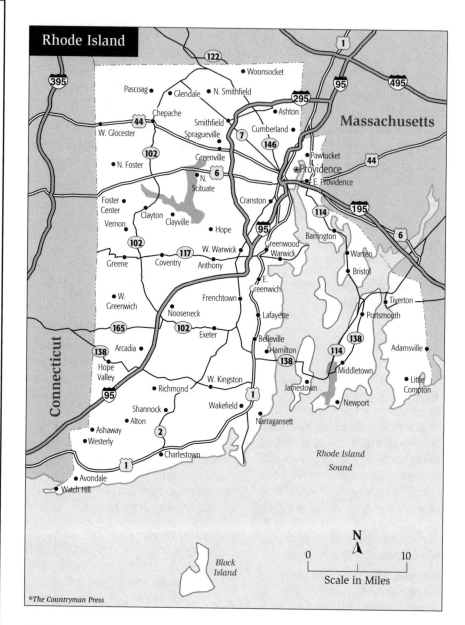

Rhode Island

Massachusetts

Connecticut

Woonsocket
Pascoag • Glendale • N. Smithfield
Chepache
W. Glocester • Smithfield • Ashton
Spragueville • Cumberland
Greenville
N. Foster • N. Scituate
Pawtucket
Providence
E. Providence
Foster Center • Cranston
Vernon • Clayton • Clayville • Hope
Greene • Coventry • Anthony
W. Warwick
Greenwood
Warwick
Barrington
Warren
Bristol
W. Greenwich • Frenchtown
Nooseneck
E. Greenwich
Lafayette
Arcadia
Hope Valley
Exeter
Belleville
Hamilton
Middletown
Tiverton
Portsmouth
Adamsville
Little Compton
Richmond
Shannock
Alton
W. Kingston
Jamestown
Newport
Ashaway
Westerly
Wakefield
Narragansett
Charlestown
Rhode Island Sound
Avondale
Watch Hill

N
0 — 10
Scale in Miles

Block Island

©The Countryman Press

Middletown

Bay Willows Inn, 1225 Aquidneck Avenue, Middletown (401-847-8400; 1-800-838-5642); $49–169 per night. The Bay Willows is one of the most affordable ways to enjoy Newport and southern Rhode Island attractions, all of which are a short drive away. The recently renovated motel has 21 guest rooms, air-conditioning, some larger suites with microwaves and refrigerators, cable TV, and smoking and nonsmoking rooms. Guests can relax with their pets in the lawn area, which has chairs and a rose trellis. Companion animals are always welcome for an extra $10 per night.

Howard Johnson Inn Middletown, 351 West Main Road, Middletown (401-849-6047); $44–199 per night. Located close to Newport, this Howard Johnson offers a swimming pool, hot tub, and sauna; cable TV with premium movie channels; and voice mail. The hotel also has an attached restaurant with outdoor seating in the summer. Companion animals are welcome in first-floor standard guest rooms for an additional $5 per pet, per night fee.

Narragansett
Four Gables Bed & Breakfast, 12 South Pier Road, Narragansett (401-789-6948); $115–135 per night. Two Bernese mountain dogs and a cat, along with innkeepers Terry and Barbara Higgins, make up the welcoming committee at Four Gables, a late-1800s home with ocean views, four fireplaces, and antiques. Pets are welcome with prior approval in the home's suite of rooms, which offers a sitting area and can accommodate up to four people.

Newport
Bannister's Wharf Guest Rooms, Bannister's Wharf, Newport (401-846-4500; guestrooms@bannisterswharf.net; www.bannisterswharf.net); $75–325 per night. Pets are always welcome at Bannister's, where guests can choose from rooms and suites, all with harbor views and a deck. The owners also rent out two-bedroom apartments nearby. There are few better locations from which to enjoy the downtown hubbub; all accommodations have air-conditioning and cable TV.

Chestnut Inn, 99 Third Street, Newport (401-847-6949; 401-846-0173; chstnut99@aol.com; www.members.aol.com./chstnut 99); $65–135 per night. In addition to a great location within walking distance of downtown Newport, the Chestnut Inn also offers four-poster beds, hardwood floors, a fenced-in backyard, a hot tub, a front porch, a barbecue grill, a washer and dryer, cable TV, and full country breakfasts. Pets are always welcome. "Our place is a dog's heaven," says innkeeper Bill Nimmo. "The property abuts a playground, and the ocean is a block away."

Motel 6 Newport, 249 Connell Highway, Newport (401-848-0600); $39–59 per night. This economy motel offers cable TV with premium movie channels, smoking and nonsmoking rooms, modem hookups, and free coffee. Kids stay free with a parent, and well-behaved pets are welcome without extra fees.

Sanford–Covell Villa Marina, 72 Washington Street, Newport (401-847-0206; www.sanford-covell.com); $60–225 per night. Pets allowed in some rooms at Sanford–Covell, a harborside B&B and marina with great water views, a wraparound porch, an entry hall with a 35-foot ceiling, a reflecting pool, a dining room, and guest rooms furnished with four-poster beds and antiques. There are no extra fees for companion animals.

Sea View Inn, 240 Aquidneck Avenue, Newport (401-846-5000; 1-800-495-2046; www.seaview-newport.com); $49–209 per night.

With water views and a large lawn area with Adirondack chairs, this two-story inn attracts pet lovers from all over. All guest rooms have two double beds or one king bed, cable TV, and air-conditioning. Visitors can borrow kites or bicycles, enjoy daily continental breakfasts, and use the swimming pool and workout equipment at the fitness center next door—all free of charge. Downtown Newport, the Cliff Walk, and the mansions are a short drive away. Pets are welcome.

Summer Cottage, 21 Catherine Street, Newport (401-848-0087; njdotterer@aol.com; www.dotterer.com); $150–165 per night. The Summer Cottage is a homey, in-town B&B with a light, bright decor, a large deck, and a living room with floor-to-ceiling windows. Four-course breakfasts are served daily on bone china; guests can choose from three guest rooms with twin-, full-, or king-sized beds. Recently bathed pets are welcome, as long as they are free of fleas and ticks.

Portsmouth
Founder's Brook Motel and Suites, 314 Boyd's Lane, Portsmouth (401-683-1244); $49–139 per night. Founder's Brook guests can choose from standard motel rooms or larger suites; some of the suites have whirlpool tubs. The motel offers a quiet, off-the-road location, in-room coffeemakers and refrigerators, and senior discounts. Pets are allowed in certain rooms for $10 per stay for short stays, or $35 per month for longer stays.

Providence
Cady House, 127 Power Street, Providence (401-273-5398; wcolaiace@aol.com); $90–100 per night. The three guest rooms at this B&B all have private baths and share access to a garden patio in the backyard. Guests can also enjoy a library, several fireplaces, cable TV, and daily breakfasts. Some pets are allowed with prior approval; there are no extra fees for animal guests.

Westin Providence, 1 West Exchange Street, Providence (401-598-8000); $229–494 per night. Most dogs won't make the cut at the Westin, which only allows pets weighing less than 10 pounds. The upscale, full-service hotel has 364 guest rooms and suites, city views, mini-bars, cable TV, alarm clocks, voice mail, and writing/computer desks. Pet owners pay a $100 deposit, $50 of which is refundable.

South Kingstown
King's Rose Bed & Breakfast, 1747 Mooresfield Road, South Kingstown (401-783-5222); $125–165 per night. This 1930s-era Colonial welcomes well-behaved pets and their owners in its seven guest rooms, most with private baths; antique furnishings provide a dignified and relaxed atmosphere, and the 2 acres of grounds allow plenty of room for exploring. "For those who packed too quickly, we have extra pet bowls, blankets, and food," says innkeeper Perry Viles.

Warren
Thomas Cole House, 81 Union Street, Warren (401-245-9768;

A PORCH OVERLOOKING THE LAWN AND WATER AT SEA VIEW INN IN NEWPORT

401-751-9109); $125–175 per night. Innkeeper Marian Clark welcomes well-behaved dogs and cats to her guest house, located in the historic district. Guests enjoy a second-floor suite with a bedroom, a bathroom, a library, and a dressing area; other amenities include full daily breakfasts, a terrace with a fountain, a dining room with a fireplace, and flower gardens.

Warwick
Holiday Inn Express Warwick–Providence, 901 Jefferson Boulevard, Warwick (401-736-5000; 1-800-HOLIDAY); $119–199 per night. There are no extra charges for companion animals at this pet-friendly Holiday Inn; just let the front-desk staff know at check-in that you're staying with a furry friend. Amenities include a business center, a wake-up service, laundry and dry-cleaning facilities, air-conditioning, a cash machine, and free airport shuttles.

MainStay Suites Warwick, 268 Metro Center Boulevard, Warwick (401-732-6667); $129–159 per night. An all-suite accommodation, MainStay offers full kitchens, complimentary breakfasts on weekdays, a basketball court, a fitness center, voice mail, alarm clocks, cable TV, air-conditioning, a hot tub, and a location that's close to downtown Providence and T. F. Green Airport. Pets are welcome for an extra $10 per night and a $100 security deposit.

Motel 6 Providence–Warwick, 20 Jefferson Boulevard, Warwick (401-467-9800); $67–69 per night.

This city motel is located 2 miles from T. F. Green Airport and has laundry facilities, free coffee, a swimming pool, cable TV with premium movie channels, smoking and nonsmoking rooms, and a "kids stay free" program. Pets are welcome.

Residence Inn by Marriott Providence, 500 Kilvert Street, Warwick (401-737-7100); $159–209 per night. Designed for long-term stays, this Residence Inn features a swimming pool, a hot tub, complimentary breakfasts, a tennis court, and studio and penthouse suites with full kitchens. Pet owners pay an extra $25 per pet, per night for one- to seven-night stays; for longer stays, the charges depend on the type of suite and the length of stay.

Westerly
Pine Lodge, 92 Old Post Road (Route 1), Westerly (401-322-0333); $75–225 per night. Accommodations at the Pine Lodge include motel efficiencies and cottages, all of which have kitchenettes, air-conditioning, satellite TV, and in-room movies. The property has a walking trail, and restaurants, shopping, beaches, and other attractions are close by. Pets are allowed in the off-season only.

Sea Shell Motel, 19 Winnapaug Road, Westerly (401-348-8337; www.seashellmotel.com); $50–110 per night. For an extra $20 per stay (not per night), your pet is welcome to join you at Sea Shell, an oceanfront motel with a hot tub, a lawn area, water views, air-conditioning, cable TV with premium movie channels, and refrigerators. Pet owners should call ahead for prior approval.

Woonsocket
Holiday Inn Express Woonsocket, 194 Fortin Drive, Woonsocket (401-769-5000; 1-800-HOLIDAY); $90–149 per night. This Holiday Inn Express location has 88 guest rooms and 16 suites, a swimming pool and a hot tub, a fitness center, air-conditioning, dry-cleaning and laundry facilities, a newsstand and gift shop, wake-up calls, and free continental breakfasts. Pets are welcome for an additional $10 per night.

Campgrounds

Campers take note: Dogs are not allowed in Rhode Island state park campgrounds.

Ashaway
Frontier Camper Park, 180 Maxson Hill Road, Ashaway (401-377-4510); call for rate information. Located close to the Connecticut border, the Frontier Camper Park offers more than 100 sites for RVs and tents, a playground, a swimming pool, rest rooms with showers, a dumping station, and a volleyball court. Pets are welcome.

Coventry
Colwell's Family Campground, 119 Peckham Lane (Route 177), Coventry (401-397-4614; 401-397-5818); $18–20 per night. Located beside Johnson's Pond, this campground has rest rooms with

metered showers; picnic tables; fire pits; telephones; a dumping station; fishing, swimming, and boating opportunities; and church services. Leashed pets are welcome as long as their owners can provide proof of vaccination.

Exeter
Peeper Pond Campground, 159 Liberty Church Road, Exeter (401-294-5540); $20–24 per night. Peeper Pond's 35 campsites for tenters and RVers are spread throughout 70 acres with picnic tables and fire pits, rest rooms with showers, a camp store, water and electricity hookups, and a volleyball courts. Dogs are allowed (one per site) as long as owners leash them, clean up after them, and never leave them unattended.

Hope Valley
Whispering Pines Campground, 41 Sawmill Road, Hope Valley (401-539-7011; wpinesri@aol.com; www.whisperingpinescamping. com); $25–31 per night. This full-service family campground has sites for tents and RVs, a swimming pool, a miniature golf course, free boat rentals, basketball and volleyball courts, a recreation hall, a camp store, laundry facilities, a playground, a snack bar, and a fishing pond. Quiet, leashed pets are allowed as long as their owners clean up after them.

Jamestown
Fort Getty Recreation Area, Fort Getty Road, Jamestown (401-423-7211; 401-423-7264); $20–30 per night. Open seasonally from May through October, this municipal campground has sites for tents

and RVs, beaches, hiking trails, ocean views, and the remains of historic Fort Getty. Campers can also enjoy a playground, a pavilion, picnic areas, and a sand volleyball court. Dogs must be leashed.

West Kingston

Wawaloam Campground, 510 Gardiner Road, West Kingston (401-294-3039); $32–34 per night. With 300 tent and RV sites on 100 acres, this large campground almost guarantees to keep everyone in the family occupied. Amenities include a swimming pool with a water slide, a playground, a miniature golf course, rest rooms with showers, picnic tables, a snack bar, and two recreation halls. Campers can bring pets, but their visitors cannot.

Homes, Cottages, and Cabins for Rent

Block Island

Crew's Hideout, 1078 West Beach, Block Island (973-575-1706; apc1275@aol.com); $2,900–6,600 per week. Rent the first floor, the second floor, or both at this Block Island property overlooking New Harbor and Montauk Point. Recently renovated, the home has six bedrooms, two kitchens, satellite TV, four bathrooms, marble floors, laundry facilities, a deck, and a patio. Pets are welcome but are not allowed in the bedrooms or on the furniture.

Middletown

Newport Summer Rental, Blissmine Road, Middletown (617-989-4392; 617-484-9087; wintersm@wit.edu); $1,900 per week or $6,800 per month. "We love pets!" says Marcia Winters, the owner of this three-bedroom home on the Newport–Middletown border. The house can accommodate up to nine people and offers a recently refurbished interior designed by a local interior designer, all-new furniture and beds, a large backyard, a washer and dryer, a barbecue grill, and a pullout couch.

Newport

Chalfin Rentals, Newport (401-848-7432; 617-244-0543; ac_account@hotmail.com); $1,100–2,450 per week. Homeowner April Chalfin welcomes pets to her two Newport rentals, both of which have a fenced-in yard for dogs. The four-bedroom home is located across from a pond and is close to downtown; the two-bedroom house has water views and is within walking distance of the beach. Pet owners pay a refundable $200 security deposit.

Portsmouth

Portsmouth Vacation Cottage, 222 Cedar Avenue, Portsmouth (603-598-5280; portia2@netzero.com); $900 per week. This two-bedroom, one-bathroom home can accommodate up to six people. It features a waterfront location on Blue Bell Cove, a sleeping loft, a fully equipped kitchen, a TV/VCR, a stereo with a CD player, and a barbecue grill. Downtown Newport attractions are about a 10-minute drive away. Pets are welcome.

Wakefield

Kagel's Cottages, Wakefield (401-783-4551; www.kagels. com); $840–1,296 per week. The Kagel family rents five waterfront cottages, ranging in size from one to three bedrooms, on its 63-acre property. Most are fully equipped with kitchens, TVs, and living areas; all sit on Salt Pond with island views and surrounding lawns and woods. Housebroken, leashed pets are welcome as long as their owners can provide proof of vaccination.

OUT AND ABOUT

Arcadia Management Area (401-539-2356). Spread throughout four southern Rhode Island towns, this sprawling 14,000-acre park has wild areas and 30 miles of trails for mountain biking, hiking, horseback riding, and cross-country skiing. Trails are identified by colored blazes: Yellow-blazed trails include the 5-mile-long **Breakheart Trail** and the 1.6-mile **John B. Hudson Trail;** white-blazed trails include the 2-mile-long **Escoheag Trail** and the 3-mile-long **Mount Tom Trail.** The trails are managed by the Narragansett chapter of the Appalachian Mountain Club; for more information, write to the club at amcri@ids.net or 15 Brayton Street in Johnston, or visit www.users.ids.net/ ~ amcri. Dogs are not allowed on designated cross-country skiing trails.

Beavertail State Park, Beavertail Road, Jamestown (401-423-9941; 401-884-2010). This 153-acre park is home of one of America's earliest working lighthouses, Beavertail Light. Visitors come for views of the ocean and rocky coastline, open and sunny grass areas, hiking trails, and saltwater fishing opportunities. Dogs are welcome on a leash.

Blackstone River Bikeway (401-723-7892). This path runs through Lincoln, North Smithfield, Woonsocket, and Pawtucket. Some of the phases of this 17-mile-long biking and walking path have been completed, and some were still under construction at the time of this writing. The former railroad lines along the Blackstone Canal are being converted to a 12-foot-wide paved path with picnic tables, rest rooms, parking lots, public telephones, and access for walkers, cross-country skiers, joggers, and dog walkers.

Block Island Greenways, Block Island. Just one of the pristine island's many walkable and scenic recreational opportunities, the Greenways are 25 miles of protected trails through open fields, woods, the Mohegan Bluffs, and wetlands. For more information and maps, call The Nature Conservancy's Block Island office at 401-466-2129.

Brenton Point State Park, Ocean Drive, Newport (401-849-4562;

401-847-2400). This is a popular spot for dog owners. Located at the site of one of Newport's former mansions, the park offers unbeatable views of the Atlantic, along with picnicking, fishing, and hiking opportunities. It's located about halfway down famous Ocean Drive.

Cliff Walk, Newport. With the world-famous Newport mansions on one side and the ocean on the other, this 3½-mile-long paved path winds along cliffs and offers some of New England's best views—both natural and man-made. Your pup is welcome on a leash. The path officially starts at Memorial Boulevard, but you can find jumping-on spots elsewhere along the route. Expect crowds and lots of other dog walkers in all seasons.

Colt State Park, Route 114, Bristol (401-253-7482). With wide views of Narragansett Bay, orchards, 4 miles of bike paths, a wedding chapel, more than 400 picnic tables, wooded trails, a salt marsh, and flower gardens, this 464-acre park is one of the most popular in Rhode Island. Rest rooms and public phones are available; dogs must be on a leash.

Downtown Newport. Thames Street and the various wharfs are lined with shops, restaurants, historic churches and greens, street vendors, and entertainers—and there's all the people-watching you can handle. It's especially crowded in the sum-

SKYE, THE RESIDENT HUSKY AT ROSECLIFF MANSION IN NEWPORT, RELAXES ON "HER" FRONT LAWN. SHE WAS ADOPTED BY THE MANSION'S GROUNDSKEEPER FROM THE LOCAL POUND JUST DAYS BEFORE SHE WAS TO BE EUTHANIZED.

mertime and during the winter holidays, when Santa makes a visit by boat to Bowens Wharf.

Fort Adams State Park, Harrison Avenue, Newport (401-847-2400). Located just off Ocean Drive and extending into Narragansett Bay, Fort Adams has 105 acres of open and scenic picnic areas, soccer fields, boat ramps, and concession stands. It's also the home of **Sail Newport,** a nonprofit sailing facility offering rentals and instruction. Every summer the park hosts blues, jazz, and folk music festivals. Dogs must be on a leash and are not allowed on the beach.

Heart and Sole Walk for the Animals, Portsmouth. This fun annual event is the major fundraiser for the **Potter League for Animals,** an advocacy and sheltering organization located in Middletown. Visitors are welcome to take part in a 1- or 3-mile walk, canine obstacle courses, cat photo contests, and contests like Best Tail Wagger, Stupid Pet Tricks, and Least Obedient Dog. The event is typically held in June at Glen Park in Portsmouth. Activities and times change from year to year; for updated information, call 401-846-8276, visit www. potterleague.org, or stop by the league's headquarters at 87 Oliphant Lane in Middletown.

Oceans and Ponds, Ocean Avenue, Block Island (401-466-5131; 1-800-ORVIS-01). Dog lovers will enjoy this outfitter's "pet corner" with animal gifts and supplies; Oceans and Ponds,

an Orvis dealer, also offers canoe rentals, sportfishing charters, fly-fishing instruction, and sailing charters from Block Island.

Photo Dog Art Gallery, Water Street, Block Island (401-466-5858). Animal lovers and photography buffs will appreciate this gallery featuring black-and-white photos of Block Island landscapes, buildings, and animals, with a focus on pets. The photographers are also available for private shoots.

Rhode Island North–South Trail. Have some extra time? This 75-mile-long byway is a great way to see the charming back roads, historic villages, and rustic hiking trails in the western part of the Ocean State. For maps, send $1 to NST Maps, 27 Post Road, Warwick, RI 02888, or check out the "Almost Official Map" at www.outdoors.htmlplanet. com/nst.

Roger Williams Park, Providence. Perhaps best known for its zoo, this 430-acre Provi-dence park also has charming, tree-lined walkways, gardens, waterways, a boathouse with paddleboats available for rent, a museum, and Carousel Village. Leashed dogs are welcome in the main park area.

Snake Den State Park, 2321 Hartford Avenue, Johnston (401-222-2632). This park's ominous name doesn't fit well with its calm and inviting atmosphere, complete with 1,000 acres, forested walking trails, a working farm, and an impressive canyon. Enter through Dame Farm or park at roadside parking areas on Brown Avenue. Dogs must be leashed.

Southland Riverboat, State Pier 3, Port of Galilee, Narragansett (401-783-2954; info@southland cruises.com; www.southland-cruises.com). Well-behaved pets are welcome on board Southland Riverboat cruises, which include fireworks, and sunset, fall foliage, and general sight-seeing tours as well as private charters. The flat-bottom riverboat can accommo-date up to 149 passengers.

WaterFire, Providence. Join the crowds at one of Rhode Island's most unique and popular events, where more than 90 bonfires are lit on specially designed floats on the waterways of downtown Providence. Artist Barnaby Evans started this still-growing event/

art exhibit in 1994; today a non-profit organization keeps the fires burning with up to 19 lightings per year. For more information and a detailed schedule visit www.waterfire.com.

WaterPlace Park and Riverwalk, Providence. This recent Providence addition played a major role in the city's well-publicized renaissance. It's a truly impressive sight: Venetian-style footbridges cross the winding canal, where gon-dolas are available for rent in the summer. Plenty of benches, walkways, and even perform-ance areas make this a fun place to hang out. The park area also serves as the location for the popular **WaterFire** exhibit (see above).

QUICK BITES

Café di Mare, 11 Bowen's Wharf, Newport (401-847-2962). For a sweet treat or something more substantial, stop in this small café serving fudge, sandwiches, wraps, and bottled drinks. Enjoy your bounty at one of the many tables outside.

Café Java Grille, 272 Thayer Street, Providence (401-276-0100). Take-out is available at this popular downtown lunch spot offering sandwiches, grill items, many vegetarian choices, desserts, and coffees. Try your hot or cold sandwich with the café's focaccia bread.

Clockwork Deli, 446 North Broad-way, East Providence (401-431-

1883). Take a load off at Clockwork Deli's outdoor seating area while enjoying stuffed deli sandwiches with turkey, chicken, roast beef, tuna, vegetables, and gourmet mustards on fresh-baked breads.

Marina Grille, Goat Island, Newport (401-848-0795). This fun Goat Island eatery has lots of casual outdoor seating, live entertainment on weekends, and dishes like fried calamari, buffalo chicken salad, grilled tuna steak, baked sole, the Marina Grille burger, lemon chicken, and of course lobster.

Payne's Dock Snack Bar, Payne's Dock, Block Island (401-466-5572). Open seasonally, this is a great casual spot to enjoy breakfast, sandwiches, chowder, ice cream, and Payne's famous homemade donuts. The dock is also the place to rent boats and buy souvenirs.

Pier Pizza Company, 126 Boon Street, Narragansett (401-792-9393). Pier Pizza has outdoor deck seating, take-out, and delivery services: Though Pier Pizza is best known for large, New York–style pizzas, the staff also cook up pasta dishes, subs, salads, and rich desserts.

Thames Street Eateries. This bustling Newport strip is lined with restaurants; many offer take-out, and a few offer outdoor seating. Try the gyros, tuna sandwiches, fruit smoothies, and ice cream at **Blue Water Wraps** or the vegetarian and classic sandwiches served on gourmet bread at the **Panini Grill** next door. On East Thames Street, **O'Brien's Pub** has a huge outdoor seating area and serves crabcakes, fish-and-chips platters, steaks, and a variety of sandwiches.

PROVIDENCE'S DOWNTOWN WATERPLACE PARK AND RIVERWALK

HOT SPOTS FOR SPOT

Delmyra Country Club for Dogs and Cats, 191 Ten Rod Road, Exeter (401-294-3247; www.delmyra.com). Pet owners are encouraged to take a tour of the facilities at Delmyra before dropping off their cat or dog for short- or long-term boarding. The Doggie Palace has indoor/outdoor runs, windows, heated floors, and air-conditioning; cats enjoy kitty condos with piped-in music. Pet food is included in the rates, and grooming and training services are also offered.

Doggie Styles Pet Spa, 1160 Charles Street, North Providence (401-727-2270). Whether you need doggie day-care or grooming services, Doggie Styles can oblige: Services include shampoos, cuts, teeth cleaning, and even canine massage and aqua therapy. Appointments are recommended, but walk-in service is also available.

Gourmet Dog, 476 Thames Street, Newport (401-841-9301; www.thegourmetdog.com). There's something for every pet and pet lover here, from "splat mats" and catnip pizza to books, greeting cards, and gourmet biscuits. The owners have installed a sink in a cleanup area that customers' pooches are free to use and have also started a pet-sitting business on the side; call for details.

Paws and Claws, 23 Narragansett Avenue, Jamestown (401-423-9677; 1-877-244-PAWS; www.pawsandclaws.com). This "pet boutique" offers doggie day care

and overnight boarding, grooming—everything from trims to "makeovers"—and pet gifts and supplies such as toys, dog sweaters, food, bowls, pet beds, catnip, collars, and leashes.

Riverside Pet Sitting, Greater Providence (401-480-7933; riv_pet@yahoo.com; www.riv-pet.com). Riverside owner Ashlee Cabral also serves as the director for the Southern New England Professional Pet Sitters Association. She provides dog walks and sitting services for cats, dogs, canaries, and any other companion animal that might need some attention while you're out. Rates start at $14 per half-hour visit.

Salty Paws, 411 Thames Street, Newport (401-849-9980). Pick up a few gifts for the animal lovers in your life at Salty Paws, which sells pet-themed stationery sets, statuary, eclectic home décor, gourmet biscuits, key chains, magnets, doggie life preservers, and stuffed animals. Your pet, of course, is welcome to browse too.

Two Cats and a Dog, Providence (401-419-0435; www.twocatsandadog.com). When you have to go out *sans* animal, owner Kristen Hudgik will come to you for pet walks and care. Certified in pet CPR and first aid, she serves pet owners in central Rhode Island with dog walks; cat-, gerbil-, and bird-sitting; feeding; administering medication; and anything else you might need.

IN CASE OF EMERGENCY

Hoffman Animal Hospital,
1338 Broad Street, Providence (401-941-7345).

Newport Animal Clinic,
541 Thames Street, Newport (401-849-3401).

North Smithfield Animal Hospital,
21 Sayles Hill Road, North Smithfield (401-766-7608).

Tiogue Veterinary Clinic,
916 Tiogue Avenue, Coventry (401-821-6927).

Turco Animal Hospital,
3 Ashaway Road, Westerly (401-596-8910).

Warren Animal Hospital,
581 Metacom Avenue, Warren (401-245-8313).

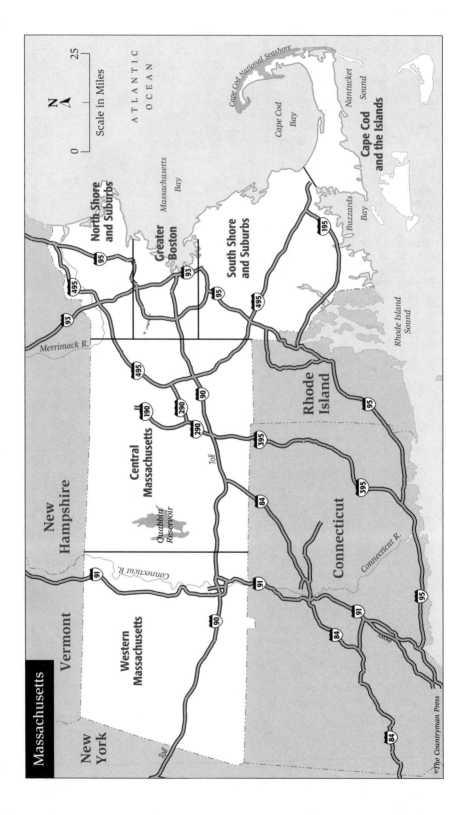

Massachusetts

THE OLD NORTH BRIDGE IN CONCORD, SITE OF THE "SHOT HEARD 'ROUND THE WORLD"

North Shore and Suburbs

PET-FRIENDLY RATING:

A curious mix of modernity and history, northeastern Massachusetts is home to top technology companies as well as many of the nation's most revered historic sites and monuments. From infamous witch hunts to Revolutionary War battles, the North Shore preserves the roots of American independence while also continuing to play a role in its advancement.

Along the coast, history and tourism take on a distinctly nautical flair. On Cape Ann, home of the country's first fishing ports, Gloucester and Rockport are havens for artists, weekenders, and seafood lovers. Nature buffs flock to Plum Island State Park, while Newburyport, Ipswich, and Essex offer plenty of upscale shopping and dining. In Lowell, riverfront mills document the early days of the Industrial Revolution. And to the south, Lexington and Concord stand as monuments to a nation's beginnings with parks, cemeteries, battle greens, and colonial-era homes and taverns. (Thoreau's famous Walden Pond makes for a wonderful day trip, but alas, pets are not allowed.) The inner suburbs are busy workaday places filled with commuters and longtime residents, many of whom can trace their ancestors back to those tumultuous times. About 3 million people live in the area, and they love to visit the seacoast and historic sites, too—expect crowds and parking hassles, especially in the summer. Preparation and patience are the keys to enjoying any trip to this remarkable slice of Americana.

ACCOMMODATIONS

Hotels, Motels, Inns, and Bed & Breakfasts

Andover

Hawthorn Suites Andover,
4 Riverside Drive, Andover (978-475-6000; 1-800-527-1133); $104–149 per night. Choose from one-bedroom or two-bedroom suites at this hotel offering free breakfast buffets, an outdoor swimming pool, a fitness center, and an outdoor barbecue area. Each suite has cable TV, free local calls, laundry service, and alarm clocks. When checking in with Fido, you'll pay a $50 initial nonrefundable charge, then $10 per night.

Residence Inn by Marriott Andover, 500 Minuteman Road, Andover (978-683-0382); $139–169 per night. Pets are welcome guests in the suites at this Residence Inn, designed for long-term stays with separate bedrooms, kitchens, and living room areas. Each suite has cable TV and a coffeemaker; amenities also include a workout room, meeting and banquet facilities, a swimming pool, and a 24-hour front desk. Animal owners pay a onetime nonrefundable fee of $100 in addition to a $10 per night charge.

Staybridge Suites Andover,
4 Tech Drive, Andover (978-686-2000); $109 per night. This hotel is a boon for night owls and time-strapped travelers: The front desk, Laundromat, workout room, and business center are all open 24 hours a day. You'll also get free food at breakfast time and during the Sundowner social hours, and the suites are fully equipped with kitchens, bedrooms, and living areas. Those traveling with a pet pay an additional $100 per stay.

Burlington

Homestead Burlington, 40 South Avenue, Burlington (782-359-9099; 1-866-238-9300); $80–109 per night. The suites at this extended-stay hotel have full kitchens stocked with cutlery and cookware, computer workstations, separate bedrooms and living room areas, and cable TV. The Burlington Mall and its

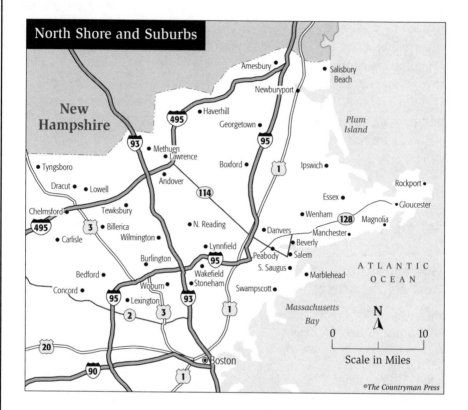

North Shore and Suburbs

©The Countryman Press

surrounding restaurants and shopping plazas are close by. Pets are welcome with a onetime nonrefundable fee of $75.

Staybridge Suites Burlington, 11 Old Concord Road, Burlington (781-221-2233); $135–233 per night. Frequented by business travelers, this all-suite residence has a 24-hour convenience store, an outdoor swimming pool, a fitness center, a sports court, and laundry facilities. Each studio is equipped with a full kitchen with utensils, cable TV, a modem hookup, a coffeemaker, and an alarm clock—though a wake-up service is also available. Animal owners pay a onetime charge of $150.

Concord
Best Western at Historic Concord, 740 Elm Street, Concord (978-369-6100). Just down the road from Concord's renowned bridge, churches, and historic homes, this Best Western offers an outdoor swimming pool, a fitness center, complimentary continental breakfasts, cable TV with premium channels, hair dryers, and data ports. Pets are welcome for an additional $10 per night.

Danvers
Motel 6, 65 Newbury Street, Danvers (978-774-8045). All Motel 6 locations are pet-friendly. On the North Shore, the Danvers location has 109 rooms with interior corridors and an indoor swimming pool. The Tewksbury facility has 92 rooms and a swimming pool, and is convenient to the University of Lowell and the Nashoba Valley ski area.

Town Place Suites by Marriott Danvers, 238 Andover Street, Danvers (978-777-6222; 1-800-257-3000); $98–130 per night. This pet-friendly, all-suite hotel is located just behind the Chili's Restaurant on Route 1; each suite has separate living room and bedroom areas, along with a kitchen. Other amenities include a swimming pool, a fitness center, laundry service, free parking, and a 24-hour front desk. Pet owners pay a onetime $50 cleaning fee, plus $10 per day.

Gloucester

Cape Ann Motor Inn, 33 Rockport Road, Gloucester (1-800-464-VIEW); $65–130 per night. You can relax in this motor inn's standard rooms or live the luxe life in the Honeymoon Suite ($170–225 per night); the building is located on the shorefront at Long Beach. Though dogs are welcome at the inn any time of the year, they're allowed on the beach itself only from Labor Day through Memorial Day.

Good Harbor Beach Inn, 1 Salt Island Road, Gloucester (978-283-1489; www.goodharborbeach-inn.com); $68–115 per night. This small red-and-white inn sits directly on the sand at Good Harbor Beach—you'd be hard-pressed to find a better location at a better price. In terms of pets, the inn welcomes them according to the same schedule as the beach itself: only during the off-season (September 15 through April 1).

Manor Inn, 141 Essex Avenue, Gloucester (978-283-0614; www.themanorinnofgloucester.

com); $69–154 per night. Animals are allowed in certain motel rooms (but not in the main manor) at this historic accommodation overlooking the Annisquam River. Many of the motel rooms have water views, and all have cable TV and air-conditioning. During the high season, guests can also enjoy free breakfasts. Pet owners pay an additional $15 per night fee.

Ocean View Inn and Resort, 171 Atlantic Road, Gloucester (978-283-6200; 1-800-315-7557; oviar@shore.net; www.ocean-viewinnandresort.com); $99–395 per night. This waterfront resort sits on nearly 6 acres with a restaurant, two swimming pools, and large decks; it's a popular spot for weddings and makes a picturesque home base for exploring the North Shore area. While not allowed in the main inn, pets are welcome in three adjacent motel buildings, Seaside, Ocean Terrace, and Cliffside, without extra fees.

Vista Motel, 22 Thatcher Road, Gloucester (978-281-3410; 1-866-847-8262; www.vistamotel.com); $65–145 per night. Choose from standard rooms, deluxe rooms, and efficiencies at this comfortable motor inn overlooking Good Harbor Beach. The landscape includes an outdoor swimming pool and more than 3 acres of waterfront lawns and gardens—perfect for exploring with Spot. Pets are welcome with prior approval.

Hamilton
Miles River Country Inn, 823 Bay Road, Hamilton (978-468-

7206; gretel@milesriver.com; www.milesriver.com); $95–175 per night. Close to the shoreline yet surrounded by 30 acres of gardens, ponds, meadows, and lawns, this impressive B&B is a haven for wildlife, human visitors, and their pet companions alike. The rambling farmhouse has a sunken living room, a breakfast room, 10 guest rooms, and great views. Well-behaved, leashed dogs and crated cats are welcome.

Lawrence
Hampton Inn North Andover, 224 Winthrop Avenue, Lawrence (978-975-4050; 1-800-HAMP-TON); $90–109 per night. Close to restaurants and shopping, this Hampton Inn offers the usual chain-hotel amenities, including an exercise room, meeting and banquet facilities, cable TV, and in-room refrigerators, irons, and ironing boards. Pets are welcome for an additional $15 per night.

Lexington
Battle Green Inn, 1720 Massachusetts Avenue, Lexington (781-862-6100; 1-800-537-8483; www.battlegreeninn.com); $79–119 per night. Located in the heart of downtown and a short walk away from Lexing-ton's famous green, this inn has the best spot in town. The guest rooms are decorated in a Colonial style and have cable TV; other amenities include on-site parking and an indoor swimming pool. Pets are welcome for an extra $20 per stay, though owners are asked not to leave them alone in the rooms.

Holiday Inn Express Lexington, 440 Bedford Street, Lexington (781-861-0852; www.hiexpress. com); $99–159 per night. This recently renovated hotel is located about a five-minute drive from the Lexington green and the downtown area. The amenities include an outdoor swimming pool, free newspapers, a concierge desk, in-room movies, free airport shuttles, cable TV, in-room coffeemakers, and hair dryers. Pets are allowed for a one-time fee of $75.

Marblehead
Seagull Inn Bed & Breakfast, 106 Harbor Avenue, Marblehead (781-631-1893; host@seagullinn. com; www.seagullinn.com); $125–225 per night. Choose from the Lighthouse Suite, the Seabreeze Suite, or the Library Suite at this home-turned-B&B on the ocean. Each suite has air-conditioning, a refrigerator, a TV/VCR, and a coffeemaker; downstairs, the Harbor Room serves as a gathering place for guests. Dogs (sorry, no cats) are welcome as long as they stay off the furniture.

Peabody
Mainstay Suites Peabody, 200 Jubilee Drive, Peabody (978-531-6632; 1-800-660-6246); $95–135 per night. This all-suite facility is located in the Centennial Business Park. Amenities include in-room movies, an indoor swimming pool, laundry and valet services, baby-sitting services, air-conditioning, cable TV, and continental breakfasts. Pet owners pay an extra $10 per pet, per night; if staying a week or more, they also pay a $150 refundable deposit.

Rockport

Carlson's Bed & Breakfast, 43 Broadway, Rockport (978-546-2770; carlson-gallery@msn.com); $90–100 per night. This picture-perfect home and art gallery allows pet guests in one of the rooms, which has a private entrance, private bath, and double bed. "Animals are welcome," says innkeeper Carol Carlson. "We even had a parrot once." Full breakfasts are served each morning in the dining room; all the sights and sounds of downtown are a walk away.

Sandy Bay Motor Inn, 183 Main Street, Rockport (978-546-7155; 1-800-437-7155; www.sandybay-motorinn.com); $76–148 per night. Animal guests are welcome for an extra $10 per night at Sandy Bay, a gray-shingle, modern inn with all the amenities: tennis courts, an indoor swimming pool and hot tub, an outdoor patio with lounge chairs, air-conditioning, cable TV, and an on-site restaurant. It's also a popular spot for functions and business meetings.

Salem

Hawthorne Hotel, on the common, Salem (978-744-4080; 1-800-SAY-STAY; www.hawthorne-hotel.com); $149–309 per night. Just like the town that surrounds it, the 1925 Hawthorne Hotel boasts a long and fascinating history. The guest rooms and dining room are decorated with antiques, lavish draperies, and period touches; there's also a gift shop, fitness room, valet, and laundry service on-site. Upon check-in, animal owners sign a pet-policy agreement that outlines the rules and regulations.

Salem Inn, 7 Summer Street, Salem (978-744-8924; salem.inn@verizon.net; www.salem-innma.com); $139–285 per night. Prepare to be bewitched: This luxurious inn will take you back in time with fireplaces, four-poster beds, Oriental carpets, three separate historic buildings (c. 1834, 1854, and 1874), and a flower-filled courtyard. Each guest room and family suite is individually decorated with period touches; pets are welcome for an additional $15 per night.

Tewksbury

Holiday Inn Tewksbury–Andover, 4 Highwood Drive, Tewksbury (978-640-9000); $114–149 per night. Convenient to both I-93 and I-495, this hotel welcomes pets and offers a concierge desk, in-room movies, complimentary morning newspapers, a fitness center, a restaurant and lounge, an indoor swimming pool and sauna, cable TV, hair dryers, and alarm clocks. Pet owners pay a refundable security deposit of $100 per stay.

Motel 6, 95 Main Street, Tewksbury (978-851-8611); $57–69 per night. (See listing under Danvers.)

Residence Inn by Marriott Tewksbury, 1775 Andover Street, Tewskbury (508-640-1003; 1-800-627-7468); $109–169 per night. The bedrooms at this all-suite hotel are separated from the living rooms with French doors; many have patios, fireplaces, and pullout sofa beds. All suites are equipped with full-sized kitchens. Pets are welcome for $10 per night, plus a $100 nonrefundable cleaning fee.

Town Place Suites by Marriott Tewskbury, 967 North Street, Tewskbury (978-863-9800; 1-800-257-3000); $95–139 per night. This all-suite hotel is popular with business travelers visiting nearby companies such as Raytheon, Hewlett-Packard, and Wang. Guests enjoy studio apartments and one- and two-bedroom suites with work areas, kitchens, and living rooms. Pets are welcome for an additional $6.50 per night and a onetime nonrefundable $100 fee.

Westford
Residence Inn by Marriott Westford, 7 LAN Drive, Westford (978-392-1407; 1-800-331-3131); $129–179 per night. Close to the Nashoba Valley ski resort and a number of large corporations, this Residence Inn has one- and two-bedroom suites, a 24-hour front desk, a swimming pool, cable TV, a fitness center, and daily free breakfasts. Pet owners pay $10 per night for 14 or fewer nights, or a flat $150 fee for more than 14 nights.

Campgrounds

North Andover
Harold Parker State Forest— Lorraine Park Campground, 1951 Turnpike Street (Route 114), North Andover (978-686-3391); $10 per night Massachusetts residents; $12 per night out-of-state residents. The goal here was to provide a semi-primitive camping experience, so the sites allow for more privacy than you'll find at most other New England campgrounds. (There are no hookups for RVs.) Each site has a picnic table and barbecue grill, and rest rooms are also available. Dogs must be on a leash. (See "Out and About" for more information on the state forest.)

Salisbury
Black Bear Family Campground, 54 Main Street, Salisbury (978-462-3183; bbcamping@aol.com; www. blackbearcamping.com); $25–35 per night. Tents, trailers, and RVs are all welcome at Black Bear, a busy family campground with a playground, a video arcade/poolroom, swimming pools, basketball courts, a camp store, laundry facilities, country-dancing nights, and rest rooms. "Small" pets (call to see if yours qualifies) are welcome, but must be on a leash at all times.

Rusnik Family Campground, Route 1, Salisbury (978-462-9551; 978-465-5295; rusnik2001@ aol.com); $30 per night. You'll find everything a family could need or want at this seacoast campground, including an outdoor swimming pool, shady and sunny sites, hookups for RVs, a miniature golf course, laundry and bathroom facilities, a duck pond, a playground, and sports courts and fields. Pets must be quiet and leashed, and owners must clean up after them.

Salisbury Beach State Reservation Campground,

Beach Road (Route 1A), Salisbury (978-462-4481); $12 per night Massachusetts residents; $15 per night out-of-state residents. Horses are allowed during the off-season, and leashed dogs are welcome year-round at this popular campground. And though horses are allowed on the beaches, dogs are not. Campers can choose from 481 campsites and make use of the recently renovated rest rooms. (See "Out and About" for more park information.)

West Gloucester

Cape Ann Camp Site, 80 Atlantic Street, West Gloucester (978-283-8683; www.capeanncampsite. com); $22 per night. This campground has a great location, spread out along 100 acres on the shores of Atlantic Ocean inlets. Tents, trailers, and RVs are welcome; hookups and monthly rates are available. Dog owners are asked to clean up after their animals, keep them on a leash, and not to leave them alone at campsites.

Homes, Cottages, and Cabins for Rent

East Gloucester

Dragonfly, 35 High Popples Road, East Gloucester (978-281-9428; patty01930@aol.com); $80–100 per night. Located about a mile from Good Harbor Beach, this 1912 English-manor-style cottage has a modernized kitchen, living room with fireplace, and master bedroom with its own bathroom. "There is conservation land across the street, which is excellent for dog walk-ing," says owner Patty Bongiorno. "We just ask that dogs be leashed."

Plum Island

Plum Island Properties, Southern Boulevard, Plum Island (c/o 711 South Dearborn Street, Chicago, IL 60605; 312-939-1490; 1-800-232-2550; robert@beach-cottage-rentals.com; www.plum-islandproperties.com); $700–1,700 per week. These three large cottages are located just a few minutes' walk from the beach: Singing Sands has three bedrooms, a wraparound deck, and a full kitchen. The Upper Cottage and the Lower Cottage are two separate apartments in the same building; each has been recently remodeled with knotty-pine walls, air-conditioning, full kitchens, decks, bikes, and beach chairs. Pet owners pay an extra $75 per week.

Rockport

Folly Cove Seasonal Rentals, Folly Cove, Rockport (978-546-7742; 1-877-943-6559; info@ follycovedesigns.com); $950–1,050 per week. The town house and cottages are available for rent individually or as a group; across the street from dog-friendly **Halibut Point State Park** (see "Out and About"), they offer by-the-sea ambience with skylights, wicker furniture, and picture windows. Shops and restaurants are within walking distance. "Very nice pets" are welcome.

Guest Chambers, c/o Karen Chambers, 25A South Street, Rockport (978-546-7893); $850 per week. This two-bedroom, fully furnished apartment offers plenty of privacy in an ultrapopular town. Guests can enjoy a full kitchen, a full bath, a dining room area, and even a washer and dryer. Pets are welcome on a case-by-case basis; owners are asked to clean up after their animals in the yard.

Pondside Cottage, Rockport (617-547-7189; millpond gardens@aol.com); $400–750 per week. This cozy cottage accommodates two people and has a full kitchen, knotty-pine walls, and a large screened-in porch that overlooks Mill Pond. It's a three-minute walk to Front Beach, though dogs are only allowed there from November 1 through May 1. Still, if it's seclusion you're looking for, you'll find it here. "Small" pets (call to see if yours qualifies) are welcome.

Rental Agencies

Patrican Real Estate, 4 Atlantic Road, Gloucester (978-283-1057; patricanre@aol.com). This agency handles rentals exclusively, and most of those are vacation and seasonal rentals. While most of their properties do not allow pets, there is always a handful of owners who welcome animals—usually with an additional security deposit. Rental options range from small cottages to large contemporary homes; call to learn about the latest listings.

OUT AND ABOUT

Captain Bill's Whale Watch and Fishing, 30 Harbor Loop, Gloucester (978-283-6995; 1-800-33-WHALE; whale watch@prodigy.net; www. captainbillswhalewatch.com). Captain Bill's allows some pets on some trips, with restrictions often based on the type of pet and the number of other passengers on board. The company offers "guaranteed sighting" humpback whale-watch trips, special-events chartered cruises, deep-sea fishing trips, and sightseeing tours.

Downtown Rockport. Known for its picturesque location and resident artists, this hub of activity attracts almost every type of visitor with its myriad art galleries, cafés, specialty shops, and scenic lookouts. While you're there, make sure to check out "Motif #1," a red lobster shack covered in buoys that has been called the most photographed building in America. Parking is always tricky: While the downtown area hums all year long, summer is especially crowded. Wear comfortable shoes and expect to take a long walk to reach the action.

Gloucester Maritime Trail, Gloucester. The Cape Ann Chamber of Commerce (33 Commercial Street, Gloucester; 978-283-1601; info@ capeann-chamber.com; www.cape annvacations.com) has recently created a "trail map" that outlines scenic and informative walks around the city's waterfront, downtown, and harbor areas. As the oldest fishing port in America (established about three years after the Pilgrims landed at the South Shore's Plymouth), the city offers more than its share of historical points of interest. Don't miss the famous Fishermen's Memorial statue on Stacey Boulevard.

Halibut Point State Park, Gott Street, Rockport. This waterfront park offers some of the best views in Massachusetts; on a clear day, you can see the shore all the way up into Maine and New Hampshire. During your visit, you can hike the trails, stop for an ocean-view picnic on the cliffs, or take a self-guided tour to learn about the Babson Farm Quarry and the history of the Massachusetts granite industry. (Guided tours are also offered during the high season.) Pets must be on a leash.

Harbor Tours—Cape Ann Cruises, Harbor Loop, Gloucester (978-283-1979; info@capeanncruises; www.capeanncruises. com); $10–20 per person. Pets are welcome and ride for free on Captain Steve Douglass's scenic harbor tours. The narrated trips take you past **Gloucester Harbor, Ten Pound Island,** the **Rocky Neck Art Colony, Norman's Woe,** and other sights that landlubbers miss. Other tours specialize in lighthouses and the **Annisquam River.**

Harold Parker State Forest, 1951 Turnpike Street (Route 114),

North Andover (978-686-3391). With 3,000 acres of forestland and ponds, Harold Parker forest (named for the first chairman of the Massachusetts State Forest Commission) is a mecca for hikers, fishermen, boaters, hunters, campers, and day-trippers. The Berry Pond day-use area, open Memorial Day through Labor Day, offers rest rooms and changing areas. Leashed pets are welcome everywhere except the beaches. (See "Accommodations—Campgrounds" for more information.)

Lexington Battle Green, Lexington. Each year on Patriots' Day (the Monday closest to April 19), actors gather on the green to reenact the events of April 19, 1775, when a ragtag group of local farmers armed themselves on this same patch of grass to try to keep British soldiers from advancing on Concord. When the first shots rang out, the first battle of the American Revolution had begun. Today, a Minuteman statue stands guard over the green, which is located in the downtown area near shops, restaurants, historic homes, and a bike trail.

Minute Man National Historical Park. The protected sites of this park are spread throughout the towns of **Lexington, Lincoln,** and **Concord** and detail some of the more fascinating happenings of the American Revolution. Highlights include the **Meriam's Corner** battle site; the **North Bridge,** site of the "shot heard 'round the world"; and the Paul Revere capture site. You can take a guided tour or wander at your own pace along the **Battle Road Trail.** Start at the visitors center at 174 Liberty Street in Concord.

Pet Mania, 1628 Massachusetts Avenue, Lexington (781-674-2200). This gift and collectibles shop is a fun stop for animal lovers; you'll find figurines of more than 130 breeds of dogs, along with mugs, T-shirts, stationery, stuffed animals, Christmas tree ornaments, and more.

Plum Island State Reservation, Parker River Wildlife Refuge Road, Plum Island, Ipswich (978-462-4481). Pets (on a leash) are allowed here only during the off-season, between October 1 and April 1, but it's just as well: Summer is extremely crowded with beachgoers, and spring and fall provide more solitude with which to enjoy the spectacular scenery and wildlife. Nature trails include boardwalks to take you through the marshes at your own pace; don't forget the binoculars! Dogs are not allowed on the beaches.

Rocky Neck Art Colony, 77 Rocky Neck Avenue, Gloucester (978-283-7978). Located just off East Main Street, the nation's oldest working art colony has evolved into a fascinating area of galleries, shops, and eateries; on

any given day, you might stumble across a poetry reading, painting demonstration, or historical lecture. The people-watching opportunities alone make it worth the trip.

Salem Walking Tours, 175 Essex Street, second floor, Salem (978-745-0666. Your dog may not be allowed inside the museums, but there are several tour companies that can tell you all you need to know about the city's "haunted" past on guided walking tours—some during the daytime, some lit only by the light of lantern at night. Contact one of these companies: **Haunted Footsteps Ghost Tour** and **Salem Historical Tours,** both at 978-745-0666; **Derby Square Tours** at 978-745-6314; or **Spellbound Tours** at 978-745-0138.

Salisbury Beach State Reservation, Beach Road (Route 1A), Salisbury (978-462-4481). While not allowed on the beach itself, leashed pets are welcome to roam the rest of this 521-acre park, including hiking trails, a picnic area, and boat ramps. Bird-watchers should keep a lookout for loons, snow buntings, ducks, northern shrikes, and grebes, among other species.

QUICK BITES

Bedford Farms Ice Cream, 18 North Road, **Bedford** (781-275-6501); 68 Thoreau Street, **Concord**

(978-341-0000). Take Rover for a well-deserved ice cream, sandwich, or other treat at either of

Bedford Farms' two locations. They're open year-round and serve more than 60 flavors of homemade ice cream and frozen yogurt. The farm itself has been running since 1880; today, it's a not-so-well-kept secret that locals would probably rather keep to themselves.

Bluwater Café, 140 High Street, Newburyport (978-462-1088). The owners of this café are dog lovers and owners (of two wirehaired pointers, Romeo and Juliet). Their menu includes seafood, pasta, salads, sandwiches, and desserts; you can take out most items and enjoy your meal at the Frog Pond across the street or on the boardwalk overlooking the Merrimack River Marina.

Boulevard Ocean View Restaurant, 25 Western Avenue, Gloucester (978-282-2949). Outside dining is available at this well-known local restaurant serving Portuguese specialties and, of course, seafood.

Carry Out Café, Route 1 South Traffic Circle, Newburyport (978-499-2240). "Home-cooked meals to go" are the specialty at this cute café offering daily specials such as southwestern chicken wraps, baked salmon with lemon and thyme, balsamic roasted chicken with red potatoes, chili, and New England clam chowdah.

Essex Seafood Restaurant and Fish Market, 143R Eastern Avenue, Essex (978-768-7233). This casual "lobster shack" has a wide variety of seafood for take-out, including clam and tuna rolls, scallop and shrimp boats,

and calamari, haddock, and lobster plates. Non–seafood eaters can order burgers, chicken fingers, and hot dogs.

Farnham's Famous Clams, Route 133, Essex (978-768-6643). Paper plates and good old-fashioned heaping portions of fried seafood and lobster are just the ticket for hungry pet owners—outside picnic tables are available.

Giuseppe's Fresh Pasta, 257 Low Street, Newburyport (978-465-2225). Owner Giuseppe C. Masia cooks up Italian favorites to eat in or take out. "I have a lot of regular customers who are pet owners and order our dinners to go," he explains. "Some of them even get dinners for their dogs, because it's all they'll eat!"

Treadwell's Ice Cream of Peabody, 46 Margin Street, Peabody (978-531-7010). Locals love the homemade flavors at this Peabody standby—for more than 50 years, they've been serving up great scoops. On any given day, you'll find about 25 flavors of ice cream, including butter crunch, mocha almond, chocolate, and vanilla, as well as low-fat frozen yogurt and sherbet.

Victoria Station, Pickering Wharf, Salem (978-745-7460). This restaurant has a scenic location on Salem Harbor and some outdoor tables on the brick patio. Seafood, prime rib, and salad are all on the menu.

Woodman's of Essex, Main Street (Route 133), Essex (978-768-6057; 1-800-649-1773). Not only does Woodman's have steamed clams, fried clams, clam cakes, and clam chowder, they also have a dog-walking area and picnic tables overlooking the salt marshes. Most customers order their lobster, shrimp, and frozen drinks from the pickup counter and enjoy their meal at the picnic tables or in their cars. The staff are happy to provide bowls of water for thirsty dogs.

HOT SPOTS FOR SPOT

Animal Krackers, 232 Main Street, Gloucester (978-283-1186). Food, toys, treats, and supplies are all available at Gloucester's only pet store. Food brands include Solid Gold, Science Diet, Eukanuba, Iams, and Breeder's Choice; nutritional supplements, flea and tick collars, leashes, collars, and doggie sweaters are also in stock.

Barking Boutique, 753 Boston Road, Billerica (978-667-6868). Pet day-care services and professional grooming, including medicated baths and nail clipping, are available at this facility, open since 1977. Cats and dogs get their own separate boarding areas.

Best Friends Pet Resort and Salon, 394 Middlesex Road, Tyngsboro (978-649-8585; www.bestfriendspetcare.com). Best Friends is a chain spread throughout the United States; the Tyngsboro location offers overnight boarding ($19–23 per night for dogs, $16 per night for cats) as well as doggie and kitty day care ($15 per day for dogs, $12 per day for cats). Your pet can get a playtime session for an extra $5 per stay, and grooming is also available.

Bone-Anza Doggie Daycare, 135 Cabot Street, Beverly (978-922-0117; www.boneanzadoggie-daycare.com). While you sightsee, your pooch can play, nap, go for walks, and socialize with the other animals and people at Bone-Anza. The staff will visit your house or hotel room ($10 per trip) to walk and water your dog, or you can bring your pet to their Cabot Street location ($20 per day) for fun and field trips to the beach and park with other pets.

Critter Care by Carol, North Reading (978-664-1308). This pet-sitting service offers dog walks, playtime, socialization, and other activities to keep your pet—large or small, common or exotic—busy while you're out. References are available, as are day and weekend hours.

Curious Creatures Pet Shop, 434 Rantoul Street, Beverly (978-922-4585). Stock up on premium cat and dog food, puppy-training products, shampoos, flea collars, chew toys, and treats at this 2,500-square-foot store in Beverly. They also have a large bird department with parrots, lovebirds, parakeets, and more.

Doggie Den, 16 Emerson Street, Haverhill (978-373-0803; doggiedenthe@aol.com). This business offers a little something for every pet owner, from grooming to training, supplies, and pet-focused photography. They even have a pickup service to save you the trip.

Paws at Play, 210 Eastern Avenue, Gloucester (978-281-PLAY; 1-866-360-PAWS). This doggie day-care facility is located in a renovated, air-conditioned farmhouse. "There's a large play-room and an enclosed porch inside, and two play yards outside," explains owner Gina Shlopak. "The dogs get lots of group play and human interaction." She plans to open an on-site cattery soon; call for updated details. Day-care rates are $14 for a half day and $22 for a full day. Overnight boarding is also available for an additional $10.

Pet Supplies Plus, 34 Cambridge Street, **Burlington** (781-273-0200); 400 Highland Avenue, **Salem** (978-740-9788). These large stores are like supermarkets for pets, stocking a wide selection of chew toys; dog, cat, bird, and small-mammal food; books; leashes and harnesses; pet beds, and more.

IN CASE OF EMERGENCY

Andover Animal Hospital,
233 Lowell Street, Andover (978-475-3600).

Beverly Animal Hospital,
303 Cabot Street, Beverly (978-927-5453).

Cape Ann Veterinary Hospital,
2 Wildon Heights, Rockport (978-546-2502).

Clipper City Animal Hospital,
419 Merrimac Street, Newburyport (978-462-7101).

Essex Animal Care Center,
229 Western Avenue, Essex (978-768-9111).

Lexington-Bedford Veterinary,
476 Bedford Street, Lexington (781-862-3670).

McGrath Animal Hospital,
31 Lexington Road, Billerica (978-667-2194).

Reading Animal Clinic,
1312 Main Street, Reading (781-944-1699).

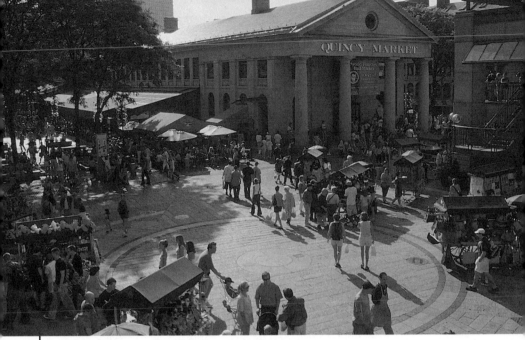

A BUSY SUMMER'S DAY AT FANEUIL HALL IN BOSTON

Greater Boston

PET-FRIENDLY RATING: 🦴 🦴 🦴 🦴

At its best, Beantown is a scenic, historic, and welcoming city. But these days, unfortunately, it is not at its best: The Big Dig massive construction and transportation project has sunk its claws into Boston for the foreseeable future, and locals and visitors alike have had to adjust to detours, orange cones, and mountains of dirt and debris. In a place that is already notoriously difficult to navigate, the project has made things even more, shall we say, interesting.

Most of the city's attractions, however, are untouched by the commotion, and Boston remains a hospitable and exciting place despite the temporary inconveniences. Best of all for pet owners, some of the region's most popular sites—from Faneuil Hall to the Freedom Trail—also happen to be outdoors. There is little you *can't* do with your pet here, except perhaps sample the cuisine at the city's many renowned restaurants. And for those occasions, there are plenty of pet-sitters and dog walkers around (see "Hot Spots for Spot") to keep an eye on your four-legged friend while you dine in style. Animal owners should note that dogs are not allowed at Boston Harbor Islands State Park; luckily the mainland offers more than enough opportunities for peering into the city's enticing past and present. Tea, anyone?

ACCOMMODATIONS

Hotels, Motels, Inns, and Bed & Breakfasts

Boston

Boston Harbor Hotel, 70 Rowes Wharf, Boston (617-439-7000; www.bhh.com); $250–830 per night. Pets are welcome at this high-end waterfront hotel that features a health club and spa, a 60-foot lap pool, a staffed business center, on-site covered parking, an indoor gourmet restaurant and an outdoor café, and a water shuttle to Logan Airport. Animals must be caged when left alone in the rooms.

Charles Street Inn, 94 Charles Street, Boston (617-314-8900; 1-877-772-8900; info@charlesstreet-inn.com; www.charlesstreetinn.com); $250–375 per night. Each room in this historic inn is named for a Victorian-era Bostonian who contributed to literature and the arts. The furnishings and surroundings are luxurious, complete with antiques, four-poster beds, and original paintings. "We have accommodated dogs ranging from 2 pounds to 100 pounds and never had a problem," explains pet-friendly innkeeper Louise Venden.

The Colonnade, 120 Huntington Avenue, Boston (1-800-962-3030; reservations@colonnadehotel.com; www.colonnadehotel.com); $165–300 per night. When it comes to making pet owners feel welcome, the Colonnade stands out from the rest. The hotel offers a VIPet program that features a dog-walking service ($15 per walk) and gifts for your animal. For its human guests, amenities include 285 contemporary rooms and 12 luxury suites, a shoe-shine service, free newspapers, laundry and valet service, a rooftop swimming pool, and a restaurant.

Eliot Hotel, 370 Commonwealth Avenue, Boston (617-267-1607; 1-800-44-ELIOT; www.eliothotel.com); $255–750 per night. This all-suite hotel was built in 1925 and offers 95 suites, room service, mini-bars, express check-in and checkout service, a fitness center, a restaurant and lounge, and a concierge service. The Eliot has no weight or size restrictions for pets and doesn't charge extra fees for them, though the management asks that you not leave your animal alone in the room.

Fairmont Copley Plaza, 138 St. James Avenue, Boston

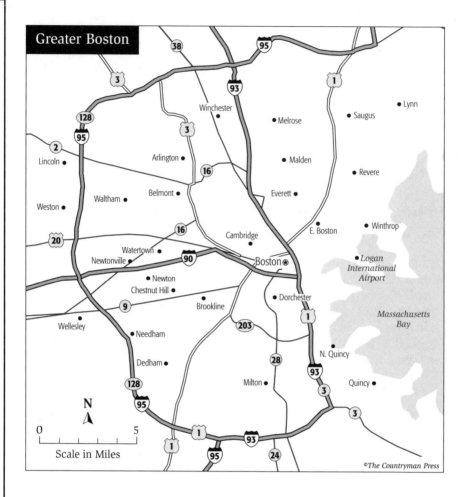

Greater Boston

©The Countryman Press

(617-267-5300; www.fairmont. com); $299–549 per night. The lavish Fairmont has been welcoming guests since 1912; on-site you'll find a fitness center, a beauty salon, 379 rooms and suites, in-room movies, 24-hour room service, desks with data ports, and baby-sitting services. Pets that weigh less than 20 pounds are welcome for an additional $25 per night.

Four Seasons Hotel,
200 Boylston Street, Boston (617-338-4400); $355–775. The Four Seasons' pet policy counts most dogs out: Only animals weighing less than 15 pounds are allowed. But pet owners looking for posh digs for their small pooch or cat will undoubtedly enjoy the "pet menu," available through room service, as well as the indoor swimming pool, 24-hour front desk, and laundry and valet services.

Hilton Boston Back Bay,
40 Dalton Street, Boston (617-236-1100); $199–400 per night. Located next to the Hynes Convention Center, this recently renovated Hilton has a fitness center, a swimming pool, two restaurants, and a business

center. Newbury Street, Copley Place, and Symphony Hall are all within walking distance. Animal owners pay a onetime fee of $40 and must keep their pets crated while in the rooms.

Hilton Boston Logan Airport,

85 Terminal Road, Boston (617-568-6700); $189–895 per night. This 600-room Hilton isn't just near the airport—it's at the airport. Walk from your room to the covered skyway and directly to your gate. Other hotel benefits include two restaurants, a café, a health club, a business center, and soundproof guest rooms. Pets are welcome without extra fees.

Howard Johnson Inn,

1271 Boylston Street, Boston (617-267-8300; 1-800-I-GO-HOJO); $115–175 per night. This is one of the best in-city bargains for pet owners and Red Sox fans: Located next to Fenway Park, the HoJo Inn has many of the same services of the fancier hotels, including a concierge service, a 24-hour front desk, free parking, a restaurant, and baby-sitting services. Animals are welcome without extra fees.

Le Meridien Boston,

250 Franklin Street, Boston (617-451-1900; www.lemeridien-boston.com); $340–650 per night. This European-style hotel was built in 1922 and originally served as the Federal Reserve Bank of Boston. Today it features a restaurant and café, 326 guest rooms, a fitness center, a business center, a concierge service, and a definite focus on luxury. Pets are welcome without extra fees, though owners are responsible for any damages.

Ramada Inn Boston,

800 Morrissey Boulevard, Boston (617-287-9100); $109–129 per night. With a free shuttle to the Boston and New England Medical Centers, a location about 5 miles from the airport, and reasonable rates, this Ramada is popular with tourists, business travelers, and other visitors. Pet owners must sign a release form and agree to follow the hotel's rules and regulations for animal guests.

Seaport Hotel,

1 Seaport Lane, Boston (617-385-4000; www.seaporthotel.com); $229–339 per night. The Seaport's 426 guest rooms and suites have water views, handcrafted furniture, and a combination of classic and modern touches. The hotel also offers an indoor swimming pool, laundry and turn-down services, airport shuttles, free shoe shines, a gift shop, and a florist. Pets are welcome without extra fees.

Sheraton Boston Hotel,

Prudential Center, 39 Dalton Street, Boston (617-236-2000); $199–519 per night. With more than 1,200 rooms, the Sheraton Boston is New England's largest hotel. The Hynes Convention Center and the Copley Place Mall are just a skywalk away; inside the Sheraton, guests can enjoy a swimming pool, restaurant and bar, room service, concierge service, and a business center. Pets are welcome without extra fees.

Swissôtel Boston,

1 Avenue de Lafayette, Boston (617-451-2600); $159–280 per night. This European-style hotel is located in the financial district close to Faneuil Hall. Each guest room

has a stocked mini-bar, cable TV, an alarm clock, and an iron and ironing board; guests can also enjoy a swimming pool, restaurant and bar, and dry-cleaning service. Pet owners must sign a release agreeing not to leave animals alone in the rooms.

Brookline

Beech Tree Inn, 83 Longwood Avenue, Brookline (617-277-1620; 1-800-544-9660); $75–160 per night. Well-behaved pets are welcome at the Beech Tree, a Victorian-style B&B with 11 guest rooms, air-conditioning, a sitting room, and a resident collie named C. K. Dexter Haven. Guests enjoy a continental breakfast each morning. Animal owners must sign a copy of the pet policy outlining the house rules.

Bertram Inn, 92 Sewall Avenue, Brookline (1-800-295-3822; innkeeper@bertraminn.com; www.bertraminn.com); $119–239 per night. Owned by a historical preservationist, this 1907 inn has 14 guest rooms on three floors; each room is individually decorated with touches like bookshelves, four-poster beds, antique walnut furniture, and cheery window swags. Pets are welcome with preapproval, though they can't be left unattended in the rooms.

Holiday Inn Boston–Brookline, 1200 Beacon Street, Brookline (617-277-1200); $189–239. For an extra $15 per night, pets can join their owners at this Holiday Inn, which features air-conditioning, an indoor swimming pool, room service, in-room movies, cable TV, in-room hair dryers, a fitness center, and a lounge. Downtown Boston is a few minutes' drive away.

Cambridge

Charles Hotel Harvard Square, 1 Bennett Street, Cambridge (617-864-1200; 1-800-323-7500); $250–3,000 per night. This ultra-deluxe hotel offers the finest of everything, including a great location. In addition to VIP rooms and services, a beauty shop, a fitness center, baby- and pet-sitting services, and room service, the hotel also has two on-site gourmet restaurants and a jazz bar. Pets are welcome without extra fees but can't be left alone in the rooms.

Residence Inn by Marriott Boston Cambridge Center, 6 Cambridge Center, Cambridge (617-349-0700); $199–349 per night. Guests enjoy a complimentary buffet breakfast, free newspapers, fax and photocopying services, and laundry facilities at this all-suite, extended-stay facility. Each suite has a separate bedroom and living room and a full kitchen. Pet owners pay an initial $100 nonrefundable fee, and then an additional $10 per night.

An Urban Homestead, 283 Windsor Street, Cambridge (617-354-3116; urbanhomestead@yahoo.com); $95–125 per night. Formerly known as **Windsor House,** this cozy, tucked-away home offers two guest rooms with double and queen beds, and can accommodate up to six people. Buffet-style breakfasts include fresh fruits, cereals, imported jams and jellies, coffee, and tea. Owner Heidi Lyons welcomes pets.

THE CHARLES HOTEL IS LOCATED IN THE HEART OF HARVARD SQUARE IN CAMBRIDGE.

Charlestown
Bunker Hill Bed & Breakfast,
80 Elm Street, Charlestown (617-241-8067; crawolff@cs.com; www.bunkerhillbedandbreakfast.com); $135 per night. A cozy alternative to the "big city" hotels, this Victorian-style B&B offers two guest rooms, an antiques-filled living room, a full kitchen and a breakfast nook, a hot tub, air-conditioning, TVs, bathrobes, slippers, and complimentary snacks. The owners are very animal-friendly and allow pets for an extra $10 per day.

Dedham
Residence Inn by Marriott Dedham, 259 Elm Street, Dedham (781-407-0999); $135–159 per night. Located in the suburbs south of Boston, this Residence Inn has suites with kitchens, a swimming pool, free parking and newspapers, a fitness center, cable TV, in-room coffeemakers, and a 24-hour front desk. Pets are allowed with a $150 nonrefundable fee and an additional $10 per night.

Newton
Holiday Inn Boston–Newton,
399 Grove Street, Newton (617-969-5300); $170–209 per night. Pets that weigh less than 30 pounds are welcome at this Holiday Inn for an extra $25 one-time fee. The hotel has a gym, in-room movies, room service, cable TV, a wake-up service, coffeemakers and hair dryers in the rooms, air-conditioning, and a concierge desk.

Sheraton Newton Hotel,
320 Washington Street, Newton (617-969-3010); $199–415 per night. This 12-story, recently renovated Sheraton is located on the outskirts of Boston. Amenities include in-room movies, a 24-hour front desk, two restaurants and a lounge, an indoor swimming pool, a fitness center, and shuttle buses that leave regularly for Faneuil Hall. Pets are welcome guests.

Revere
Hampton Inn Logan Airport,
230 Lee Burbank Highway, Revere (781-286-5665); $79–139 per night. As its name implies, this hotel is just north of the airport and 3 to 6 miles from most Boston attractions. On-site, you'll find an indoor swimming pool and hot tub, satellite TV, and a fitness club. The hotel also offers a free airport shuttle service. "Small" pets (call to see if yours qualifies) are welcome without extra fees.

Saugus
Colonial Traveler Motor Court,
1753 Broadway, Saugus (781-233-6700); $55–82 per night. This simple and clean motor inn is located about 6 miles north of Boston and offers standard rooms, one- and two-bedroom suites, cable TV with premium movie channels, refrigerators, and coin-operated laundry facilities. Pets are welcome for an additional $10 per night.

Waltham
Summerfield Suites Boston–Waltham, 54 Fourth Avenue, Waltham (781-290-0026); $99–209 per night. Each of the one- and two-bedroom suites at this extended-stay facility has a desk with data ports, separate bedroom and living room areas,

cable TV, and VCRs. Pet owners will pay an extra $25 per night if staying for less than four nights; for stays longer than four nights, the hotel charges a onetime non-refundable fee of $150.

Winthrop

Inn at Crystal Cove, 600 Shirley Street, Winthrop (617-846-9217; ccove@tiac.net; www.inncrystal-cove.com); $89–129 per night. Located on a peninsula just outside Boston, this inn has great views of the city skyline and harbor. Each of the 30 guest rooms has air-conditioning, cable TV, and free local calls; some also have balconies and water views. "We have lots of open spaces for dogs to run around," says manager Karl Sticker. "We also have parks nearby and a gigantic boulevard for dog walking." Pets are enthusiastically welcomed.

Woburn

Radisson Hotel Woburn, 15 Middlesex Canal Park Road, Woburn (781-935-8760); $119–159 per night. Formerly known as the **Ramada Inn Woburn,** this hotel sits next to a 17-screen Showcase Cinema movie theater in the Boston suburbs. Amenities include a restaurant and lounge, a swimming pool, air-conditioning, cable TV,

and in-room coffeemakers. Pet owners pay a $150 deposit: $100 of that fee is refundable.

Red Roof Inn Boston Woburn, 19 Commerce Way, Woburn (781-935-7110; 1-800-RED-ROOF); $85–114 per night. This suburban economy hotel is located close to the train and bus stations and makes a good home base for visiting Boston or any of the large companies in the surrounding I-95 corridor. Guests can take advantage of express checkout services, free local calls, cable TV, and free newspapers. Pets that weigh less than 80 pounds are welcome.

Rental Agencies

Bed & Breakfast Associates Bay Colony, Boston (1-888-486-6018; info@bnbboston.com; www.bnbboston.com). This reservations service can help you find short- and long-term housing in the Boston area; at any given time, a few of their accommodations allow pets. At the time of this writing, animal-friendly listings included "The Studio," a contemporary South End town house, and "Emma's Garden," a one-bedroom Beacon Hill apartment with a kitchenette and a brick patio.

OUT AND ABOUT

Arnold Arboretum of Harvard University, intersection of Centre Street (Route 1) and the Arborway (Route 203), Boston (617-524-1718). This is a fantastic destina-

tion for any visitor—one that just happens to allow your pets to come along, too. The 365-acre research and educational arboretum contains one of the best woody plant collections in the world. Highlights include a bonsai garden, a lilac collection, the Chinese Path, and 130 types of maple trees. (If you arrive in early October, you'll enjoy a fiery show of foliage.) Dogs must be leashed, and owners are expected to clean up after their animals.

Boston Common. Like many of New England's commons and greens, this one was once used to graze cattle. Today, of course, it is better known as one of the oldest public parks in America. Comprising 50 acres, it includes the **Boston Public Garden,** fountains, the Make Way for Ducklings sculptures, and the famous Swan Boats. Dogs must be on a leash.

Boston Walk for Animals, Boston. The **Massachusetts Society for the Prevention of Cruelty to Animals (MSPCA)** puts on this walk every autumn. The dates and locations change periodically; call 617-522-7400 or visit www.mspca.org for the latest information. The society also hosts a fun Animal Hall of Fame fund-raising dinner each year—all are welcome to attend.

Charles River Canoe and Kayak, Artesni Park (off Soldiers Field Road), Cambridge (617-965-5110). Rent a canoe and explore the harbor with your favorite adventurous canine. The waterway is typically crowded with kayaks, sailboats, motorboats, and the boats of rowing teams at practice, so use caution, especially near the Boston University Bridge.

Charles River Reservation, Boston. Managed by the Metropolitan District Commission, this 17-mile-long stretch of park winds its way around the river with views of rowers, sailboats, and the Cambridge and Boston skylines. The pathways, especially popular with joggers and dog walkers, run past the **Hatch Shell** (where the Boston Pops give their annual Fourth of July concerts), **Mount Auburn Cemetery,** and **JFK Memorial Park,** among other spots. The park runs alongside Storrow Drive, Memorial Drive, and Soldier's Field Road.

Christopher Columbus Waterfront Park, Boston. After a visit to the North End, take a stroll over to this green and garden-filled area located between Commercial and Long Wharfs. Keep traveling south toward Central Wharf and the **New England Aquarium,** and you'll find plenty of spots to stop and enjoy the views. (If you're lucky, you'll also see the seals hanging out in the aquarium's outdoor habitat.) Dogs must be on a leash.

Faneuil Hall and Quincy Market, Boston. This large outdoor gathering place and vendor area has cart after cart selling scarves, cookbooks, hats, oatmeal cookies, clam chowder, flowers, T-shirts, trinkets, rubber stamps, and a seemingly endless array of other items and foods. (There's inevitably at least one cart selling pet-related fun stuff.) Additions in recent years have included indoor shopping malls and chain stores, but there's still plenty to do outside with your pooch in tow. Walk the cobblestone streets, enjoy a hot pretzel from a vendor, or just relax on a bench and watch the world go by. The marketplace is tucked between North, Congress, and State Streets.

First Night, Boston. The city streets fill with people, ice sculptures, and celebration every New Year's Eve in Boston and Cambridge. There are usually more than 250 indoor and outdoor shows, entertainers, and artists, along with fireworks. If your pooch doesn't mind crowds and loud noises, this is a must-see.

Freedom Trail, Boston. This self-guided trail of Boston's historic sites is one of the city's most popular attractions—and, like all of the best things in life, it's absolutely free. Start at the Visitor Information Center on the Boston Common and follow the red brick/red paint line as it winds through the streets. Medallions on the ground mark each of 16 notable sites, including the **Old South Meeting House,** the Boston Massacre site, and the **Paul Revere House.** The 2½-mile-long trail ends at the **Bunker Hill Monument.**

Harvard Square, Cambridge. Park your car here and wander for a bit; this bustling commercial area has about 20 bookstores, 10 music stores, 9 museums, 5 theaters, and street performers around every corner. There are plenty of students around, but people from every conceivable walk of life also find themselves drawn to the activity and discussions at the small cafés and sidewalk benches. To get there, just head for JFK Street and follow your nose around the winding and crowded streets.

Lynn Woods, Pennybrook Road, Lynn (781-477-7123; www.flw. org). "Lynn Woods is dog's paradise," says park ranger Dan Small. "We have 40 miles of hiking trails and fire roads." Because the on-site ponds are part of the local reservoir system, dogs aren't allowed to swim, and they must be on a leash at all times. Popular landmarks include the stone tower, Dungeon Rock, the rose garden, and Wolf Pits.

The North End, Boston. This Italian enclave is slowly becoming more of a melting pot of different peoples, but it's still the place Bostonians go to get a taste of Italy. In addition to myriad restaurants, cafés, and pastry shops, you'll also find the **Paul Revere house, Copp's Hill Burying Ground,** and the famous **Old North Church** on these narrow, historic streets. The neighborhood stretches throughout Hanover, Salem, Parmenter, Richmond, Fulton, and Prince Streets, roughly located between Faneuil Hall and the wharfs.

Petoberfest, Boston. **The Animal Rescue League of Boston** holds this rollicking event each October with games, crafts tables, family activities, and, of course, lots of food (for people and pets). Other annual events include the **That Doggone Walk** fund-raising trek in June, and the **Holiday Dinner for Horses,** a salute to the city's working equines, in December. Dates and locations vary from year to year; for updated information, contact the league at 617-426-9170 or visit www.arl-boston.org.

Provincetown–Boston Ferry, Boston Harbor Cruises, Long Wharf Ferry Terminal, Boston (617-227-4321; www.boston-harborcruises.com); $39–49 per person, round trip. Take a scenic shortcut from Boston to one of Cape Cod's most interesting towns. Boston Harbor Cruises' "fast ferry" welcomes animals on board for this 90-minute journey on the Atlantic; the boat is the biggest passenger ferry in the United States. (For more information on Provincetown, see "Cape Cod and the Islands.")

QUICK BITES

Absolutely Asia, 864 Main Street, Waltham (781-891-1700). Order your Chinese and Thai food to go or have it delivered; specialties include Yu Hsiang–style pork and beef, Hong Kong–style pan-fried noodles, jumbo shrimp in black bean sauce, and Thai-style spicy seafood soup.

Brigham's, 50 Congress Street, **Boston** (617-523-9372); 109 High Street, **Boston** (617-482-3524); 499 East Broadway, **South Boston** (617-269-9706); 172 School Street, **Everett** (617-389-9315). This local chain is a long-time Boston-area favorite. You can eat inside or order ice cream, frozen yogurt, and other treats from the take-out window. These are just a few of the locations; as you explore the region, you're bound to pass more.

El Pelon, 92 Peterborough Street, Boston (617-262-9090). Locals love this tiny Mexican restaurant, where most of the items are available as take-out and everything is very reasonably priced. House specialties include fish tacos and burritos, taquitos, and extra-hot sauce.

Faneuil Hall Marketplace, 3 Faneuil Hall Market Place, Boston. If you're craving it, you'll probably find it here. Many of the restaurants have outdoor seating on the cobblestones, and the marketplace itself has a huge selection of take-out-only eateries serving everything from seafood to pizza, gelato, and cheesecake. You can't bring your dog inside the walk-through marketplace, but outside there are plenty of benches to be found for enjoying your bounty.

Il Panino Express, 264 Hanover Street, Boston (617-720-5720). This North End restaurant offers great walk-around food, including calzones, sandwiches, subs, and pizza slices. They're open daily for lunch and dinner; at the time of this writing, the company was planning to open a satellite location on Massachusetts Avenue in Harvard Square in Cambridge.

New England Soup Factory, 2 Brookline Place, Brookline (617-739-1899). When you're tired of sandwiches, stop by this take-out shop for a cup of chili or soup with every imaginable combination of ingredients. The menu changes daily. And if you're *not* sick of sandwiches, they have those, too, along with desserts.

Parish Café, 361 Boylston Street, Boston (617-247-4777). Located just around the corner from the Public Garden, this upscale café has some outdoor seating and serves sandwiches on gourmet bread with ingredients such as prosciutto, lobster salad, roast beef, and arugula.

Veggie Planet, 47 Palmer Street, Cambridge (617-661-1513). This vegetarian restaurant and pizzeria in Harvard Square bakes its pizzas on organic pizza dough with varieties such as Mexican bean, caramelized fennel and onion, and red-peanut curry. Coffee, tea, and Italian sodas are also available.

HOT SPOTS FOR SPOT

Animal Spirit, 2362 Massachusetts Avenue, Cambridge (617-876-9696; animalspirit@hotmail.com). Take your pooch for a visit to this grooming spa and pet health-supply store near Porter Square. Pampering services include herbal shampoos and a Hydro-Surge bathing "spa treatment." You'll also find a full line of gourmet pet foods, toys, and treats.

Best Friends Pet Resort and Salon, 15 Main Street, Wakefield (781-245-1237; www.bestfriends-petcare.com). This branch of the national pet-sitting chain offers overnight boarding for dogs ($16–22 per night) and cats ($11 per night). Doggie and kitty day care is also available, as are grooming services. You can purchase playtime sessions for your pet during her stay for an extra $5 per session.

Four Paws and a Leash, Dorchester (617-288-6751; dennis@fourpawsandaleash.com; www.fourpawsandaleash.com). Owner Dennis Saccoach runs his pet-caretaking business out of Dorchester and serves the entire Greater Boson area. Services include dog walks, play sessions, and at-home pet care; the prices vary with each individual situation, though half-hour walks are typically $10, and one-hour walks are $17.

Linda's Critter Corral, 73 Bessom Street, Lynn (781-599-7387). If you run out of pet food or supplies on the road, stop by Linda's. This well-stocked shop has everything you might need for cats, dogs, gerbils, birds, and other animals, as well as toys, gifts, and collectibles for animal owners.

Morning Paws, Boston (617-338-8178; morningpaws@mail.com; www.morningpaws.com). This Boston-based company specializes in "dog walks and cat care" in the **Back Bay, Bay Village, Beacon Hill,** and the **South End.** Owner Philip Schwartz also offers short-term boarding for small to medium dogs, as well as house-sitting and pet-sitting services. Dog-walking rates are $10–12 per dog; for cat care, owners pay $12–15 per visit. Overnight boarding is $40 for 24 hours of care.

Partners in Pet Care, 260 Beacon Street, Somerville (617-547-2992; dogspetcare@netscape.net; www.partnersnpetcare.com). This animal-centered business offers 40-minute pet-sitting, walks, and play sessions for Boston-area residents as well as visitors who would like to enjoy a nice dinner while someone else keeps an eye on Fluffy. The rates are $13 per walk and $10 per visit for cat-sitting. Dogs are always walked individually, not in groups.

Pet-Estrian Services, Belmont (617-484-2489; pet-estrian@aol.com; www.pet-estrian.com). Based in Belmont, this animal-focused business offers daily dog walks, pet-sitting services, and daily Leader of the Pack play groups that offer dogs a chance to socialize and exercise while their owners are otherwise occupied. Owner Lesley Sager Levine even publishes an online newsletter for her clients.

Pet Shop Girls, 472 Shawmut Avenue, Boston (617-262-7387). This is one of the South End's busiest stops for animal lovers. Pet Shop Girls is a doggie daycare center, groomer, and pet-supply store rolled up into one—they even offer pet massages from licensed massage therapist Arnold Katz.

Skipton Pet Center, 70 Southampton Street, Boston (617-541-0520; 1-800-PET-MENU; petmenu@rcn.com; www.1800-petmenu.com). This company offers a most unusual service in the pet-supply world—they deliver! You can call the 800 number and get dog and cat food, treats, toys, and other supplies delivered to your door, or you can visit their Southampton Street store Monday through Friday from 9 AM to 7 PM.

IN CASE OF EMERGENCY

Angell Memorial Animal Hospital,
350 South Huntington Avenue, Jamaica Plain (617-522-7282).

Arlington Animal Clinic,
191 Broadway, Arlington (781-646-0758).

Brookline Animal Hospital,
678 Brookline Avenue, Brookline (617-277-2030).

Cambridge Veterinary Care,
1724 Massachusetts Avenue, Cambridge (617-661-6255).

Charles Street Animal Clinic,
158 Charles Street, Boston (617-227-0153).

Everett Animal Clinic,
456 Ferry Street, Everett (617-387-6777).

Union Square Veterinary Clinic,
37 Union Square, Somerville (617-628-2644).

PLYMOUTH ROCK AND THE *MAYFLOWER II* ARE BOTH VISIBLE FROM THIS SHADY PARK IN DOWNTOWN PLYMOUTH.

South Shore and Suburbs

PET-FRIENDLY RATING: 🦴 🦴 🦴

Visiting pet owners aren't likely to complain about the South Shore's peaceful scenery, quaint shopping villages, and lovely public parks—but they just might grumble a bit about the small number of pet-friendly accommodations offered in this busy corner of the state. Likewise, those who came to Massachusetts to delve into real-life history lessons will be disappointed to learn that many of the region's most popular attractions, including Battleship Cove, Edaville USA, and Plimoth Plantation, are off-limits to pets. (Luckily, you and your furry friends can still check out the *Mayflower II* and Plymouth Rock from the sidewalk: See Pilgrim Memorial State Park under "Out and About.")

Most of the South Shore's tourism appeal is centered along its coast, starting in the north with picturesque towns like Scituate and Duxbury and working down to the historically significant Plymouth; the near-Cape communities of Wareham, Marion, and Fairhaven; the southern havens of Dartmouth and Westport; and the bustling port cities of New Bedford and Fall River. Visitors don't typically venture into the suburbs, though there are more than enough parks and attractions there to keep you busy. Many first-time Massachusetts visitors find the South Shore's tourist-friendly location—midway between the Cape and Boston—to be an ideal home base for covering both ends of the vacation spectrum.

ACCOMMODATIONS

Hotels, Motels, Inns, and Bed & Breakfasts

Braintree

Motel 6, 125 Union Street, Braintree (781-848-7890); $59–75 per night. Like other Motel 6 locations, the Braintree and Seekonk motels welcome pets. The Braintree site is located about 10 miles from Cambridge and offers premium movie channels, laundry facilities, and free coffee. In Seekonk, guests are right across the river from Providence, Rhode Island, and enjoy similar amenities.

Brockton

Residence Inn by Marriott Brockton, 124 Liberty Street, Brockton (508-583-3600; 1-800-627-7468); $139–169 per night. Designed for long-term stays, the Brockton Residence Inn has suites with kitchens, desks, and separate bedroom and living room areas. On-site, you'll also find a swimming pool, a fitness center, and valet service. Pet owners pay a onetime cleaning fee of $150, then an additional $10 per night.

Fairhaven

Holiday Inn Express Fairhaven, 110 Middle Street, Fairhaven (508-997-1281); $71–149 per night. This Holiday Inn Express has 80 guest rooms, an on-site fitness center, air-conditioning, laundry facilities, photocopying and fax services, and free continental breakfasts. It's located on the scenic waterfront, close to restaurants, shops, and the Fairhaven Historic District. Pets are welcome for an additional $10 per night.

Huttleston Motel, 128 Huttleston Avenue, Fairhaven (508-997-7655); $50–80 per night. This clean, quiet motel is family owned and operated, offering an affordable lodging alternative in the coastal community of Fairhaven. The motel is located right outside New Bedford and about 20 minutes from the Cape Cod Canal. Pets are welcome with prior approval for an additional $5 per day; animals cannot be left alone in the rooms.

Foxboro

Residence Inn by Marriott Foxboro, 250 Foxboro Boulevard,

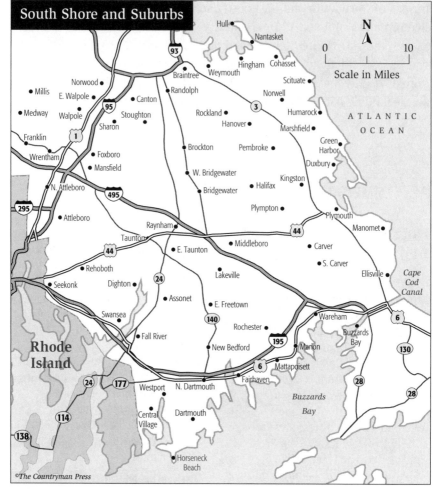

South Shore and Suburbs

Hull • Nantasket
Hingham Cohasset
Norwood • Braintree Weymouth
• Millis E. Walpole • Scituate •
Randolph Norwell •
• Canton
• Medway Walpole Stoughton Rockland • Humarock •
Sharon Hanover • Marshfield •
Franklin Green •
Wrentham • Foxboro • Brockton Pembroke • Harbor
• Mansfield Duxbury •
N. Attleboro W. Bridgewater Kingston
• Halifax •
Bridgewater
Plympton • Plymouth
• Attleboro Manomet •
Raynham •
Taunton 44 • Middleboro Carver
• E. Taunton • S. Carver
• Rehoboth Lakeville Ellisville • Cape Cod Canal
• Seekonk Dighton •
Assonet E. Freetown Wareham
Swansea Rochester • Buzzards Bay
• Fall River New Bedford Marion
Rhode Mattapoisett
Island Westport N. Dartmouth Fairhaven Buzzards Bay
Central Dartmouth
Village
Horseneck Beach

N
0 10
Scale in Miles

ATLANTIC
OCEAN

Rhode Island

Buzzards Bay

©The Countryman Press

Foxboro (508-698-2800); $119–165 per night. You can choose from a studio or a one- or two-bedroom suite at this Residence Inn, which also offers a swimming pool, free breakfast buffets, and a rental-car desk. Pet owners staying one to five nights will pay an additional flat fee of $150; those staying more than five nights will pay $100 plus an additional $10 per night.

Franklin

Hawthorne Suites Hotel,
835 Upper Union Street, Franklin (508-553-3500; 1-800-527-1133;

www.hawthornsuites-ma.com); $79–219 per night. Choose from one- and two-bedroom executive or luxury presidential suites at Hawthorne Suites, a full-service hotel offering free buffet breakfasts, an indoor swimming pool and hot tub, a fitness center, and a meeting space for business travelers. Pet owners pay a $75 nonrefundable deposit and $5 per night, up to 30 nights.

Kingston

Inn at Plymouth Bay, Route 3, Kingston (781-585-3831; 1-800-941-

0075; inn@plymouthbay.com; www.plymouthbay.com); $99–139 per night. Families are welcome at this well-appointed inn (children under 18 stay free). Amenities include indoor and outdoor swimming pools, a hot tub and sauna, color TVs with free movies, private balconies, microwaves, and refrigerators. Pets are allowed in designated smoking rooms only.

Mansfield
Holiday Inn Mansfield,
31 Hampshire Street, Mansfield (508-339-2200); $124–144 per night. The Mansfield Holiday Inn offers an indoor swimming pool, hot tub and sauna, outdoor tennis courts, laundry and valet services, in-room movies, free morning newspapers, a restaurant and lounge, room service, and in-room coffeemakers and hair dryers. Pets are allowed for an additional $10 per night.

Red Roof Inn Mansfield/Foxboro,
60 Forbes Boulevard, Mansfield (508-339-2323; 1-800-RED-ROOF); $59–71 per night. You can take in a Patriots' football game in Foxboro and then relax at this Red Roof Inn, part of the national chain of economy motels. Guests enjoy a swimming pool, cable TV, laundry facilities, express checkout, and free local calls. Pets are welcome with no extra fees, though owners have to sign a pet-policy agreement form.

Middleboro
Days Inn Plymouth–
Middleboro, 30 East Clark Street, Middleboro (508-946-4400); $61–99 per night. Animals are welcome for an additional $3 per night at this Days Inn, which is close to Plymouth attractions and features a 24-hour front desk, cable TV, free morning newspapers, in-room hair dryers, and laundry services. Some rooms also have refrigerators and microwaves. Guests enjoy a continental breakfast each morning.

New Bedford
Captain Haskell's Octagon House,
347 Union Street, New Bedford (508-999-3933; stay@the octagonhouse.com; www.the-octagonhouse.com); $70–125 per night. This extremely pet-friendly B&B welcomes animals of all shapes and sizes; owners Ruth and Chuck Smiler even offer a discount to pet owners who have adopted their animal from a shelter. The historic home features antiques-filled guest rooms, private baths, a cozy parlor, and formal gardens. Ruth and Chuck also have plenty of suggestions for four-legged outings in the area.

Plymouth
Beach House Bed & Breakfast,
45 Black Pond Lane, Plymouth (508-224-3517; 1-888-BNB-CLIF; denise@beachhousebandb.com; www.beachhousebandb.com); $90–140 per night. Located directly on the ocean, this modern, weathered-shingle B&B has wicker deck furniture and lounge chairs, a private beach, bright interior furnishings, hardwood floors, cable TV, and great views. In the fall and winter months you can often see seals; golf courses and other attractions are nearby. Pets are welcome.

Hall's Bed & Breakfast,
3 Sagamore Street, Plymouth (508-746-2835); $65–80 per

night. For an extra $5 per night, dogs can join their owners at this downtown Victorian B&B located close to everything Plymouth has to offer, including shops, restaurants, and historic sites. A full country breakfast is included in the rate, as is parking.

Raynham

Days Inn Taunton, 164 New State Highway, Raynham (508-824-8647); $80–95 per night. Located close to several malls and movie theaters and about 20 minutes from Plymouth, this Days Inn has a gym, cable TV, laundry facilities, a restaurant, and a 24-hour front desk. Pets are welcome without extra fees.

Rehoboth

Five Bridge Inn Bed & Breakfast, 154 Pine Street, Rehoboth (508-252-3190; info@fivebridgeinn.com; www.fivebridgeinn.com); $88–145 per night. Dine on complimentary wine and cheese while you relax in your guest room or common areas at this spacious and luxurious B&B. On-site, you'll also find a lap pool, a screened-in gazebo, a tennis court, and hiking trails on the inn's 80 acres. Five Bridge specializes in weddings and other events. Pets are welcome.

Rockland

Holiday Inn Express Rockland, 909 Hingham Street, Rockland (781-871-5660); $55–139 per night. For an additional $6 per night, your pet can join you at this hotel featuring free continental breakfasts, air-conditioning, a laundry service, hair dryers, irons and ironing boards, in-room

movies, and a wake-up service. Rockland is a short drive from Boston as well as the scenic coastal towns of Scituate, Cohasset, and Hingham.

Scituate Harbor

Inn at Scituate Harbor, 7 Beaver Dam Road, Scituate Harbor (781-545-5550; 1-800-368-3818; www.innatscituateharbor.com); $79–189 per night. Guests at this contemporary inn can relax on the outdoor deck overlooking the harbor, walk to downtown shops and restaurants, or swim in the indoor swimming pool. All rooms have cable TV, air-conditioning, and water views; two of them are available for pet owners for an additional fee of $20 per day, per pet.

Seekonk

Motel 6, 821 Fall River Avenue, Seekonk (508-336-7800); $59–75 per night. (See listing under Braintree.)

Ramada Inn Seekonk, Route 114A, Seekonk (508-336-7300; 1-800-298-2054); $84–95 per night. Close to Brown University and Providence College, this hotel is popular with campus visitors and business travelers alike. Amenities include an airport shuttle, an on-site restaurant, room service, a swimming pool, free local calls, and a 24-hour front desk. Pets are welcome for an extra $10 per night.

Somerset

Quality Inn Somerset, 1878 Wilbur Avenue, Somerset (508-678-4545; 1-800-228-5151); $99–119 per night. Located across the water from Fall River, this Quality Inn has a restaurant and lounge, free continental breakfasts, an indoor swimming pool, laundry facilities, room service, and cable TV with in-room movies. Animal owners will no doubt appreciate the hotel's pet-friendly policies (no extra fees) as well as its picnic area in the yard.

Wareham

Little Harbor Guest House, 20 Stockton Short Cut Street, Wareham (508-295-6329); $77–87 per night. Golfers will fall hard for this cute B&B: It's surrounded on all sides by the Little Harbor Country Club par-3 golf course. The Cape-style home offers large, sunny guest rooms, full country breakfasts, a swimming pool, and a hot tub. The beach is a half mile away. There are no extra fees for pets, though they can't be left alone in the rooms.

Campgrounds

East Mansfield

Canoe River Campground, 137 Mill Street, East Mansfield (508-339-6462); $20–26 per night. Leashed, quiet pets are welcome at Canoe River, a family campground with 200 sites for tenters and RVers. The wooded grounds offer swimming pools, a pond, an arcade, boat rentals, and lots of scheduled activities. The site is close to the Rhode Island border and about a half hour's drive from Boston in one direction and Plymouth in the other.

East Taunton

Massasoit State Park Campground, 1371 Middleboro

Avenue, East Taunton (508-822-7405); $10 per night Massachusetts residents; $12 per night out-of-state residents. Open from Memorial Day through Columbus Day, this campground welcomes leashed pets to its 120 sites for tents and RVs. Campers can take advantage of showers, flush toilets, picnic tables, and fire pits at each site and a dumping station. The state park (see "Out and About" for more information) also has a boat ramp and hiking trails.

Foxboro

Normandy Farms Family Camping Resort, 72 West Street, Foxboro (508-543-7600; camp@normandyfarms.com; www.normandyfarms.com); $19–57 per night or $127–326 per week. Bring your tent or RV to Normandy Farms for a full resort-style camping experience. Facilities include a gift shop, a snack bar, modern rest rooms and laundry areas, scheduled children's activities, swimming pools, and the Recreation Lodge. Pets are always welcome but must stay on a leash and cannot be left alone.

Hingham

Wompatuck State Park Campground, Union Street, Hingham (781-749-7160; 781-749-7161); $10 per night Massachusetts residents; $12 per night out-of-state residents. Choose from 450 campsites (many with hookups) at this large campground offering rest rooms with showers, a dumping station, fireplaces and picnic tables at each site, hiking trails, and a boat ramp. (See "Out and About" for more information about the park.)

Middleboro

Boston South–Middleboro–Plymouth KOA, 438 Plymouth Street, Middleboro (508-947-6435; 1-800-562-3046); $22–39 per night. Tenters and RVers are welcome at this centrally located campground; quiet, leashed pets are welcome at campsites but not in the Kamping Kabins. The KOA has a swimming pool and sundeck, volleyball and basketball courts, a game room, dances and movie nights, and a playground.

Plymouth

Sandy Pond Campground, 834 Bourne Road, Plymouth (508-759-9336; 508-224-6121; www.sandypond.com); $23–30 per night. With 200 campsites, canoe rentals, sports fields, two beaches, hiking trails, and a playground, Sandy Pond offers families plenty to do. The camp store stocks all the basics, including firewood and food. Quiet pets are welcome as long as they stay on leashes, although the campground bans certain breeds; call for details. There is a $5 per night fee for animals weighing more than 25 pounds.

Rochester

Gateway to Cape Cod Resort, 90 Stevens Road, Rochester (508-763-5911); $25 per night. Of the 143 sites at this membership campground, 110 accommodate pull-throughs and all have full hookups. Gasoline and propane are available, as well as a camp store, a snack bar, a recreation hall, tennis and volleyball courts,

and a playground. Pets are welcome without extra fees but cannot be left unattended at a site.

South Carver

Myles Standish State Forest Campground, Cranberry Road, South Carver (508-866-2526); $10 per night Massachusetts residents; $12 per night out-of-state residents. This 14,000-acre park (see "Out and About") near Plymouth has nearly 500 campsites for tenters and RVers, along with hookups, a dumping station, rest rooms with hot showers, picnic tables, and fire pits. There are also five "group camping" sites that can accommodate 50 persons each.

Westport Point

Horseneck Beach State Reservation Campground, Route 88, Westport Point (508-636-8817; 508-636-8816); $12 per night Massachusetts residents; $15 per night out-of-state residents. Run by the Massachusetts Department of Environmental Management, the Horseneck Beach campground is open seasonally with 100 campsites, picnic areas, a boat ramp, rest rooms with showers, and a dumping station. Pets must be on a leash and are not allowed at the beach. (For more information on the reservation, see "Out and About.")

Homes, Cottages, and Cabins for Rent

Plymouth

Oceanfront Home on Plymouth Bay, Plymouth (508-747-0883; 617-696-6284; ed1091@attbi.com); $2,500–3,000 per week.

Steps from the beach, this large house has water views, a wraparound deck, a fireplace, and satellite TV. "Allowing animals has worked out well for us," explains owner Mary Dutkiewicz. "I usually find that people who travel with their pets take extra precautions to make sure they won't ruin the experience for anyone who follows them!"

Summer Cottage, Plymouth (617-698-7651; rgatnik@scci-bos.com); $900–1,000 per week. Well-behaved, quiet pets are welcome at this coastal rental located close to all of Plymouth's attractions and several golf courses. The house accommodates six people and has three bedrooms, a living room with a fireplace, a patio, a breakfast room, and access to a private beach.

South Middleboro
Tispaquin Pond Home, Tispaquin Pond, South Middleboro (407-932-3470; richhlan2@juno.com); $600–1,200 per week.

This modern Colonial sits directly on the water with a dock, a rowboat, a Jacuzzi, a fireplace, a barbecue grill, cable TV, a VCR, and a stereo with CD player. Relax by the pond, head into town for antiquing, or visit the nearby Cape and Plymouth. "Small" pets (call to see if yours qualifies) are allowed.

Rental Agencies

The Absent Innkeeper, 631 State Road, Plymouth (508-224-6728; innkeeper@absentinnkeeper.com; www.absentinnkeeper.com). This agency specializes in short-term, vacation, and corporate rentals; some of the listed properties do allow pets, though the exact number varies from season to season. Most of the homes are directly on the water or close to it, and rates range from about $850 to about $3,000 per week. Call or visit the web site to see the latest listings.

OUT AND ABOUT

Feast of the Holy Ghost, Fall River. This huge street fair and celebration takes place during the last week of every August in downtown Fall River. Visitors can enjoy a traditional procession, music, street performances, and of course *lots* of food. If you're not in town during the festival, you can still check out the **Maritime Heritage Trail** and the **Columbia Street Historic District,** where

you'll find shops, restaurants, and historic brick architecture.

F. Gilbert Hills State Forest, Mill Street, Foxboro (508-543-5850). Local mountain biking enthusiasts know the way to this 1,000-acre preserve spread throughout Foxboro and Wrentham; it was named for a former state park employee who created many of Massachusetts's first state park maps. The forest has 23 miles of trails for hiking, biking, horseback riding, and cross-country skiing. Dogs must be on a leash.

Fort Phoenix State Reservation, Green Street, Fairhaven (508-992-4524). The first sea battle of the Revolutionary War was fought in this spot; today, the small park offers visitors a half-mile stretch of beach with wonderful views, and a chance to see the remnants of the once mighty fort. Dogs are welcome but must be on a leash.

Freetown Fall River State Forest, Slab Bridge Road, Assonet (508-644-5522). Pass the day-use area's picnic tables and rest rooms and wander along more than 50 miles of trails and dirt roads at this oasis just outside the city of Fall River. The farm is especially popular with those who like to go the distance, such as mountain bikers, snowmobilers, and horseback riders, though dog walkers will feel welcome as well.

Friends of the Plymouth Pound, Plymouth. This nonprofit organization holds fun fund-raising events each year to benefit homeless animals in the South Shore area. Visitors are always welcome at the group's annual **Memorial Weekend Carnival** at the Armstrong Skating Arena in Plymouth and the yearly **Pet Walk,** usually held on the first Saturday in September at Morton Park in Plymouth. For more information, call 508-224-6651 or visit www.gis.net/~fpp.

Horseneck Beach State Reservation, Route 88, Westport

Point (508-636-8817; 508-636-8816). When you see the stretches of beach and salt marshes at Horseneck, you'll understand why it's one of the most popular parks in Massachusetts—especially in the summer. Though pets are not allowed on the beach itself, they are welcome at the campground (see "Accommodations—Campgrounds"), on rocky outcrops, and on trails.

Lloyd Center for Environmental Studies, 430 Potomska Road, South Dartmouth (508-990-0505; www.thelloydcenter.org). Wander along the **Chaypee Woods Trail,** the **Osprey Point Trail,** the **Hardscrabble Farm Loop,** or other paths at this research and environmental center. "Our outdoor property of 55 acres of coastal estuary and upland habitat and its trails are open for free, dawn to dusk, 365 days a year," explains Geoffrey Garth, public affairs coordinator for the center. "We do allow pets to come along with their owners as long as they stay on a leash."

Massasoit State Park, 1371 Middleboro Avenue, East Taunton (508-822-7405). This park is a popular gathering place for local dogs and their owners, who enjoy hiking, biking, cross-country skiing, and romping on the scenic trails—if you arrive in the fall, be sure to look for the bright cranberry bogs. The park also offers a campground (see "Accommodations—Campgrounds"), horseback riding, picnic areas, and opportunities for nonmotorized boating.

Myles Standish Monument State Reservation, Crescent Street, Duxbury (508-866-2580). This wonderful picnic spot (tables are available) has wide views of the coastline's beaches, harbors, and lighthouses; a 14-foot statue of Captain Myles Standish of the original Plymouth Colony; and walking paths through the forest.

Myles Standish State Forest, Cranberry Road, South Carver (508-866-2526). Visitors can camp overnight at Myles Standish (see "Accommo-dations—Campgrounds") or just explore for the day to enjoy forest scenery, picnics, boating, and swimming at any of the park's 16 ponds. Separate biking, hiking, and horse-riding trails ensure something for nearly everyone.

New Bedford/Martha's Vineyard Ferry, 1494 East Rodney French Boulevard, New Bedford (508-997-1688); adult one way $10; child one way $5. Take your favorite leashed pooch or feline on board the ferry *Schamonchi* for a relaxing ride to Martha's Vineyard. The 150-foot boat has a snack bar, beer and wine, bike storage, picture windows, and plenty of seating for 640 passengers.

New Bedford Whaling National Historical Park. Visitor Information Center: 33 William Street, New Bedford (508-996-4095). Spread throughout 20 blocks in the restored historic district, this park enables visitors to stroll through the city's renowned whaling past. Among the notable points of interest are

the **Seamen's Bethel Chapel** (which Herman Melville called the Whaleman's Chapel in *Moby Dick*), **Waterfront Park,** and the hardy **schooner *Ernesta*.** As you walk the cobblestone streets, you'll also pass by eateries, shops, and other diversions.

Pilgrim Memorial State Park, Water Street, Plymouth (508-866-2580). You and your pooch can catch a glimpse of the *Mayflower II* at the State Pier and Plymouth Rock from this small shady green with benches, picnic tables, a gift shop, and public rest rooms.

Plymouth Breakwater, Plymouth. This long wall of stone makes for a fun and scenic jaunt: Walk out to sea and turn back to see the *Mayflower II* and the downtown area. Start the journey at the pretty bridge located at the entrance to the Leo F. DeMarsh Boat Ramp.

Scituate Light, Cedar Point, Scituate Harbor. This is a popular spot with kite fliers, sight-seers, and local residents looking for a peaceful respite. The 50-foot bright white tower, constructed in 1811, is made of granite and brick and is managed today by the **Scituate Historical Society** (781-545-1083). Just around the corner from the light you'll find a picturesque downtown area with restaurants, antiques shops, boutiques, and plenty of boats bobbing in the harbor.

Village Landing Marketplace, 170 Water Street, Plymouth. Do some window-shopping at this visitors village with cobblestone streets, boutiques, bakeries, ice cream stands, and a view of the harbor.

Walk for Animals, Sharon. The **Neponset Valley Humane Society** in Norwood holds this fund-raising event each year (2003 marks the walk's 10th anniversary). Complete with prizes, entertainment, and refreshments, it's usually held on the Sunday after Mother's Day at Borderland State Park in Sharon; for updated information, call the society at 508-261-9924 or visit www.nvhumanesociety.org.

Wompatuck State Park, Union Street, Hingham (781-749-7160; 781-749-7161). This 3,500-acre park has a boat ramp and miles of trails for biking, hiking, cross-country skiing, and horseback riding. One of Wompatuck's best-known landmarks is the **Mount Blue Spring,** a source of fresh water. Dogs must be on a leash and cannot swim in the reservoir. To reach the park, follow the signs from Route 228.

QUICK BITES

Barnacle Bill's Seafood, 3126 Cranberry Highway, Wareham (508-759-1822). Dogs like fish too: You can order both of your favorite seafood meals or sandwiches and enjoy them out on Barnacle Bill's picnic tables.

Cape Cod Café, 979 Main Street, Brockton (508-583-9420). This dine-in and take-out restaurant specializes in gourmet pizzas. Choose from traditional favorites and more exotic toppings, including tomato and feta, Tex-Mex, buffalo chicken, Greek sausage, and roasted red pepper.

Chester's Restaurant and Mill Wharf Pub, 150 Front Street, Scituate (781-545-3999). Choose from the dinner or pub menu at Chester's, an eatery with wonderful views of the harbor and an outdoor deck seating area.

Fireking Bakery and Bistro, 15 North Street, Hingham (781-740-9400). Stop into the bakery for fresh-baked breads and treats, or linger on the outdoor patio for lobster rangoons, teriyaki grilled chicken, or angelhair pasta with shrimp.

Jamie's Pub and The Gannett Grill, 360 Gannett Road, North Scituate Village (781-545-6000). Every item on Jamie's extensive menu is available for take-out, from nachos and wings to steaks, seafood, pizza, club sandwiches, and burgers.

Lobster Hut, Town Wharf, Plymouth (508-746-2270). Leashed, well-behaved dogs are welcome on the outdoor patio at Lobster Hut. Order a fried seafood plate, burger, lobster, or chicken fingers from the indoor window and then enjoy your meal while overlooking the water.

New York Bagel, 1572 President Avenue, **Fall River** (508-677-4767); 272 State Road, **North Dartmouth** (508-990-3350). New York Bagel's two locations offer sandwiches on your choice of fresh-baked bread, rolls, or bagel varieties such as whole wheat, garlic, rye, sun-dried tomato, blueberry, and salsa. You can also choose from more than six varieties of cream cheese.

Pilgrim Path Café, South Park Avenue, Plymouth (508-746-6483). This casual eatery serves breakfast, specialty sandwiches, calzones, burgers, pasta, home-made breads, and desserts; you'll find a few outdoor tables with a view of the *Mayflower II* and the beach.

HOT SPOTS FOR SPOT

Abby's Dog Depot, 104 State Road, Westport (508-730-1199). Abby's has doggie day care, all-natural foods and supplies, grooming and aromatherapy for all breeds, obedience and obstacle-course training, animal-related gifts, and virtually anything else a canine lover could want or need. Day-care "dog dues" are $18 per day.

Belmont Pet, 108 Torrey Street, Brockton (508-586-0043). Pick up all the basics for your cat, dog, gerbil, or other companion animal at Belmont Pet, which stocks foods and supplies from companies such as Rio Vista, Lupine Pet, and Zoo Med.

Best Friends Pet Resort and Salon, 1014 Pearl Street, Brockton (508-583-8555; www.bestfriends petcare.com). Grooming, pet day care, and overnight boarding are all available at the Brockton location of the Best Friends chain. In addition to the standard fees ($12–20 per night for boarding and $10–12 per day for day care), you can also purchase extra play sessions that allow your pooch to socialize and stretch his legs.

Bite Me! Biscuits, 687 North Bedford Street, East Bridgewater (508-350-0200; 1-888-451-8880; info@bite-me-biscuits.com). After one visit, this all-natural doggie bakery will no doubt become your canine's favorite South Shore stop. Treats include Dog House Cookies with carob chips, Gingerbread Mailmen, Bonanza Bones, and Lollipups. A line of Bite Me! Apparel is also available for animal fans.

Down to Earth, 751 Kempton Street, New Bedford (508-996-1995). Down to Earth is a natural-food store for pets as well as people; the shop specializes in holistic foods, supplements, and all-natural pet products such as Oma's Pride, Wellness, and Wysong pet-food brands.

Homeward Bound, New Bedford (508-998-7557; amyhoubre@ yahoo.com). Amy Houbre, a veterinary technician, has run this pet-care business for about two years. She provides dog-walking and pet-sitting services for $12 per half hour or $25 per day for in-house care. Fully insured and bonded, she'll be happy to keep an eye on your favorite canine or feline while you're visiting the area.

Patnaude's Aquarium and Pet Super Store, 1193 Ashley Boulevard, New Bedford (508-995-0214; 1-800-927-3872; www.patnaudespets.com). This is a large store with lots of choices in pet food, toys, treats, accessories, cages and kennels, and doghouses. Originally specializing only in aquarium supplies and fish, the store has since branched out to include everyone's favorite land animals as well.

The Pet Nanny, 76 Kilby Street, Hingham (781-749-HELP; 617-413-3017; info@thepetnanny.com; www.thepetnanny.com). Animal-sitting, dog walking, play groups, pet shuttles: Pet Nanny owner Nancy Labriola does it all. She gave up a career in the corporate world to pursue a job that would allow her to spend more time with animals, and her clients (both two- and four-legged varieties) are the beneficiaries.

A Pet's Peeve, 310 Lincoln Street, Hingham (781-749-8668). Unless your pet dislikes a good grooming, this business's name is a bit of a misnomer. Formerly known

as **For Your Paws Only,** the company offers straightforward clipping and washing services for all breeds.

Pet World, 60 Providence Highway, East Walpole (508-668-4300). The owners of this pet-store-with-a-conscience offer toys, bowls, biscuits, leashes, litter, food, rawhide, and more; they also support local spay-and-neuter programs and operate a Kitty City shelter for cats in need of homes.

Preppy Puppy Bakery, 12 Kendrick Road, Wareham (508-291-7555; www.preppypuppy-bakery.com). Treat your canine to Rover Roll-Ups, Springer Sprinkles, Boston Terrier Pie, Poodle Puffs, Corgi Cannoli, and other doggie treats at this fun bakery. They can even custom-make Rover a sugar-free birthday cake—with his name, of course. If you can't make it to the store, you can also order any of their treats online.

Under My Wings, Plymouth (508-747-4259; 1-877-PET-SITR). It's a tricky situation: You want to visit Plimoth Plantation, but pets aren't allowed—you're also not allowed to leave your pet alone in the hotel room. No problem. Janet and Bob Depathy, owners of Under My Wings pet-sitting service, will be happy to visit your pet wherever you're staying and keep her busy while you're out.

IN CASE OF EMERGENCY

Brockton Animal Hospital,
386 Belmont Street, Brockton (508-588-4142).

Buttonwood Pet Hospital,
922 Kempton Street, New Bedford (508-996-3159).

Norwood Animal Hospital,
437 Walpole Street, Walpole (508-660-3011).

Old Derby Animal Clinic,
124 Old Derby Street, Hingham (781-749-2800).

Plymouth Animal Hospital,
345 Court Street, Plymouth (508-746-4232).

Roberts Animal Hospital,
516 Washington Street, Hanover (781-826-2306).

Wessels Animal Hospital,
96 Summer Street, Taunton (508-822-2981).

Cape Cod and the Islands

PET-FRIENDLY RATING:

New Englanders love their Cape and its two bucolic islands, Nantucket and Martha's Vineyard, with a ferocious loyalty. Sure, they're crowded. Sure, they're pricey. But if you're looking for a picture-postcard view of the quintessential New England seashore, this is where you'll find it.

The Cape's many towns have diverse personalities, from the miniature golf, arcades, and campgrounds of the upper and mid-Cape to genteel, quieter spots near the bend of the "elbow." At the tip, the art colony of Provincetown (a very pet-friendly town) attracts visitors with an open mind and a sense of adventure. In Woods Hole, scientists from around the world delve into the latest deep-water discoveries at the Woods Hole Oceanographic Institution. This is also the spot where most people catch a ferry to Martha's Vineyard, a jovial, tourist-friendly island with breath-taking beaches, harbors, and architecture. Nantucket is a bit smaller and farther away from the mainland and, as a result, enjoys a slightly more escapist and adventurous ambience.

All three areas burst at the seams during the summer season; pet owners are often better off waiting until spring or fall, when more accommodations allow animals and the sidewalks have a bit more room for roaming. The beach rules vary from town to town, but in general your pooch will probably not be allowed at all between 8 AM and 6 PM on most town beaches in the summer. But take heart: Leashed dogs are allowed on most beaches at the Cape Cod National Seashore (see "Out and About"). You'll have plenty of luck at dinnertime—Cape Cod and both islands have an abundance of restaurants with outdoor seating areas offering lobstah, chowdah, and other seafood delights. You'll also find numerous kennels and pet-sitters, opportunities for getting out into the open ocean, and of course spectacular views around every corner.

ACCOMMODATIONS

Hotels, Motels, Inns, and Bed & Breakfasts

Barnstable

Lamb and Lion Inn, Route 6A, Barnstable (508-362-6823; 1-800-909-6923; info@lambandlion.com; www.lambandlion.com); $125–250 per night. Laid-back luxury is the goal at the Lamb and Lion, where the amenities include a swimming pool, a hot tub, fireplaces, and three resident Yorkies to keep an eye on things. Guest rooms have private entrances and vary in size and style. Pets weighing less than 40 pounds are welcome for an additional $15 per pet, per night.

Buzzards Bay

Bay Motor Inn, 223 Main Street, Buzzards Bay (508-759-3989; baymotorinn@yahoo.com; www.capecodtravel.com/bay-motorinn); $52–120 per night. Pets are welcome for an additional $10 per night at Bay Motor Inn, located along the edge of the Cape Cod Canal. There are 7 miles of hiking trails within walking distance, and the inn offers cable TV, free coffee and local calls, and air-conditioning. The accommodations include standard rooms, efficiencies, and cottages.

Fox Run Bed & Breakfast, 171 Puritan Road, Buzzards Bay (508-759-1458; foxrun@capecod.net; www.bbhost.com/foxrun); $80–185 per night. Certified with the National Wildlife Federation's Backyard Habitat Program, Fox Run B&B is surrounded by wetlands, cranberry bogs, and plenty of great bird-watching spots. The

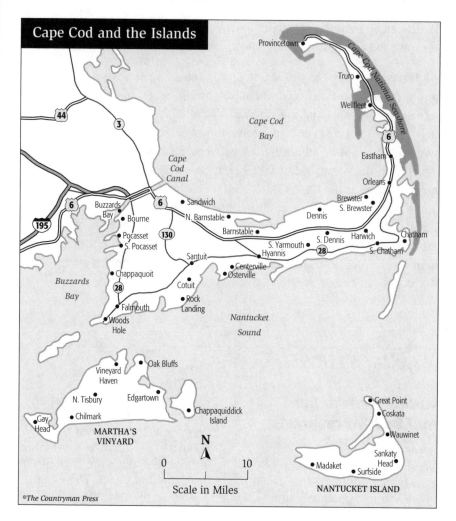

Cape Cod and the Islands

three guest rooms are decorated with turn-of-the-20th-century, French Provincial, and Old Cape Cod themes. Pets are welcome during the off-season only.

Centerville

Inn at Centerville Corners, 1338 Craigville Beach Road, Centerville (508-775-7223; info@centervillecorners.com; www.centervillecorners.com); $50–180 per night. For an extra $5 per night, your pet is welcome to join you at this cozy motor inn located in the small village of Centerville. Amenities include an indoor heated pool and sauna, free continental breakfasts each morning, cable TV, air-conditioning, and in-room refrigerators. Efficiency units are also available.

Eastham

Cottage Grove, P.O. Box 821, Eastham (508-255-0500; 1-877-521-5522; www.grovecape.com); $70–185 per night or $650–1,700 per week. Blending the privacy of cottage living with the pleasures of a B&B, Cottage Grove is a unique, pet-friendly accommoda-

A COZY GUEST ROOM AT WINGSCORTON FARM INN IN EAST SANDWICH

tion on the outer Cape. Each cottage has heat and air-conditioning, cable TV, and antique furnishings. "We are all about community and experience here, and fully believe that people should be able to vacation with their pets," explains owner Greg Wolfe.

East Sandwich

Earl of Sandwich Motel, Old King's Highway (Route 6A), East Sandwich (508-888-1415; 1-800-442-EARL; www.earlofsandwich.com); $55–109 per night. Set on a pond and surrounded by lawns and flower beds, the Earl of Sandwich offers 24 individually decorated rooms (some with canopy beds), free continental breakfasts, an outdoor swimming pool, air-conditioning, and cable TV. Pets are allowed in certain rooms; advance notice is required.

Wingscorton Farm Inn, 11 Wing Boulevard, East Sandwich (508-888-0534); call for rate information. Your pet will fit right into the menagerie at Wingscorton, a working farm with sheep, goats, chickens, geese, and other animals. Built in 1758, this historic home offers a library, dining area, guest rooms, and a carriage-house apartment, all furnished with antiques. Full country breakfasts include specialties such as rhubarb pie, fruit turnovers, fresh eggs, and a variety of juices. Rooms have four-poster beds and fireplaces, along with modern touches like TV and full, private baths. Well-behaved children and companion animals are welcome.

Hyannis

Cascade Motor Lodge, 201 Main Street, Hyannis (508-775-9717; www.cascademotorlodge.com); $44–175 per night. Choose from standard rooms and efficiencies at this Hyannis motel featuring full baths, air-conditioning, cable TVs and VCRs, smoking and nonsmoking rooms, and kitchenettes. You can also rent movies and bicycles at the main office. Well-behaved pets are welcome.

Comfort Inn Hyannis,

1470 Route 132, Hyannis (508-771-4804); $69–189 per night. This centrally located Comfort Inn offers all the most popular amenities, including air-conditioning, free continental breakfasts, premium movie channels, an indoor swimming pool with a hot tub and sauna, a fitness center, and Nintendo for the kids. Pets are welcome at this 104-room hotel.

Hyannis Port
Simmons Homestead Inn,

288 Scudder Avenue, Hyannis Port (1-800-637-1649; simmons-homestead@aol.com; www.simmonshomesteadinn.com); $120–280 per night. Built in the early 1800s, this recently renovated inn features animal-themed rooms, full breakfasts each morning, a barn housing the owner's collection of antique red sports cars, and a relaxed, hospitable atmosphere. All rooms have private baths. Dogs (sorry, no cats) are welcome for an additional $25 per night.

Martha's Vineyard
Brady's Bed & Breakfast,

10 Canonicus Avenue, Oak Bluffs, Martha's Vineyard (508-693-9137; 1-888-693-9137; www.sunsol.com/bradys); $65–167 per night. The resident cocker spaniel at Brady's will probably greet you when you arrive. This relaxed and quaint

seaside inn has a huge porch facing the ocean, Downeast-style furnishings, upscale bedding, and a weathered-shingle exterior. Well-behaved, well-traveled dogs (sorry, no cats) are welcome without extra fees: "I only charge one bottle of Absolut," says innkeeper E. Brady Aikens.

Duck Inn, 10 Duck Pond Way, Aquinnah (Gay Head), Martha's Vineyard (508-645-9018); $85–225 per night. Pets are welcome in one room at this cozy farm and B&B originally designed by a whaler. Gourmet breakfasts include specialties such as crêpes, fresh eggs, and fruit; the house features private baths in some rooms, fireplaces, a hot tub, and peaceful views. The designated pet room has a private entrance.

Island Inn, Beach Road, Oak Bluffs, Martha's Vineyard (508-693-2002; 1-800-462-0269; www.islandinn.com); $85–355 per night. You can bring your pet along at the Island Inn during every month except July and August. Accommodations include a studio, one- and two-bedroom suites, a condo suite, a town house, and a cottage. The inn also has an outdoor freshwater pool, tennis courts, a barbecue and picnic area, a playground, and more than 7 acres to explore.

Martha's Vineyard Surfside Motel, P.O. Box 2507, Oak Bluffs, Martha's Vineyard (508-477-8600; reservations@mvsurfside.com; www.mvsurfside.com); $65–295 per night. "We're one of the few lodging establishments

on the island that welcomes pets, and it almost never comes back to bite us!" jokes Bob Emerson, Surfside's manager. The motel offers standard rooms as well as suites, all of which are clean, bright, and cheerily decorated. Pets must stay on a leash on the property and can't be left alone in the rooms.

Point Way Inn, Main Street and Pease's Point Way, Edgartown, Martha's Vineyard (1-888-711-6633; info@pointway.com; www.pointway.com); $150–600 per night. Pets are welcome in two of the rooms at this historic inn and former sea captain's home. The Garden Room has a private entrance, a queen bed, and a daybed; the Deck Suite has two sleeping areas, a living room, a breakfast room, and an oversized tub. Animal owners pay an additional $25–50 per night.

Shiretown Inn, North Water Street, Edgartown, Martha's Vineyard (508-627-3353; 1-800-541-0090; paradise@shiretown-inn.com); $59–750 per night. Listed on the National Register of Historic Places, the Shiretown's buildings were constructed in 1795 as whaling captains' quarters and carriage houses. Pets are welcome at the inn's Garden Cottage room; it has a queen-sized bed, cable TV, a full private bathroom, and air-conditioning.

North Truro
Outer Reach Resort, Route 6, North Truro (1-800-942-5388); $59–159 per night. Outer Reach is proud to be pet-friendly and welcomes your animal for an

additional $15 per night. The large motel-style resort is located on 12 acres with views of Cape Cod Bay. Choose from waterfront- and park-view rooms, some with air-conditioning and others with fans. There are also plenty of outdoor picnic areas and decks.

Orleans
Orleans Inn, 3 Old Country Road, Orleans (508-255-2222; info@orleansinn.com; www. orleansinn.com); $75–250 per night. A former sea captain's estate, the Orleans Inn has a rich history as well as modern touches such as private bathrooms, cable TV, and a guest kitchen. The 11 rooms are individually decorated with quilts and new furniture; the waterfront suites also have living areas with pullout couches. Pets are welcome without restrictions.

Skaket Beach Motel, 203 Cranberry Highway (Route 6A), Orleans (508-255-1020; 1-800-835-0298; skaket@c4.net; www.skaketbeachmotel.com); $58–175 per night. Pets are welcome here during the off-season (defined as March through June 30, and September 2 through November 23) for an additional $9 per night. Guests can choose from standard and deluxe rooms or apartments; some are poolside. All rooms have cable TV with premium movie channels, air-conditioning, and refrigerators.

Provincetown
Breakwater Motel, Motor Inn, and Apartments, 716 Commercial Street, Provincetown (508-487-1134; 1-800-487-1134); motel

and motor inn $59–135 per night; apartments $550–925 per week. These three separate accommodations are all located near each other in Provincetown; the 11 apartments each have a kitchen, air-conditioning, and cable TV. The motel and motor inn are located across from the harbor and offer some waterfront rooms. "Small" pets (call to see if yours qualifies) are welcome, but can't be left unattended.

Cape Inn, 698 Commercial Street, Provincetown (508-487-1711); $69–179 per night. Formerly known as the **Best Inn,** this 78-room hotel is located across from the bay and about a mile from the downtown area. Amenities include a swimming pool, cable TV, in-room coffee-makers and refrigerators, nightly movies in the lounge, and smoking and nonsmoking rooms. Pets are welcome without extra fees.

Four Gables, 15 Race Road, Provincetown (1-866-487-2427; info@fourgables.com; www.four-gables.com); $72–192 per night (off-season); $1,000–1,500 per week (summer). This pet-, gay-, and family-friendly lodging offers cottages and apartment-style units with kitchens, covered decks and porches, air-conditioning, lawns, and gardens. "We think of your pet as being on vacation, too, so we've installed gates on the porches so pets can be outside in a protected area and see what's going on," says owner Bob McCandless.

Gabriel's Guestrooms and Apartments, 104 Bradford Street, Provincetown (508-487-3232; 1-800-9MY-ANGEL; gabrielsma@aol.com; www.gabriels.com); $95–350 per night. From the moment you arrive at the well-landscaped courtyard at Gabriel's, you know you're visiting someplace out of the ordinary. Each of the apartments and guest rooms is named for a notable woman, including Emily Dickinson, Dian Fossey, and Amelia Earhart. Continental vegetarian breakfasts often include blueberry pancakes, oatmeal, fruit salad, and bagels; you'll also find a hot tub, sauna, outdoor sundecks, individually decorated rooms, and private baths. Your pets are always welcome and will feel right at home with the resident animals: three cats and a dog.

Ireland House, 18 Pearl Street, Provincetown (508-487-7132; info@irelandhse.com; www.irelandhse.com); $85–140 per night. Misty the Samoyed and Harley the parrot already live at Ireland House; visiting pets are welcome with prior approval for an additional $10 per night. The inn offers two deluxe suites with sitting areas, double beds, pine floors, exposed beams, quilted bedspreads, robes, and air-conditioning. Daily continental breakfasts are included in the rates.

Sandwich

Sandwich Lodge and Resort, 54 Route 6A, Sandwich (508-888-2275; 1-800-282-5353; sandwichlodge@hotmail.com; www.sandwichlodge.com); $55–240 per night. Guests at the Sandwich Lodge can enjoy two heated

THE FLOWER-FILLED COURTYARD AT GABRIEL'S GUESTROOMS AND APARTMENTS IN PROVINCETOWN

pools (one indoor, one outdoor), nice views, and free continental breakfasts. Pets are allowed in the motel-style standard rooms; each room has a private entrance and direct access to a large field. Animal owners pay an additional $15 per night.

South Harwich

Stone Horse Motel, 872 Main Street, South Harwich (508-430-2220; info@stonehorsemotel. com; www.stonehorsemotel. com); $65–165 per night. The sign hanging in front of this cute motel tells passersby about its pet-friendly policies; companion animals are welcome in Stone Horse rooms. Accommodations include standard double rooms, double rooms with kitchenettes, and suites with kitchenettes.

The motel sits on 3 acres with a heated swimming pool.

South Yarmouth

Brentwood Inn, 961 Main Street, South Yarmouth (1-800-328-8812; www.brentwoodinncapecod.com); $35–110 per night or $275–900 per week. Choose from town houses, cottages, and motel rooms at this versatile facility, where the amenities include an indoor swimming pool, a hot tub and sauna, a lounge area, a picnic area with barbecue grills, and a sundeck. Dogs are allowed for an additional $10 per night.

Motel 6 South Yarmouth, 1314 Route 28, South Yarmouth (508-394-4000; 1-800-4-MOTEL6); $46–82 per night. Pets are always welcome at Motel 6; the South

Yarmouth location offers a swimming pool, nonsmoking rooms, premium movie channels, free coffee, and a "kids stay free" feature. It's located just down the road from Cape Cod Community College.

West Dennis

Barnacle Motel, 219 Main Street, West Dennis (508-394-8472; www.sunsol.com/barnacle); $60–140 per night. This recently remodeled lodging has an outdoor swimming pool, a convenient location, air-conditioning, free coffee each morning, and cable TV with premium movie channels. Some rooms have kitchenettes, and the owners offer spring, fall, and family specials. Well-behaved pets are welcome.

West Harwich

Cape Cod Claddagh Inn, 77–79 West Main Street, West Harwich (508-432-9628; 1-800-356-9628; info@capecod claddaghinn.com; www.capecod-claddaghinn.com); $95–195 per night. Surrounded by 2 acres, the Claddagh Inn specializes in Irish hospitality with nine guest rooms, a swimming pool, a tiki bar, a wraparound porch, air-conditioning, in-room refrigerators, and cable TV. The on-site Claddagh pub and restaurant, and the intimate Kerry Room, serve fine food and drink. Pets are welcome with prior approval.

Yarmouth Port

Colonial House Inn, Route 6A, Yarmouth Port (508-362-4348; info@colonialhousecapecod.com; www.colonialhousecapecod.com); $90–135 per night. The rates at this c. 1820s inn include breakfast as well as dinner; the menu is à la carte with your choice of up to 14 entrées. The antiques-filled guest rooms in the main house and restored carriage house all have pleasant views and share access to the indoor swimming pool. Pets are welcome for an additional $5 per night.

Campgrounds

Bourne

Bay View Campground, 260 MacArthur Boulevard, Bourne (508-759-7610; www.bay-viewcampground.com); $30–38 per night. In addition to the usual campground amenities such as rest rooms, showers, and a camp store, campers at Bay View will also find an ice cream parlor, Internet-access stations, three swimming pools, two playgrounds, a baseball field, and a tennis court. Dogs are allowed on a leash, as long as owners clean up after them and don't leave them alone in the rooms.

Bourne Scenic Park, 370 Scenic Highway, Bourne (508-759-7873; scenicpark@capecod.net; www. bournerecauth.com/bsp); $25–27 per night. This RV-friendly campground features a picnic area, hot showers, a saltwater swimming pool, paved roads, canal fishing, a tenting area, playgrounds, a camp store, scheduled family activities, and a game room. Quiet pets are welcome, but owners must keep them on a leash and clean up after them.

Brewster

Nickerson State Park Campground, Route 6A, Brewster (508-896-3491); $12 per night Massachusetts residents; $15 per night out-of-state residents. Choose from more than 400 campsites at this 1,900-acre forested campground in a park with enough recreational opportunities to satisfy all the adults and children in your clan (see "Out and About"). The campground has rest rooms, hot showers, picnic tables, tent sites, and RV sites with hookups.

Sweetwater Forest Family Camping Resort, Route 124, Brewster (508-896-3773; sweeth-2orv@aol.com; www.sweetwater-forest.com); $20–35 per night. Well-behaved pets are welcome at this peaceful family campground; the staff even offer boarding services in case you need someone else to look after your furry friend for a while. Campground amenities include separate tenting and RV areas, 60 acres of woods and lakefront scenery, recreation for the kids, and hot showers.

Buzzards Bay

Scusset Beach State Reservation Campground, 140 Scusset Beach Road, Buzzards Bay (508-888-0859); $12 per night Massachusetts residents; $15 per night out-of-state residents. Most of the 103 sites at this campground have hookups; campers will also find flush toilets, showers, and a dumping station. Tent camping is offered from May through Columbus Day, though RV camping is available year-round. Scusset Beach also offers Safari Camping for RV clubs. (For more information on the park, see "Out and About.")

East Falmouth

Cape Cod Campresort, 176 Thomas Landers Road, East Falmouth (508-548-1458; www.resortcamplands.com); $22–28 per night. Campers at this East Falmouth facility can rent boats or tepees, relax in the teen game room or adult lounge, shop in the camp store, splash in the swimming pool, and romp at the playground. Choose from 200 wooded and open sites for tents and RVs. Pet owners pay an additional fee of $4 per night.

Falmouth

Washburn Island Camping, Waquoit Bay National Estuarine Research Reserve, Falmouth (508-457-0495; 1-877-I-CAMP-MASS; www.waquoit-bayreserve.org); $5 per night Massachusetts residents; $6 per night out-of-state residents. Those looking for an out-of-the-ordinary experience won't mind the extra effort it takes to reserve a spot and reach this secluded campground. First, you'll need to secure a permit; then you'll need your own boat to reach one of the seven sites (there's no ferry). You'll also have to learn to avoid the deer ticks and poison ivy that are both plentiful. Dogs must be on a leash. (See "Out and About" for information on the reserve.)

Sandwich

Dunroamin' RV Resort, 14 John Ewer Road, Sandwich (508-477-

0541); $30 per night or $200 per week. No tent camping is allowed at this facility, which caters strictly to RVs. Pets are welcome without extra fees, though owners must keep them on a leash and show proof of vaccination. Amenities include full hookups and a picnic table at each site, laundry facilities, a playground, and planned activities in the summer.

Peters Pond Campground, 185 Cotuit Road, Sandwich (508-477-1775; info@peterspond. com;www.peterspond.com); $29–42 per night or $183–265 per week. Leashed pets are allowed at this large campground only from mid-April through July 1, and from Labor Day through mid-October, though a limited number of campers in self-contained vehicles are allowed to bring pets during the summer months. Amenities include a camp store, rest rooms, two beaches, two playgrounds, and walking trails.

Shawme-Crowell State Forest Campground, Route 130, Sandwich (508-888-0351). Camping is the draw at this popular 700-acre reserve (see "Out and About" for more information about the forest). The campground has nearly 300 sites for tents and RVs, along with rest rooms, showers, and picnic tables. Pets are welcome, but as in all state parks they must be leashed, and owners must clean up after them.

Homes, Cottages, and Cabins for Rent

Brewster
Long Pond Cottage, Brewster (781-383-0188; 781-383-0235; dpz@attbi.com); $2,200–2,850 per week. Eight people can comfortably stay at this three-bedroom home located directly on a private Long Pond beach. Other amenities include cable TV, a full kitchen, wraparound decks, beach chairs, and a fireplace. The Cape Cod bike trail is a short walk—or bike ride—away. "Small" pets (call to see if yours qualifies) are welcome.

Chatham
Waincroft, Emery Lake, Chatham (941-774-4212; waincroft@aol. com); $1,250–2,200 per week. Waincroft, a contemporary home with a sunken living room, patio, and pond views, can accommodate up to eight people. The house has a lobster steamer, washer and dryer, full kitchen, cable TV and a VCR, a charcoal grill, and patio furniture. Pet owners pay a $250 deposit in addition to the standard security deposit.

Martha's Vineyard
Edgartown Compound, West Tisbury Road, Edgartown, Martha's Vineyard (508-627-3998; printease@aol.com); $2,200–2,500 per week. Secluded on 3 acres, this hideaway has post-and-beam architecture; a master bedroom suite; a game room with TV/VCR, puzzles, board games, and other rainy-day activities; a woodstove; and a large deck with a barbecue grill

and patio furniture. Dogs (sorry, no cats) are welcomed by owner Betsy Harrington.

Oak Bluffs Home, Oak Bluffs, Martha's Vineyard (843-881-0796; miltonw1@msn.com); $2,500–4,500 per week. With seven bedrooms, this large house can accommodate groups for family reunions, weddings, or other events. Pets are welcome as long as they stay off the furniture. The home's features include a huge wraparound porch, a roomy TV/gathering room, and a full kitchen. It's located about two blocks from the beach.

Patterson Guest House, West Tisbury, Martha's Vineyard (508-693-0871; 508-693-8163); $700–1,400 per week. With two bedrooms and a sleeper sofa, this secluded cottage can accommodate up to six people. Pet owners will appreciate the dog run in the backyard, along with the hammock, picnic table, kitchen, barbecue grill, washer and dryer, and cable TV. Guest animals must be treated with flea and tick medications and should have their own pet bed.

Vineyard Haven Home, Vineyard Haven, Martha's Vineyard (617-924-1827; 617-312-6598; mwk4619@gis.net); $1,800–2,250. This three-story contemporary house has large rooms, a den, three bedrooms and a master suite, private balconies, a rooftop and main-level deck, a full kitchen, TV with a VCR/DVD player, and a washer and dryer. The beach and downtown areas are a half mile away.

Housebroken pets that have been treated for fleas and ticks are welcome.

Nantucket

Boomerang, Surfside, Nantucket (508-221-8424; boomerangnantuck@aol.com); $1,400–2,600 per week. This adorable Cape-style home has weathered shingles, sunny and spacious rooms, a large backyard, a fireplace, and one queen and four twin beds. New features include an outdoor shower, a back deck, and patio furniture. One well-behaved adult dog at a time (sorry, no cats) is allowed, provided your pet is crated when left alone.

North Chatham

Cannon Hill Home, North Chatham (310-277-1926; 310-488-5979); $2,500–3,800 per week. Located in the Cannon Hill Association residential area, this large Cape-style house has a formal dining room, a large kitchen, four bedrooms, an exercise area, air-conditioning, patio furniture, a fireplace, and access to the association's private beach. Well-behaved pets are always welcome.

North Eastham

Waterfront Eastham Cottages, North Eastham (781-784-8934; pioneer@sria.com); $1,200–2,500 per week. Complete with a private beach, these two cottages have a dramatic oceanfront location. One has two bedrooms and a sleeping loft; the other has three bedrooms. Both have cable TV, a kitchen, a large deck, and a barbecue grill. Pets are welcome, though the owners usually request a larger security deposit from guests who bring animals.

Orleans

Skaket Beach Home, 9 Gull Lane, Orleans (508-255-7374; cindy.cape@verizon.net); $900–1,400 per week. Located a half mile from Skaket Beach, this Orleans Cape-style home has a furnished outdoor patio with a barbecue grill, a large backyard abutting a wildlife conservation area, and air-conditioning. Bikes are also available for use; a bicycle/walking trail is nearby. One leashed dog (sorry, no cats) is welcome per group.

Provincetown

Beachfront Cottage, Provincetown (508-487-9791; 917-882-8635); $1,500–4,400 per week. Located directly on the water, this home can accommodate up to eight people; the owner prefers to rent to families rather than groups of singles. Amenities include four bedrooms, two bathrooms, a fireplace, cathedral ceilings, and a TV with VCR/DVD player. Due to a growing flea problem in Provincetown, flea treatment is essential for the cottage's visiting pets.

East End Home, Provincetown (508-255-3612; 508-240-0700); $1,350 per week. Featuring post-and-beam construction, wood floors, a sleeping loft, a hot tub, and a laundry room, this two-bedroom, two-bathroom house can accommodate up to four people. The large windows look out into the surrounding woods, and there's also cable TV, a VCR, a CD player, a full kitchen, and a barbecue grill. Well-behaved pets are welcome.

Labrador Landing, 47 Commercial Street, Provincetown (917-597-1500; www.labrador-landing.com); $750–2,500 per week. With a name like Labrador Landing, they'd have to allow pets. Harley, the resident Chihuahua, will be on hand to welcome you and your four-legged friends to these two luxury waterfront accommodations—a boathouse cottage and a two-story cottage. Pet owners pay a $100 refundable deposit in addition to the standard security deposit.

South Orleans

Ocean Bay View Lodge Cottages, 116 Portanimicut Road, South Orleans (508-255-3344); $500–875 per week. These nine housekeeping cottages are spread throughout 9 acres on Little Pleasant Bay. They vary in size, are fully furnished with kitchens and living rooms, and share access to a private beach, a salt marsh, a playing field, and two boats. Well-behaved dogs and cats are welcome to join their owners.

Truro

Truro Cottage, 14 Mill Pond Road, Truro (212-988-8934; 508-349-2652); $450–650 per week. Owners Daisy and David Paradis offer this two-bedroom rental in a quiet neighborhood; it has a large deck with a picnic table, grill, and marsh view, and is located within a 15-minute walk of the harbor and a half-hour walk of the beach. Dogs (sorry, no cats) are welcome as long as they stay off the furniture.

Wellfleet

Pine Moorings, Wellfleet (508-349-7467; 315-789-9250); $350–975 per week. Pine Moorings offers four rental units ranging in size from one to three bedrooms (two are waterfront). Each accommodation has a full bathroom and kitchen, a TV and VCR, coffeemakers, and a deck or patio with a barbecue grill. Pets are welcome provided they've been treated for fleas; all dogs must be crated when left alone.

OUT AND ABOUT

Ara's Tours, Nantucket (508-221-6852; ara@arastours.com; www.arastours.com). "Lap pets" are welcome to join their owners on a tour of Nantucket's lighthouses, historic streets, and architecture with local resident Ara Charder. Trips in the air-conditioned vehicle last for about 1½ hours and cost $12 per person; private charters are also available.

Beebe Woods, Falmouth. This is a great spot for peaceful walks through the woods; you'll almost always bump into other pooches along the trails. From the village Green, take Palmer Avenue to Depot Avenue; follow Depot all the way to the end for parking at the Cape Cod Conservatory and Highfield Theatre. (For a trail map, visit the nearby chamber of commerce at Main Street, or call 508-548-8500; info@falmouth-capecod.com.)

Cape Cod Light, Light House Road, North Truro. You'll see the signs on Route 6 for this historic lighthouse. It was moved back from the eroding cliff in recent years, leaving a scenic boardwalk from the light to the edge of the ocean. The lighthouse grounds are surrounded by the Highland Golf Links, one of the East Coast's oldest courses. Pets are allowed on the grounds but not in the gift shop.

Cape Cod National Seashore: Province Lands Visitor Center, Provincetown (508-487-1256); **Salt Pond Visitor Center,** Eastham (508-255-3421). This 43,000-acre national park comprises much of the outer reaches of the Cape. Renowned for its beaches and dune landscape, the preserve is home to many endangered and threatened wildlife species, historic buildings, picnic areas, and photogenic overlooks. The rules for pets here are the opposite of those found in many other parks: Pets are welcome on beaches (except those staffed by a lifeguard) but are not allowed on trails. Dogs must be on a 6-foot leash at all times. The Province Lands Visitor Center is located on Race Point Road off Route 6 in Provincetown; the Salt Pond Visitor Center is located at the corner of Nauset Road and Route 6 in Eastham. Both centers can provide maps, orientation, and ranger-guided activities, and staff members are available to answer questions.

Craig's Motor Boat Rentals,
Waquoit Bay, Route 28, East Falmouth (508-548-9283); $130–275 per day. Bring your four-legged first mate along for a cruise in Cape Cod waters. Craig's rents fiberglass and hulled boats. Safety vests, first-aid kits, and tarps are included, and you can also rent fishing gear.

Dolphin Fleet Whale Watch,
Standish Street, Provincetown (508-349-1900; 1-800-826-9300; www.whalewatch.com); $20 per adult. Well-behaved pets are welcome aboard the Dolphin Fleet's whale-watching trips in Cape Cod Bay. Each trip is led by a naturalist from the Center for Coastal Studies, and an on-board galley provides food and drinks.

Hy-Line Cruises, Ocean Street Dock, Hyannis (508-778-2600; 1-800-492-8082; www.hy-line-cruises.com). Leashed pets are welcome aboard Hy-Line cruise vessels (with the exception of a few first-class areas) to join the fun on ferry trips to Nantucket and Martha's Vineyard. The company's boats are also available for private charters.

Island Water Sports, 100 Lagoon Pond Road, Vineyard Haven, Martha's Vineyard (508-693-7767; boatmv@adelphia.net; www.boatmv.com). Pets are welcome aboard all power-, sail-, and paddleboats at this rental facility; some kayaks are even large enough to accommodate a dog. You can also rent fishing rods, water skis, and float tubes.

The company's owner, Alice Seaton, just asks that all pets be willing participants in the ocean journey and can fit comfortably inside the vessel.

Magellan Sportfishing Charters,
Route 28, Harwich Port (508-430-7437; 1-800-848-TUNA; magellan@flash.net; www.capecod-sportsmen.com). Well-behaved pets are welcome on full- or half-day charters in search of cod, pollack, striped bass, bluefish, or bluefin tuna. The boat accommodates a maximum of six people; prices range $450–875 per group.

Nantucket Air, Barnstable Municipal Airport, 660 Barnstable Road, North Ramp, Hyannis, MA; 1-800-635-8787; on Nantucket: 508-228-6234). You can bring your pet along for the scenic flight to or from Nantucket as long as you give the airlines advance notice. Frequent fliers take Rover for free; all others pay $10 per pet each way.

Nickerson State Park, Route 6A, Brewster (508-896-3491). You can camp overnight at Nickerson (see "Accommodations—Campgrounds") or just spend the day. On-site, you'll find an 8-mile-long bicycle path, hiking trails, trout-stocked fishing ponds, picnic areas, horseback-riding and cross-country skiing trails, boat launches, and handicapped accessible facilities. Dogs must be on a leash at all times.

Scusset Beach State Reservation, 140 Scusset Beach Road, Buzzards Bay (508-888-0859). Fishermen frequent this 380-acre park on the Cape Cod Canal. The park's attractions include a campground (see "Accommodations—Camp-grounds"), a fishing pier, picnic areas, biking and hiking trails, and plenty of spots to stop and enjoy the views. Dogs must be on a leash and are not allowed on the 1½-mile-long stretch of beach.

Shawme-Crowell State Forest, Route 130, Sandwich (508-888-0351). Horseback riders love this 700-acre patch of reserved land located near the entrance to Cape Cod. The park has more than 15 miles of trails that meander through the woods—often used by cross-country skiers in the wintertime. You'll also find picnic and barbecue areas and an on-site campground (see "Accommodations—Campgrounds").

Shearwater Excursions, Nantucket (508-228-7037; www. explorenantucket.com). This eco-tour company welcomes dogs on board its 26-foot catamaran. (Captain Blair Perkins has found that the dogs actually attract the attention of seals and make them come closer to the boat!) Trips take passengers into the scenic bays and inlets of Nantucket and neighboring small islands. The boat holds a maximum of six passengers at a time.

Steamship Authority Ferries, Route 28, **Woods Hole** (508-548-3788); South Street Dock, **Hyannis** (508-771-4000); $5.50–13 per adult, one way; $34–165 per vehicle, one way. Steamship ferries are the most popular choice for journeys to and from Woods Hole on Cape Cod, and Vineyard Haven on Martha's Vineyard; you can also use them for travel between Hyannis on Cape Cod, and Nantucket. Crated or leashed pets are welcome without extra fees. Reservations are necessary.

Stephen Huneck Gallery, Dock and Kelly Streets, Edgartown, Martha's Vineyard (508-627-4666). Dog lovers shouldn't miss this gallery featuring lithographs, woodcuts, and furniture by renowned dog lover and artist Stephen Huneck; he's also the author of the popular series of children's books featuring his black Lab, Sally.

Waquoit Bay National Estuarine Research Reserve, Route 28, Falmouth (508-457-0495; www. waquoitbayreserve.org). Pets are welcome on a leash at this impressive 2,500-acre preserve, though owners are advised to take extra precautions against deer ticks—a growing problem in the area. Also, as this is a wildlife preserve with an abundance of hatchlings, dogs are not allowed on or near the beach. You can camp at the **Washburn Island** sites (see "Accommodations—Campgrounds") or explore **South Cape Beach State Park, Waquoit Bay,** numerous ponds, and the **Quashnet River Property.** Start at the headquarters on Route 28 for maps and other information.

Wellfleet Drive-In, Wellfleet (508-349-7176; wellfleetcinemas@ hotmail.com); $6.50 per adult. Bring your pup along in the backseat and take in new releases and double features at this old-fashioned drive-in movie theater. There's also a snack bar and playground on-site. Campers and oversized vehicles (defined as SUVs, minivans, and pickup trucks) are welcome but must park in a designated area so as not to obscure others' views.

QUICK BITES

Cape Cod

Beehive Tavern, 406 Route 6A, Sandwich (508-833-1184). This is mostly an indoor kind of place, but the tavern does have a few outdoor tables as well. Meal choices include steaks, fish, pasta, large salads, club sandwiches, burgers, and daily specials.

Box Lunch, various locations, Cape Cod. You can find a Box Lunch on Main Street in **Orleans,** Patriot Square in **Dennis,** and Main Street in **Falmouth,** along with six other locations throughout the Cape. The local chain specializes in "rollwiches," travel-friendly wraps made with any combination of chicken, turkey, ham, roast beef, and vegetables you can dream up.

Bubula's by the Bay, 185 Commercial Street, Provincetown (508-487-0773). At Bubula's, you can choose from sandwiches and salads at lunchtime and upscale entrées at dinner. Recommended by local innkeepers, it has a great location and plenty of outdoor seating by the sidewalk.

Carbo's Bar and Grill, 681 Falmouth Road, Mashpee (508-477-5238). Located in a shopping center, this casual restaurant has outdoor patio seating with umbrellas and serves pizza and grill favorites.

Emack and Bolio's Ice Cream, Route 6A, Orleans (508-255-5844). There's lots of outdoor seating at this shop serving gourmet ice cream, smoothies, and espresso. The shop sits next to Mill Pond Co. Painted Furniture, which welcomes dogs inside for browsing.

Governor Bradford Restaurant, 312 Commercial Street, Provincetown (508-487-2781). Sit at one of the many outdoor tables at this bustling downtown restaurant and choose from wings, steamers, sandwich plates, salads, and fried seafood platters.

Landfall Restaurant, Luscombe Avenue, Woods Hole (508-548-1758). After a long ferry ride, relax at this scenic harborfront restaurant with outdoor seating. Specialties include shrimp cocktail, burgers, lobster, and seafood platters.

Lobster Pound, 157 Cranberry Highway, Orleans (508-240-1234). Pick your own lobster and enjoy your meal outdoors at one of the patio picnic tables.

Marley's of Chatham, 1077 Main Street, Chatham (508-945-1700).

The cat on the sign will lead you to this restaurant with an outdoor patio serving chicken, seafood, steaks, and vegetarian dishes. If you can't stay, take-out is also available.

Seafood Sam's, various locations, Cape Cod. Located on Coast Guard Road in **Sandwich,** and on Route 28 in **Harwichport, Falmouth,** and **Yarmouth,** this local chain serves broiled and fried fish, along with other treats. Covered outdoor tables are available.

Sweet Tomatoes, 148 Route 6A, Sandwich (508-888-5220). Grab a slice or a whole pie at Sweet Tomatoes, which serves Neapolitan-style pizza and has outdoor seating at picnic tables.

Village Café, 188 Main Street, Falmouth (508-540-5234). Watch the world go by from the sidewalk seating area while you enjoy breakfast or lunch at this busy downtown restaurant.

Martha's Vineyard
The Bite, Basin Road, Menemsha, Martha's Vineyard (508-645-9239). Order chicken wings, potato salad, french fries, clam rolls, and fried seafood platters at the take-out window at this ultra-casual, fun restaurant with outdoor tables.

Stripers Restaurant, 52 Beach Road, Vineyard Haven, Martha's Vineyard (508-693-8383). Just a short walk from the ferry, Stripers has a casual atmosphere and outdoor deck seating. Choose an appetizer such as grilled octopus or shrimp chowder, or an entrée such as baked Cornish hen or steamed lobster with yucca.

Nantucket
Bartlett's Ocean View Farm Market Kitchen, Bartlett Farm Road, Nantucket (508-228-3906). Grab a sandwich or meal on your way to the beach or a picnic. Bartlett's offers many vegetarian selections along with salads, breakfast treats, and desserts.

Cioppino's Restaurant and Bar, 20 Broad Street, Nantucket (508-228-4622). "We have a lovely patio and welcome pets," says Cioppino's Tracy Root. "Our staff bring a bowl of water right away to travelers who choose to bring a dog or cat or parakeet to dine outside." The menu includes items such as pan-seared crabcakes, smoked trout, Tuscan mozzarella salad, and carpaccio of beef.

HOT SPOTS FOR SPOT

Cape Cod
Animal Inn, Route 130, Sandwich (508-477-0990). Owned by a veterinarian, the Animal Inn boarding facility has outdoor runs, heated indoor kennel areas, playtime programs, a pet-supply shop, piped-in music, and a separate area for cats. Grooming and obedience training are also available.

"We've boarded everything from potbellied pigs to ferrets, bunnies, iguanas, a goose, and a goldfish, to name a few!" says staffer Barbara Ferguson.

Big Bow Wow and Little Meow, 372 Commercial Street, Provincetown (508-487-2907). A portion of the sales at this cute shop supports local greyhound rescue organizations; items include pet-themed collectibles, clothing and jewelry for two-legged customers, and treats, bandannas, and accessories for the four-legged variety.

Cloverleaf Kennel, 558 Carriage Shop Road, East Falmouth (508-540-PETS; petboarding@cloverleafkennel.com; www.cloverleaf-kennel.com). The staff at this boarding and grooming facility give each dog several walks each day and board cats in a separate second-floor space. The kennel is heated and air-conditioned. You'll need proof of vaccination before boarding a pet, and reservations are strongly recommended. Fees range from $9 per night for cats to $12 and $13 per night for dogs.

Comforts of Home Pet Sitting, 13 Pond Street, Dennis (508-385-8941). A member of Pet Sitters International, Sue Baudanza provides dog walks and pet-sitting services for locals as well as visitors to the Cape. "We are happy to sit for summer visitors at a home or rental property, or at a hotel if management has agreed to it," she says. A typical charge is $10 per half-hour visit, and $15 for a one-hour visit.

Derbyfield Country Kennel, 556 Depot Street, North Harwich (508-432-2510). Recommended by locals, this family-run boarding facility has a pickup service, piped-in music for the animals, indoor and outdoor runs, a separate cattery, heat in the winter, and nightly treats.

KC's Animal Resort, 79 Shank Painter Road, Provincetown (508-487-7900; kcl@capecod.net; www.ptownpets). Located beside a veterinary clinic, KC's offers 22 private kennels, heated floors and air-conditioning, outdoor runs, and a play yard. Your pet can also get a complete grooming—including a bath, ear cleaning, and nail clipping—during her stay. Rates range $19–22 per night; play sessions and walks are $4 extra.

Nauset Kennels, 2685 Nauset Road, North Eastham (508-255-0081). Nauset offers doggie day care as well as overnight boarding. The facility has several play yards, heat and air-conditioning, pickup and delivery, and a separate boarding area for cats.

Paws and Whiskers, 256 Commercial Street, Provincetown (508-487-3441). This "dog bakery and pawticulars" shop sells everything from gourmet, fresh-baked treats to toys, collars, leashes, hats, and bowls.

Paws 'n' Claws, Brewster (508-385-3638). Patti McGan owns this pet-sitting business that serves **Brewster, Hyannis, Barnstable,** and other nearby towns. For about $15 per hour, she can visit your motel, B&B, hotel, or cottage for midday walks, doggie day trips, and simple sitting while you're out having dinner.

Martha's Vineyard
Black Dog General Store,
480 State Road, Vineyard Haven, Martha's Vineyard (508-696-8182). When thinking of the Vineyard, many people call to mind the ubiquitous Black Dog silhouette logo of this wildly popular tavern, bakery, and store. Inside, you can find T-shirts, mugs, socks, golf balls, hats, and nearly everything else emblazoned with the dark pooch's picture. You can also browse dog bowls, biscuits, backpacks, and other good stuff for your four-legged companions. The Black Dog donates a portion of its profits to the ASPCA and to the National Education for Assistance Dog Service (NEADS).

Good Dog Goods, 79 Circuit Avenue, Oak Bluffs, Martha's Vineyard (508-696-7100). Owner Kerry Scott calls her shop "a celebration of dogs"; your pup is welcome to join you inside as you browse the wide selection of items designed especially for dogs and their owners.

Nantucket
Cold Noses, The Courtyard at Straight Wharf, Nantucket (508-228-KISS). This fun boutique sells dog and cat toys, nautical- and Nantucket-themed collars, leashes, and tags, breed-specific gift items, T-shirts, tote bags, Christmas tree ornaments, books, and more.

Nantucket MSPCA (Massachusetts Society for the Prevention of Cruelty to Animals), 21 Crooked Lane, Nantucket (508-228-1491). In addition to caring for local domestic and wild animals, the Nantucket MSPCA can also board and groom your pet in its newly built facility during your visit to the island. Staffed with volunteers and veterinarians, the society also offers humane education, wildlife rehabilitation, and homeless-animal adoption programs.

IN CASE OF EMERGENCY

Barnstable Animal Hospital, 157 Airport Road, Hyannis (508-778-6555).

Deer Run Veterinary Services, 168 Teaticket Highway, East Falmouth (508-548-3406).

Herring Cove Animal Clinic, 79 Shank Painter Road, Provincetown (508-487-6449).

Nantucket MSPCA, 21 Crooked Lane, Nantucket (508-228-1491).

Pleasant Bay Animal Hospital, Route 137 and Queen Ann Road, East Harwich (508-432-5500).

Sandwich Animal Hospital, 492 Route 6A, East Sandwich (508-888-2774).

Vineyard Veterinary Clinic, 276 Vineyard Haven Road, Edgartown, Martha's Vineyard (508-627-5292).

COGGSHALL PARK IS AN OASIS FOR DOG WALKERS AND HIKERS IN FITCHBURG.

Central Massachusetts

PET-FRIENDLY RATING: ✔ ✔ ✔

For travelers planning a trip to New England, central Massachusetts may not be high on the to-do list: Some say it lacks the glamour of the seacoast and the lure of covered-bridge landscapes in places like Vermont and New Hampshire. But pet owners will find the area awash with things to do and places to go, including apple orchards, parks, mountains, winding back roads and city streets. Whether you're hoping to spend a week at a lakefront campground, paddle a canoe or simply take a nice drive to look at the changing leaves, this often overlooked section of the state can provide a peaceful escape in an otherwise crowded commonwealth.

Unfortunately, the region is not as accommodating to animal lovers as it used to be. In January, 2003, the living history museum and popular tourist attraction Old Sturbridge Village reversed its pet-friendly policies—dogs are no longer allowed to accompany their owners through the museum's many outdoor exhibits and displays. Hopefully Sturbridge's many animal-inclusive hotels and campgrounds won't follow suit, but it would be worthwhile to double-check current policies before making reservations. Travelers should also note that central Massachusetts' most noteworthy natural feature, the enormous Quabbin Reservoir, is a public water supply and therefore off-limits to pets.

ACCOMMODATIONS

Hotels, Motels, Inns, and Bed & Breakfasts

Auburn
Baymont Inn and Suites, 444 Southbridge Street, Auburn (508-832-7000; www.baymont-inns.com/auburn); $79–109 per night. Guests at Baymont enjoy free continental breakfasts, newspapers, and local calls, along with interior corridors, voice mail, express checkout services, and cable TV with premium movie channels and pay-per-view films. Children under 18 stay free, and pets are welcome without extra fees.

Barre
Jenkins Inn, 7 West Street, Barre (978-355-6444; jenkinsinn@juno.com); $135–185 per night. Listed on the National Register of Historic Homes, this antique farmhouse offers private bathrooms, country breakfasts, air-conditioning, parking, color TVs, and in-room telephones. Dogs (sorry, no cats) are welcome at Jenkins Inn for an additional $5 per night, provided they are not left alone in the rooms.

Fitchburg
Best Western Royal Plaza Hotel, 150 Royal Plaza Drive, Fitchburg (978-342-7100); $89–169 per night. Pets are allowed at the Royal Plaza on a "limited basis" at the general manager's discretion for an additional $10 per night. Amenities include a swimming pool, a restaurant and lounge, a fitness center, laundry facilities, cable TV, a 24-hour front desk, a business center, and room service.

Framingham
Motel 6 Framingham, 1668 Worcester Road, Framingham (508-620-0500); $51–59 per night. Pets are allowed at all Motel 6 locations; the Framingham site offers premium movie channels, laundry facilities, elevators, free morning coffee, and a location that's convenient to restaurants and shopping. Kids stay free with their parents.

Red Roof Inn Framingham, 650 Cochituate Road, Framingham (508-872-4499; 1-800-RED-ROOF); $61–93 per night. Amenities include cable TV, free newspapers, alarm clocks, a 24-hour front desk, express checkout services, free local calls, modem lines, and plenty of parking. Framingham is home to hundreds of independent and chain

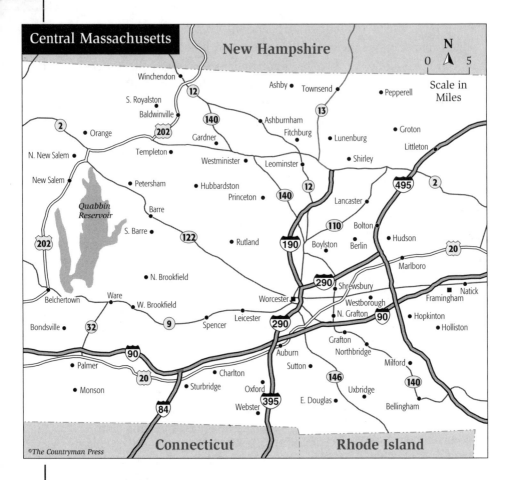

Central Massachusetts

New Hampshire

N

0 — 5

Scale in Miles

Connecticut

Rhode Island

stores, restaurants, businesses, and a hospital. Pets are welcome without extra fees.

Residence Inn by Marriott Boston Framingham, 400 Staples Drive, Framingham (508-370-0001; 1-800-627-7468); $99–179 per night. Stay long- or short-term at the Residence Inn, where suites take the place of traditional hotel rooms. At the Framingham location, guests can take advantage of free newspapers, a swimming pool, a fitness center, laundry facilities, studios, and one- and two-bedroom suites. Pet owners pay a onetime $150 nonrefundable fee.

Leominster
Motel 6 Leominster,
48 Commercial Street, Leominster (978-537-8161); $49–59 per night. Located about 5 miles from Fitchburg, the Leominster Motel 6 amenities include an outdoor swimming pool, a restaurant, nonsmoking rooms, laundry facilities, free morning coffee, and premium movie channels. Well-behaved pets are welcome without extra fees.

Marlboro
Super 8 Motel Marlboro,
880 Lynch Boulevard, Marlboro (508-460-1000; 1-800-698-1011); $59–104 per night. Guests at this

65-room, two-story Super 8 location can enjoy free 15-item continental breakfasts, interior corridors, and satellite TV. General Manager Karen Bradshaw is an animal lover and owns two poodles herself. "We'll go out of our way to make your pet's stay comfortable," she says. Animals are allowed in smoking rooms with a $30 refundable deposit.

Milford

Days Inn Milford, 3 Fortune Boulevard, Milford (508-634-2499); $69–94 per night. Free coffee is available at this Days Inn location, which also offers a 24-hour front desk, modem lines, free local calls, a fitness center, and cable TV. Animals are welcome for an extra $25 per night.

Orange

Executive Inn, 110 Daniel Shays Highway, Orange (978-544-8861); $50–85 per night. This motel, located near three fishing lakes and a driving range, offers 28 recently remodeled rooms and free continental breakfasts. The Mohawk Trail is about 10 miles away. Pets are allowed for an extra $7 per night.

Travel Inn, 180 Daniel Shays Highway, Orange (978-544-2986); $55–75 per night. Pets are welcome for an additional $5 per night at this motel with a 24-hour front desk, free continental breakfasts, cable TV with premium movie channels, alarm clocks, and free local calls. Refrigerators and microwaves are available upon request.

Southborough

Red Roof Inn Southborough, 367 Turnpike Road, South-

borough (508-481-3904; 1-800-RED-ROOF; $59–75 per night. At this Red Roof Inn location, guests can enjoy cable TV; express checkout services; a 24-hour front desk; and free newspapers, local calls, and parking. Pets are welcome without extra charges.

Sturbridge

Best Western American Motor Lodge, 350 Main Street, Sturbridge (508-347-9121); $79–109 per night. Located just around the corner from Old Sturbridge Village, this hotel features 55 rooms, cable TV, an indoor swimming pool and sauna, a playground, a game room, a restaurant and lounge, laundry facilities, and meeting rooms. Pets that weigh less than 60 pounds are allowed.

Days Inn Sturbridge, 66–68 Haynes Street, Sturbridge (508-347-3391; 1-800-544-8313); $55–85 per night. Set in the woods, this Days Inn is located about a mile from Old Sturbridge Village and offers a swimming pool, cable TV, express checkout services, and in-room coffeemakers and alarm clocks. Pets are allowed for an additional $7 per night.

Green Acres Motel, 2 Shepard Road, Sturbridge (508-347-3496); $55–139 per night. With 16 rooms, this Sturbridge motel has a quiet location, a swimming pool, in-room refrigerators, non-smoking rooms, and cable TV. Pets are welcome for $5–8 per night, depending on the season.

Publick House Country Motor Lodge, on the common, Route

131, Sturbridge (508-347-3313; 1-800-PUBLICK; info@publick-house.com; www.publickhouse. com); $79–104 per night. These motel buildings are located just up the hill from the historic Publick House Inn and Tavern; a walkway connects the two areas. Though pets are not allowed in the main inn, they are welcome in motor-lodge rooms for an additional $5 per night. Each room has a balcony and cable TV, and shared access to a swimming pool.

Sturbridge Host Hotel, 366 Main Street, Sturbridge (508-347-7393; 1-800-582-3232; www.sturbridge-hosthotel.com); $139–199 per night. Designed to accommodate those traveling for business as well as pleasure, the Sturbridge Host has suites and guest rooms, Colonial decor (including canopy beds and fireplaces in some rooms), and in-room hair dryers and coffeemakers. Pet owners staying for one night pay an extra $15; those staying for two or more nights pay a onetime fee of $25.

Thomas Henry Hearthstone Inn, 453 Main Street, Sturbridge (1-888-781-7775; thhearth@aol. com;www.hearthstonestur.com); $129–279 per night. Built by the current owners, this elegant country inn has homey touches, like in-room whirlpools, as well as modern conveniences. The Great Hall Dining Room serves breakfast and dinner; and tea, wine, and brandy are served in front of the fireplaces. Pets are welcome with prior approval.

Sudbury
Arabian Horse Inn Bed & Breakfast, 277 Old Sudbury Road, Sudbury (978-443-7400; 1-800-ARABIAN; joanbeers@aol. com); $159–299 per night. Not only are dogs welcome at this 1880 lavish estate, but there's also "room at the inn" for your horse in Arabian's stables. Innkeepers Joan and Rick Beers allow animals in the on-site one-bedroom cottage; it has two floors, a king-sized bed, a kitchenette, a living room area, a private garden, a hot tub, and views of the horse pastures.

Westborough
Residence Inn by Marriott Boston Westborough, 25 Connector Road, Westborough (508-366-7700); $139–189 per night. The Westborough Residence Inn offers a swimming pool, laundry services, a fitness center, free morning newspapers and continental breakfasts, cable TV, and a 24-hour front desk. Like all Residence Inns, the hotel caters to long-term stays. Pet owners pay a onetime non-refundable fee of $150.

Wyndham Westborough, 5400 Computer Drive, Westborough (508-366-5511; www. wyndham.com/westborough); $129–189 per night. Pets are welcome with a $50 refundable deposit at this four-story Westborough hotel. Guests can take advantage of a fitness center, an indoor swimming pool, a hot tub and sauna, voice mail, data ports, in-room hair dryers and coffeemakers, free newspapers,

THE HISTORIC PUBLICK HOUSE IN STURBRIDGE WELCOMES PETS IN ITS COUNTRY-MOTEL ANNEX.

and cable TV with premium movie channels.

Westford

Residence Inn by Marriott Boston–Westford, 7 LAN Drive, Westford (978-392-1407; 1-800-331-3131); $129–179 per night. This Residence Inn location has a fitness center, a swimming pool, laundry services, and in-room modem hookups. The suites have separate sleeping and living areas and kitchens. Animal owners staying longer than two weeks pay a $150 nonrefundable deposit; those staying less than two weeks pay $10 per night.

Westford Regency Inn, 219 Littleton Road, Westford (978-692-8200; info@westfordregency.com; www.westfordregency.com); $95–239 per night. This upscale hotel houses 193 rooms and suites decorated in Colonial New England style; an on-site health club offers an indoor swimming pool, fitness classes, racquetball courts, and a weight room. One adult dog (sorry, no cats) is allowed per room with a $25 non-refundable fee and a $100 refundable deposit.

Worcester

Holiday Inn Worcester, 500 Lincoln Street, Worcester (508-852-4000); $111–165 per night. This fairly new, full-service hotel offers an indoor swimming pool and sauna; a concierge desk; in-room hair dryers, irons, and coffeemakers; wake-up and turn-down services; room service; a fitness center; and a lounge. Free airport shuttles are also available. Pets are welcome for an extra $25 per night.

Regency Suites Hotel, 70 Southbridge Street, Worcester (508-753-3512); $89–155 per night. The Regency Suite does allow pets, though its policy is a bit too restrictive for most pet owners: Only animals weighing less than 15 pounds are allowed. If you do have a small pup or cat, you can enjoy the hotel's studios and one- and two-bedroom suites, along with an outdoor swimming pool, fitness center, beauty shop, and convenience store.

Campgrounds

Ashby
Willard Brook State Forest Campground, Route 119, Ashby and Townsend (978-597-8802); $10 per night Massachusetts residents; $12 per night out-of-state residents. There are 21 campsites at this state forest campground, complete with picnic tables, fire pits, and flush toilets (but no showers). Open Memorial Day through Labor Day only, the campground offers opportunities for fishing, swimming, hiking, and picnicking. (For more information on Willard Brook, see "Out and About.")

Baldwinville
Otter River State Forest Campground, New Winchendon Road, Baldwinville (978-939-8962); $10 per night Massachusetts

residents; $12 per night out-of-state residents. In addition to 83 traditional campsites for tents and RVs, Otter River also has two group camping areas that can each accommodate up to 25 people. Other amenities include hiking trails, picnic tables, fire pits, and rest rooms with showers. (See "Out and About" for more state forest information.)

Littleton
Northwest–Concord–Salem KOA, Route 2A, Littleton (978-772-0042; 1-800-562-7606; minuteman@ma.ultranet.com); $22–34 per night. Pets are allowed at RV and tent campsites but not at Kamping Kabins at KOA. Campers can relax in the outdoor swimming pool and set up their home-away-from-home at wooded or sunny sites. Hookups are available.

Monson
Sunsetview Farm Camping Area, 57 Town Farm Road, Monson (413-267-9269; camp@sunsetview.com; www.sunsetview.com); $22–28 per night. Wagon rides, bingo games, classic-car shows, and guided nature walks are just some of the activities at Sunsetview, where tenters and RVers can enjoy a swimming pool, rest rooms with showers, game courts, and a snack bar. Quiet, leashed family pets are welcome as long as their owners clean up after them. There is a limit of two dogs per site.

Oakham
Pine Acres Family Camping Resort, 203 Bechan Road, Oakham (508-882-9509; 1-866-571-

6048; camp@pineacresresort. com; www.pineacresresort.com); $17–44 per night. Tucked-away tent sites and full-hookup RV sites are available at Pine Acres, a lake-front campground with three beaches, boat docks and launching areas, a playground, rest rooms with showers, a camp store, laundry facilities, and trails for cross-country skiing, hiking, and biking. Pets are welcome for an extra fee of $2 per pet, per night.

Phillipston
Lamb City Campground, 85 Royalston Road, Phillipston (978-249-2049; 1-800-292-LAMB; lambcity@tiac.net; www.lambcity. com); $18–40 per night or $110–240 per week. Tent and RV campers at Lamb City can make use of a camp store, lake views, swimming pools, and hayrides. Nicki, the resident pooch, will welcome you as you arrive. The Blake family welcomes friendly dogs at their campground, provided their owners can show proof of vaccination.

Sturbridge
Jellystone Park Sturbridge, River Road, Sturbridge (508-347-9570; rsmith@jellystone sturbridge.com); $26–45 per night. With live bands, two swimming pools, a hot tub, a water slide, a snack shop, miniature golf, a video arcade, and two playgrounds, families should find plenty to do at this Jellystone Park campground located near Old Sturbridge Village. Dogs are welcome, but must be on a leash at all times.

Wells State Park Campground, Route 49, Sturbridge (508-347-

9257); $10 per night Massachusetts residents; $12 per night out-of-state residents. The 60 campsites at this state park have fire pits and picnic tables and share access to a dumping station and rest rooms with hot showers. Popular park activities (see "Out and About") include hiking, swimming, hunting, canoeing, and fishing.

Webster
Webster–Sturbridge KOA, 106 Douglas Road, Webster (508-943-1895); $23–31 per night. Located about 10 miles outside Worcester, this KOA features a swimming pool, and tent and RV sites. Hookups, cable TV, firewood, and modem data ports are all available with an extra charge. Leashed, well-behaved dogs are welcome at sites.

West Townsend
Pearl Hill State Park Campground, New Fitchburg Road, West Townsend (978-597-8802; 978-597-2850); $10 per night Massachusetts residents; $12 per night out-of-state residents. The 51 tent and RV campsites at this 1,000-acre park (see "Out and About") each have fire pits and picnic tables, and access to freshwater spigots and rest rooms with showers. The campground, like the park itself, is only open to the public seasonally.

Winchendon
Lake Dennison State Recreation Area Campground, Route 202, Winchendon (978-939-8962); $10 per night Massachusetts residents; $12 per night out-of-state residents. The campground at this large state reservation has 151

campsites, fire pits, picnic tables, a dumping station, and rest rooms with showers. The lake offers swimming and boating activities; nearby trails and picnic tables provide a peaceful escape. (For more information on the recreation area, see "Out and About.")

OUT AND ABOUT

Arrowhead Acres, 92 Aldrich Street (Route 98), Uxbridge (508-278-5017). Though officially a Christmas tree farm, Arrowhead Acres offers family activities year-round on its 73 acres. Visitors can enjoy hayrides, a petting farm, horseshoe pits, a swimming pool, badminton and shuffleboard courts, a large pavilion for group outings, a pumpkin patch, and of course Christmas tree tagging in the winter. Pet owners are asked to clean up after their animals and keep them on leashes.

Berlin Orchards, 200 Central Street (Route 62), Berlin (978-838-2400). Dogs on a leash are welcome in the outdoor areas at this large orchard, farmer's market, and gift shop located along Route 62. Come for apple picking in the fall, maple sugaring in the spring, and special events throughout the year.

Breezelands Orchards, Southbridge Road, Warren (413-436-710). During the fall, leashed pets are allowed to join their owners in the pick-your-own orchard at Breezelands, where apples, peaches, and pears are the most popular fruits. Inside, the shop sells cider donuts, pies, jellies, fruit baskets, and cheese.

Coggshall Park, 244 Mount Elam Street, Fitchburg (978-343-9892). This beautiful 200-acre city park has extensive hiking trails, a scenic pond, and a gazebo that's a popular spot for wedding-day photos. Leashed dogs are welcome, though they're not allowed on the perimeter of the pond or in the playground.

Fruitlands Museums, 102 Prospect Hill Road, Harvard (978-456-3924; www.fruitlands. org). Leashed pets are welcome at Fruitlands, an outdoor history museum with miles of nature trails, archaeological-dig sites, historic homes, and exhibits on Native Americans in New England, Shakers, and other early inhabitants of the area. Animal owners are asked to clean up messes and to not leave their pets alone in parked cars or tied up on the property.

Hyland Orchard and Brewery, 199 Arnold Road, Sturbridge (1-877-HYLANDS; www.hyland-brew.com). "Hyland's a very pet-friendly place!" says Business Manager Beth Damon. "Our only restriction is that pets not be left in vehicles during the warm months and that they are leashed when on our property." Activities include apple picking in the orchard, picnicking in the recreation area, watching maple syrup demonstrations, and joining in at the Peach Festival and haunted-orchard rides.

Lake Dennison State Recreation Area, Route 202, Winchendon (978-939-8962). In addition to campsites (see "Accommodations—Campgrounds"), this park also offers a boat ramp; a beach; trails for hiking, horseback riding, and cross-country skiing; and picnic areas with barbecue grills. Of the 10,000 acres managed by the Army Corps of Engineers as a flood-control project, about 4,000 acres are available for public use. Leashed dogs are welcome but are not allowed on the beach.

Otter River State Forest, New Winchendon Road, Baldwinville (978-939-8962). You can stop by for the afternoon or stay overnight in the campground (see "Accommodations—Campgrounds") at this 12,000-acre park located near the New Hampshire border. Visitors will find a baseball field, picnic areas with shelters and barbecue grills, and trails for hiking, biking, and cross-country skiing. Dogs must be on a leash.

Paws in the Park, Framingham. **Save a Dog,** a Framingham-based animal rescue organization, hosts this annual dog-walk fund-raiser each year, usually on a Saturday at the end of June. Local and visiting pet lovers are welcome to attend. In addition to the walk, there are dog contests, games, food, and obedience demonstra-

tions. For more information, contact Save a Dog at P.O. Box 1108, Framingham, MA 01701, or at saveadog@saveadog.org or www.saveadog.org.

Pearl Hill State Park, New Fitchburg Road, West Townsend (978-597-8802; 978-597-2850). Open seasonally from Memorial Day through Labor Day, this 1,000-acre park has a 5-acre pond, a campground (see "Accommodations—Campgrounds"), a beach, picnic areas with barbecue grills and shelters, and trails where hiking and cross-country skiing are permitted. Dogs must be on a leash and are not allowed on the beach.

Walk 'N Wag, Sturbridge. Held each September in Sturbridge, this fun dog-walking event is a fund-raiser for the **Second Chance Animal Shelter** in East Brookfield. Out-of-towners are more than welcome to attend; for more information on this year's dates and times, visit www.secondchanceanimals.org or call the shelter at 508-867-5525.

Wells State Park, Route 49, Sturbridge (508-347-9257). There are 10 miles of trails in this 1,400-acre park; you can use them for horseback riding, hiking, dog walking, cross-country skiing, or mountain biking. Wells also has a campground (see "Accommodations—Campgrounds"), a beach, picnic areas, and a boat ramp and launch area for motorized and nonmotorized vessels. Dogs must be leashed and are not allowed on the beach.

Willard Brook State Forest, Route 119, Ashby and Townsend (978-597-8802). Located just across the road (Route 119) from **Pearl Hill State Park** (see above listing), this somewhat larger park has more than 2,000 acres; a campground (see "Accommodations—Campgrounds"); myriad trails with permitted uses such as cross-country skiing, hiking, biking, and horseback riding; picnic areas with barbecue grills; and boating and fishing opportunities. Dogs must be on a leash.

QUICK BITES

Bagel Time, 194B Park Avenue, Worcester (508-798-0440). This friendly city stop offers baker's dozens along with deli and roll-up sandwiches, fresh-brewed coffees, and cool smoothies.

Barber's Crossing, 175 Leominster Road, Sterling (978-422-8438); 325 West Boylston Street, Worcester (508-852-3435). Most people enjoy their Barber's meal inside the Colonial-themed dining rooms, but those with a pooch in tow can also order lunch and dinner to go. Menu items include sandwiches, burgers, poultry, steaks, seafood, salads, and dessert.

Farm at Baptist Common, 342 Baldwinville Road, Templeton (978-939-8146). When you concentrate on one thing, you're bound to do it well. The farm offers more than 30 flavors of its well-known fudge for an after-dinner (or after-anything) treat.

Herd Rock Calfe and Moo Moo's Ice Cream, Davis' Farmland, 145 Redstone Hill, Sterling (978-422-MOOO). On a hot day, take a break for premium ice cream or snacks like pizza, chicken fingers, and hot dogs—the child-friendly café even has baby food on hand.

Howard's Drive-In, Route 9, West Brookfield (508-867-6504). Walk up to Howard's window and order fisherman's platters, seafood samplers, lobster rolls, tuna sandwiches, burgers, frappes, floats, and ice cream sundaes.

Meadowbrook Orchards Farm Stand and Bakery, 209 Chase Hill Road, Sterling (978-365-7617). Choose from sweets and fresh-baked treats or more substantial lunch meals like sandwiches and soups at this country farm stand. You can also pick up frozen ready-to-heat-and-eat meals on your way out.

Nancy Chang, 372 Chandler Street, Worcester (508-752-8899). With an emphasis on healthy ingredients, such as brown rice, olive and soybean oils, and herbs, Nancy Chang restaurant offers Chinese food for take-out, delivery, or eat-in service.

Rom's Restaurant, Route 131, Sturbridge (508-347-3349). Open seven days a week, Rom's offers eat-in or take-out services and serves Italian and American favorites. A kid's menu is available.

HOT SPOTS FOR SPOT

Barking Lot, 71 West Main Street, Hopkinton (508-435-6633). Take your pooch for a bath or pick up food, toys, treats, and other animal-friendly items at this grooming and pet-supply facility.

Clip and Dip Dog Grooming, 19 Pond Street, Natick (508-653-7425). All breeds of canines are welcome at Clip and Dip, which has been offering bathing, cuts, flea dips, hot-oil treatments, and more for more than 12 years. You'll need to make an appointment before stopping by.

Critter Sitters, 49 Lawrence Street, Milford (508-478-9844; thecrittersitters@hotmail.com). Critter Sitters' owner Emmie L. Himmelman will happily keep your pet busy for a few hours if you can't be there; she serves **Milford, Bellingham, Franklin, Medway,** and other nearby towns and has provided pet care for cats, dogs, geckos, hamsters, and ferrets. The charge is $15 per visit or $35 for overnight care.

Doggie Den, 14 Blake Street, Northboro (508-393-6970; www.thedoggieden.net). Canine boarding, grooming, training, and day care are all available at this Northboro facility. An on-site boutique carries pet-care items as well. Day-care rates range $17–22 per day.

Gemini Dog Training and Daycare, 53-B Ayer Road, Littleton (978-486-9922; www.geminidogs.com). The doggie day-care facilities at Gemini include fenced-in play areas, afternoon snacks, and staff members who give each animal lots of attention. Reservations are required.

Harvard Kennels, 259 Ayer Road, Harvard (978-772-4242). Reservations are required at this popular kennel located about halfway between Worcester and Lowell. Boarding rates are $8 per night for cats and $14–16 per night for dogs, depending on size.

Pet Barn, 310 Park Avenue, Worcester (508-831-0262). This small family-operated business has a holistic approach to pet care; the Pet Barn carries gourmet and name-brand foods, homeopathic remedies, herbal supplements, toys, chewies, and other supplies. Special orders are welcome.

Pet Supplies 'N' More, 78 River Street, Fitchburg (978-343-4892). If you run out of anything on the road for your bird, cat, dog, gerbil, hamster, or fish, chances are you'll find it at this large pet store. Grooming, pet photos, and obedience classes are also offered.

Pet World, 1262 Worcester Road, Natick (508-653-9221). This large, well-stocked store carries treats, food, and accessories for dogs, cats, birds, and small animals; it's also the home of Kitty City, a shelter for homeless cats in the Greater Framingham area.

IN CASE OF EMERGENCY

Adams Animal Hospital,
1287 South Main Street, Athol (978-249-7967).

Littleton Animal Hospital,
29 King Street, Littleton (978-486-3101).

Metrowest Veterinary Associates,
207 East Main Street, Milford (508-478-7300).

Quabbin Animal Hospital,
180 Ware Road, Belchertown (413-323-7203).

Slade Veterinary Hospital,
334 Concord Street, Framingham (508-875-7086).

Sturbridge Veterinary Hospital,
6 Cedar Street, Sturbridge (508-347-7374).

Westside Animal Clinic,
546 Mill Street, Worcester (508-756-4411).

Western Massachusetts

PET-FRIENDLY RATING: 🦴 🦴 🦴 🦴

Unfortunately, many of the things that western Massachusetts is famous for, including Tanglewood, the Eastern States Exposition (Big E) and fair, the Norman Rockwell Museum, and the Yankee Candle Company factory, are off-limits to animals. But on the bright side, this beautiful, culturally rich region is also blanketed with vast, pet-friendly state parks and forest preserves; more than any other region in the state, this is a naturalist's heaven.

It's also one of New England's most popular destinations for those look-ing to get a peek at the changing autumn leaves; from the renowned Mohawk Trail to Routes 7 and 41 and every byway in between, this end of the state has scenic vistas to rival those in the better-known Vermont to the north. Stockbridge draws music, dance, and theater fans from around the country with its many festivals and shows, and the Amherst–Northampton area, otherwise known as the Five College

Region, holds its own with busy downtown shopping areas, brew pubs, and intellectual discourse. Your pup may have to wander on the edges of all that culture, but once he sees the mountains, waterfalls, hiking trails, and shady parks around every corner, he probably won't mind.

ACCOMMODATIONS

Hotels, Motels, Inns, and Bed & Breakfasts

Amherst

Lord Jeffery Inn, 30 Boltwood Avenue, Amherst (1-800-742-0358; info@lordjefferyinn.com; www.lordjefferyinn.com); $89–209 per night. A popular setting for weddings and other special events, this historic inn and tavern offers 40 guest rooms as well as eight suites, which have attached sitting rooms and sofa beds. The inn is close to four colleges, the University of Massachusetts, bike trails, and shopping. Pets are allowed in designated smoking rooms for an additional $15 per night.

University Lodge, 345 North Pleasant Street, Amherst (413-256-8111); $55–139 per night. Located close to Amherst College, the University of Massachusetts, and downtown Amherst's shops and restaurants, the University Lodge has 20 rooms (each with two double beds), cable TV, and in-room coffeemakers. Pets are welcome without extra fees.

Bernardston

Windmill Motel, Route 10, Bernardston (413-648-9152); $48–61 per night. Choose from single or double rooms (one bed or two) at this clean 16-unit motel located close to the interstate and the Northfield Mount Hermon School campus. Breakfast is served each morning in an on-site cafeteria. Dogs are welcome without extra fees, though they must be crated when left alone in the room.

Blandford

Pleasure Horse Paso Fino Farm and Bed & Breakfast, 43 Russell Stage Road, Blandford (413-848-2214); $40–90 per night. Your horse, pig, dog, rabbit, or any other pet is welcome at this active B&B in the countryside. Breakfast is included in the rates; the home has eight stalls for horses and 12 acres of scenic pastures. Pets must housebroken and well behaved. Dog and cat owners pay an extra $10 per night—the fee for all other animals is an additional $15 per night.

Buckland

Restful Crow Bed & Breakfast, 6 Cross Street, Buckland (413-625-9507; dpoland@therestfulcrow.com; www.therestfulcrow.com); $65–110 per night. "I accept pets with pleasure," says Restful Crow

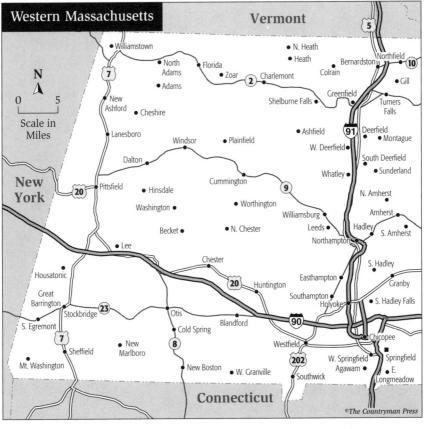

Western Massachusetts

Vermont

New York

Connecticut

©The Countryman Press

innkeeper Diane Poland. "Well-mannered pets are more than welcome." Located a hop, skip, and jump from the Mohawk Trail, this historic B&B offers two guest rooms and one suite, all furnished with antiques. The main house has fireplaces, cathedral ceilings, and gathering rooms.

Chicopee

Motel 6 Springfield–Chicopee,
36 Burnett Road, Chicopee (413-592-5141); $41–52 per night. Like all Motel 6 locations, this one welcomes pets without extra charges. Guest amenities include laundry facilities, cable TV with premium movie channels, free local calls, and free morning coffee. Kids stay free with their parents.

Ramada Inn Chicopee,
357 Burnett Road, Chicopee (413-592-9101); $49–79 per night. For an extra $10 per night, pets are welcome guests at this Ramada Inn featuring an outdoor swimming pool, a playground, express checkout services, microwaves, refrigerators, alarm clocks, and in-room hair dryers and ironing boards.

Florida

Whitcomb Summit Motel,
229 Mohawk Trail, Florida (1-800-547-0944; www.whitcomb-summit.com); cabins, $45–65 per night. Pets are allowed in the

cabins, but not in the main motel building, at this strategically located motel along the Mohawk Trail. Each cabin can accommodate up to six people with private baths, mountain views, and access to a swimming pool and campfire sites.

Great Barrington

Barrington Court Motel, 400 Stockbridge Road, Great Barrington (413-528-2340); $55–200 per night. Pets are welcome with prior approval at Barrington Court, a motel with 23 traditional rooms and two larger one-bedroom suites, landscaped grounds, a swimming pool, a bocce-ball court, and in-room coffeemakers and refrigerators.

Chez Gabrielle, 320 State Road (Route 23), Great Barrington (413-528-2799; chezgay@aol. com); $125–175 per night. Pets are welcome in Chez Gabrielle's two cheery guest rooms; each has a private bath. You'll also find a large fenced-in yard for dogs to roam, sunrooms, a deck, fireplaces, and a hot tub. There's a dog already living on the premises, so make sure your pup enjoys the company of other canines.

Turning Point Inn, 3 Lake Buel Road, Great Barrington (413-528-4777; turningpointinn@aol.com; www.turningpointinn.com); cottage, $130–249 per night. Owned and run by a chef, the Turning Point Inn is actually a 100-year-old tavern that has been refurbished to include six guest rooms. Though pets are not allowed in the main house, they are welcome in the neighboring

large cottage that has two bedrooms, a kitchen, and a sunporch. The inn has a fenced-in area where dogs are free to run.

Hadley

Howard Johnson Inn, 401 Russell Street, Hadley (413-586-0114); $59–149 per night. Guests at this HoJo Inn will find cable TV with premium movie channels, a swimming pool, free newspapers, a 24-hour front desk, alarm clocks and meeting/business rooms. Pets are allowed in designated smoking rooms only for an additional $20 per night.

Lenox

Walker House, 64 Walker Street, Lenox (413-637-1271; 1-800-235-3098); $80–220 per night. "We have cats and always hated to think of leaving them in a kennel, so we understand when pet lovers want to bring their animals along," says Walker House owner Peggy Houdek. The well-landscaped, historic inn has a welcoming front porch, Victorian decor, eight guest rooms named for composers, and full country breakfasts. Pets must be housebroken and quiet.

Richmond

A Bed & Breakfast in the Berkshires, 1666 Dublin Road, Richmond (413-698-2817; 1-800-795-7122; www.abnb.com); $125–195 per night. Doane Perry, who also owns A Bed & Breakfast in Cambridge, welcomes children and pets to this western Massachusetts getaway with perennial gardens, large lawns, a screened-in porch, air-conditioning, down comforters, and private baths. The rates include a full country breakfast and afternoon tea and sherry.

Sheffield
Birch Hill Bed & Breakfast, 254 South Undermountain Road, Sheffield (413-229-2143; 1-800-359-3969; info@birchhillbb; www.birchhillbb.com); $130–215 per night. The Birch Hill farm-house dates back to the era of the American Revolution. In addition to seven country-themed guest rooms with private baths, the inn also has a gathering room, a swimming pool, and res-ident greyhounds. Your pet is also welcome provided she stays on a leash, stays out of the gar-dens, and is not left unattended.

Race Brook Lodge, Route 41, Sheffield (1-888-RB-LODGE; www.rblodge.com); $95–245 per night. This post-and-beam lodge fits right into the western Massachusetts landscape with a gathering barn, cathedral ceilings, a wine bar, fireplaces, hardwood floors, and warm, "chintz-free" guest rooms. The designated pet-friendly rooms are all on the first floor with private entrances; ani-mal owners pay an additional $25 per stay (not per night).

South Deerfield
Red Roof Inn South Deerfield, 9 Greenfield Road, South Deerfield (413-665-7161); $62–69 per night. This Red Roof Inn loca-tion offers clean and simple guest rooms, free morning newspapers, a swimming pool, alarm clocks, cable TV, laundry facilities, and a 24-hour front desk. Pets are wel-come without extra charges.

Springfield
Holiday Inn Springfield Downtown, 711 Dwight Street, Springfield (413-781-0900); $119–169 per night. Located near the intersection of I-91 and I-90, this conveniently located hotel has a lobby bakery, an indoor swimming pool, room service, cable TV with pay-per-view movies, in-room hair dryers and irons, laundry facilities, and a fit-ness center. Pets are welcome for an additional $35 per stay (not per night).

Super 8 Chicopee, 463 Memorial Drive, Springfield (413-592-6171); call for rate information. Formerly known as the Best Western Chicopee, this budget motel is located just off I-90 and has 106 rooms with tra-ditional décor, a heated swim-ming pool, cable TV, and smok-ing and nonsmoking rooms. Pets are welcome for an additional $25 per stay (not per night).

Stockbridge
Pleasant Valley Motel, Route 102, Stockbridge (413-232-8511); $39–175 per night. Pets are wel-come for an additional $10 per night at Pleasant Valley, a 16-room motel with a swimming pool, cable TV, in-room micro-waves and refrigerators, and smoking and nonsmoking rooms. During the high season, guests can also enjoy free continental breakfasts.

Tyringham
Sunset Farm Bed & Breakfast, 66 Tyringham Road, Tyringham (413-243-3229; 413-243-0730; mchale@vgernet.net; www.sun-

setfarminn.com); $90–110 per night. Guests at Sunset Farm enjoy homemade country breakfasts and a relaxing, laid-back environment—some stay one night, some stay for the whole summer. "We have many fields and areas for owners to walk their pets, and the Appalachian Trail runs right through the property," explains innkeeper Mary Hale. Pets should be friendly, not left alone in rooms, and should sleep on their own bed or blanket.

West Springfield

Knights Inn West Springfield, 1557 Riverdale Street, West Springfield (413-737-9047); $50–67 per night. Pets are welcome guests—without extra charges—at this Knights Inn, which offers free local calls, a swimming pool, a restaurant, cable TV, free parking, hair dryers, and smoking and nonsmoking rooms.

Red Roof Inn West Springfield, 1254 Riverdale Street, West Springfield (413-731-1010); $47–75 per night. There are no extra fees for animals at this Red Roof Inn, where the amenities include premium movie channels, exterior corridors, free local calls, photocopying and fax services, snack machines, and alarm clocks.

Regency Inn and Suites, 21 Baldwin Street, West Springfield (413-781-2300); $59–150 per night. Located across from the Big E fairgrounds, this Regency Inn and Suites (formerly known as the Ramada Ltd. and Suites) has an indoor swimming pool, premium movie channels, in-room hair dryers, coffeemakers, irons,

microwaves and refrigerators, and hot tubs in some suites. Dogs and cats are welcome for an extra $10 per night.

Residence Inn by Marriott West Springfield, 64 Border Way, West Springfield (413-732-9543); $89–139 per night. Designed for long-term stays, this Residence Inn has studios and one- and two-bedroom suites with kitchens and separate living and sleeping areas. The West Springfield location also offers a fitness center, cable TV, and a swimming pool. Pet owners pay a onetime $75 fee and then an additional $10 per night.

West Stockbridge

Williamsville Inn, Route 41, West Stockbridge (413-274-6118; williamsville@taconic.net); $140–150 per night. Well-behaved pets are welcome at the Williamsville Inn, a historic B&B with 13 guest rooms, two suites, and full country breakfasts served each morning in the Garden Room. (At the time of this writing, the inn was undergoing a possible change in ownership; call to confirm its pet-friendly status if you'd like to visit.)

Williamstown

Cozy Corner Motel, 284 Sand Springs Road, Williamstown (413-458-8006); $45–135 per night. Guests at this 12-room motel enjoy clean, simple rooms, cable TV, in-room refrigerators, and free continental breakfasts each morning. A VCR is also available upon request. Pet owners pay an extra $10 per night and sign a pet-policy agreement upon check-in.

A SECLUDED RENTAL CABIN AT THE JERICHO VALLEY INN IN WILLIAMSTOWN

Jericho Valley Inn, 2541 Hancock Road, Williamstown (413-458-9511; 1-800-JERICHO; jvinn@bcn.net); cottages, $138–238 per night. Pets are welcome in the cottages at this friendly and clean inn, which also offers standard motel rooms and suites. Tucked away near two ski resorts and two golf courses, Jericho Valley has a scenic hilltop location, complimentary breakfasts, air-conditioning, an outdoor swimming pool, and cable TV. The cottages are roomy and bright with fireplaces, kitchenettes, full bathrooms, and separate bedrooms and living rooms. The surrounding forests and lawns provide plenty of room for roaming.

Campgrounds

Charlemont
Mohawk Trail State Forest Campground, Route 2, Charlemont (413-339-5504); $10 per night Massachusetts residents;

$12 per night out-of-state residents. Campers at Mohawk Trail's 56 sites have access to rest rooms with showers, picnic tables, fire pits, and camping cabins (each can accommodate 3 to 4 people); group camping sites (up to 50 people) are also available. Open seasonally, the park also offers guided family programs, trails, and boating (see "Out and About").

East Brimfield
Quinebaug Cove Campground, 49 East Brimfield–Holland Road, East Brimfield (413-245-9525; info@quinebaugcove.com; www.quinebaugcove.com); $28–35 per night. Campers at Quinebaug enjoy scheduled activities like hayrides, fishing derbies, boat races, and bingo nights, in addition to an Olympic-sized swimming pool, a boat ramp, a recreation center, and a camp store. Pet owners must clean up messes, show

proof of vaccination, and cannot leave their animals unattended.

Gill

Barton Cove Campground, Route 2, Gill (413-863-9300); $15 per night. Located on a peninsula at the **Northfield Mountain Recreation and Environmental Center** (see "Out and About"), this campground is owned by Northeast Utilities and offers rustic tent camping (sorry, no RVs) with picnic tables, fire pits, and hibachis. Nearby, you'll find trails through the woods, a boat ramp, and a dinosaur-quarry archaeological area. Leashed dogs are welcome.

Goshen

DAR State Forest Campground, Route 112, Goshen (413-268-7098); $10 per night Massachusetts residents; $12 per night out-of-state residents. Popular as a day-use area (see "Out and About"), this state forest also offers 52 campsites from Memorial Day through Columbus Day for those who would like to stay overnight. The campground has rest rooms with showers, fire pits, picnic tables, and one group camping site that can accommodate up to 75 people.

Granville

Prospect Mountain Campground, 1349 Main Road (Route 57), Granville (1-888-550-4PMC); $24–35 per night. Though dogs are not allowed in the cabins or rental trailers at Prospect Mountain, they are welcome at tent and RV sites provided they stay on a leash and their owners pick up after them. Campground amenities include two ponds, playing fields, a playground, a pavilion, a swimming pool, a nature trail, and rest rooms.

Lanesboro

Mount Greylock State Reservation Campground, Route 7, Lanesboro (413-499-4262); $5 per night Massachusetts residents; $6 per night out-of-state residents. This fairly small campground is quiet and remote with 35 sites, outhouses, picnic tables, and fire pits. The **Appalachian Trail** runs through this notable park (see "Out and About"), where hiking, hunting, and cross-country skiing are allowed.

Lee

October Mountain State Forest Campground, Woodland Road, Lee (413-243-1778); $10 per night Massachusetts residents; $12 per night out-of-state residents. The 46 sunny sites at this campground have picnic tables and fire pits and share access to rest rooms with showers; some sites are wheelchair accessible. Five group sites can accommodate up to 25 people each. Campers will no doubt enjoy roaming the park (see "Out and About") and relaxing at the picnic areas and on the trails.

Monterey

Beartown State Forest Campground, 69 Blue Hill Road, Monterey (413-528-0904); $10 per night Massachusetts residents; $12 per night out-of-state residents. This rough-it campground has just 12 sites, picnic tables, fire pits, and plenty of peace and quiet. Campers can also enjoy boating, swimming, fishing, hiking, and more at this huge, wild park (see "Out and About") located in the southwest corner of the state.

North Adams

Savoy Mountain State Forest Campground, 260 Central Shaft Road, North Adams–Florida (413-664-9567); $10 per night Massachusetts residents; $12 per night out-of-state residents. The 45 campsites at Savoy Mountain are nestled in a former orchard. Pets on a leash are welcome. Campers can take advantage of flush toilets, picnic tables, and fire pits along with nearby hiking trails, boat-launch areas, ponds, and waterfalls. (See "Out and About" for more park information.)

Pittsfield

Bonnie Brae Cabins and Campsites, 108 Broadway, Pittsfield (413-442-3754; smith llddsmith@aol.com; www.bonnie-braecampground.tripod.com); $27 per night or $162 per week. Rent a cabin or bring your tent or RV to Bonnie Brae for wooded campsites, full hookups, an outdoor swimming pool, rest rooms with hot showers, and laundry facilities. Leashed, quiet pets are welcome as long as their owners don't leave them alone at a site.

Pittsfield State Forest Campground, Cascade Street, Pittsfield (413-442-8992); $10 per night Massachusetts residents; $12 per night out-of-state residents. Picnic tables, flush toilets, and fire pits are available at this state forest campground near the New York border. In addition to the 30 sites, the preserve (see "Out and About") also provides opportunities for boating, hiking, bird-watching, and swimming.

Tolland

Tolland State Forest Campground, 410 Tolland Road, P.O. Box 342, East Otis, MA 01029 (413-269-6002); $10 per night Massachusetts residents; $12 per night out-of-state residents. You can camp right at the water's edge at Tolland State Forest, a park that is located alongside a 1,000-acre reservoir (see "Out and About"). The campground itself is located on a peninsula and has 92 campsites, rest rooms with showers, picnic tables, fire pits, and a dumping station. This one fills up quickly; make your reservations early.

Windsor

Windsor State Forest Campground, River Road, Windsor (413-684-0948); $10 per night Massachusetts residents; $12 per night out-of-state residents. Campers at Windsor State Forest have access to 24 individual sites, one group camping site that can accommodate up to 25 people, outhouses, picnic tables, and fire pits. Walking trails and waterfalls are nearby. (See "Out and About" for more park information.)

Homes, Cottages, and Cabins for Rent

Berkshires Carriage House, Great Barrington (617-424-1050; 617-424-8963; daveh@bwinc. com); $2,500 per week. This hilltop home is available for rent during the summer months; the house can accommodate up to eight people and has three bedrooms, two bathrooms, a full kitchen with a dishwasher, a fireplace, a great room, and a screened-in porch. House-trained pets are welcome with prior approval as long as owners clean up after walks on the property.

Lakefront Cabin, Norwich Lake, Huntington (323-964-8123; mischa joyner@aol.com); $650 per week. Set back on 1 private acre, this rental cabin has a private dock, two bedrooms, one bathroom, an enclosed porch, a fireplace, a pullout sofa, cable TV, a barbecue grill, and kitchen appliances. Well-behaved, housebroken, quiet pets are welcome with no extra fees.

OUT AND ABOUT

Beartown State Forest, 69 Blue Hill Road, Monterey (413-528-0904). Extremely popular with cross-country skiers, Beartown has 12,000 acres and plenty of trails for those who prefer to travel on skis, snowmobiles, horses, bikes, or their own two feet. There's also a campground on-site (see "Accommodations—Campgrounds"), along with a boat ramp, a beach, a 35-acre pond, picnic areas, and rest rooms. Pets must be leashed and are not allowed at the beach.

Bridge of Flowers, 22 Water Street, Shelburne Falls. Come spring and summer, local gardening enthusiasts cover this early-1900s trolley bridge with an astounding array of flowers in bloom. Located just off Route 2 (the Mohawk Trail), it's a great stop for a picture.

DAR State Forest, Route 112, Goshen (413-268-7098). This 1,700-acre forest preserve includes trails for horseback riding, hiking, biking, and cross-country skiing, along with Upper and Lower Highland Lakes, where nonmotorized boating is allowed. There are also several shaded picnic areas with great views. Dogs must be on a leash and are not allowed at the beach. (See "Accommodations—Campgrounds" for campground information.)

Downtown Northampton. This is where it's all happening in Northampton, otherwise known as NoHo, home to college students, artists, and a thriving cultural scene. The downtown area is centered along Main Street, which is lined with cafés, bookstores, clothing shops, and park benches that are perfectly suited for people-watching.

Dr. Seuss National Memorial, State and Chestnut Streets, Springfield. Surrounded by museums at the Quadrangle, this sculpture garden celebrates a hometown hero (Theodor Seuss Geisel, aka Dr. Seuss, was born in Springfield) on a peaceful and shady green. The fanciful bronze sculptures include a 14-foot Horton the Elephant and a tower of 10 turtles from Seuss's book *Yertle the Turtle.*

Historic Deerfield, Routes 5 and 10, Deerfield (413-774-5581; www.historic-deerfield.org). This 330-year-old village is home to preserved and restored 18th- and 19th-century homes and buildings, offering a snapshot of what life may have looked like in early rural New England. Though pets are not allowed in the historic buildings or museums, the public street is a wonderful place to stroll, admire the architecture, and imagine a former period in our nation's history.

Look Memorial Park, 300 North Main Street, Florence (413-584-5457). There's a lot going on at this 157-acre park, which boasts picnic areas, special events like crafts fairs and Easter egg hunts, a steamer railroad, a lake and pedal boats, tennis courts, a water-spray park, and walking paths. Dogs are permitted on a leash as long as their owners clean up after them. The entry fee is $2–10 per vehicle (depending on the day and the number of people in the car), and there are extra charges for some of the attractions once you're inside the park.

Mohawk Trail. Locals call it the Highway of History; visitors know it as one of the best leaf-peeping roads in all of New England. The Mohawk Trail is the stretch of Route 2 in northwestern Massachusetts between Williamstown and Orange. Most people try to make stops at the **Mount Greylock** and **Whitcomb** summits, the **Bridge of Flowers** in Shelburne Falls, the **Bissell Covered Bridge** in Charlemont, and the famous **hairpin turn** (use caution: It really is sharp) in North Adams.

Mount Greylock State Reservation, Route 7, Lanesboro (413-499-4262). In the northwestern corner of the state, Mount Greylock is not only the highest peak in Massachusetts (at 3,491 feet) but also its first official state park. You can drive or hike to the summit. There are also 45 miles of trails and a campground on-site (see "Accommodations—Campgrounds"). Dogs are welcome on a leash.

Natural Bridge State Park, Route 8, North Adams (413-663-6312). Bring your camera to this unusual state park, which is home to the only marble dam in North America. The "natural bridge" of its name refers to a marble arch that has been worn down over the centuries by water rushing through the gorge below. Once privately owned, the land became a state preserve in the mid-1980s.

Northfield Mountain Recreation and Environmental Center. Visitors Center: 99 Millers Falls Road (Route 63), Northfield (1-800-859-2960). Owned and managed by Northeast Utilities, this huge swath of green along the Connecticut River has 26 miles of trails, a campground (see **Barton Cove** under "Accommodations—Campgrounds"), guided walks, and family nature programs. The area is popular with horseback riders, mountain bikers, and hikers. You can get maps and other information at the visitors center; dogs must be on a leash.

Norwottuck Rail Trail, Connecticut River Greenway State Park, Warren Wright Road, Amherst–Belchertown (413-586-8706). Dogs are welcome on a 6-foot leash on this 10-mile-long paved trail, a former railroad line. Use caution with your pooch, as the trail is populated by fast-moving bicyclists, runners, in-line skaters, and cross-country skiers.

October Mountain State Forest, Woodland Road, Lee (413-243-1778). This is the largest state forest in Massachusetts; visitors will find more than 16,000 acres with a campground (see "Accommodations—Camp-grounds"); a section of the **Appalachian Trail** and other trails for hiking, cross-country skiing, and mountain biking; the renowned and scenic **Schermerhorn Gorge;** and plenty of wildlife-viewing opportunities. Leashed pets are welcome.

Pittsfield State Forest, Cascade Street, Pittsfield (413-442-8992). A 13,000-acre preserve, Pittsfield State Forest attracts nature lovers with its 30 miles of trails (mountain biking, horseback riding, hiking, and cross-country skiing are all approved uses), **Berry Mountain**'s scenic vistas, picnic areas, the famous **Balance Rock** geological phenomenon, water-falls, and abundant wildlife. Dogs must be leashed and are not allowed on the beach.

Precious Paws, 18 Crafts Avenue, Northampton (413-585-WOOF; info@precious pawsinc.com). Your pet is more than welcome inside this do-good gift shop founded by Elizabeth Frechette, a dog lover and breast cancer survivor who

AT THE PRECIOUS PAWS GIFT STORE IN NORTHAMPTON, PROCEEDS BENEFIT ANIMAL WELFARE ORGANIZATIONS AND BREAST CANCER RESEARCH.

wanted to find a creative way to raise funds for research. All of the gift items, including towels, clothing, and kitchen and bath accessories, feature fun dog-themed designs (including the shop's Colors of Hope black-Lab logo), and 20 percent of all profits go to benefit breast cancer research as well as local humane societies.

Savoy Mountain and Mohawk Trail State Forests, Route 2, North Adams and Charlemont (413-664-9567; 413-339-5504). Located right next to each other along the Mohawk Trail (Route 2), these two forest preserves comprise a total of 23,000 acres and offer campgrounds (see "Accommodations—Camp-grounds") and opportunities for canoeing, hiking, hunting, picnicking, swimming, horseback riding, and mountain biking.

Stanley Park, 400 Western Avenue, Westfield (413-568-9312). Stanley Park's 300 acres include miles of walking trails, a pond, a playground, and a picnic area with barbecue grills. Dogs on a leash are welcome but are not allowed in the rose garden area.

Storrowton Village Museum, 1305 Memorial Avenue, West Springfield (413-787-0136). Located on the grounds of the Big E state fair, this village is made up of nine 19th-century buildings that were gathered here and assembled around a shady green. Though pets are not allowed on the grounds or inside the buildings during the September fair, you can still stroll by to look at exteriors of the meetinghouse, blacksmith shop, farmhouse, and other buildings during the rest of the year.

Summer Arts and Crafts in Stockbridge Show. This annual outdoor show is typically held in August and features artisans from all over New England. The dates and location vary from year to year; for more information, contact the Stockbridge Chamber of Commerce at 413-298-5200 or info@stockbridgechamber.org.

Tolland State Forest, 410 Tolland Road, P.O. Box 342, East Otis, MA 01029 (413-269-6002). This isn't the largest of western Massachusetts's state parks, but it is one of the most interesting. Located along the **Otis Reservoir,** the preserve has great water views; long and leisurely trails for hiking, biking, and cross-country skiing; a campground (see "Accommodations—Campgrounds"); and a boat launch. Dogs are not allowed on the beach and must stay on a leash.

Walk for Animals, Springfield. This annual fund-raiser is organized by the Springfield branch of the **Massachusetts Society for the Prevention of Cruelty to Animals** (MSPCA); it's usually held in downtown Springfield on a Sunday in May and has attracted as many as 500 animal lovers and their pets. Another popular yearly event is the society's **Happy Endings Winter Gala,** which takes place every January and includes dinner, dancing, and a silent auction. For up-to-date information on this year's times and locations, call 413-736-2992 or visit the society at 171 Union Street in Springfield.

Windsor State Forest, River Road, Windsor (413-684-0948). This 1,700-acre preserve is frequented by fishermen, hunters, hikers, bird-watchers, horseback

riders, snowmobilers, and cross-country skiers. The park's most famous feature is the 80-foot-high waterfall at **Windsor Jambs Gorge.** The forest also has a campground (see "Accommodations—Campgrounds"), picnic areas, and rest rooms.

QUICK BITES

Antonio's, 31 North Pleasant Street, Amherst (413-253-0808). Every local college student knows about this downtown pizza haven, where you can get a slice of cheese pizza, or ham and pineapple, veggie, pepperoni, or lots of other traditional and adventurous combinations. Enjoy your slice with Fluffy on one of the benches that line bustling North Pleasant Street.

Atkins Farms Country Market, Route 166 and Bay Road, South Amherst (413-253-9528; 1-800-594-9537). Stop in for lunch at Atkins Farms' deli or snack bar and stay for apple picking. "We have a pavilion, picnic tables, and an orchard where people often bring their dogs to exercise," explains staffer Jen Adams. Cheese, fudge, cider, baked goods, coffee, and ice cream are just some of the items for sale at this old-fashioned market.

Barrington Brewery, 420 Stockbridge Road, Great Barrington (413-528-8282). In addition to homemade beers, the

Barrington Brewery also offers an outdoor dining area with casual, family-friendly American fare.

Bricker's Restaurant, Route 2 and I-91, Greenfield (413-774-2857). Bricker's American-style dishes, including chicken, steak, seafood, and pasta, are available for takeout. The restaurant is casual and has a full bar.

Catherine's Chocolate Shop, 260 Stockbridge Road, Great Barrington (1-800-345-6052). Got a hankering for a chocolate-dipped strawberry? Stop to Catherine's for homemade confections made with the main ingredient that's everyone's favorite guilty pleasure.

Coolidge Park Café, 36 King Street, Northampton (413-584 3100). Located at the Hotel Northampton, this café serves appetizers, burgers, salads, sandwiches, pasta, and other entrées at indoor and outdoor dining areas.

Glendale River Grille, Route 183, Glendale (413-298-4711). In addition to its main restaurant, Glendale also specializes in boxed lunches to go, featuring salads, fresh bread, sandwiches, and soups. Each lunch comes with springwater, fruit, and dessert.

Gus and Paul's, 1500 Main Street at Tower Square, Springfield (413-781-2253). This deli serves breakfast, lunch, and dinner, and specializes in New York–style sandwiches and fresh-baked desserts. Outdoor patio dining is available seasonally.

Samel's Deli, 115 Elm Street, Pittsfield (413-442-5927). Samel's offers "overstuffed" sandwiches, like tuna melts, Reubens, and

specialty concoctions, along with veggie burgers, salads, fried seafood platters, and roll-ups.

Shelburne Falls Coffee Roasters, 1207 Mohawk Trail, Shelburne (413-625-0116). After you sneak a peek at the Bridge of Flowers, stop in here for java, soup, sandwiches, and pastries to go.

Vermont Country Deli and Café, 48 Main Street, Northampton (413-586-7114). There are a few covered tables on the sidewalk outside this extremely popular stop for locals as well as visitors. Inside, you can choose from a huge selection of gourmet deli items, sandwiches on fresh-baked bread, and baked goods.

HOT SPOTS FOR SPOT

All Caring Animal Center, 440 Stockbridge Road, Great Barrington (413-528-8020). Pet-centered acupuncture, nutritional supplements, and herbal therapy are some of the holistic services offered at this pet-care center, which also provides more traditional veterinary services.

Allen Heights Critter Corner, 301 Dalton Avenue, Pittsfield (413-448-8090). This grooming and retail shop sells pet health-care items and food, including brands like Innova, Blue Seal, and Diamond. In addition to full grooming services, you can also choose the "bathe your own" option for $13.99 per half hour: Shampoo, towels, and hair dryers are provided.

Blue Moon Kennel, 35 Glendale Road, Housatonic (413-274-6674; www.bluemoonkennel.com). This facility, located just outside of Stockbridge, bills itself as a "resort hotel, beauty salon, and boutique" for dogs and cats. Animals enjoy playtimes, an optional TLC program, grooming services, indoor and outdoor runs, and a full line of pet supplies. Reservations are required. Rates are $20 per night for dogs and $10 per night for cats.

For Animals, 44 West Mountain Road, Lenox (413-445-8843; www.trainingforanimals.com). In addition to group and private training and obedience classes, For Animals also offers pet-sitting and "home-style" overnight boarding, in which pets are allowed to travel freely throughout the house and yard (unless you prefer that the animal be crated). The service is limited to three pets at a time, so reservations are essential.

Fur and Feathers Pet Sitting, serving Easthampton, Northampton, Southampton, and Westhampton; (413-527-8488). This unique service offers short-term pet sitting ($14 per visit for dogs, $12 per visit for cats) in your home as well as overnight or longer-term pet care at its "bed & breakfast" for animals, where your pet can roam free and get plenty of personalized attention. The B&B charge is $18 per night for dogs, $12 per night for cats, and $8 per night for birds.

Good Dog, 18 Center Street, Northampton (413-586-5242). Browse a fun selection of pet gifts and supplies, including mugs, leashes, collars, wall hangings, biscuit jars, and T-shirts, at this downtown shop.

Mount Tom Boarding Kennel and Grooming Salon, 320 Easthampton Road, Holyoke (413-532-3918; 413-533-0217). Mount Tom's two main services for pet owners are overnight boarding in a kennel facility and complete grooming for all breeds of dogs and cats, including cuts and flea baths. Call for an appointment.

IN CASE OF EMERGENCY

Bilmar Veterinary Services,
776 Main Street, Great Barrington (413-528-1180).

Boston Road Animal Hospital,
1235 Boston Road, Springfield (413-783-1203).

Greylock Animal Hospital,
1028 State Road, North Adams (413-663-5365).

Pioneer Valley Veterinary Hospital,
571 Bernardston Road, Greenfield (413-773-7511).

Pittsfield Veterinary Hospital,
1634 West Housatonic Street, Pittsfield (413-499-1580).

Valley Veterinary Hospital,
320 Russell Street, Hadley (413-584-1223).

Vermont

THE WINDHAM COUNTY COURTHOUSE AND TOWN GREEN IN NEWFANE

Southern Vermont

PET-FRIENDLY RATING: 🦴 🦴 🦴

Although southern Vermont is famous for its Green Mountains, the color many people associate with the area is white, white, white. This region is a haven for skiers, offering steep mountain resorts like Stratton, Mount Snow, Haystack, and Okemo as well as hundreds of miles of quiet cross-country trails. In the autumn, of course, visitors come in search of fiery colors, and they're never disappointed with the show.

Unfortunately for skiers with pets, pet-friendly accommodations are not abundant in these parts, nor are there many kennels and pet-sitters willing to watch your pooch while you hit the slopes. Pet owners may be better off waiting until spring or summer, considered the off-season in southern Vermont, when you can spend your days *with* your dog at a state park, hiking trail, covered bridge, campground, mountain peak, or quaint town green. You'll find all these and more in this picturesque "welcome center" of the Green Mountain State.

ACCOMMODATIONS

Hotels, Motels, Inns, and Bed & Breakfasts

Andover

Inn at High View, 753 East Hill Road, Andover (802-875-2724; hiview@aol.com; www.innathighview.com); suites, $175 per night. "Small- to medium-sized" dogs (call to see if yours qualifies) are welcome in High View's two suites. Located on the top of East Hill, the restored farmhouse offers daily full breakfasts and weekend dinners in its dining room, cross-country skiing trails on 72 acres, a library with a fireplace, a sauna, and a friendly resident cocker spaniel.

Arlington

Valhalla Motel, Route 7A, Arlington (802-375-2212; 1-888-258-2212; stay@valhallamotel.com; www.valhallamotel.com); $40–75 per night. The 12 guest rooms at Valhalla have air-conditioning, cable TV, phones, refrigerators, and private baths. Guests can also splash around in an outdoor swimming pool. Pets are welcome.

Bennington

Bennington Motor Inn, 143 West Main Street, Bennington (1-800-359-9900; www.coolcruisers.net/benningtonmotorinn); $76–102 per night. Pets are allowed in designated smoking rooms at the Bennington Motor Inn for an additional $20 per night. Remodeled in 2002, the inn has new furnishings, 16 guest rooms, cable TV with premium movie channels, air-conditioning, and a convenient location close to shops, restaurants, and cross-country skiing trails.

Darling Kelly's Motel, RR 1, Bennington (802-442-2322); $42–81 per night. A few of the rooms at Darling Kelly's are designated for pet owners, "and we've never had a problem," says owner Ed Diamond. The motel offers a swimming pool, lawn areas and yard games, in-room movies, and refrigerators. Animals are welcome as long as they stay off the furniture and are not left alone in the rooms.

Knotty Pine Motel, 130 Northside Drive, Bennington (802-442-5487; kpine@sover.net; www.bennington.com); $44–89 per night. "I'd say 99 percent of pet owners have been great guests," say Knotty Pine proprietor Thomas C. Bluto. He welcomes animals, provided their owners are willing to follow the motel's posted rules of "petiquette." Guests can enjoy a swimming pool, air-conditioning, cable TV, in-room coffeemakers and refrigerators, and some efficiency units.

Brattleboro

Econo Lodge Brattleboro, 515 Canal Street, Brattleboro (802-254-2360); $56–69 per night. For an extra $10 per night, pets are welcome at this Econo Lodge with free continental breakfasts,

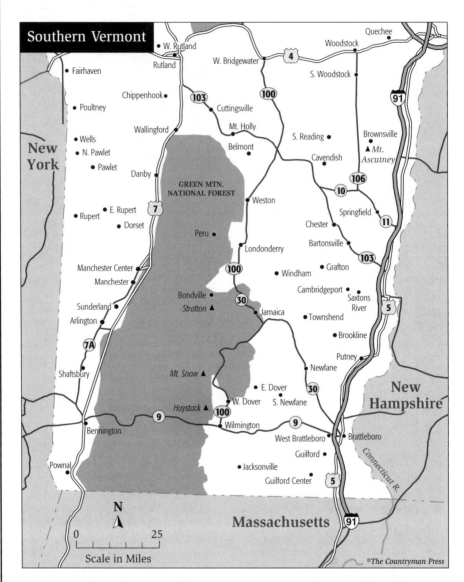

Southern Vermont

Quechee
Woodstock
W. Rutland
W. Bridgewater
4
Rutland
S. Woodstock
Fairhaven
100
91
Chippenhook
103
Cuttingsville
Poultney
Mt. Holly
Brownsville
Wallingford
S. Reading
▲ Mt.
Wells
Belmont
Ascutney
New
N. Pawlet
Cavendish
York
Pawlet
Danby
106
GREEN MTN.
10
NATIONAL FOREST
Weston
Springfield
E. Rupert
7
Chester
11
Rupert
Dorset
Bartonsville
Peru
103
Londonderry
Manchester Center
100
Grafton
Manchester
Windham
Cambridgeport
Bondville
Saxtons
Sunderland
30
River
Stratton ▲
Jamaica
5
Arlington
Townshend
7A
Brookline
Putney
Newfane
New
Shaftsbury
Mt. Snow ▲
Hampshire
30
E. Dover
Haystack ▲
W. Dover S. Newfane
100
9
Wilmington
Bennington
9
Brattleboro
West Brattleboro
Guilford
Jacksonville
Pownal
Guilford Center
5

N

0   25

Scale in Miles

Massachusetts
91

Connecticut R.

©The Countryman Press

in-room coffeemakers, a wake-up service, laundry facilities, an outdoor swimming pool, cable TV, refrigerators, photocopying and fax services, and alarm clocks.

Forty Putney Road Bed & Breakfast, 192 Putney Road, Brattleboro (802-254-6268; 1-800-941-2413; frtyptny@sover.net; www.putney.net/40putneyrd); $108–230 per night. This spacious B&B is surrounded by lawns, gardens, and fountains; inside, you'll find antiques-filled common rooms, guest rooms, a suite, and a cottage. Snacks, wine, and beer are served indoors in the winter and on the patio in the summer. Well-behaved, housebroken pets are welcome for an additional fee of $15 per stay (not per night).

Motel 6 Brattleboro,
1254 Putney Road, Brattleboro

(802-254-6007); $39–46 per night. This Motel 6 offers premium movie channels, smoking and nonsmoking rooms, free morning coffee, free local calls, large-vehicle/truck parking, telephones, and a "kids stay free" program. Well-behaved pets are welcome.

Brownsville

Pond House Inn Bed & Breakfast, Bible Hill Road, Brownsville (802-484-0011; pond house0011@yahoo.com; www. pondhouseinn.com); $150–185 per couple, per night. The Pond House's three guest rooms are secluded on a 10-acre farm with cozy touches like imported soap, fresh flowers, tile and marble baths, gourmet breakfasts, and complimentary afternoon cheese and fruit. Outside, you can relax in the garden or by the spring-fed pond. "Polite" dogs and horses are welcome. The Pond House also occasionally offers "puppy weekends" with special events and trips for dogs and their owners.

Chester

Stone Hearth Inn, 698 Route 11 West, Chester (802-875-2525; 1-888-617-3656; www.thestonehearthinn.com); $79–139 per night. This historic inn and tavern offers a glimpse into Vermont's past while also providing modern amenities such as private bathrooms, fine linens and towels, a recreation/TV room, alarm clocks, and a hot tub. With prior notice, pets are welcome in designated rooms for an additional $30 per night.

Grafton

Grafton Homestead, 499 Route 121 East, Grafton (802-843-1111; vacation@graftonhomestead.com; www.graftonhomestead.com); $100–122 per night. Pets are welcome with prior approval for an additional $25 per night at the Grafton Homestead, which offers a large suite for rent with a living room, bedroom, full kitchen, private bath, and private entrance. Historic Grafton is a short walk away, and hiking trails, cross-country skiing trails, golf courses, and antiques shops are nearby.

Jamaica

Ascent of Nature Bed & Breakfast, 23 Turkey Mountain Road, Jamaica (802-874-4424; reservations@ascentofnature.com; www.ascentofnature.com); $75–95 per night. Your pet is welcome to join the two cats and a dog already living at this historic farmhouse, as long as she's friendly and well behaved. The B&B offers gourmet country breakfasts, including homemade sausage, seven-grain pancakes, eggs, and Vermont maple syrup, along with a gathering room, gardens, and an outdoor fireplace.

Londonderry

Frog's Leap Inn, 107 Route 100, Londonderry (802-824-3019; 1-877-FROGSLEAP); $90–345 per night. Chloe the beagle and Sammy the cat, along with innkeepers Kraig and Dorenna Hart, enjoy welcoming four-legged visitors to their country inn. The expansive grounds boast 32 acres with hiking and cross-country ski trails, a swimming pool, a tennis court, picnic areas, and relaxing gardens. The guest rooms have handmade quilts and private baths.

Ludlow

Combes Family Inn Bed &

Breakfast, 953 East Lake Road, Ludlow (802-228-8799; 1-800-822-8799; info@combesfamily-inn.com; www.combesfamily-inn.com); $65–154 per night. Well-behaved pets are welcome in five rooms at the Combes Family Inn. Each room has pine furniture, air-conditioning, a view of Okemo Mountain, and access to a shared sunporch. The main inn building has a gathering room with a fireplace, a TV room, and a dining room, where guests enjoy full country breakfasts each morning.

Timber Inn Motel, Route 103, Ludlow (802-228-8666; timber-inn@tds.net; www.timberinn-motel.com); $64–99 per night. For an extra $10 per night, dogs (sorry, no cats) are allowed at the Timber Inn during certain times of the year; call for details. The motel offers knotty-pine guest rooms with one or two bedrooms, an apartment with an outdoor deck, a hot tub, a sauna and an outdoor heated pool, cable TV with premium movie channels, and a playground.

Manchester Center
Four Winds Country Motel, 7379 Route 7A, Manchester Center (1-877-456-7654; fwmotel@sover.net; www.vtweb.com/fourwinds); $66–120 per night. Pets are sometimes allowed at Four Winds with prior approval (call for details). The 18 standard and deluxe guest rooms have patios with tables and chairs, cable TV, hair dryers, alarm clocks, tables, coffeemakers, and telephones. A cottage house/

recreation room offers table tennis and card tables, books, board games, and a TV/VCR.

Marlboro
Colonel Williams Inn, Marlboro (802-257-1093); carriage house $125 per night. Built in 1769, this historic B&B is a favorite for weddings, civil unions, and weekend getaways. For an additional fee of $25 per stay (not per night), pets are welcome in the efficiency apartments located in the inn's Carriage House building. The rates include a full breakfast.

Peru
Johnny Seesaw's, Route 11, Peru (802-824-5533; 1-800-424-CSAW; jseesaws@sover.net; www.jsee-saw.com); $50–99 per person, per night. The emphasis is on fun at Johnny Seesaw's, billed as one of America's first ski lodges. Accommodations include lodge rooms, family suites, and cabins; a shuttle service brings you to nearby Bromley Mountain. Pets are welcome for an extra $10 per night; they must be leashed, quiet, well behaved, and not left alone in rooms.

Putney
Camp Gone to the Dogs, Putney (802-387-5673; www.camp-gone-tothe-dogs.com); summer sessions, $900–1,050 per week with housing or $800 per week without housing. Designed by and for dog lovers, this one-of-a-kind camp is an accommodation and activity center all rolled up into one. Attendees stay in dorms with single, double, or triple rooms; cabins; or Marlboro

North, a former private hotel. Some rooms share baths. For more information about the camp's programs here in Putney, see "Out and About." (You can also attend fall and midsummer camp sessions in Stowe; see "Out and About" in "Northern Vermont.")

Putney Inn, Depot Road, Putney (802-387-5517; 1-800-653-5517; www.putneyinn.com); $88–158 per night. For an extra $10 per night, your pet is allowed in any of the 25 rooms at the Putney Inn—though the innkeepers recommend first-floor rooms as the most convenient for animal owners. Each room has a private bath, private entrances, and period furnishings, including four-poster beds. The inn is perhaps best known for its gourmet dining room.

Sandgate
Green River Inn, 3402 Sandgate Road, Sandgate (1-888-648-2212; stay@greenriverinn.com; www. greenriverinn.com); $100–160 per night. For an extra $10 per night, pets are welcome in two of the Green River Inn's comfortable, antiques-filled rooms: One has a king-sized bed and private bath with a two-person shower; the other offers a king-sized bed and a private bath with a whirlpool tub. You and Fluffy can also roam on the inn's 450 acres, including 4 miles of trails.

Shaftsbury
Serenity Motel, 4379 Route 7A, Shaftsbury (802-442-6490; 1-800-644-6490; serenity@sover.net; www.thisisvermont.com/pages/

serenity); $50–75 per night. Animals are welcome without extra charges at Serenity, where each neatly painted, yellow-and-blue cottage unit has a telephone, a covered porch, air-conditioning, a refrigerator, and a coffeemaker. Some of the units are adjoining to accommodate groups. Shaftsbury State Park and the Battenkill River are both nearby.

Springfield
Holiday Inn Express Springfield, 818 Charlestown Road, Springfield (802-885-4516; 1-800-465-4329); $77–179 per night. Located about 20 minutes from the Okemo and Ascutney ski areas, this Holiday Inn Express welcomes pets in designated smoking rooms with a $200 refundable deposit. The hotel has 88 guest rooms, a restaurant, laundry facilities, air-conditioning, extended-stay suites with kitchenettes, a fitness center, and an indoor swimming pool.

Sunderland
Arcady at the Sunderland Motor Lodge, 6249 Route 7A, Sunderland–Arlington (802-362-1176; 1-800-362-1151; innkeeper@ arcadyvt.com; www.arcadyvt. com); $68–130 per night. The large guest rooms at Arcady have coffeemakers, private entrances, refrigerators, and porches. Other amenities include air-conditioning, cable TV, and complimentary buffet breakfasts. Pets (a maximum of two) are welcome for an additional fee of $15 per pet, per night; they should be leashed and quiet, and they should stay off the furniture.

West Dover

Gray Ghost Inn, Route 100 North, West Dover (802-464-2474); $48–184 per night. Kenai, the resident pooch, will greet you and your pet when you arrive at this cozy inn with 26 guest rooms, private baths, a gathering room with a fireplace, a game room, cable TV, and a sauna. Pets are welcome throughout the year, except on peak winter and holiday weekends; call for details. There are no extra fees for animal guests.

Snow Goose Inn at Mount Snow, Route 100, West Dover (802-464-3984; reservations@snowgooseinn.com; www.snowgooseinn.com); $150–250 per night. Two of the luxurious Snow Goose Inn rooms are designated as pet-friendly: They have private baths, feather beds, whirlpool tubs, and fireplaces. Guests and their pups can also take advantage of 3 acres of woods, trails, and gardens, full country breakfasts, and complimentary wine and snacks in the evening.

Wilmington

Inn at Quail Run, 106 Smith Road, Wilmington (802-464-3362; 1-800-343-7227; quailrunvt@aol.com); $90–200 per night. "We are indeed a happy pet-friendly inn, and happen to enjoy our pet guests and their owners a bit more than the others!" says enthusiastic innkeeper and dog owner Lorin Streim. Your pooch can munch complimentary doggie biscuits and run free on 15 acres of property, while you can enjoy gourmet breakfasts and large rooms, including the Ilene,

the Charlotte, and the Olivia, with bright decor, air-conditioning, and designer linens.

Campgrounds

Ascutney

Wilgus State Park Campground, Route 5, Ascutney (802-674-5422); $13–22 per night. Get your feet wet at this small state campground located next to the Connecticut River. You'll find 25 sites, a rest room with showers, a group camping area, a playground, and a picnic area. Pets are welcome, as long as they stay on a leash and have proof of vaccination.

Bennington

Greenwood Lodge and Campsites, P.O. Box 246, Bennington (802-442-2547; grnwd@compuserve.com; www.campvermont.com/greenwood); $17–21 per night. Choose from hostel rooms or 40 wooded campsites at Greenwood, which offers 120 acres, three ponds, a recreation room, rest rooms with showers, a playing field, and a volleyball court. "Quiet, good-natured pets" are welcome as long as their owners bring proof of vaccination and don't leave them unattended.

Woodford State Park Campground, 142 State Park Road, Bennington (802-447-7169; 1-800-658-1622); $13–22 per night. One of southern Vermont's larger state campgrounds, Woodford State Park has more than 80 wooded sites for tents and trailers, in addition to 20 lean-to sites. Campers also have access to rest rooms with showers and a dumping station. Don't forget proof of vaccination for your pet—you'll need it.

Brattleboro
Fort Dummer State Park Campground, 434 Old Guilford Road, Brattleboro (802-254-2610; 1-800-299-3071); $13–22 per night. Campers at Fort Dummer can experience a bit of history (see "Out and About") as well as fun in the outdoors. The campground offers 51 sites for tents and RVs, two rest rooms with showers, a dumping station, hiking trails, lawn areas, and a playground. RV owners should note that there are no hookups, and pet owners must show proof of vaccination.

Dummerston
Hidden Acres Campground, 792 Route 5, Dummerston (802-254-2098); $20–30 per night. All of the 40 sites at this campground have a picnic table and a fire pit; other amenities include rest rooms with showers, hiking trails, an 18-hole miniature golf course, a swimming pool, a camp store, playing fields, a game room, and laundry facilities. Pets must be leashed, and certain breeds are not allowed; call for details.

East Dummerston
Brattleboro North KOA, 1238 Route 5, East Dummerston (802-254-5908; 1-800-562-5909); $24–35 per night. Campers at this KOA can enjoy a swimming pool, pull-through sites with hookups, a gift shop, and recreation areas. Attractions like Santa's Land, miniature golf, and

Putney Village are nearby. Quiet, well-behaved pets are welcome at campsites but not in Kamping Kabins.

Jamaica
Jamaica State Park Campground, 285 Salmon Hole Lane, Jamaica (802-874-4600; 1-800-299-3071); $13–22 per night. Two rest rooms with showers, 43 campsites, 18 lean-to sites, a picnic area, and a nature center are among the man-made attractions at this campground located in a state park (see "Out and About" for more park information). Pets are not allowed in picnic areas or other day-use areas, and owners must show proof of vaccination before entering the park.

Winhall Brook Campground at Ball Mountain Lake, 25 Ball Mountain Lane, Jamaica (802-874-4881; 1-877-444-6777); $13–17 per night. This U.S. Army Corps of Engineers property has a day-use area (see **Ball Mountain Lake** under "Out and About") as well as a campground with 88 tent and pop-up trailer sites and 23 RV sites with hookups. Campers can also use rest rooms with showers, a dumping station, playgrounds, and nearby hiking trails.

Newfane
Kenolie Village Campground, 16 Kenolie Campground Road, Newfane (802-365-7671); $15–18 per night. This large family campground has 150 wooded and sunny sites, rest rooms with showers, laundry facilities, a camp store, scheduled activities, and a nearby river for fishing, boating, and swimming. Pets are

welcome without extra fees, though owners are expected to clean up after them. Kenolie Village is open in the spring, summer, and fall.

Plymouth
Calvin Coolidge State Park Campground, 855 Coolidge State Park Road, Plymouth (802-672-3612 ; 1-800-299-3071); $13–22 per night. This historically significant park (see "Out and About") also abounds with outdoor adventurers; the on-site campground has more than 50 sites, five rest rooms with showers, a playground, a dumping station, numerous hiking trails, and secluded "wilderness" camping areas. There are no RV hookups, and pet owners must show proof of vaccination.

Pownal
Pine Hollow Campground, RR 1, Pownal (802-823-5569); $20–27 per night. Leashed, quiet pets are welcome at Pine Hollow, where you'll find 60 sunny and wooded sites for tents and RVs, a group camping area, catch-and-release fishing, bathrooms with showers, hiking and biking trails, a pond, horseshoe pits, and shuffleboard courts.

Townshend
Townshend State Park Campground, 2755 State Forest Road, Townshend (802-365-7500; 1-800-299-3071); $13–22 per night. You'll need a leash and proof of vaccination to bring your pet along to this popular campground, which offers 30 tent and RV sites, four lean-to sites, bathrooms with showers,

hiking trails, a recycling area and Dumpster, firewood, and a picnic area.

Wilmington
Molly Stark State Park Campground, 705 Route 9 East, Wilmington (802-464-5460; 1-800-299-3071); $13–22 per night. Tent and trailer campers will feel right at home at this small, quiet campground, where amenities include 23 standard and 11 lean-to sites, rest rooms, a playground, and a picnic pavilion. Some hiking trails into the state park (see "Out and About" for more information) begin at the campground. Bring proof of vaccination for your pet.

Windsor
Ascutney State Park Campground, 1826 Back Mountain, Windsor (802-674-2060; 1-800-299-3071); $13–22 per night. Hang gliders arriving at Ascutney in search of the park's well-known launch spot at Brownsville Rock might want to consider staying the night at the on-site campground; overnight campers can choose from 39 wooded standard sites in addition to 10 lean-to sites, a dumping station, and rest rooms with showers. Bring proof of vaccination for your pet.

Homes, Cottages, and Cabins for Rent

Bromley Mountain
Ski Area A-Frame Home, Bromley Mountain area (609-758-1444; jgrinkevich@ushwy1.com); $100–200 per night.

There's a five-night minimum at this rental house, a classic A-frame near Stratton, Bromley, and Magic Mountain. The Appalachian Trail and Long Trail are within walking distance. Amenities include cable TV, a VCR, a fireplace, two bedrooms and a sleeping loft, firewood, and a kitchen. Pets are welcome without restrictions.

Lake St. Catherine

Waterfront Cottage, Lake St. Catherine (802-325-2416; mre jag69@vermontel.com); $780 per week. Well-behaved and house-trained pets are welcome at this lakefront home, which can accommodate up to four people and has two bedrooms and one bathroom. All linens and towels are provided, along with a barbecue grill, satellite TV, a VCR/DVD player, a doghouse, small boats, a deck, and a coffeemaker.

Mount Snow

Mount Snow Area Rental, Mount Snow (860-344-9600; ellen@solutionspr.com); call for rate information. "We have a 70-pound golden retriever, so we understand how difficult it is to travel and find suitable accommodations with a pet," says homeowner Ellen Ornato. Your pet is welcome at her three-bedroom Mount Snow house rental, which also has a dog run, a hot tub, a woodstove, cable TV, a sleep sofa, and a large family room.

Ski Chalet, Dover, Mount Snow (518-346-8478; 518-377-8834; marilynmstevens@aol.com); $600–700 per week or $1,700–2,000 per month. This tucked-away large chalet can accommodate up to 10 people; it's located about a mile from Mount Snow and is connected to many snowmobile trails. The home has a fireplace, a VCR, a deck, and a game room with rainy-day activities like table tennis and bumper pool. "Small" pets (call to see if yours qualifies) are allowed.

Pawlet

Southern Vermont Log Home, Pawlet (603-772-7857; dlshirleyjr@attbi.com); $500–600 per week. This Manchester-area cabin has mountain views, three bedrooms, a fireplace, a washer and dryer, a kitchen with all the usual appliances, and a TV with VCR. Outside, 5 acres provide plenty of room for dog walks and runs. Renters are welcome to bring their animal as long as they follow reasonable rules of pet etiquette.

Plymouth

Restored Farmhouse, Plymouth (212-326-1098; 914-725-4676; clemle@studley.com); $325–550 per night in winter; $1,000 per week in summer and fall. Located about halfway between Okemo and Killington, this four-bedroom, three-bathroom house is set on 5 acres and backs up into the Calvin Coolidge State Forest. Amenities include an outdoor hot tub, a washer and dryer, a kitchen, cable TV and a VCR, and a woodstove. A snowmobile trail runs next to the property.

South Londonderry

Farm House Rental, South Londonderry (203-661-3630; nick@lanirock.com; www.vermontfarmhouse.com); $200–500 per night. Nick Adamson, the owner of this pond-front farmhouse, travels with his two German shepherds and welcomes your pet to his rental: "If only some of the people guests would behave as well as the guest dogs," he jokes. The historic home is surrounded by 80 acres of land with three ponds and offers two fireplaces, a sauna, and satellite TV.

Springfield
Christmas Tree Plantation Cottage, Springfield (802-885-9597; 1-877-817-0810; mollica@christmastreesofvt.com); $500–700 per week. The name is accurate: This cozy one-bedroom cottage is located right in the middle of a 70-acre Christmas tree farm beside the Connecticut River. Amenities include a swimming pool, a porch with a barbecue grill, one bathroom, and satellite TV. Pet owners pay a $150 security deposit and an extra $10 per day, per pet.

Wallingford
Country Home, Wallingford (802-773-6681; 903-561-8204; advtemp@tyler.net); $700–800 per week. Located about a half hour's drive from Killington and Okemo, this Wallingford ranch home can accommodate up to eight people and has four bedrooms, two bathrooms, a deck, a kitchen, a woodstove, and an open floor plan. "Being pet lovers ourselves, it was an easy decision to make our rental pet-friendly," says owner Larry Williams.

Rental Agencies

Mountain Resort Rentals, Route 100, West Dover (802-464-1445; rentverm@sover.net; www.mountainresortrentals.com). This property management company can help you locate a town house, chalet, home, apartment, or condo in or near the Mount Snow–Haystack ski area. "About 80 percent of the time, pets are no problem," explains co-owner Richard Schuler. Most of the rental units are located within resort communities and are available year-round.

OUT AND ABOUT

Ball Mountain Lake, 88 Ball Mountain Lane, Jamaica (802-874-4881). Managed by the U.S. Army Corps of Engineers, this dam and lake recreation area hosts about 175,000 visitors each year; hikers, boaters, and day-trippers enjoy mountain views while photographing wildlife, sitting down for a picnic, or walking the dog. The access road is open seasonally. Whitewater rafters congregate near the dam each spring for the annual planned water release for boaters. There's also an on-site campground (see **Winhall Brook Campground** under "Accommodations—Campgrounds").

Calvin Coolidge State Forest and Park, 855 Coolidge State Park Road, Plymouth (802-672-3612; 1-800-299-3071). This vast protected forest is made up of more than 16,000 acres in seven towns along scenic Route 100; the 500-acre state park is tucked within it. The park is frequented by overnight campers (see "Accommodations—Hotels, Motels, Inns, and Bed & Breakfasts"), hikers, gold panners, and history buffs who want to check out 19 log cabin lean-tos from the original Calvin Coolidge homestead.

Camp Gone to the Dogs, Putney (802-387-5673; www.camp-gone-tothe-dogs.com); summer sessions, $900–1,050 per week with housing or $800 per week without housing. "Campers" at this unique program can stay on-site (see "Accommodations—Campgrounds") or off: Either way, they're sure to have a tail-waggin' good time. Created by animal lover Honey Loring, Camp Gone to the Dogs is just that: a canine-centered place where you and your pup can take part in seemingly boundless activities or just loll around on the lawn with other like-minded visitors. The rates include meals, classes, lectures, and group activities, including obedience, agility, breed handling, herding, fly ball, Frisbee, doggie costume parties, arts and crafts, and all varieties of "just for fun" contests. The summer sessions are held in Marlboro, though you can also attend fall and midsummer sessions in Stowe (see "Out and

About" in "Northern Vermont"). Sit, stay!

Downtown Brattleboro. Like many college towns, this one offers plenty of clothing shops, restaurants, bookstores, pharmacies, bakeries, and downtown sidewalk benches. A nearby pretty park provides a shady spot to take a rest from all that people- and dog-watching.

Fort Dummer State Park, 434 Old Guilford Road, Brattleboro (802-254-2610; 1-800-299-3071). Fairly small as far as state parks go, this 217-acre historical spot commemorates one of Vermont's earliest settlements. The trails are heavily wooded and populated by deer, grouse, and other native wildlife species. There's also a campground on-site (see "Accommodations—Campgrounds"). Dogs must be leashed but are otherwise welcome.

Green Mountain National Forest. Look at any map of southern Vermont, and you'll notice an enormous swath of green running right down the middle: This vast wilderness is home to ski mountains, hundreds of miles of trails, including the **Long Trail** (see listing below) and the **Appalachian Trail,** steep cliffs, majestic views, endangered wildlife, and enough autumn color to take your breath away. There are limitless opportunities for adventure—far more than we could ever fit here. Some of the most popular hiking and walking trails include: the **Green Mountain Trail,** a fairly tough 6-mile loop that starts at the Big Branch

Picnic Area on Forest Road 10 in Danby; the **Griffith Lake Trail,** a level 4-mile trip off Forest Road 58 in Peru that's popular with snowmobilers and cross-country skiers; the **Hapgood Pond Trail,** an easy 0.8-mile-long nature walk located off Forest Highway 3 just north of Peru; and the **White Rocks/Ice Beds Trail,** a fairly easy walk to some fascinating geological features that begins on Route 140 East, just past Wallingford Four Corners. For information, more trail descriptions, directions, and maps, contact the Manchester Ranger District in Manchester Center at 802-362-2307, visit the Green Mountain National Forest Headquarters on 231 North Main Street in Rutland, or visit www.fs.fed.us/r9/gmfl.

Jamaica State Park, 285 Salmon Hole Lane, Jamaica (802-874-4600; 1-800-299-3071). This 756-acre park is a favorite among fishermen, who enjoy throwing their line at the **West River.** Hikers and cross-country skiers come for the winding trails, and kayakers and canoeists arrive in April and September to take advantage of the water release from the **Ball Mountain Dam.** Your pup is welcome to come with you for the day or stay overnight at the campground (see "Accommodations— Campgrounds"), as long as he's on a leash.

Long Trail. More than 270 miles long, this renowned and rugged trail stretches from Canada to Massachusetts, passing directly through the Green Mountains of

Vermont. The southern part of the trail is considered to be the least difficult, though it is still challenging and recommended for experienced hikers and backpackers. (This is also the part of the state where the Long Trail meets the **Appalachian Trail** for about 100 miles.) You can find a shelter about every 6 miles along the way; in southern Vermont, the two largest are at **Stratton Pond** and **Spruce Peak.** Access the start of trail in North Adams, Massachusetts, or Williamstown, Massachusetts, or jump in at popular spots such as the **Bromley Mountain** and **Spruce Peak Trails,** starting 5 miles east of Manchester Center on Routes 11 and 30; the busy **Stratton Pond Trail,** located off Kelley Stand Road in Stratton; or the **Homer Stone Brook Trail,** located off Homer Stone Road in South Wallingford. For more information, maps, hiking tips, and directions, contact the Green Mountain Club at 802-244-7037 or visit www.greenmountainclub.org.

Lowell Lake State Park, 1756 Little Pond Road, Londonderry (802-824-4035; 1-800-299-3071). The main attraction here is the **Lowell Lake Trail,** a meandering 3½-mile-long loop that wraps all the way around the lake. There aren't many steep spots, so it's ideal for pooches looking for an afternoon trot. Parking is available at the Lowell Lake Road boat launch.

Mayfest, downtown Bennington

(www.bennington.com). Held each year on Memorial Day weekend, this downtown festival attracts arts, crafts, and food vendors from around New England. Wander the closed-off streets to browse pottery, paintings, woodcrafts, jewelry, and other one-of-a-kind creations.

Molly Stark State Park, 705 Route 9 East, Wilmington (802-464-5460; 1-800-299-3071). Located about halfway between Brattleboro and Bennington along Route 9 (otherwise known as the Molly Stark Trail), this park is home to hiking and biking trails, large fields, a campground (see "Accommodations—Campgrounds"), and **Mount Olga,** where a still-standing old fire tower affords wonderful views. Dogs must be on a leash and are not allowed in picnic areas.

Newfane Town Center and Green, Route 30, Newfane. Newfane is home to the well-known **Windham County Courthouse,** the **Village Union Hall,** and other historic buildings clustered around a picture-perfect green; it's a wonderful spot to stretch your legs and let Rover sniff around the scenery. If you pass by at mealtime, the market across the street from the courthouse offers the ingredients for a picnic (see **Newfane Market** and **Newfane Country Store** under "Quick Bites").

Scott Bridge, Route 30, Townshend. In a landscape filled with quaint covered bridges, this one stands out from the rest: The Scott is the longest covered bridge in Vermont, with both Town lattice and kingpost trusses still holding it together. The 276-foot-long bridge has seen better days (repairs and replacement boards are obvious), but the hardy old girl still makes for a fun and adventurous on-foot crossing.

Summer Concerts on the Green, town green, Route 7A, Manchester. From blues to classical and rock, these warm-weather musical concerts usually take place on Friday nights from 6:30 to 8. Admission is free. Bring a blanket or a lawn chair, and make sure your pooch isn't the howling type before settling in. For updated schedules, call the Manchester and the Mountains Chamber of Commerce at 1-800-362-4144 or visit their web site at www.manchestervermont.net.

Townshend State Park, 2755 State Forest Road, Townshend (802-365-7500; 1-800-299-3071). Perhaps best known for its hiking trails that lead to the peak of **Bald Mountain,** this park also attracts visitors with its waterfalls, small pools, picnic areas, scenic views, and wildlife-viewing opportunities. In the summer, overnighters also flock to the campground (see "Accommodations—Campgrounds"). Dogs are not allowed in day-use areas and must be leashed.

Wilgus and **Ascutney State Parks,** Ascutney (1-800-299-3071). Both located in and around the town of Ascutney near the New Hampshire border, these two state parks offer campgrounds (see "Accommodations—Campgrounds"), picnic areas, scenic views, and hiking and biking trails. Wilgus, located off Route 5, straddles the **Connecticut River** and is especially popular among canoeists; Ascutney, located on Route 44A in Windsor, offers challenging and steep hiking routes, such as the **Summit Road.**

Woodford State Park, 142 State Park Road, Bennington (802-447-7169; 1-800-658-1622). Located within the **Green Mountain National Forest** along Route 9, the 400-acre Woodford State Park is located at a 2,400-foot-high mountain plateau and houses a

campground (see "Accommodations—Campgrounds"), a beach, a picnic area, public rest rooms, and walking and hiking trails. You can also rent a canoe, paddleboat, or rowboat for use on the surrounding **Adams Reservoir.** Pets must be leashed and are not allowed in picnic areas.

Yankee Dog, Bowser Publications, P.O. Box 144, Jacksonville 05342. This free quarterly newspaper ("all the news that's fit to sniff") is published locally and distributed throughout New England. *Yankee Dog*'s publisher, Debra Theriault, is a great source for southern Vermont doggie information; for more details or to subscribe, call 802-368-7660 or e-mail Theriault at bowser@sover.net.

QUICK BITES

Al Ducci's Italian Pastry, Elm Street, Manchester (802-362-4449). You can order any of Al Ducci's pasta meals, sandwiches, fresh bread, and baked goods to go and wash them down with coffee, a cold drink, or wine.

Apple Barn and Country Bake Shop, Route 7, South Bennington (1-888-8-APPLES). In addition to the 30 varieties of apples grown in the on-site orchards, the Apple Barn also serves up homemade jellies and jams, maple syrup, classic Vermont cheddar, sweet baked treats, and cold drinks.

Chelsea Royal Diner, Route 9 and Marlboro Road, West Brattleboro (802-254-8399). Order

your sandwich or meal at the take-out window at this convenient Route 9 stop and eat at one of the many picnic tables.

Daniel's Café, 92 Main Street, Grafton (802-843-2245). Located at the Old Tavern at Grafton, this café has outdoor seating and take-out service; choose from a variety of salads, sandwiches, and soups. Well-behaved pets are welcome.

Frankie's Pizzeria, 145 Harmony Place, Brattleboro (802-254-2420). Staying in Brattleboro with dog in tow? You're in luck— Frankie's delivers. You can also order a pizza, pasta dinner, or salad as take-out.

THE SCOTT BRIDGE IN TOWNSHEND IS LONGEST COVERED BRIDGE IN VERMONT.

Happy Crab, Main Street, Manchester (802-362-4650). Rest a while at one of the many picnic tables and dine on this restaurant's famous crabcakes. Shopping is nearby.

Jamaica Coffee House, 3863 Route 30, Jamaica (802-874-7085). The resident pooch, Belle, will greet you when you stop in this eclectic shop serving up baked treats, java, espresso, cappuccino, and cold drinks. You can relax with your refreshments at one of the tables out on the porch.

Newfane Market and **Newfane Country Store,** Route 30, Newfane; Country Store (802-365-7916). These two stores sit next to each other and across from the picturesque green and Windham County Courthouse; the market sells deli sandwiches, baked goods, cold drinks, and convenience items; the Country Store offers fudge, candy, gifts, and other fun treats.

HOT SPOTS FOR SPOT

The Corner Pantry and More, 733 Main Street, Bennington (802-442-8417). You'll find any pet items you might run out of on the road at this shop, including food, treats, toys, shampoos, wormers, odor removers, flea and tick collars, and tie-outs. Because the Corner Pantry also serves as a gas station, you can't beat the hours: 6 AM to 9 PM, seven days a week.

One Stop Country Pet Supply, 648 Putney Road, Brattleboro (802-257-3700). From standard supplies like food and leashes to hard-to-find items like doggie life jackets, animal first-aid kits, and temporary ID tags (a must for on-the-road pets), this Brattleboro shop stocks all the necessities and luxuries you might need while traveling.

Petcetera, Routes 11 and 30, Manchester Center (802-362-5447). Located in historic Manchester Center, this fun shop stocks treats and chewies, leashes, collars, food, toys, breath fresheners, and pet-themed stationery and gifts. It's sure to be one of your dog's favorite stops.

Puppy Acres Boarding Kennels, 930 Lee Road, Guilford (802-254-5496). This family-owned and -operated kennel offers overnight boarding on 110 acres of property. There's room for up to 80 dogs, and each pooch has 60 square feet of space to use, including an indoor tiled space and a covered outdoor run. Cats stay in a separate boarding area. The rates are $8 per night for dogs and $6 per night for cats; food is included unless you'd prefer to bring your own.

Tavern Hill Pet Care Center, 296 River Road South, Putney (802-387-5073). This animal-centered place has its all: overnight boarding, doggie day care, grooming, and even a retail shop with collars, leashes, treats, and other basics. Overnight stays are $14 for dogs and $10 for cats; doggie day-care rates are typically $12 per day. Grooming rates vary, based on the pet and the services required.

Wundrland Pet Lodge, junction of Routes 7 and 103, North Clarendon (802-773-8011). "We're like a play camp for dogs," says Wundrland owner Nancee Schaffner. "We're different in that we allow the dogs to play with each other." You'll want to call early: The kennel usually fills up three months in advance of holidays and popular ski weekends. Overnight boarding costs $14 per night for dogs and $8 per night for cats. Doggie day care is also available for $7 per day.

IN CASE OF EMERGENCY

Deerfield Valley Veterinary, 85 Route 100, West Dover (802-464-0641).

Green Mountain Veterinary Hospital, 48 Treat Hill Road, Manchester Center (802-362-2620).

Mount Anthony Veterinary Hospital, 832 West Road, Bennington (802-442-4324).

Poultney Veterinary Services, 330 East Main Street, Poultney (802-287-9292).

Springfield Animal Hospital, 346 River Street, Springfield (802-885-2505).

Windham Veterinary Clinic, 687 Putney Road, Brattleboro (802-254-9412).

Central Vermont

When pet owners take to the outdoors, many head first to state parks—often the only places where you can relax with a picnic, a great view, and your pooch by your side. But visitors may be surprised (and disappointed) to learn that Vermont state parks, unlike those in many other states, do not allow companion animals into day-use areas, including picnic areas. Leashed pets are allowed on hiking trails and in state campgrounds; still, this bit of bad news can throw a wrench into your plans, especially if you had hoped to spend your day hovering over a barbecue grill in the great outdoors.

But central Vermont, luckily, offers much more than state parks. The town of Woodstock, often called "the prettiest little village in America," seduces photographers and antiquers with its small-town charm. To the west, Rutland is a surprisingly pet-friendly small city, even offering a B&B designed especially for dogs and their owners. The college town of

Middlebury is welcoming and surrounded by picture-perfect farmland (the poet Robert Frost once called the area home; see "Out and About"). Then, of course, there are all those beautiful Green Mountains, charming visitors with their scenic vistas, ski resorts, challenging hiking trails, and hidden waterways. The best way to see it all is to get lost: Roll down the window, throw away the map, and see where all those intriguing back roads can take you.

ACCOMMODATIONS

Hotels, Motels, Inns, and Bed & Breakfasts

Barre

Knoll Motel, 1015 North Main Street, Barre (802-479-3648; knollmotel@charter.net; www.knollmotel.com); $50–75 per night. "Some small dogs" (call to see if yours qualifies) are allowed to stay at this motel, which recently celebrated its 50th anniversary. Rooms have one queen-sized bed or two double beds, irons and ironing boards, microwaves, refrigerators, and cable TV. One family suite is also available.

Maplecroft Bed & Breakfast, 70 Washington Street, Barre (802-476-0760; maplecroftvermont@hotmail.com; www.maplecroft-vermont.com); $75–100 per night. The resident dog and two cats will welcome your pet to Maplecroft with just two caveats: You must give at least 24 hours' advance notice and provide a sleeping crate—no animals are allowed on innkeeper Marianne Kotch's handmade quilts. The historic home has three guest rooms, an antiques-filled front parlor, and a dining room.

Brandon

Lilac Inn, 53 Park Street, Brandon (802-247-5463; 1-800-221-0720; lilacinn@sover.net; www.lilacinn.com); $135–300 per night. One of the grandest Vermont accommodations to allow pets, the Lilac Inn is a fully restored, early-1900s mansion with wide lawns, gardens and fountains, and large, individually decorated rooms and suites: The Bridal Suite is the most requested. Pets are welcome in designated rooms with prior approval.

Bridport

Champlain Valley Alpacas and Farmstay, 326 Fiddler's Lane, Bridport (802-758-3276; alpaca@wcvt.com; www.wcvt.com/~alpaca); $55–255 per night. Bring your horse, dog, or other animal along to this tranquil accommodation where you can get an up-close look at a working alpaca farm. Choose from a suite with a queen-sized bed or a furnished two-bedroom apartment. Hiking and biking trails are nearby, and guests are welcome to participate

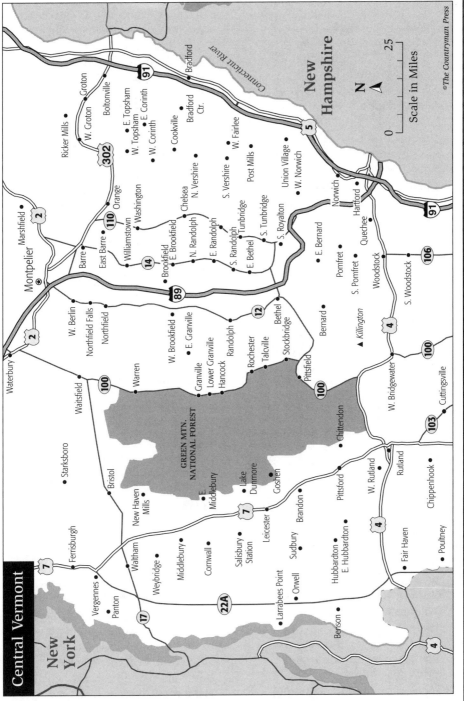

Central Vermont

©The Countryman Press

Scale in Miles

N

0   25

New Hampshire

New York

Connecticut River

GREEN MTN. NATIONAL FOREST

▲ Killington

in the day-to-day workings of the farm as well.

Bristol

Firefly Bed & Breakfast, Bristol (802-453-2223; info@fireflybb. com; www.fireflybb.com); $70–79 per night. Bring your horse or well-behaved small- to medium-sized pet (dogs up to the size of a Lab are welcome without extra fees) to Firefly, where you'll enjoy full country breakfasts, hiking trails, a pond, and a swimming pool. The three guest rooms have quilts and king-sized or double beds; two share a bath and one has a private bath.

Fairlee

Silver Maple Lodge and Cottages, 520 Route 5 South, Fairlee (802-333-4326; 1-800-666-1946; smlodge@localnet.com; www.silvermaplelodge.com); $79–94 per night. Your well-behaved pet is welcome in the Silver Maple Lodge's seven cottage rooms. All have knotty-pine walls and floors, and some have fireplaces, kitchenettes, and sleep sofas. Guests enjoy free continental breakfasts, picnic tables, and a wraparound screened-in porch. (The innkeepers also offer hot-air ballooning/accommodation packages.)

Killington

Butternut on the Mountain, Weathervane Road, Killington (802-422-2000); $64–160 per night. This friendly motor inn has 17 guest rooms, airport shuttles, cable TV with in-room movies, an indoor swimming pool, a restaurant, and lounge and laundry facilities. Pets are allowed in the summer only; there are no extra fees.

Cascades Lodge, 58 Old Mill Road, Killington (802-422-3731; 1-800-345-0113; www.cascades-lodge.com); $69–219 per night. Pets are welcome at Cascades in the summer and fall only; pet owners pay an additional fee of $25 per stay or $10 per night. The full-service lodge has a fitness center, an indoor swimming pool, a sauna, a restaurant and pub, and mountain-view rooms and suites. Killington's hiking and skiing trails are a short walk or shuttle ride away.

Cortina Inn and Resort, 103 Route 4, Killington (802-773-3333; cortina1@aol.com; www. cortinainn.com); $95–249 per night. Located on 32 landscaped acres, the Cortina Inn has a pond, tennis courts, an indoor swimming pool, 96 rooms and seven deluxe suites, two restaurants, a fitness center, public areas with fireplaces, and two reading rooms. Pets are welcome for an additional $10 per night, provided owners adhere to pet-policy rules they'll receive at check-in.

Inn at Long Trail, Route 4, Killington (1-800-325-2540; ilt@vermontel.net; www.innat-longtrail.com); $68–114 per night. The designated pet rooms at this rustic inn are the two-room fireplace suites with private entrances; the inn also offers a redwood hot tub, a gathering room with a fieldstone fireplace, hardwood floors, and Adirondack-style furnishings.

Pets must be quiet, leashed, and crated if left alone in a suite.

Mendon

Econo Lodge Killington Area, 51 Route 4, Mendon (802-773-6644; 1-800-553-2666); $65–97 per night. The 30 guest rooms and efficiencies at this Econo Lodge have cable TV and air-conditioning; guests can also take advantage of free continental breakfasts, two lounges with fireplaces, a reading loft with almost 1,000 books, a swimming pool and hot tub, picnic areas, and a game room. Pets are allowed for an extra $10 per night.

Middlebury

Middlebury Inn, Court House Square, Middlebury (802-388-4961; 1-800-842-4666; midinnvt@sover.net; www.middleburyinn.com); $110–175 per night. Pets are welcome in the Contemporary Motel rooms at Middlebury Inn at no extra charge. This historic inn is located across from the town green and offers four levels of accommodations; the motel rooms have air-conditioning, free local calls, cable TV, private bathrooms, pullout sofa beds, and in-room coffeemakers.

Quechee

Quality Inn at Quechee Gorge, 5817 Woodstock Road, Quechee (802-295-7600; 1-800-228-5151); $65–190 per night. For an extra $10 per night, your pet is welcome to join you at this Quality Inn, which features a swimming pool, cable TV with in-room movies, a restaurant, laundry facilities, fax and photocopying services, and hair dryers and ironing boards. Outside, you'll find a jogging track and a picnic area with tables.

Rutland

Harvest Moon Bed & Breakfast, 1659 North Grove Street, Rutland (802-773-0889; llpink@sover.net; www.harvestmoon.com); $75–125 per night. The two guest rooms at Harvest Moon each have a private bath, antiques, comfortable country furnishings, vintage wallpaper, quilts, and views of the nearby mountains, farmland, and sugarhouse. Gathering areas include a parlor and dining room. Well-behaved, housebroken pets are welcome for an additional fee of $10 per pet, per night.

Holiday Inn Rutland–Killington, 476 Route 7 South, Rutland (802-775-1911); $107–159 per night. You'll find a swimming pool, in-room movies, and room service at this Holiday Inn, where pets are welcome for an additional fee of $10 per night, per pet. Other amenities include laundry facilities, a concierge desk, a lounge, air-conditioning, cable TV, a sauna, and free airport shuttles.

Ramada Limited of Rutland, 253 South Main Street, Rutland (802-773-3361; 1-888-298-2054); $72–129 per night. Guests at the Rutland Ramada enjoy a swimming pool, a business center, a fitness center, a 24-hour front desk, cable TV, laundry facilities, free local calls, and alarm clocks. Pets are welcome for an additional $25 per stay, provided they are not left alone in the rooms.

**Red Roof Inn Rutland–
Killington,** 378 South Main
Street, Rutland (802-775-4303);
$67–75 per night. Formerly
known as the **Howard Johnson
Rutland,** this Red Roof Inn has
an indoor heated swimming pool
and sauna; complimentary breakfasts, coffee, and newspapers;
laundry facilities; alarm clocks;
smoking and nonsmoking rooms;
and voice mail. Leashed pets are
welcome without extra fees.

Waitsfield

The Garrison, Route 17,
Waitsfield (802-496-2352; 1-800-
766-7829); $65–450 per night.
This unique accommodation offers
motel-style rooms or entire condominiums for rent, varying in size
from one to four bedrooms with
room for 1 to 12 people. Guests in
any unit can enjoy the swimming
pool, a common area with a game
room, a fitness center, and laundry facilities. Pets are welcome for
an additional $20 per night.

Hyde Away Inn, 1428 Millbrook
Road (Route 17), Waitsfield (1-
800-777-HYDE; hideaway@
madriver.com; www.hydeaway-
inn.com); $89–139 per night. The
Hyde Away has a laid-back,
bustling atmosphere with après-
ski fun, a casual restaurant, and
free breakfasts each morning. The
rooms vary in size and style and
can each accommodate one to
five people. Pets are welcome in
the rooms that have private
entrances for an additional $10
per night.

Millbrook Inn, 533 Mill Brook
Road, Waitsfield (802-496-2405;
1-800-477-2809; millbrkinn@aol.

com; www.millbrookinn.com);
$40–110 per night. Mo, the resi-
dent mixed-breed pooch at
Millbrook, enthusiastically welcomes other dogs to his cozy inn
and large backyard—no barkers,
please. Each of the seven guest
rooms has a private bath and
handmade quilt; other amenities
include living rooms, a fireplace,
an on-site restaurant, and nearby
skiing and hiking trails.

Warren

Golden Lion Riverside Inn,
731 Route 100, Warren (802-496-
3084; 1-888-867-4491; gldnlion@
madriver.com; www.gmavt.net/
~gldnlion); $55–94 per night.
Pets are welcome in some rooms
at the Golden Lion for an extra
$5 per night; the property has an
outside pen with a doghouse and
a nearby beach where pets can
swim. The modern motel rooms
have cable TV and telephones,
and guests can also enjoy free
breakfasts and an outdoor hot
tub. Dogs must be crated when
left alone in rooms.

Powderhound at Sugarbush,
Warren (802-496-5100; 1-800-548-
4022; phound@madriver.com;
www.powderhoundinn.com); call
for rate information. Dogs, cats,
rabbits, and even gerbils have
stayed at this Mad River Valley
lodging, whose name and skiing-
doggie logo reveal its pet-friendly
nature. The converted historic
farmhouse offers two-room
suites, a swimming pool and hot
tub, tennis courts, **Michael's
Restaurant** and the **Doghouse
Pub,** and woods and fields for
exploring.

THE PAW HOUSE INN, A DOG-CENTERED B&B IN WEST RUTLAND

West Rutland

Paw House Inn, 1376 Clarendon Avenue, West Rutland (1-866-PAW-HOUSE; info@pawhouse-inn.com; www.pawhouseinn.com); $135–155 per night. Every traveling dog owner should make a point of visiting this unique B&B at least once. Conceived, designed, and managed exclusively for pooches and their people, the Paw House has human *and* dog bedding in each room, personalized doggie treats upon arrival, and an on-site kennel—known as Mario's Playhouse—where your mutt has her own spot for relaxing while you ski, shop, dine, or catch a movie. You'll also find an exercise area in the backyard, a nearby walking path, full breakfasts each morning, and comfortable common rooms where you can socialize with other two- and four-legged visitors.

White River Junction

Best Western at the Junction, 306 North Hartland Road, White River Junction (802-295-3015; 1-800-870-7234); $64–79 per night. Close to ski mountains, Dartmouth College, and the village of Woodstock, this Best Western offers amenities such as a swimming pool, a fitness center, in-room coffeemakers, cable TV, laundry services, a 24-hour front desk, and a restaurant. You can bring your pet along for an additional $10 per night.

Ramada Inn White River Junction, 259 Holiday Drive, White River Junction (802-295-3000; 1-888-298-2054); $75–95 per night. Pets are allowed in designated smoking rooms at this Ramada Inn, which offers a fitness center; a swimming pool; cable TV; microwaves and refrigerators; alarm clocks; and in-room hair dryers, ironing boards, and coffeemakers. There are no extra fees for animals.

Williamstown

Autumn Harvest Inn, Clark Road, Williamstown (802-433-1355; autumnharvest@aol.com; www.centralvt.com/web/autumn); $79–139 per night. Snow-mobilers, hikers, and horseback riders will appreciate this comfortable and historic accommodation, which is located close to many trails. The former dairy farm also offers spacious rooms and suites, private baths, meals in the adjoining restaurant, and a relaxing wraparound porch. Leashed, well-behaved dogs are allowed in certain rooms.

Woodstock

Three Church Street Bed & Breakfast, 3 Church Street, Woodstock (802-457-1925); $85–115 per night. This riverfront B&B has 11 guest rooms, 2 acres of lawn and gardens, a swimming pool, a tennis court, a music room, a library, and a porch overlooking the water. Downtown Woodstock is a short walk away, and golf, hiking trails, and antiques shops are nearby. Dogs are welcome for an additional $5 per night.

Winslow House, 492 Woodstock Road, Woodstock (802-457-1820); $85–165 per night. The friendly innkeepers at Winslow House offer a romantic atmosphere in the heart of Woodstock; the historic farmhouse is located about a mile from the village green. The spacious rooms feature antique furnishings, queen-sized beds, cable TV, refrigerators, ceiling

fans, and air-conditioning. You can also enjoy a full breakfast in the dining room, a workout in the exercise room, and cookies in the living room. Pets are welcome.

Campgrounds

Addison

DAR State Park Campground, 6750 Route 17, Addison (802-759-2354; 1-800-658-1622); $15–22 per night. Named for the Daughters of the American Revolution, the organization that donated the park's land, DAR has a designated dog-walk trail, 70 sites for RVs and tents (including 24 lean-tos), and rest rooms with showers. This is also the filming site for the movie *What Lies Beneath.* Animals are not allowed in the day-use area. Bring proof of vaccination.

Fair Haven

Bomoseen State Park Campground, 22 Cedar Mountain Road, Fair Haven (802-265-4242; 1-800-658-1622); $15–22 per night. This seasonal waterfront campground, popular for picnics and boating, is located beside Lake Bomoseen (see "Out and About" for more park information). Campers can choose from 66 shady or sunny campsites, each with a picnic table and fire pit and access to rest rooms with showers. Pet owners must bring proof of vaccination.

Gaysville

White River Valley Campground, Route 107, Gaysville (802-234-6780; river@sover.net; www.sover.net/~river); $20–29 per night. The White River offers plenty of opportunities for recreation at this family campground; you can rent inner tubes, swim, fish, and boat. On-site, you'll also find a camp store, 100 sites for tents and RVs, 21 acres of woods, basketball and volleyball courts, a playground, and a recreation room. Owners must leash dogs and clean up after them.

Hubbardton
Half Moon State Park Campground, 1621 Black Pond Road, Hubbardton (802-273-2848; 1-800-658-1622); $15–22 per night. Located near the Bomoseen State Park Campground in the Bomoseen State Forest (see above listing and "Out and About"), this campground focuses on tent camping with 59 quiet and shady sites. A playground, walking trails, and rest rooms with showers are also available. Dog owners must show vet records as proof of vaccination.

Leicester
Country Village Campground, 40 Route 7, Leicester (802-247-3333); $13–21 per night. This pet-friendly campground, located about 3 miles north of Brandon, has a dog-walk area, a camp store, and wooded and sunny sites with picnic tables and fire pits. Leashed, quiet dogs are welcome, provided their owners have proof of rabies vaccination and clean up after them.

Salisbury
Branbury State Park Campground, 3570 Lake Dunmore Road (Route 53), Salisbury (802-247-5925; 1-800-658-1622); $15–22 per night. This state park campground has more than 30 sites, rest rooms with showers, picnic tables and fire pits, woods and open fields, hiking trails, and mountain streams. Animal owners must use a leash and show vet records as proof of vaccination. Pets are not allowed in the day-use picnic and swimming area.

Kampersville Lake Dunmore, Lake Dunmore Road, Salisbury (802-352-4501; 1-877-250-2568; e-mail@kampersville.com; www. kampersville.com); $19–34 per night. Tenters and RVers will find scheduled family activities, 200 campsites, a miniature golf course, two swimming pools, a recreation hall, boat rentals, rest rooms with showers, and a camp store at this large, active campground. Pets are welcome on a leash as long as their owners clean up after them and show proof of vaccination.

Vergennes
Button Bay State Park Campground, 5 Button Bay State Park Road, Vergennes (802-475-2377; 1-800-658-1622); $15–22 per night. This former farmland area is now a 253-acre park with 73 campsites for RVs and tents. Campers can use rest rooms with showers, a dumping station, picnic tables, a swimming pool, and a playground, and they can rent boats. Dogs are not allowed in the day-use areas, but they are welcome on a leash on nature trails. Don't forget proof of vaccination.

White River Junction
Quechee State Park Campground, 190 Dewey Mills Road, White River Junction (802-295-2990; 1-800-299-3071); $15–22 per night. Managed by the U.S. Army Corps of Engineers, this campground has 47 sites for tents, pop-up trailers, and RVs (no hookups); rest rooms with showers; a dumping station; a playground; and a playing field. Quechee Gorge and the North Hartland Flood Control Dam are nearby.

Williamstown
Limehurst Lake Campground, 4104 Route 14, Williamstown (802-433-6662; 1-800-242-9876); $19–25 per night. Most breeds (call to see if yours qualifies) are welcome at Limehurst, a family campground with a private lake, primitive tent sites, RV sites with hookups, lean-tos, and cottages. Campers can also enjoy a beach, rental boats, a playground, scheduled activities, and camp store. Owners must leash their pets and clean up after them.

Homes, Cottages, and Cabins for Rent

Cabot
Lakefront Home, Cabot (802-563-2217; hanzer@sover.net); $100–150 per night or $400–600 per week. "We've had no problems with pets in the two years we've been allowing them," says homeowner Betsy Hanzimanolis, whose lakeside house has three bedrooms, two bathrooms, a full kitchen, a screened-in porch, children's toys and books, and a boat for guests' use. Renters are required to pay a local cleaner for a complete vacuuming and cleaning when they leave.

Chelsea
Central Vermont Home, Chelsea (860-447-8695; vtnest@snet.net); $95 per night or $500 per week. This affordable rental house has three bedrooms, a combination living and dining room with a woodstove, one bathroom, a garage, a washer and dryer, a kitchen, and satellite TV and a VCR. House-trained pets are welcome. Dogs will enjoy running around on the fields that surround the house and nearby pond.

Killington
Killington Chalet, Killington–Pico Ski Area (732-920-8368; russ1293@aol.com); $575–1,550 per week. The owners of this mountain home are animal lovers, and welcome pets to their three-bedroom rental. Amenities include a kitchen, a mudroom, dining and living rooms, a wraparound deck, a fireplace, a washer and dryer, a barbecue grill, and satellite TV. Skiing and golfing are both close by.

Lake Bomoseen
Lakeshore, Lake Bomoseen, West Castleton area (802-446-2640; 802-273-2222; mobrien@vermontel.net); $1,385–1,685 per week. This pet-friendly luxury property sits right on the edge of the water and has two bedrooms, two bathrooms, and two large decks. "Our previous dog guests gave it four paws up!" says owner Mary Ellen O'Brien. "We

sometimes also provide pet-sitting for a nominal charge." Multiple pets are welcome without extra fees. (Mary Ellen offers another pet-friendly rental on Joe's Pond in West Danville; see "Accommodations—Homes, Cottages, and Cabins for Rent" in "Northern Vermont" for more information.)

Neshobe Canal Cabins, Lake Bomoseen (802-438-9868; nunzia @sover.net); $500–700 per week. Affordable and pet-friendly, these rustic cabins are available for rent from June through October. "We have had such wonderful experiences as a result of having dogs in our lives, and we know there are many people who feel that their pets are part of their families," explains owner Nan Sevigny. The rentals have screened-in porches, barbecue grills, woodstoves, two double beds, and sleeper sofas.

Lake Fairlee
Lake House, Lake Fairlee (802-333-4684; 802-333-9488; ifsrental @aol.com); $1,800–2,200 per week. Pets are welcome with prior approval at this four-bedroom home offering all the luxuries, including a tennis court, a boat dock, a wet bar, a sunroom and patio, a fireplace, an after-swim outdoor shower, and a children's playhouse. Five acres of the property are equipped with invisible fencing; dog owners are just asked to clean up after their animals.

South Woodstock
Leave No Trace Cabin, South Woodstock (301-834-9711; equusbambi@aol.com; home

town.aol.com/equusbambi/VT-LNT.html); $125–150 per night or $700 per week. Resembling something like a gingerbread house made of logs, this quaint woodland cabin has two bedrooms, two bathrooms, a whirlpool tub, satellite TV, woodstoves, a washer and dryer, a kitchen, and an outdoor barbecue grill. Pets are welcome; two extra-large dog crates are provided, and you can even bring your horse to the on-site paddock.

Vershire
Country Estate, Vershire (802-765-4869; 802-765-4376; mbaldwin@sover.net); $350 per night or $1,450–2,000 per week. Looking for luxury? This rambling, historic brick home can accommodate up to 15 people and has six bedrooms and four bathrooms. Guests can bring their dogs inside or take advantage of the luxury, heated dog kennels on the property. Three horse stalls are also available for visiting equines. Other amenities include 100 acres of trails and woods, a swimming pond, two kitchens, fireplaces, and woodstoves.

Washington
Caleb Atwell House, Washington (860-349-1293; 860-349-2430; ltorelli@tiac.net; http://home.tiac. net/ ~ ltorelli/vermont1.htm); $600 per week or $2,300 per month. Located beside a small pond, this secluded, historic home has original wide-plank floorboards and beamed ceilings; two bedrooms; a fieldstone fireplace; a living room, den, and kitchen; and appliances such as a microwave, washer and dryer,

and TV/VCR. Pets are welcome for an additional $25 per week.

West Brookfield

Post and Beam Cottage, West Brookfield (802-728-4835; 802-728-5903; smorris@sover.net); $450 per week. Responsible pet owners are welcome at this brand-new

Cape-style cottage with one bedroom. Ideal for couples or small families, the home has a kitchen, a fireplace and woodstove, an outdoor barbecue grill, and a stereo and CD player. Mountain biking and cross-country skiing trails start on the property.

OUT AND ABOUT

Art in the Park Foliage Festival, Rutland. As you might guess, this fall-color spectacular takes place each October. It has been attracting visitors for more than 40 years with crafts artisans, food vendors, music, and children's activities. For more information, call 802-775-0356.

Auction for the Animals, Woodstock. This annual event usually takes place in August at the **Lucy MacKenzie Humane Society** shelter in Woodstock; a yard sale is followed by an auction of items such as furniture, rugs, antiques, art, and glassware. The shelter's annual **Walk-A-Thon** is typically held in May. For more information, visit the shelter at Cox District Road or call 802-457-3080.

Barre Bike Path, South Barre. You can access this 1-mile-long paved pathway at Fairview Street, Bridge Street, or Parkside Terrace in South Barre. Dogs are welcome on a leash.

Bomoseen State Forest, 22 Cedar Mountain Road, Fair Haven (802-265-4242; 1-800-658-1622). With

more than 2,800 acres, this state forest contains the smaller **Bomoseen State Park,** myriad hiking trails, boat rentals, a beach, many quiet corners, and wildlife-viewing opportunities. Dogs are not allowed in day-use areas but are allowed in the campground (see "Accommodations—Campgrounds").

Branbury State Park, 3570 Lake Dunmore Road, Salisbury (802-247-5925; 1-800-658-1622). Pets are not allowed in the most popular section of this state park, a wide grassy area with lake access and picnic areas. But ask the rangers for directions to the hiking areas around the corner and you'll find yourself in the company of other dog walkers, horseback riders, and nature lovers enjoying the smooth, quiet trails to scenic vistas. Pets are also allowed in the park's campground (see "Accommodations—Campgrounds").

Chimney Point State Historic Site, Routes 125 and 17, Lake Champlain Bridge, Addison (802-759-2412; www.historic vermont.org). This former Native

American camping area beside Lake Champlain became a regional trade center in 1,000 B.C. and continued in that role well into the 1600s. Today, the site commemorates that period as well as the 1700s-era French settlements and fort in what is now known as Chimney Point. Dogs are welcome on a leash but are not allowed in the visitors center.

Dead Creek Wildlife Management Area, Route 17, Addison. Migratory birds, including geese, red-winged blackbirds, owls, and hawks, are plentiful in this 2,800-acre refuge during the spring and fall. For a great view, bring your binoculars to the sheltered viewing area along Route 17 on the drive from Vergennes to Addison; the shelter even provides pictures and descriptions of the birds you're likely to see.

Green Mountain National Forest. The pride of Vermont, the Green Mountain National Forest makes up a huge section of the southern part of the state and continues up into central Vermont with ponds, trails, flora and fauna, primitive campsites, and majestic, untouched forestland. Try one of the following hikes: the **Abbey Pond Trail,** a 2-mile-long route with a waterfall and secluded pond, located about 5 miles north of Middlebury; the **Mount Horrid/ Great Cliff Trail,** a fairly steep slope to a lookout point, starting at Route 73 at Brandon Gap; or the **Lincoln Gap West Vista Trail,** a short and easy walk to great views with parking located at

Lincoln Gap Road. There are many more: For further description and directions, visit the Green Mountain National Forest Headquarters on 231 North Main Street in Rutland, call 802-747-6700, or visit www.fs.fed.us/r9/gmfl.

Kingsland Bay State Park, 787 Kingsland Bay State Park Road, Ferrisburgh (802-877-3445; 1-800-658-1622). This relatively new state park is the former site of a girls' camp; today it encompasses 265 undeveloped acres with walking and hiking paths beside Lake Champlain. It's a popular area for picnics and boating.

Long Trail. This famous Canada-to-Massachusetts trail passes through the entire state of Vermont. Those who hike the whole trail are called End to Enders. For those who just want to explore a section, the central Vermont portion provides some of the most challenging terrain. Among the best-known sites are the **Camel's Hump** (elevation: 4,083 feet), **Mount Abraham** (elevation: 4,000 feet), and **Skylight Pond. Skyline Lodge** is the largest shelter; others are spaced every 6 to 8 or so miles. For more information, maps, and trail descriptions, contact the **Green Mountain Club** at 802-244-7037 or visit www.green-mountainclub.org.

Mad River Greenway, Waitsfield. This 4-mile-long thin trail is popular with locals; you can hop on just off Route 100 at Tremblay Road or Meadow Road. Dogs must be well behaved and leashed.

Quechee. This small, picturesque town is home to a number of central Vermont's most popular attractions, including **Quechee Gorge** (aka the Grand Canyon of New England), the Quechee Gorge Village shopping area, and the annual **Quechee Balloon Festival,** held each June. The 600-acre **Quechee State Park** is located in nearby White River Junction at 190 Dewey Mills Road; for more park information, call 802-295-2990 or 1-800-299-3071. For more information on Quechee events and attractions, call the chamber of commerce at 802-295-7900.

Robert Frost Wayside Area and Trail, Route 125, Ripton (802-388-4362). Talk about poetic: This wonderful spot, located near Middlebury College's Bread Loaf campus, has a picnic area and short walking trail lined with mounted plaques bearing excerpts from some of Robert Frost's noted poems. The famous writer once lived in a cabin on the grounds.

Rock of Ages Quarries, 773 Graniteville Road, Graniteville (Barre) (802-476-3119; www.rock-ofages.com). Leashed pets are welcome in the shop and on the grounds at Rock of Ages, a 50-acre, 600-foot-deep working quarry with amazing views of the trenches and massive slabs of granite as they are cut and removed. On hot days, the staff are sometimes also willing to watch your pup in the air-condi-

tioned office while you explore the grounds. Pets are not allowed on the bus tours.

Scenic Drives. Dirt roads outnumber their paved counterparts in Vermont, and visitors often agree that the best way to explore the state is to wander with no particular destination in mind. For some ideal starting places for a journey, try these: **Route 5** along the Vermont border through the towns of Newbury, Wells River, and Ryegate; **Route 4** from Rutland to Woodstock; **Route 100,** alongside the Green Mountain National Forest, from Killington to Waitsfield; and **Route 125** from Middlebury to Chimney Point.

Stephen Huneck Gallery, 49 Central Street, Woodstock (802-457-3206). Four-legged customers are welcome at this art gallery featuring the works of Vermont native Stephen Huneck, a sculptor, furniture maker, woodcut printmaker, and author specializing in (often humorous) animal themes. For more information on his home gallery and popular attraction **Dog Mountain** in St. Johnsbury, see "Out and About" in "Northern Vermont."

Union Village Dam and Recreation Area, entrances in Union Village and Thetford Center. Like the Ball Mountain Lake recreation area (see "Southern Vermont"), this is a U.S. Army Corps of Engineers property offering ample opportunities for fishing trips, picnics, and hikes. The site encompasses about 6 miles of fish-stocked river, as well as picnic tables, barbecue grills, and rest rooms. Pets are welcome.

QUICK BITES

Baba's Market and Deli, 54 College Street, Middlebury (802-388-6408). There's plenty of outdoor seating at this local college favorite with wood-fired pizza ovens, sandwiches, grocery items, and cold drinks of every variety. Look carefully and you might also find dog treats at the checkout counter.

Bridge Restaurant, Route 17, Chimney Point (802-759-2152). Located next to the Champlain Bridge to New York and the Chimney Point State Historic Site, this family restaurant serves simple, tasty meals and offers lots of outdoor seating.

Kampersville Deli and Ice Cream Parlor, Lake Dunmore Road, Salisbury (802-352-4223). Right around the corner from **Branbury State Park** (see "Out and About") and myriad boating opportunities on Lake Dunmore, this snack bar has take-out service offering your favorite summertime treats.

La Brioche Bakery and Café, 89 Main Street, Montpelier (802-229-0443). This locally renowned eatery serves gourmet sandwiches and pastries indoors, on the patio, or for take-out. Choose from soups, fresh-baked breads with meats and cheeses, scones, cinnamon buns, croissants, muffins, and more.

Main Scoop, 61 Main Street, Vergennes (802-877-6201). This take-out ice cream stand makes for a refreshing stop on your travels through scenic Vergennes. There are outdoor picnic tables and a good variety of flavors—including vanilla—for your favorite pooch.

New Village Snack Bar, West Street, Rutland (802-775-2712). Order at the window and eat outside at the picnic tables at this casual restaurant serving burgers, french fries and onion rings, seafood, chicken sandwiches, and ice cream.

Pizza Jerks, 1307 Killington Road, Killington (802-422-4111). At this New York–style pizzeria, you can eat in, order a slice or a whole pie to go, or bring home an uncooked pizza to bake in your own oven. In addition to specialties like the Heart Stopper (double cheese, double sausage, and double pepperoni), the "jerks" also cook up calzones, strombolis, and subs.

Woodstock Farmer's Market, 468 Woodstock Road, Woodstock (802-457-3658). Stop in this produce, meat, and seafood market for fresh sandwiches to go. In-house specialties include Ann's California Roll-Up (turkey with cheese, tomatoes, avocado, and pesto-mayo) and the vegetarian Quechee Gorge (cheese and tomato with mustard, served grilled with cheddar-herb bread).

HOT SPOTS FOR SPOT

Catamount Pet Supply,
296 Route 4 East, Rutland (802-773-7642). Owned and run by veterinarians, this pet shop specializes in offering all-natural foods without by-products or fillers. In addition to foods and treats, the store stocks toys, crates, and other supplies for dogs, cats, and small animals. Grooming is also available.

Diamond Brook Kennel and Pet Country Club, 4597 Route 30, Brandon (802-273-2941; www.diamondbrook.com). Your four-legged friend will get top-of-the-line treatment at Diamond Brook, where the trainers provide obedience classes, supplies, grooming, and boarding. The inside/outside runs are roomy: 56 to 90 square feet for each animal. Complete grooming services are also available; rates vary according to size and services.

Falls General Store, Route 12, Northfield Falls (802-485-8044). Though this shop doesn't specialize in pet supplies, it is a fun and interesting place to pick up animal food and treats. While you're there for Rover, you can also grab a fishing license, sandwich, slice of pizza, or a Vermont souvenir for yourself.

Lucky Dog Day Care and Boarding Facility, 60 Pike Hill Road, Warren (802-496-5944). There are no cages or kennels at Lucky Dog: just an acre of land, a playroom, and a deck where the dogs romp and play together while their "parents" are off skiing, vacationing, or sightseeing. Pickup and delivery of your pooch is included in the rates, which range $18–25 per day.

Middlebury Boarding and Grooming Kennel, 2819 South Street Extension, Middlebury (802-388-9643; mbgk@sover.net; www.mbgk.com). You can make reservations online for this Middlebury kennel offering overnight boarding ($12 per night for dogs and $8.50 per night for cats), doggie day care ($8.50 per day), and grooming for all sizes and breeds. Obedience classes and agility training are also available.

Pet Deli, 1284 Route 302, Berlin Suite #8, Barre (802-479-4307). Also known as **All About Pets,** this animal-supply store specializes in high-quality foods and nutritional supplements for all types of companion animals. Your furry friend will appreciate the wide selection of rawhide bones and smoked products at the Doggie Deli counter, not to mention the bulk biscuit bar full of treats.

Rebecca's Professional Paw Sitting, Case Street, Middlebury (802-388-2224). Have to run an errand? Can't leave your pet alone? Rebecca's short-term pet-care service can step in. Each 20-minute appointment costs $12, which includes walks, playtime, feeding, brushing, hugging, and whatever else your dog, cat, or gerbil might need.

Sunshine Pet Sitting, Norwich (802-649-3309). Owner Melinda Meyerhoff keeps herself busy with her popular pet-sitting services. "I'm turning away business at times, and I love what I do!" she says. Meyerhoff can walk, feed, and play with your pet while you're out: The typical base rate for sitting is $12 per hour.

IN CASE OF EMERGENCY

Country Animal Hospital,
2472 Route 107, Bethel (802-234-5999).

Eastwood Animal Clinic,
298 Route 4, Rutland (802-773-7711).

Middlebury Animal Hospital,
139 Washington Street Extension, Middlebury (802-388-2691).

Northfield Animal Clinic,
138 King Street, Northfield (802-485-5580).

River Valley Veterinary Hospital,
3890 Route 5, Newbury (802-866-5922).

Woodstock Veterinary Hospital,
1217 Route 12, Woodstock (802-457-2229).

Northern Vermont

From dog chapels to canine camps, northern Vermont is a nearly ideal spot for those whose travel plans include a pet. In addition to its many animal-friendly accommodations, the region also boasts big-city attractions; sweeping views of water, mountains, and rolling farmland; secluded campgrounds; ski resorts; and enough hiking trails to keep you and Spot busy for days—or weeks.

Most of the activity is centered on the Burlington and Stowe areas; the former is home to the University of Vermont, spectacular Lake Champlain, great restaurants, and a bustling pedestrian mall; the latter plays host to famous festivals and hopping ski resorts. (Skiers will be pleased to find numerous dog-sitting options and pet-friendly lodgings nearby.) Boaters and fishermen make the most of northern Vermont's seemingly endless waterways, the largest of which is the mighty Lake Champlain. To the northeast, the more rural areas offer perhaps the most accurate glimpse of Old Vermont, from the quaint Lake Willoughby region to the movie-set-like village of Craftsbury Common. Scenic roads (complete with covered bridges, of course) wind through it all, making almost any drive fun in any season. Canadians can count their blessings for the close proximity; for the rest of us in the lower 48, the destination more than justifies the long ride.

ACCOMMODATIONS

Hotels, Motels, Inns, and Bed & Breakfasts

Averill

Quimby Country Lodge and Cottages, P.O. Box 20, Averill (802-822-5533; quimbyc@ together.net; www.quimby-country.com); $51–151 per night. Located in the northeast corner of Vermont along the Canadian border, Quimby Country welcomes dogs and cats to its 600-acre lakefront resort. Accommodations include private cottages with kitchens and maid service; in the high season, the rates include three meals each day and planned family activities. Boat and Windsurfer rentals are free.

Barnet

Inn at Maplemont Farm, 2742 Route 5, Barnet (802-633-4880; 1-800-230-1617; mplmnt@ together.net; www.maplemont. com); $90–110 per night. Two enthusiastic Bernese mountain dogs, Yuri and Cooper, are the bellhops-in-training at this warm and friendly B&B with a wrap-around porch and rocking chairs, deluxe breakfasts, farm animals, four guest rooms, antiques, a

BERNESE MOUNTAIN DOG YURI IS THE OFFICIAL GREETER AT THE INN AT MAPLEMONT FARM IN BARNET.

dining room, and a relaxing common room. The inn's 43 acres have plenty of hills and pastures for exploring, and the nearby Connecticut River provides canoeing and kayaking opportunities. Pets are always welcome without extra fees, provided they are not left alone in the rooms.

Bolton Valley

Black Bear Inn, 4010 Bolton Access Road, Bolton Valley (802-434-2126; 1-800-395-6335; blk-bear@wcvt.com; www.black-bearinn.com); $53–185 per night. For an additional $10 per day, Black Bear Inn guests can make use of an on-site kennel, other-

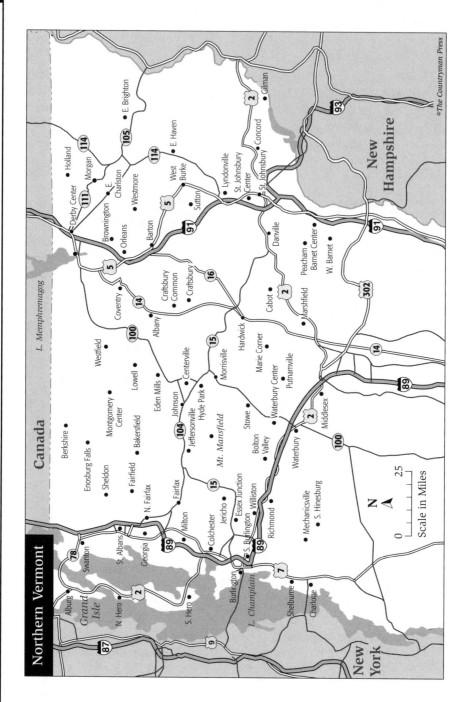

Northern Vermont

Canada

New Hampshire

New York

©The Countryman Press

Scale in Miles
0   25

N

L. Champlain

L. Memphremagog

Mt. Mansfield

wise known as the **Bone and Biscuit Inn**. The kennel is open seasonally and offers private indoor/outdoor runs for each animal. Human visitors can enjoy tennis courts, a swimming pool, and individually decorated guest rooms with private baths.

Burlington

Clarion Hotel Burlington, 1117
Williston Road, Burlington (802-
658-0250; www.clarionvermont.
com); $109–179 per night. The
staff at this animal-friendly hotel
can recommend local pet-sitters
and will present you with their
pet policies upon arrival. The
Clarion has an indoor swimming
pool, a fitness center, a restaurant
and lounge, room service, and
premium movie channels. There's
a limit of two dogs per room;
those paying with cash must
leave a $50 security deposit.

Holiday Inn Burlington,
1068 Williston Road, Burlington
(802-863-6363); $89–164 per
night. For an additional $10 per
stay (not per night), you can
bring your pet along at the
Burlington Holiday Inn. The
hotel offers two swimming pools
and a sauna; laundry facilities;
room service; a fitness center;
alarm clocks; in-room movies,
irons, and coffeemakers; a
lounge; and a concierge service.

**Sheraton Burlington Hotel and
Conference Center,** 870 Williston
Road, Burlington (802-865-6600;
1-800-325-3535); $125–229 per
night. The Sheraton Burlington
has a convenient location close to
downtown and Lake Champlain,
a swimming pool, a restaurant
and room service, express checkout services, a fitness center,
cable TV, a 24-hour front desk,
laundry facilities, and a lounge.
Pets are welcome, provided they
are not left alone in rooms.

Town and Country Motel,
490 Shelburne Road, Burlington
(802-862-5786); $49–104 per
night. This clean, no-frills motel
is close to everything you might
want to see in the Burlington
area; several ski resorts are also
within an hour's drive. Smoking
and nonsmoking rooms are available, and dogs (sorry, no cats)
are welcome for an additional fee
of $5 per dog, per night.

Craftsbury Common

Craftsbury Outdoor Center,
Craftsbury Common (802-586-
7768; 1-800-729-7751; stay@crafts-
bury.com; www.craftsbury.com);
$230 per night. Friendly pets are
allowed in the cottages at the
Craftsbury Outdoor Center, a fun
facility offering activity-filled
vacations for those interested in
hiking, mountain biking, kayaking, yoga, swimming, sculling,
running, and skiing. Pet owners
pay a onetime $25 cleaning fee
and are asked to keep their animals under control at all times.

Inn on the Common, Route 14,
Craftsbury Common (802-586-
9619; 1-800-521-2233; info@innon
thecommon.com; www.innothe-
common.com); $119–320 per
night. Located beside its town's
historic common, this 16-room,
1700s inn is set on 10 acres with a
tennis court, swimming pool, gardens, and fields. Gourmet breakfasts and dinner are served in the
dining room, and the rooms are
furnished with antiques, woodstoves, fireplaces, and four-poster
beds. Pets are welcome for an
extra $15 per night.

Derby

Mac's Cottages, Lake Salem,
Derby (802-334-6807); $375 per

week. These two-bedroom, fully furnished rental cabins provide cable TV, screened-in porches, kitchens, and bedding. The grounds have nice views, a beach for swimming and relaxing, and a dock for boating and fishing. Pets are welcome.

Essex Junction
Homeplace Bed & Breakfast, 90 Old Pump Road, Essex Junction (802-899-4694); $85 per night. "I've been extremely lucky so far with guest pets," says Homeplace innkeeper Mariot Huessy. "My dogs love to play with other dogs." The country B&B has four guest rooms, books and games, farm animals, European antiques, and full country breakfasts. Dogs are welcome with prior approval for an additional $10 per night, as long as they are not left alone in the rooms.

Fairfax
Inn at Buck Hollow Farm, 2150 Buck Hollow Road, Fairfax (802-849-2400; inn@buckhollow.com; www.buckhollow.com); $63–103 per night. Your pets are always welcome with prior notice at Buck Hollow, a gracious and low-key inn where the resident dogs, Isham and Chelsea, and several resident cats will be on hand to show you around. Set on 400 acres of horse fields, forests, lawns, and fields, the farm has an on-site antiques shop, four-poster beds, a swimming pool, a hot tub, and full country breakfasts. (Ask for the Yellow Room, which has a sliding door leading out onto a private porch and the large backyard.)

Grand Isle
By the Lake Motel, Lake Shore Drive, Grand Isle (802-372-6134); $65 per night. The five housekeeping efficiencies at By the Lake have lake access and boat-launching rights. Each can accommodate up to four people, and pets are welcome. Weekly and other long-term rentals are also available.

Jeffersonville
Mannsview Inn, 916 Route 108, Jeffersonville (802-899-8321; 1-888-937-MANN; rsvp@mannsview.com; www.mannsview.com); $75–185 per night. This animal-friendly inn has its own on-site kennel (see **Canine Care** under "Hot Spots for Spot") that guests and others can make use of while visiting the area. The inn itself offers seven guest rooms with four-poster beds, quilts, antiques, and a mix of private and shared baths. Guests can also enjoy full breakfasts, a hot tub, a sunroom, and a library.

Morgan Center
Seymour Lake Lodge, 28 Valley Road, Morgan Center (802-895-2752; seymourlodge@fcgnetworks.net; www.seymourlakelodge.com); $55 per night, single occupancy. Guests at the waterfront Seymour Lake Lodge can enjoy free use of canoes or rent powerboats, kayaks, or rowboats; other amenities include an on-site gift shop and free continental breakfasts. Pets are welcome without extra fees in four of the seven lodge rooms and in the neighboring boathouse cottage.

DOGS, HORSES, AND CATS WILL WELCOME YOU AND YOUR PET TO THE INN AT BUCK HOLLOW FARM IN FAIRFAX.

North Hero

Shore Acres Inn and Restaurant, Route 2, North Hero (802-372-8722; vtshacres@ aol.com; www.shoreacres.com); $89–155 per night. Shore Acres guests have access to boat docking, tennis courts, a swimming pool, a golf course and putting green, horseshoe pits, shuffleboard courts, and croquet. Most of the rooms have water views; all have cable TV, air conditioners, and contemporary furnishings. Pets are welcome for an extra $10 for one night and $5 each additional night.

Orleans

WilloughVale Inn on Lake Willoughby, 793 Route 5A, Orleans (802-525-4123; info@ willoughvale.com; www.willoughvale.com); $79–249 per night. With wonderful water views, eight individually decorated rooms, two luxury suites, four lakefront cottages with decks and private docks, an on-site restaurant, and a lounge, the Willough-Vale is a relaxed inn designed for quiet getaways. With prior approval, one pet weighing less than 50 pounds is welcome in each room or cottage.

St. Johnsbury

Fairbanks Inn, 401 Western Avenue, St. Johnsbury (802-748-5666); $59–110 per night. Dogs of any size (sorry, no cats) are welcome at this small motel for an additional $5 per night. Amenities include a swimming pool, laundry facilities, cable TV with in-room movies, modem lines, and in-room microwaves and coffeemakers. Animals should not be left unattended in the rooms.

Holiday Motel, 25 Hastings Street, St. Johnsbury (802-748-8192); $42–95 per night. Dogs (sorry, no cats) are allowed in certain rooms at the Holiday Motel, where amenities include clean guest rooms, an exercise room, and laundry services. Smoking and nonsmoking rooms are available. Pet owners pay an additional $10 per night.

Shelburne
Econo Lodge and Suites,
3164 Shelburne Road, Shelburne (802-985-3377; 1-800-553-2666); $44–119 per night. The Econo Lodge provides accommodations for long- and short-term stays with standard rooms and suites offering air-conditioning, cable TV, an outdoor swimming pool, laundry facilities, continental breakfasts, in-room movies, a restaurant, a wake-up service, and a picnic area. Pets are allowed in smoking rooms for an extra $10 per night.

South Burlington
Best Western Windjammer Burlington,
1076 Williston Road, South Burlington (802-863-1125; 1-800-371-1125; www.bestwestern.com/windjammerinn); $71–114 per night. Pets are welcome at the Windjammer for an extra fee of $5 per pet, per night. Amenities at the full-service hotel include an indoor and an outdoor swimming pool, a restaurant and pub, free continental breakfasts, a fitness center, a sauna, laundry services, fax and photocopying services, in-room movies, and cable TV with premium movie channels.

University Inn and Suites,
5 Dorset Street, South Burlington (1-800-808-4656); $49–199 per night. Pets are allowed in smoking rooms only at the University Inn, a hotel with a swimming pool, hot tub and sauna, a fitness center, free morning newspapers,

a business center, a video arcade, air-conditioning, and a spa. There are no extra fees for animals.

Stowe
Andersen Lodge: An Austrian Inn,
3430 Mountain Road, Stowe (802-253-7336; 1-800-336-7336; trude@stoweaccess.com); $50–120 per night. For an extra $5 per night, dogs are welcome to join their owners at the Andersen Lodge, a European-influenced inn and restaurant with 17 guest rooms, a sauna, a swimming pool, tennis courts, a hot tub, a game room, a formal dining room, and two living rooms. Innkeepers Dietmar and Trude Heiss lend the Austrian hospitality of their homeland.

Burgundy Rose, Route 100, Stowe; (802-253-7768; 1-800-989-7768; info@theburgundyrose.com; www.theburgundyrose.com); $59–99 per night. Burgundy Rose innkeeper Mary Kamm enjoys welcoming pet owners to her cozy country-style motor inn offering value, standard, and deluxe rooms with quilts, rocking chairs, free local calls, air-conditioning, and custom shampoos and soaps. Kamm also offers a pet-friendly vacation home for rent called the **Hidden Rose** (see "Homes, Cottages, and Cabins for Rent" for more information).

Commodores Inn, 823 South Main Street, Stowe (802-253-7131; 1-800-44-STOWE; www.commodoresinn.com); $98–162 per night. Animals are welcome without restrictions at this full-service, hotel-style inn with king- and queen-sized beds, air-conditioning, cable TV, a restaurant and lounge, a fitness room, an indoor swimming pool, and two hot tubs. Common areas include a living room with a fireplace and a reading room with board games.

Innsbruck Inn, 4361 Mountain Road, Stowe (802-253-8582; 1-800-225-8582); $104–219 per night. This Bavarian-style inn offers unusual amenities such as a paddle-tennis court and an on-site scuba diving school. Guests can choose from superior and standard rooms, suites, efficiency units, and a five-bedroom chalet. Pets are welcome for an additional $10 per night, provided they are not left unattended at any time.

Mountaineer Inn, 3343 Mountain Road, Stowe (802-253-7525; www.stowemountaineer-inn.com); $95–150 per night. Each room at the Mountaineer Inn has its own deck and shares access to an indoor swimming pool, a large hot tub, a dining room, a lounge, and landscaped grounds along the West Branch River. Guests can choose from basic, standard, and family-style rooms that accommodate up to eight people. Pets are welcome.

Northern Lights Lodge, 4441 Mountain Road, Stowe (802-253-8541); $58–98 per night. Dogs and "well-behaved owners" are always welcome for an extra $10 per stay at Northern Lights, a ski lodge in a pine forest, offering indoor and outdoor swimming pools, a hot tub and sauna, movie and game rooms, a breakfast room with a fireplace, cross-country

skiing trails, air-conditioning, and complimentary full breakfasts for all guests.

Ten Acres Lodge, 14 Barrows Road, Stowe (1-800-327-7357; tenacres@stowevt.net; www.tenacreslodge.com); $115–440 per night. Pets are welcome in the cottages at Ten Acres Lodge, a converted 1840s farmhouse B&B with a gourmet dining room and lounge, a hot tub, and artwork collections hanging on the walls of the library and gathering rooms. The roomy cottages offer two or three bedrooms, living rooms, and kitchenettes.

Topnotch at Stowe Resort and Spa, 4000 Mountain Road, Stowe (802-253-8585; 1-800-451-8686; topnotch@topnotch-resort.com; www.topnotch-resort.com); $170–815 per night. Tennis, golf, spa treatments, massage, restaurant and bistro dining, cross-country skiing, snowshoeing, hiking, child care, and more are all available at Topnotch, a deluxe accommodation in the mountains. Lodging choices include hotel rooms and town-house rentals. Pets are welcome with prior approval. Meal packages are also available.

Waterbury

Grunberg Haus, 94 Pine Street (Route 100), Waterbury (802-244-7726; 1-800-800-7760; grunhaus@aol.com; www.grunberghaus.com); $125–175 per night. Though not allowed in the main inn, pets are welcome in the Grunberg Haus cabins. The cabin units are set in the woods with decks, vaulted ceilings, private bathrooms, queen-sized beds, ceiling fans, and woodstoves. Hiking and cross-country skiing trails wind through the property. The resident collie, Grace, will give you and your pooch a warm hello.

Campgrounds

Brownington
Will-O-Wood Campground,
227 Willowood Lane, Brownington (802-525-3575; www.will-o-woodcampground.com); $17–23 per night. Overlooking Lake Willoughby, this family campground has sites for tents and RVs, 100 acres of fields and woods, rest rooms with showers, a swimming pool, a camp store, a recreation hall, and laundry facilities. Quiet, leashed pets are welcome, as long as their owners clean up after them and don't leave them unattended.

Burlington
North Beach Camping,
60 Institute Road, Burlington (802-862-0942; 1-800-571-1198); $20–30 per night. Tents, pop-up campers, and RVs will all find a home at this lakefront campground operated by the city of Burlington's Department of Parks and Recreation. Leashed, well-behaved pets are welcome, as long as their owners clean up after them and don't leave them unattended. Campers can enjoy a beach, a snack bar, and bathrooms with showers.

Colchester
Malletts Bay Campground,
88 Malletts Bay Campground Road, Colchester (802-863-6980);

$22–29 per night. Malletts Bay offers a waterfront location on Lake Champlain, tent and RV sites, picnic tables, laundry facilities, rest rooms with showers, a swimming pool, a dumping station, a camp store, tennis courts, basketball courts, and a playground. Pets are welcome, but they must be leashed and quiet, and owners must clean up after them.

Danville
Sugar Ridge RV Village and Campground, 24 Old Stagecoach Road (Route 2), Danville (802-684-2550; www.sugarridgerv park.com); $22–29 per night or $133–173 per week. Open seasonally, Sugar Ridge is a fairly new campground located just west of St. Johnsbury with two swimming pools and a kiddie pool, a miniature golf course, 111 sites for tents and RVs, rest rooms with showers, a snack bar, laundry facilities, a pond, hiking trails, and wagon rides. Most dog breeds (call for more information) are welcome.

Derby
Char-Bo Campgrounds, Hayward Road, Derby (802-766-8807; charbo@together.net; www.char-bo.com); $18–23 per day. This very pet-friendly campground allows dogs on the beach; there are also 150 acres for running and exploring. Campsites at Char-Bo each have views of Lake Salem and the surrounding mountains, and share access to a swimming pool, an on-site pitch-and-putt golf course, picnic and field areas, and horseshoe pits.

Eden Mills
Lakeview Camping Area,
4902 Route 100, Eden Mills
(802-635-2255; 802-527-1515;
elhugh@together.net; www.lake-
viewcampingarea.com); $19 per
night. From tents to pop-up
campers and 33-foot RVs, everyone will find a spot at this North
Country campground. Most sites
have views of Lake Eden; all
have picnic tables and fire pits.
Guests can also take advantage
of beaches, playgrounds, a
dumping station, and a gift
shop/camp store. Pets are welcome without extra fees.

Enosburg Falls
**Lake Carmi State Park
Campground,** 460 Marsh Farm
Road, Enosburg Falls (802-933-
8383; 1-800-252-2363); $13–22
per night. The state's largest
campground, Lake Carmi offers
140 sites for tents and RVs (no
hookups), 35 lean-to sites, rest
rooms with showers, a dumping
station, rental boats, and walking
trails in the state park (see "Out
and About" for more park information). Animals are not allowed
in day-use areas or on the beach,
and dog owners must bring proof
of vaccination.

Grand Isle
**Grand Isle State Park
Campground,** 36 East Shore
South, Grand Isle (802-372-4300;
1-800-252-2363); $13–22 per
night. This lakefront park and
campground is the most visited
in the state with 120 sites for
tents and RVs, and 36 more with
lean-tos. Other amenities include
rest rooms with showers, a boat-
launching ramp, boats for rent,
a volleyball court, and walking
trails. Pets are not allowed in
day-use areas or on the beach,
and pet owners must bring proof
of vaccination.

Guildhall
**Maidstone Lake State Park
Campground,** 4858 Maidstone
Lake Road, Guildhall (802-676-
3930; 1-800-658-6934); $13–22 per
night. Pets are welcome to join
their owners at this 73-site campground provided they have proof
of vaccination and stay off the
beach. Sites for tents, trailers, and
RVs (no hookups) are provided,
along with flush toilets, showers,
a dumping station, and hiking
trails. (For more park information,
see "Out and About.")

Island Pond
**Brighton State Park
Campground,** 102 State Park
Road, Island Pond (802-723-4360;
1-800-658-6934); $13–22 per
night. Looking to get away from
it all? There's not much to do at
this Northeast Kingdom campground except enjoy the wildlife,
forest, water, and peace and
quiet. Campers can choose from
63 sites for tents and RVs, and
21 sites with lean-tos. Amenities
include rest rooms with showers,
a dump station, and hiking trails.
Dogs are not allowed on the
beach, and owners must bring
proof of vaccination.

South Hero
Apple Island Resort, Route 2,
South Hero (802-372-5398);
$22–45 per night or $130–270 per
week. Tent sites, RV sites, and
cabins are all available at Apple
Island, where campers can take
advantage of a swimming pool,

laundry facilities, a game room with a TV, a playground, a camp store, and a nearby marina and deli. Quiet, leashed, well-behaved dogs are always welcome.

Camp Skyland on Lake Champlain, 398 South Street, South Hero (802-372-4200); $18 per night. There are no extra fees for pets at this family campground, but owners are required to use a leash, clean up after their animals, and not leave them unattended at any time. Campers can enjoy boat rentals, rest rooms with showers, laundry facilities, a game room, and a lending library. Rustic cabins are also available for rent; call for details.

Underhill Center
Underhill State Park Campground, Underhill Center (802-899-3022; 1-800-252-2363); $13–22 per night. Ideal for tent campers looking for a quiet spot, this fairly small campground has 11 sites for tents and 6 sites with lean-tos. A separate camping area with nine lean-to sites is reserved for groups. The campground has flush toilets and water, but no showers. Dogs must have proof of vaccination. (For more information on the state park, see "Out and About.")

Waterbury
Little River State Park Campground, 3444 Little River Road, Waterbury (802-244-7103; 1-800-658-6934); $13–22 per night. This large campground set inside Mount Mansfield State Forest offers 81 sites for tenters

and RVers (no hookups), along with 20 lean-to sites, rest rooms with showers, a playground, a boat launch, boat rentals, and hiking trails. Dogs are not allowed in day-use areas, and pet owners must show proof of vaccination.

Homes, Cottages, and Cabins for Rent

Eden Mills
Eden Mountain Lodge and Cottage, 1390 Square Road, Eden Mills (802-635-9070; edenlodge@ sover.net; www.edenmountain-lodge.com); $950–1,400 per week. "Dogs are number one at this place," says Eden Mountain Lodge owner Jim Blair, a champion musher who provides dogsledding lessons and trips for interested guests. Choose from the log cabin–style lodge or the cottage. Each is fully furnished, can accommodate up to six people, and has porches and modern kitchens.

North Hero
Beachfront Home, North Hero (802-658-8358; bernsconi@-adelphia.net); $1,500–1,800 per week. A sandy beach, three bedrooms, picture windows, a dock, a mooring, and a boat launch are all available to renters at this Lake Champlain house. Other amenities include air-conditioning, a full kitchen, a fireplace, a TV/VCR, a stereo and CD player, and lake views. Pets are welcome with an additional security deposit.

Stowe

Edson Hill View, Edson Hill Road, Stowe (802-253-4337; obrienoslo@aol.com; www.obrienoslo.bizland.com); $500–700 per night. This 3,500-square-foot home has four bedrooms, Scandinavian furnishings, several fireplaces, a two-car garage, a living room, a den, whirlpool tubs in the bathrooms, and a hot tub outside. Surrounding the house are 5 acres of woods, fields, and mountain views. In the summer, the owners operate it as a B&B for $85–110 per night. Pets are welcome.

Hidden Rose, c/o the Burgundy Rose, Route 100, Stowe (802-253-7768; 1-800-989-7768; info@theburgundyrose.com; www.theburgundyrose.com); $400–450 per night or $2,400–2,700 per week. This four-bedroom, three-bathroom vacation home can accommodate up to 10 people with a full kitchen, a whirlpool bath, TV and VCR, laundry facilities, a piano, and 9 acres for exploring. Two horses live on-site; your pet is also welcome and can feel free to use the dog run and doghouse. The owner also runs a neighboring inn called the **Burgundy Rose** (see page 200 for more information).

Restored Antique Cape, Stowe (802-253-7055; eroberts@pshift.com); $500–550 per night. Located close to Mount Mansfield State Forest, ski areas, and Stowe Village, this cheery yellow home has three bedrooms, two bathrooms, a full kitchen, a washer and dryer, a fireplace, a stereo and CD player, and a canoe for guests' use. Most pets are welcome with prior approval.

Waterbury Center

1836 Cabins, Route 100, Waterbury Center (802-244-8533; cabin1836@together.net); www.1836cabins.com); $79–139 per night or $475–955 per week. Located on 200 private acres, the furnished cabins at this Stowe-area property have living rooms and dining rooms, full kitchens and bathrooms, decks with barbecue grills, and color TVs. The deluxe versions are larger with a few more amenities. Cross-country ski trails wind through the woods, and leashed pets are welcome.

West Danville

Waterfront Cottage, Joe's Pond, West Danville (802-446-2640; 802-273-2222; mobrien@vermontel.net); $985 per week. Dogs are always welcome at this one-bedroom cottage overlooking Joe's Pond and the surrounding landscape. Ideal for a couple, the cottage has satellite TV, a kitchen, air-conditioning, a woodstove, an outdoor barbecue grill, and a canoe available for guests' use. (The owner, Mary Ellen O'Brien, offers another pet-friendly rental on Lake Bomoseen; see "Accommodations—Homes, Cottages, and Cabins for Rent" in "Central Vermont" for more information.)

Rental Agencies

Stowe Country Rentals, 56 Park Street, Stowe (802-253-8132; 1-800-639-1990; rent@stowe-countryrentals.com; www.stowe-countryrentals.com). "We have many pet-friendly properties," explains Stowe Country Rentals owner Mary Beth Quinn. The agency can help you locate short- and long-term rental apartments, homes, condominiums, and estates throughout the Stowe area. Check the web site for updated listings and rates.

OUT AND ABOUT

Camp Gone to the Dogs, Stowe (802-387-5673; www.camp-gone-tothe-dogs.com). Though headquartered in the southern Vermont town of Putney (see "Accommodaions—Hotels, Motels, Inns, and Bed & Breakfasts" in "Southern Vermont"), this pooch-centered camp holds its midsummer and fall sessions in Stowe. Campers and their dogs can stay on-site or at local hotels, and enjoy all meals and activities included in the camp rates, which range 850–1,250 per week. Participants can spend their time relaxing and throwing a Frisbee around or take part in as many scheduled events and classes as they want. Some of the options include guided walks and shopping trips, grooming demonstrations and workshops, obedience classes, nutrition and training lectures, "beauty" and skills contests, and costume parties. For more information, inquire with camp founder and director Honey Loring at the phone number above.

Church Street Marketplace, Burlington. This outdoor shopping area and gathering place has fountains, food vendors, restaurants with outdoor seating (see "Quick Bites"), and more than 40 clothing boutiques, art galleries, salons, bookshops, and jewelry stores. It's an upbeat place to while away an afternoon window-shopping or people-watching. Parking is available at one of the nearby garages or metered lots.

Dog Mountain, Spaulding Road, East St. Johnsbury (802-748-2700). This one-of-a-kind attraction is a must-see for all visiting (and local) dog lovers. Artist and author Stephen Huneck has transformed the hillside of his home into a studio and gallery for his canine-themed, whimsical works, which alone would be interesting enough for most of us. But the highlight of the site is the **Dog Chapel,** a nondenominational house of worship for people and their pets. Spaulding Road is located just off Route 2.

Kingdom Trails Network. Long valued by mountain bikers, this vast network of trails snakes over mountains, past meadows, and through forests for about 100 miles, offering visitors a chance to experience all the varied terrain the Northeast Kingdom has to offer. Not only bikers but also hikers, snowshoers, and cross-country skiers have taken advantage of the scenic country byways protected and maintained by the **Kingdom Trails Association.** For more information, write to the association at P.O. Box 204, East Burke, VT 05832; call 802-626-3215; e-mail info@kingdomtrails.org; or visit www.kingdomtrails.org.

Lake Carmi State Park, 460 Marsh Farm Road, Enosburg Falls (802-933-8383; 1-800-252-2363). A great spot for boating, this 7½-mile-long lake is more than 30 feet deep in some spots and is home to walleyes and northern pike. Roads leading to the campground (see "Accommodations—Campgrounds") cut through scenic bogs, forests, and wetlands: Bird-watchers, bring your binoculars. Dogs must stay off the beach and out of day-use areas.

Lake Champlain Ferries. Headquarters: King Street Dock, Burlington (802-864-9804; lct@ferries.com; www.ferries.com). Leashed or crated pets are allowed on board Lake Champlain Transportation Company's ferries, which run on three main routes: Burlington, Vermont, to Port Kent, New York; Grand Isle, Vermont, to Plattsburgh, New York; and Charlotte, Vermont, to Essex, New York.

Long Trail. Created and maintained by the **Green Mountain Club** (GMC), this Canada-to-Massachusetts trail winds its way throughout Vermont and is the oldest long-distance hiking trail in the United States. In the northern part of the state, the GMC recommends the hike past **Lake Willoughby** and **Mount Hor;** the **Babcock Trail** and **Big Muddy Pond** area near Belvidere Center; and the **Lake Mansfield Trail** in the Stowe area. For more hiking ideas and maps, call 802-244-7037 or visit www.greenmountain-club.org.

Maidstone Lake State Park, 4858 Maidstone Lake Road, Guildhall (802-676-3930; 1-800-658-6934). One of wildest parks in Vermont, Maidstone provides visitors with plenty of opportunities for hiking, boating, fishing, and swimming. Wildlife-watchers will want to keep an eye out for endangered loons, which rear their chicks in the deep Maidstone Lake. Dogs are not allowed in day-use areas or on the beach.

Mutt Strutt, Stowe. An annual fund-raising event organized by the **North Country Animal League,** the Mutt Strutt usually takes place in Stowe in July and includes crazy costume contests, pet-supply vendors, entertainment, and children's activities. For up-dated information on this year's date and location, call the league at 802-888-5065, stop t their office at 3524 Laporte Road in Morris-ville, or visit www. ncal.com.

St. Albans Drive-In Theater, Route 7, St. Albans (802-524-2468). One of New England's few remaining drive-ins, the St. Albans theater provides a bit of Hollywood in northern Vermont.

Your pooch might be hoping for *Snow Dogs* or *101 Dalmations,* but we can't promise anything.

Scenic Drives. So many lovely roads, so little time . . . For starters, try **Route 2** through Grand Isle and Lake Champlain; **Route 5** from Barton to West Burke; **Route 105** from Newport to Island Pond; and **Route 100** through Stowe and Morrisville.

Stoweflake Hot Air Balloon Festival, Stowe. One of Vermont's most popular annual events, this Stowe festival draws thousands of spectators to its colorful show of hot-air balloons rising into the summer sky. For updated dates and times, call 802-253-2232 or visit www.stoweflake.com.

Stowe Recreational Path, Stowe. This much-loved, 5.3-mile-long path is frequented year-round by bikers, walkers, joggers, cross-country skiers, in-line skaters, and anyone else looking for breath of fresh air. With wonderful mountain views, the trail winds through woods, open areas, and the shops at Stowe Village. Dogs are welcome on a leash.

Underhill State Park, Underhill

Center (802-899-3022; 1-800-252-2363). This park is best known for its hiking trails that climb the challenging **Mount Mansfield.** You can climb all the way to the top or take more leisurely loops; the famous **Long Trail** (see previous page) passes through here, as well. Dogs are not allowed in day-use areas. If you plan to stay a while, consider the on-site campground (see "Accommodations—Campgrounds").

Vermont City Marathon, Burlington. Get your paper cups of water ready for this huge annual event drawing runners from around the world. The 26.2-mile-long race is sponsored by KeyBank and takes place in downtown Burlington each May. For more information, call 1-800-880-8149 or visit www.vcm.org.

Waterfront Boat Rentals, Perkins Pier, Maple Street, Burlington (802-864-4858; 1-877-964-4858). Set out onto Lake Champlain with a rowboat, kayak, canoe, skiff, or Boston Whaler: All are available for rent at this full-service facility. Rates range $10–60 per hour, $25–150 for four-hour trips, and $35–225 for eight-hour trips.

QUICK BITES

Apple Farm Market, Route 2, South Hero (802-372-6611). Take a break for an ice cream, snack, or meal at the Apple Farm Market's outdoor picnic tables, or stop in for fresh Vermont-made food and products.

Bagel Depot, 1216 Railroad Street, St. Johnsbury (802-748-8215). This is a quick stop for fresh-baked bagels, either toasted with cream cheese, butter, jelly, or other toppings or made into thick deli-style sandwiches.

B&W Snack Bar, Route 5, Orleans (802-754-8579). B&W offers affordable finger foods, sandwiches, seafood, burgers, and other roadside snacks; grab a meal to go and hit the road.

Bonz, Brooklyn Street, Morrisville (802-888-6283). No, it's not for dogs; despite the canine-enticing name, Bonz is actually a barbecue and sandwich restaurant designed just for humans. The inexpensive, tasty dishes are available for take-out.

Church Street Marketplace, Burlington. If you're going to be in the Burlington area, this is the place to go for food and fun with your pooch. The marketplace is lined with food vendors and outdoor restaurants, including (just to name a few) the Liquid Energy Café, Uncommon Grounds Coffee and Tea, Bimini Bill's, Ben & Jerry's, and the Church Street Tavern. Park in one of the nearby garages or metered lots.

Greenstreet's, 30 Main Street, Burlington (802-862-4930). Enjoy seasonal outdoor dining at this waterfront café serving soups, salads, burgers, gyros and panini sandwiches, beef and chicken, pasta, vegetarian dishes, and seafood; for dessert, check out the ice cream bar.

Hi Boy Sandwich Shop, 60 Broad Street, Lyndonville (802-626-8685). Take-out is a popular option at Hi Boy, a sandwich shop and restaurant where you can order hot and cold meat, cheese, and veggie creations along with pizza and snacks.

Pub Outback, 482 Route 114, East Burke (802-626-1188). Pet owners often take advantage of the outdoor seating area at this casual, friendly restaurant; menu selections include "fajita pitas"; Texas, Mexican, and veggie burgers; steaks, chicken, and seafood dishes; and special kids' meals.

Warner's Snack Bar, Route 7, St. Albans (802-527-2377). This ultra-casual spot offers fried foods, sandwiches, cold drinks, and other nourishment for hungry travelers: Enjoy your meal with your pet at the outdoor picnic tables.

HOT SPOTS FOR SPOT

Canine Care, Mannsview Inn, 916 Route 108, Jeffersonville (802-899-8321; 1-888-937-MANN; rsvp@mannsview.com; www. mannsview.com). Located on the property of the historic **Mannsview Inn B&B** (see "Accommodations—Hotels, Motels, Inns, and Bed & Breakfasts"), this new kennel provides boarding and day care for visiting and local canines. The dogs have indoor and outdoor play areas, and owners can take advantage of flexible hours for drop-off and pickup.

Doggie Daycare, 59 Industrial Avenue, Williston (802-860-1144; pat@doggiedaycare.com; www.doggiedaycare.com). This active and *inter*active facility has four play yards, climbing and playground equipment, wading pools, and grooming facilities. Dogs play together and socialize with staffers while their owners are out and about. Day-care rates range from about $13 per day to $58 per week. Overnight boarding rates range from $25 per night to $150 per week.

Dogs Etc. Grooming and Pet Care, 782 South Main Street, Stowe (802-253-2547). This grooming shop offers cuts, clips, and shampoos along with a doggie day-care service ($2 per hour), a small retail shop selling food and supplies, and a self-service dog wash area where you can scrub your pooch yourself and leave the mess behind.

Johnson Farm and Garden, 1442 Route 15, Johnson (802-888-7282). As the biggest pet-supply store in the region, this shop sells food and supplies for companion and farm animals along with plants, yard tools, and other outdoor necessities.

Noah's Ark Pet Center, 6 Roosevelt Highway, Colchester (802-655-0421; ewoody1229@aol.com). With 10,000 square feet of treats, shampoos, chew toys, catnip, animal-care books, leashes and collars, bowls and food, this full-line pet shop has

everything you might need for your dog, cat, fish, reptile, bird, or hamster.

Pet Food Warehouse, 2455 Shelburne Road, **Shelburne** (802-985-3302; www.pfwvt.com); 2500 Williston Road, **South Burlington** (802-862-5514; www.pfwvt.com). These two locally owned shops sell biscuits, rawhides, dog and cat beds, animal coats and sweaters, kennels and crates, grooming supplies, cat litter, bird food, magazines and books, and more than 25 brands of pet food. The South Burlington location also offers a Pet Wash Express service, in which owners wash their own pets in the store's tubs.

See Spot Run, 3357 Route 108, Jeffersonville (802-644-8055; dogkeep@sover.net). Canines get their own vacation at this active "dog camp" and day-care service in Jeffersonville. Four-legged visitors interact and play with each other in a 1-acre fenced area complete with two wading pools and indoor areas where dogs are welcome on the furniture. Previsit interviews and reservations are necessary: "I don't just take anyone," explains owner Tracie Korol. "And I pick favorites for house time and go-to-the-back-and-get-a-cookie-day." Rates are typically $20 per day.

IN CASE OF EMERGENCY

Companion Animal Care,
54 Western Avenue, St. Johnsbury (802-748-2855).

Green Mountain Animal Hospital,
1372 North Avenue, Burlington (802-658-3739).

Lamoille Valley Veterinary Services,
278 Route 15, Hyde Park (802-888-7911).

Newport Veterinary Hospital,
246 Route 45, Newport (802-334-2655).

Tanneberger Veterinary Hospital,
997 Fairfax Road, St. Albans (802-524-2001).

New Hampshire

Southern New Hampshire

PET-FRIENDLY RATING: 🦴 🦴 🦴

Hoping to visit the New Hampshire seashore with your pet? Good luck. This small stretch of coastline, long popular with sunbathers, is about as pet-*un*friendly as a place can be. There's a hotel or motel around every corner in the Hampton Beach area, but most innkeepers and motel owners don't allow pets. In addition, animals are not welcome on the beaches or at the nearby Strawbery Banke outdoor living-history museum and the waterfront Prescott Park, both in Portsmouth.

Inland, pet-loving travelers fare slightly better. The Merrimack Valley region, home of the state capital, Concord, and the cities of Nashua and Manchester, does offer a few chain-style accommodations, though this isn't a popular area for tourism. Your best bet for a vacation is the Monadnock region, located in the southwest corner of the state, which offers the vast majority of the area's animal-friendly lodgings. Many of those that do swing open their doors (and doggie doors) to you and your four-legged friends boast homey atmospheres in country settings, friendly innkeepers, and antique architecture. And once you've found a place to stay, you and Rover can set out for mountain hiking, canoeing, covered-bridge crossing, leaf peeping, and other outdoorsy pursuits. Day trips across the border to Vermont are also popular with visitors to the Quiet Corner of New Hampshire.

ACCOMMODATIONS

Hotels, Motels, Inns, and Bed & Breakfasts

Ashuelot
Crestwood Chapel and Pavilion, 400 Scofield Mountain Road, Ashuelot (603-239-6393; info@ crestwood-e.com; www.crest-wood-e.com); $250–350 per night. This luxury retreat is surrounded by flower gardens, fruit trees, and 200 acres of walking paths and woods. B&B guests stay at either the pavilion or the chapel; both include a daily breakfast cooked to order, afternoon snacks, feather beds, kitchens, satellite TV, and whirlpool baths. Massage, beauty, and fitness services can also be arranged. Pets are always welcome.

Bedford
Wayfarer Inn and Conference Center, 121 South River Road, Bedford (603-622-3766; 1-877-489-3658); $89–169 per night. Located at the historic site of John Goffe's Mill, the Wayfarer Inn has 194 guest rooms with in-room cof-feemakers, irons, and hair dryers. Other inn amenities include a covered bridge, a pond, water-falls, daily breakfasts, indoor and outdoor swimming pools, a fit-ness center, and a restaurant and lounge. Pets are welcome for an extra $25 per night.

Chesterfield
Chesterfield Inn, Route 9, Chesterfield (603-256-3211; 1-800-365-5515; chstinn@sover.net; www.chesterfieldinn.com); $150–275 per night. This upscale country inn offers whirlpool baths, private decks and terraces, fireplaces, landscaped grounds with gardens, scenic views, refrigerators, air-conditioning, and full gourmet breakfasts made with herbs from the garden and local produce. Pets are welcome in 6 of the inn's 15 guest rooms.

Concord
Best Western Concord, 97 Hall Street, Concord (603-228-4300; 1-800-528-1234); $79–119 per night. For an extra $10 per night, your pet can join you at this Concord hotel with a swimming pool, a fitness center, laundry facilities, in-room coffeemakers and alarm clocks, cable TV, and free morning newspapers. Smoking and nonsmoking rooms are available.

Comfort Inn Concord, 71 Hall Street, Concord (603-226-4100;

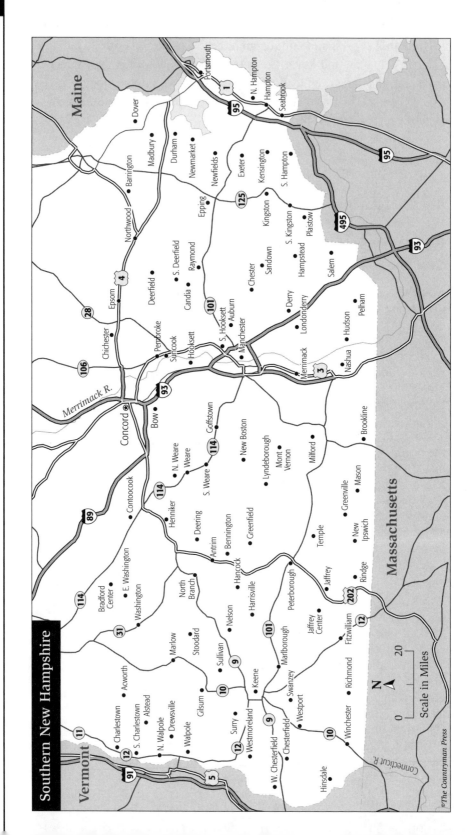

Southern New Hampshire

©The Countryman Press

1-800-228-5150); $69–149 per night. Located in the state capital, this Comfort Inn offers an indoor swimming pool, cable TV and in-room movies, free continental breakfasts, laundry facilities, and a car-rental desk. Pets are welcome for an additional $10 per night.

Durham
Hickory Pond Inn and Golf Course, 1 Stagecoach Road, Durham (603-659-2227; 1-800-658-0065; hickorypondinn@aol.com; www.hickorypondinn.com); $69–129 per night. This longtime pet-friendly inn has a relaxed atmosphere, individually decorated guest rooms, cozy gathering rooms, and a greenhouse-style dining room where continental breakfasts are served each morning. The historic building sits next to a par-3 golf course, where a dog-walking path winds through the greens. Guests can also enjoy computer workstations, air-conditioning, cable TV, and private baths. Pets are welcome in designated rooms without extra fees.

Exeter
Colonial Hearthside Inn, 137 Portsmouth Avenue (Route 108), Exeter (603-772-3794; www.colonialhearthside.com); $85–115 per night. This seacoast-area hotel offers its guests a swimming pool and 32 rooms with cable TV, microwaves, refrigerators, double beds, air-conditioning, and data ports. Exeter Academy, outlet shopping, and Hampton Beach are all nearby. Animal owners sign a pet-policy agreement form and pay an extra $10 per night.

Francestown
Inn at Crotched Mountain, 534 Mountain Road, Francestown (603-588-6840); $70–140 per night. Children and pets are always welcome at this homey, 13-room country inn. The three resident English cocker spaniels will show you around the 1800s home and the property's on-site walking and cross-country skiing trails, flower and vegetable gardens, swimming pool, and tennis courts. Guests will also enjoy the views of the mountain and surrounding valley.

Hampton
Inn of Hampton, 815 Lafayette Road, Hampton (603-926-6771; 1-800-556-4638); $110–190 per night. Amenities at this coastal hotel include an indoor swimming pool, a hot tub, a fitness center, a restaurant, and a lounge. Guests can choose from standard guest rooms, executive-level rooms, or deluxe suites. Pets are permitted in smoking rooms without extra charges.

Stone Gable Inn, 869 Lafayette Road, Hampton (603-926-6883; 1-800-737-6606); $59–89 per night. The Stone Gable offers economy lodging near the action of Hampton Beach with cable TV; in-room refrigerators, microwaves, and coffeemakers; air-conditioning, and free local calls. Pets are welcome for short-term stays only (one or two nights) with a refundable deposit of $25.

Hancock
Hancock Inn, 33 Main Street, Hancock (1-800-525-1789; innkeeper@hancockinn.com; www.hancockinn.com); $215–235 per night. Dating to 1789, the Hancock Inn is New Hampshire's oldest continuously operating accommodation. Pet

guests are welcome in the Drovers Room, a suite on the first floor with a patio, antique furniture, a king-sized bed, and a fireplace. Guests also enjoy full country breakfasts, gathering room parlors, and a tavern.

Keene

Holiday Inn Express Keene, 175 Key Road, Keene (603-352-7616); $69–123 per night. Pets are allowed in smoking rooms for an extra $10 per night at this Holiday Inn Express, which features a 24-hour front desk, a fitness center, a swimming pool, laundry facilities, cable TV, and free local calls and morning newspapers.

Manchester

Center of New Hampshire Holiday Inn, 700 Elm Street, Manchester (603-625-1000); $108–165 per night. Pets are allowed at the Manchester Holiday Inn for an extra $25 per night; the hotel offers a gift shop, a fitness center, an indoor swimming pool and sauna, cable TV and in-room movies, a wake-up service, air-conditioning, alarm clocks, and in-room coffeemakers and irons.

Comfort Inn Manchester, 198 Queen City Avenue, Manchester (603-668-2600; 1-800-228-5150); $79–109 per night. This hotel caters to southern New Hampshire travelers with an indoor pool and sauna; laundry facilities; cable TV and VCRs; in-room microwaves, hair dryers, and irons; a newsstand; and free continental breakfasts. Pet owners must stay in smoking rooms and pay with a credit card.

TownePlace Suites by Marriott Manchester, 690 Huse Road, Manchester (603-641-2288; 1-800-627-7468); $60–140 per night. Designed for long-term stays, this Marriott facility has studio apartments and one-and two-bedroom suites; all accommodations have full kitchens. Other amenities include a swimming pool, a fitness center, valet laundry services, modem lines, and cable TV. Pets are allowed with a onetime nonrefundable fee of $175.

Merrimack

Days Inn Merrimack, 242 Daniel Webster Highway, Merrimack (603-429-4600; 1-800-544-8313); $59–89 per night. This Days Inn's amenities include in-room coffeemakers and hair dryers, a 24-hour front desk, cable TV, free local calls, laundry facilities, and modem lines in each room. Pets weighing less than 25 pounds are allowed with an extra fee of $25 per night.

Nashua

Holiday Inn Nashua, 9 Northeastern Boulevard, Nashua (603-888-1551); $89–119 per night. Companion animals are welcome without extra fees at the Nashua Holiday Inn, where the amenities include an outdoor swimming pool, room service, a fitness center, in-room coffeemakers, a wake-up service, and in-room movies. Air-conditioning, a restaurant, and a lounge are also available.

Red Roof Inn Nashua, 77 Spitbrook Road, Nashua (603-888-1893); $49–69 per night. This economy motel has clean rooms, cable TV, laundry facilities, alarm clocks, a 24-hour front desk, in-room modem lines, free newspapers, express checkout services, and free local calls. Pets are welcome without extra fees.

New London
Maple Hill Farm, 200 Newport Road, New London (603-526-2248; 1-800-231-8637; info@ maplehillfarm.com; www.maple-hillfarm.com); $90–125 per night. Pets are allowed in one designated room at Maple Hill Farm, a country-inn B&B. The room has a king-sized bed (or two twins) with antique furniture, air-conditioning, a porch, and a private entrance. Guests can enjoy homemade breakfasts (choose from continental or traditional), a hot tub, fireplaces, gathering rooms, and a deck.

Newton
Carriage Barn Equestrian Center, 6 Sarah's Way, Newton (603-382-2119; gpcnewton@aol. com; www.carriage-barn.com); $85 per night. Bring your dog or your horse to Carriage Barn, a B&B located in a restored carriage barn at Sarah's Way, a "planned equestrian community." Guests without horses can also arrange private riding lessons with the resident equines upon request. Dog owners pay an additional $10 per stay; horse owners pay an additional $25 per night for stabling.

Peterborough
Peterborough Manor Bed & Breakfast, 50 Summer Street, Peterborough (603-924-9832; himanor@weaver.mv.com; www.peterboroughmanor.com); $60–65 per night. "Well-behaved

humans and small dogs" (call to see if yours qualifies) are welcome for an extra $5 per night at this historic B&B offering sunny guest rooms with private bathrooms, quilted bedspreads, TVs, queen-sized beds, a dining room, and a library. A continental-style breakfast is served each morning.

Portsmouth
Motel 6 Portsmouth, 3 Gosling Road, Portsmouth (603-334-6606); $49–69 per night. Kids stay for free at this Motel 6, which offers cable TV, premium movie channels, laundry facilities, a swimming pool, modem hookups, and a convenient location near downtown shopping and restaurants. Pets are welcome without extra fees.

Residence Inn by Marriott Portsmouth, 1 International Drive, Portsmouth (603-436-8880; 1-800-331-3131); $189–259 per night. Business travelers are the most frequent guests at Residence Inns, which are designed for long-term stays. The Portsmouth location offers studio apartments and one- and two-bedroom suites, a swimming pool, a 24-hour front desk, a fitness center, and valet laundry services. Pets are allowed with a onetime nonrefundable deposit of $250.

Rindge
Woodbound Inn, 62 Woodbound Road, Rindge (603-532-8341; 1-800-688-7770; info@woodbound.com; www. woodbound.com); $135–199 per night. Dogs and cats are welcome guests at the Woodbound Inn's waterfront cabins. The one- and two-bedroom cabins

ONE OF SEVERAL LAKEFRONT CABIN RENTALS AT THE WOODBOUND INN IN RINDGE

are located near the main inn and have picture windows, small decks, Franklin stoves, king-sized beds, and daybeds. Guests enjoy complimentary buffet-style breakfasts in the inn's dining rooms and share access to a private sandy beach, a gift shop, the Woodbound Inn's par-3 golf course, and 18 kilometers of hiking and cross-country skiing trails in a country setting.

Salem

Red Roof Inn Salem, 15 Red Roof Lane, Salem (603-898-6422); $60–90 per night. Pets are welcome at the Salem Red Roof Inn, which offers express checkout services, cable TV, free newspapers and local calls, alarm clocks, and a 24-hour front desk. There are no extra fees for companion animals.

Temple

Auk's Nest Bed & Breakfast, East Road, Temple (603-878-3443; auksnest@cs.com); $50–70 per night. This 1700s B&B is located next to 350 protected acres with hiking and cross-country skiing trails. The three guest rooms have views of gardens and an orchard. The home also has antiques, a screened-in porch, a common room with a fireplace, and three resident dogs and a cat. Pets are welcome for an extra $5 per night; bring proof of vaccination.

Troy

Inn at East Hill Farm,
460 Monadnock Street, Troy
(603-242-6495; 1-800-242-6495;
info@east-hill-farm.com; www.
east-hill-farm.com); $78–94 per
adult, per night; $58–70 per child,
per night. This family-centered
resort keeps kids and adults busy
with three swimming pools, a
sauna, a lake beach, tennis and
shuffleboard courts, children's
recreation programs, boats, cross-
country skiing, horseback riding,
and interaction with the on-site
farm animals. Leashed dogs are
welcome in designated rooms for
an extra $10–20 per night.

Westmoreland

**Maples of Poocham Bed &
Breakfast,** Poocham Road,
Westmoreland (603-399-8457;
1-800-659-6810; host@themaples-
ofpoocham.com; www.themaples-
ofpoocham.com); $50–75 per
night. Dogs (sorry, no cats) are
welcome with prior approval at
the Maples of Poocham, provided
they are treated for fleas and
ticks, not left alone, and not
aggressive toward the resident
cats. The B&B has two guest
rooms, a front porch with chairs,
stained-glass bay windows,
antique furniture, and semi-
private bathrooms.

Wilton Center

**Stepping Stones Bed &
Breakfast,** Bennington Battle
Trail, Wilton Center (603-654-
9048; 1-888-654-9048; www.
steppingstonesbb.com); $65–75
per night. This 1700s-era restored
farmhouse B&B is surrounded by
flower gardens, walking paths,
and wildlife. Guest rooms are
decorated with colors and tex-
tures inspired by nature.
Breakfasts are served in the
sunny garden room. Your leashed
dog (sorry, no cats) is welcome
to join the dog and two cats that
already live at Stepping Stones.

Campgrounds

Allenstown

**Bear Brook State Park
Campground,** Route 28,
Allenstown (603-485-9869);
$15 per night. The 98 sites for
tents and RVs (no hookups) at
this seasonal campground are
clustered around Beaver Pond.
Camp amenities include laundry
facilities, rest rooms with showers, and a camp store. Leashed
dogs are welcome, but they are
not allowed on the beach. (See
"Out and About" for more park
information.)

Deering

Oxbow Campground, 8 Oxbow
Road, Deering (603-464-5952;
oxbow@conknet.com; www.
ucampnh/oxbow); $25–31 per
night. Along with private sites
for tents and RVs, Oxbow has a
swimming pond, a beach, a
playground, a recreation hall,
scheduled family activities, and
two camping cabins. Pets should
be leashed, quiet, and not left
unattended. "We just had an
Amazon parrot in our tenting
area, but most of our visiting
pets are dogs," explains owner
Brenda Hansen.

Greenfield

**Greenfield State Park
Campground,** Route 136,
Greenfield (603-271-3628); $16

per night. Certain sections of this large 257-site campground and park (see "Out and About") are designated for pet owners. Facilities include boat rentals, rest rooms with showers, and a camp store. RVs are welcome, though the campground has no hookups. Pets must be leashed and are not allowed on the beach.

North Hampton
Shel-Al Campground, 115 Lafayette Road, North Hampton (603-964-5730; www.shel-al.com); $18–25 per night. Tenters and RVers will both find sites at Shel-Al, a family-run campground located near beaches and other coastline attractions. Campers can also enjoy a playground, shuffleboard courts, a camp store, and rest rooms with showers. Leashed pets are welcome, provided their owners clean up after them and don't leave them alone at a site.

Rindge
Woodmore Campground, 117 Woodbound Road, Rindge (603-899-3362; info@woodmore-campground.com; www.wood-morecampground.com); $20–26 per night. The McLay family runs this waterfront campground located on Lake Contoocook; campers will find a swimming pool, tennis and basketball courts, a game room, picnic areas, a camp store, boat rentals, a playground, and scheduled activities on weekends. Dogs are welcome, but they must be leashed and owners must clean up after them.

West Swanzey
Swanzey Lake Camping Area, 88 East Shore Road, West Swanzey (603-352-9880; lobo@monad.net; www.swanzey-lake.com); $18–24 per night or $105–150 per week. "We are pet people and very much enjoy those special members of the family," says Swanzey Lake co-owner Jill Amadon. The 88 campsites can accommodate tents as well as RVs. Lake swimming, hanging out at the dock, boating, and shopping at the camp store are popular activities. Pets are not allowed on the beach or on the lawn.

Homes, Cottages, and Cabins for Rent

Harrisville
Silver Lake Cottage, Silver Lake, Harrisville (413-584-5898); $350 per night or $1,400 per week. Located on 13 acres with lake frontage, this pet-friendly rental can accommodate up to 16 people and has eight bedrooms and five bathrooms. The home also has a front porch and rocking chairs, a kitchen, a canoe and a rowboat, a fireplace, and picnic tables. "The lake is great for dogs who love to swim!" says home-owner Ruth Jacobson-Hardy.

Warner
Gossler Camps, 18 Fourth Road, Warner (603-456-3679; gossler camps@msn.com); $425–500 per week. Guests have been visiting the Gossler cabins for more than 60 years. They vary in size, but each is fully furnished with a bathroom and a kitchen, and offers views of Tucker Pond. Sailboats, canoes, kayaks, rowboats, and paddleboats are all available to guests. Leashed, quiet dogs are welcome.

OUT AND ABOUT

Abby Fund Yard Sale, Nashua. This annual gathering of shoppers and animal lovers is held each summer to benefit the **Humane Society of Greater Nashua.** Volunteers are always needed to donate items and run booths. For updated information on this year's location and date, contact the society at 24 Ferry Road, call 603-889-BARK, or visit www.hsfn.com.

Ashuelot Covered Bridge, Bolton Road, Winchester. One of the most visited covered bridges in New Hampshire, this elaborate and unique crossing was built in 1864. Its bright red roof covers two spans and lattice openings along the 169-foot-long sides.

Bear Brook State Park, Route 28, Allenstown (603-485-9874; 603-485-9869). Leashed pets are welcome (though not on the beach) at this 10,000-acre park with a campground (see "Accommodations—Campgrounds") and extensive day-use facilities, including 40 miles of hiking trails for horseback riders, hikers, dog walkers, and mountain bikers. Boat rentals, several fishing ponds, a fitness course, and target and archery ranges are also available.

Chesterfield Gorge Natural Area, Route 9, Chesterfield (603-239-8153). This relatively small 13-acre park has great views; a walking trail winds past **Wilde Brook** and the impressive **Chesterfield Gorge.** Picnic tables provide nice spots for a rest and a snack. Pets must be on a leash.

Greenfield State Park, Route 136, Greenfield (603-547-3497). Hike, boat, fish, bird-watch, or have a picnic at the 400-acre Greenfield State Park, which offers walking trails, ponds, wetlands, and forestlands. Pets are allowed in designated areas; watch for signs. The park's best-known feature is its campground (see "Accommodations—Campgrounds" for more information).

Hampton State Pier, off Route 1A, Hampton (603-436-1552). If you're in town with your pet and dying for some ocean views, the dogs-allowed pier might be one of your only chances. Located next to the Seabrook Bridge, this popular fishing and boat-launching area is a fun place to hang out and watch the busy harbor activities.

Harbour Trail, Portsmouth. Winding throughout Portsmouth's downtown and historic areas, this self-guided tour of the city takes you past the waterfront, quaint back streets, shops, restaurants, and 17-, 18th-, and 19th-century homes and churches. Guided tours are available on some weekends, and the Portsmouth Chamber of Commerce sells a Harbour Trail map for $2. For more information, call 603-436-3988 or visit www.portsmouthnh.com.

Miller State Park, Route 101, Peterborough (603-924-3672). You can drive or hike to the 2,290-foot summit of majestic **Pack Monadnock mountain,** the centerpiece of this popular park that's open daily in warm weather and on weekends in the spring and fall. Once you get to the top, there are plenty of well-marked trails of varying lengths for hikers of all abilities. Or just relax and enjoy the summit views and have a picnic at one of the provided tables. (Note: Don't confuse this mountain with the better-known Mount Monadnock down the road, where dogs are not allowed.)

Monadnock Humane Society Adoption and Learning Center, Route 10, West Swanzey. With walking trails, agility programs, doggie play areas, and a retail shop (see **Animal Tracks** under "Hot Spots for Spot"), this 74-acre site is a friendly home for local shelter animals and a fun stop for visiting pet owners. The society's annual **Walk for Animals** is its primary fund-raiser; usually held in September, the day has something for every cat and dog lover, including talent contests, a sponsored walk, and a Canine Carnival. For more information, visit www.monad-pets.com or call 603-352-9011.

Pisgah State Park, Routes 19 and 10, Chesterfield and Winchester (603-239-8153). With more than 13,000 acres, this rugged park is New Hampshire's largest. Leashed dogs are welcome to join their owners as they explore forested paths, ponds, wetlands, and marsh ecosystems. Hiking, biking, and fishing are among the most popular activities; motorized vehicles such as snowmobiles and all terrain vehicles (ATVs) are also allowed.

Urban Forestry Center, 45 Elwyn Road, Portsmouth (603-431-6774). This local gem's facilities include a 95-acre forest with self-guided trails, a tree-farm and forestry demonstration area, salt marshes, dense woodlands, and gardens filled with native wildflowers. The nature and education center is designed to promote the healthy management of New Hampshire's forest resources. Dogs are welcome on a leash; the staff even provides environmentally friendly "mutt mitts" to clean up messes.

QUICK BITES

Albees On Amherst, 36 Amherst Street, Manchester (603-623-6907). Whether you're staying in Manchester or just passing through, Albees is a good bet for fresh deli sandwiches, snacks, coffee, and cold drinks to go. Locals praise the friendly service in particular.

Barley House, 132 North Main Street, Concord (603-228-6363). Visiting the State House for business or pleasure? The Barley House is right across the street. You can order lunch or dinner to go from its pub-style menu, with items like firecracker shrimp cocktail, the State House Caesar salad, and smoked pork chops.

Café Brioche, 14 Market Square, Portsmouth (603-430-9225). This downtown café is best known for its pastries and desserts, though you can also enjoy soups, stews, bisques, salads, pizza, and deli sandwiches at the outdoor sidewalk seating.

Keene Fresh Salad, 44 Main Street, Keene (603-357-6677). Here's a healthy stop for greens, veggies, hot and cold drinks, soups, and a good selection of quick entrées. Grab a take-out lunch to enjoy on your hike—or drive—up Pack Monadnock.

Kimball Farm, Route 124, Jaffrey (603-532-5765). If you passed through the Monadnock region without a visit to Kimball's, you'd

be among the minority; this famous ice cream shop serves its cool treats (more than 40 homemade flavors) from take-out windows with plenty of outdoor picnic tables. Expect a crowd.

Lucky Panda, 2 Pauls Way, Amherst (603-598-6555). If you're staying nearby, the Lucky Panda will deliver; if you're just driving through, stop in for take-out Chinese meals made with chicken, beef, seafood, and rice (and a fortune cookie, of course).

Main Street Restaurants, Durham. Popular with the local college crowd, this strip of coffee shops, bars, and restaurants offers plenty of sidewalk seating in warm weather and take-out meals year-round. Try a slice at **Joe's NY Style Pizza** and watch all the local dogs trot by.

HOT SPOTS FOR SPOT

Animal Tracks, Monadnock Humane Society (MHS), Route 10, West Swanzey (603-352-9011; www.monadpets.com). Located at the **MHS Adoption and Learning Center** (see "Out and About"), this well-stocked retail shop has gift items like mugs and picture frames, along with pet toys, beds, bowls, leashes and collars, and food. All proceeds benefit the animals at the shelter.

At Home With Rover, East Swanzey (603-313-4663). Erik Salyer, the owner of this pet-

sitting business, can provide short-term care for your pet, including walks, feedings, and playtimes, while you're involved with humans-only activities: He charges $10 per half-hour visit and $3 for each additional 15 minutes.

Canine Cupboard Gourmet Dog Treats, 102 State Street, Portsmouth (603-431-0082). Barkin' Brownies, carob-flavored muffins, pooch-friendly cupcakes, and peanut butter pies are just some of the gourmet canine treats you'll find at this State Street bakery for dogs. Gift items for pet lovers are also available.

Granite State Dog Training Center, 90 Route 101A, Amherst (603-672-DOGS). In addition to its extensive training programs, Granite State also offers overnight boarding and doggie day care in heated and air-conditioned indoor/outdoor runs, as well as shampoos, cuts, clips, and other grooming services.

It's Raining Cats and Dogs, 13 Commercial Alley, Portsmouth (603-430-9566). Located in a shady, shop-filled alley in the downtown area, this cozy store offers breed-specific gifts, treats for dogs and cats, magnets, greeting cards, T-shirts, housewares, and other fun items for animal lovers.

Nestled Inn Boarding Kennel, 537 Old Homestead Highway, East Swanzey (603-357-3300; www.nestledinnboardingkennel.com). Dogs and cats are welcome at this Monadnock-region kennel, which offers seven-day-a-week service with overnight boarding and doggie day care in indoor/outdoor kennels, in addition to full grooming services.

Noah's Animal Care, Manchester area (603-623-6624; cmoore@nac-nh.com; www.nac-nh.com). The staffers at this pet-sitting service, owned by Bill and Carolyn Moore, will come to you at your rental home or hotel room to walk your pet, feed him, administer medication, or perform other necessary services. Rates vary depending on the services requested.

Proper Canine Training and Boarding, 759 Daniel Webster Highway, Merrimack (603-424-6166; www.properk9.com). This heated and air-conditioned kennel has indoor/outdoor runs for dogs and a separate area for cats. Training programs are also available, as are brushing, clipping, washing, and other grooming services. Boarding rates start at $14 per night for dogs and $10 per night for cats.

IN CASE OF EMERGENCY

Animal Hospital of Nashua,
168 Main Dunstable Road, Nashua (603-880-3034).

Court Street Veterinary Hospital,
686 Court Street, Keene (603-357-2455).

Great Bay Animal Hospital,
31 Newmarket Road, Durham (603-868-7387).

Jaffrey–Rindge Veterinary Clinic,
109 River Street, Jaffrey (603-532-7114).

North Hampton Animal Hospital,
83 Lafayette Road, North Hampton (603-964-7222).

Russell Animal Hospital,
286 Pleasant Street, Concord (603-224-2361).

Central New Hampshire

Lake Winnipesaukee's busy shoreline has attracted New England visitors for years with affordable accommodations, water slides, video arcades, go-cart tracks, campgrounds, boat rentals, and other family-centered activities and events. Finding a place to stay here is not a problem—unless you're visiting with Rover. "There must be a hundred motels within a mile of us," says one animal-friendly motel owner, "and only one or two allow pets." Still, with that many accommodations to start with, the odds are in your favor of finding at least one "pets allowed" lodging you'll like—and one is all you need. Hotels and motels are not as plentiful in the western reaches, home to renowned Dartmouth College and Lake Sunapee, but this quieter area appeals to those looking to escape the Winnipesaukee crowds.

Activities for pet owners are not plentiful in central New Hampshire. Many of the attractions are indoors, and even most of the outdoor nature centers, boat tours, and town fairs ban companion animals. Also, don't assume that a STATE PARK sign is a green light for dogs: Only certain state parks allow pets (see "Out and About"), and then only on a leash. That's not to say there's nothing to do in central New Hampshire with your dog: Scenic drives, canoe trips, quiet walks in the woods, geology lessons, and bustling downtown scenes are plentiful enough to fill up at least one restful and fun vacation in this beautiful region of the state.

ACCOMMODATIONS

Hotels, Motels, Inns, and Bed & Breakfasts

Ashland
Black Horse Motor Court, Route 3, Ashland (603-968-7116; www.blackhorsemotorcourt.com); $48–79 per night. Black Horse offers a wide variety of accommodation choices, including motel suites, one-room cottages, and one- and two-bedroom cottages. Guests have access to a sandy beach, rowboats, and shuffleboard courts; hiking trails, golf courses, and ski resorts are nearby. Pets are allowed for an extra $10 per night or $40 per week.

Bradford
Mountain Lake Inn, Bradford (603-938-5622; 1-800-662-6005; innkeeper@mountainlakeinn.com; www.mountainlakeinn.com); $70–85 per night or $600 per week. The Mountain Lake Inn dog, Snoopy, and two cats, Midnight and Trouble, welcome your pooch (sorry, no cats) to their 1800s Colonial set on 168 hilltop acres. The B&B has a

Currier and Ives decor, nine guest rooms with private baths, a barbecue area, hiking trails, and a private beach. Two rooms and a cabin are set aside for pet owners.

Bradley Lake
Owl's Nest Lodge and Conference Center, Bradley Lake, Andover (603-735-5159; owlsnest@tds.com; www.whoooo.com); cottages, $600 per week; lodge, $55 per person, per weekend. Well-behaved pets are welcome in the Owl's Nest's two cottages, which have private docks, canoes, kitchens, and porches, as well as at the lodge, which is designed to accommodate large groups (up to 50 people) with seven bunk rooms, a dining area, a large kitchen, and a deck. Dogs must be on a leash.

Center Harbor
Kona Mansion Inn, Kona Road, Center Harbor (603-253-4900); $105 per night or $495–795 per week. Pets are welcome in one of the inn's rooms, all four cottages, and both A-frame chalets. Set beside Lake Winnipesaukee, the

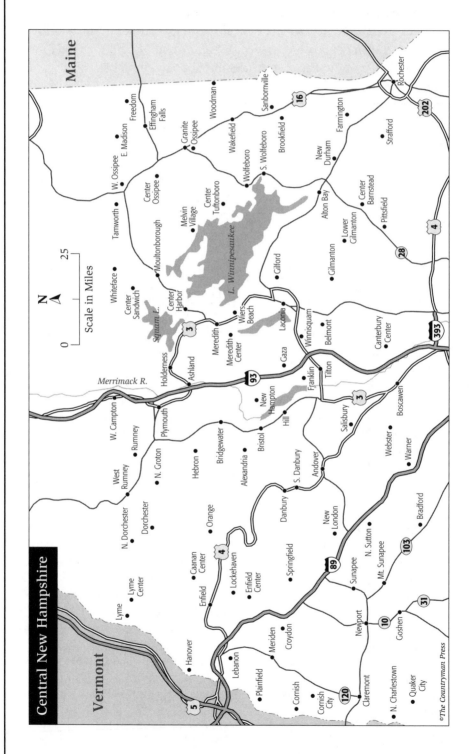

Central New Hampshire

©The Countryman Press

resort offers a private beach and docks, a par-3 golf course, tennis courts, dining rooms, and a lounge. Each chalet has three bedrooms and a kitchen; the cottages range in size from one to two bedrooms, all with kitchens.

Lake Shore Motel and Cottages, Route 25, Center Harbor (603-253-6244); $100–150 per night. Choose from motel rooms and cottages at this family-oriented accommodation. Each cottage unit has a screened-in porch, a full kitchen, and cable TV. The motel building has efficiencies and two- and three-room suites, all with air-conditioning. Well-behaved dogs are welcome as long as their owners clean up after them.

Enfield

Mary Keane House, Route 4A, Lower Shaker Village, Enfield (1-888-239-2153; mary.keane. house@valley.net; www.mary-keanehouse.com); $95–155 per night. Over the years, the Mary Keane House has welcomed dogs, cats, guinea pigs, and one cockatiel; animals are welcome in the first-floor suite, called Griselda, which features a private entrance, a queen-sized bed, antique furnishings, Victorian decor, and a separate sitting room with a pullout couch and a covered porch with a glider swing.

Franklin

D. K. Motel, 390 North Main Street, Franklin (603-934-3311); $60–85 per night. For an additional $5–10 per night, your pet is welcome in smoking rooms at D. K. Motel (so named because it

offers double and king-sized beds). The motel is located at the end of a dead-end road and has a large fenced-in yard; Sky, a Siamese cat, and four parakeets already call D. K. home.

Georges Mills

Georges Mills Cottages, Georges Mills (603-763-2369; info@georgesmillscottages.com; www.georgesmillscottages.com); $75–145 per night or $395–795 per week. Leashed dogs (sorry, no cats) are welcome in the cottages, suites, and town houses at this waterfront family resort between Otter Pond and Lake Sunapee. Some units have screened-in porches and balconies; all have kitchens, living rooms, and dining rooms. Guests share access to a beach and docks. Dogs should be with their owners at all times.

Loudon

Lovejoy Farm Bed & Breakfast, 268 Lovejoy Road, Loudon (603-783-4007; 1-888-783-4007; info@lovejoy-inn.com; www.love-joy-inn.com); $74–99 per night. This tastefully decorated accommodation has antique furnishings, Oriental rugs, original stenciling, and four-poster beds; all the modern amenities are available as well. Full country breakfasts are served in the dining room each morning. Well-behaved pets are welcome as long as they are not left alone in the rooms.

Red Roof Inn, 519 Route 106, Loudon (603-225-8399; 1-800-RED-ROOF); $62–69 per night. One "small" pet (call to see if yours qualifies) per room is welcome at this Red Roof Inn, which offers an indoor swimming pool, interior corridors, complimentary continental breakfasts, alarm clocks, and cable TV with premium movie channels.

Meredith

Town Line Motel, 4 Daniel Webster Highway, Meredith (603-366-5570); $49–89 per night. "We have pets and we travel, so we know how tough it is to find a place," explains Town Line Motel owner Nancy Brown, who manages and cleans the 16-room motel with her husband. Amenities include an outdoor swimming pool, color TVs, and air-conditioning. Pets are welcome without extra fees.

Mount Sunapee

Mount Sunapee Best Western Sunapee Lake Lodge, 1403 Route 103, Mount Sunapee (603-763-2010; 1-800-606-5253; info@sunapeelakelodge.com; www.sunapeelakelodge.com); $89–229 per night. This hotel has a good location for those hoping to explore the Dartmouth–Sunapee Lake region. The lodge's features include a swimming pool, a fitness center, free continental breakfasts, a restaurant and lounge, standard rooms and deluxe suites, cable TV, and air-conditioning. Leashed pets are allowed in designated rooms with advance notice.

Newport

Newport Motel, Route 11, Newport (603-863-1440; 1-800-741-2619; info@newportmotel-nh.com; www.newportmotelnh.com); $60–80 per night. Shang, the Newport Motel's resident pooch and "staff member," was rescued from the local animal shelter. He'll welcome you and your canine to this clean, welcoming motel, which offers continental breakfasts, a snack and coffee counter, and standard and deluxe rooms. The motel's most unusual feature is its rates, which don't go up in the summer.

Plymouth

Pilgrim Inn and Cottages, 307 Main Street (Route 3), Plymouth (603-536-1319; www.pilgriminn.com); $40–145 per night. For an extra $10 per night, you're welcome to bring your pet to the cottages at Pilgrim Inn. Some units have kitchens. The innkeepers can also arrange "golf and stay" packages with three nearby courses, and "ski and stay" packages with Tenney Mountain and Waterville Valley ski areas. Animal must be crated when left alone in cottages.

Rochester

Anchorage Inn, 13 Wadleigh Road, Rochester (603-332-3350; www.anchorageinns.com); $59–109 per night. Pets are welcome for an additional $10 per night at the Anchorage Inn's Rochester location, which offers a swimming pool, cable TV with premium movie channels, air-conditioning, standard rooms, and kitchenette units. You and Spot can roam the property's walking trails and wide lawns, and enjoy its pond during your visit.

Governor's Inn, 78 Wakefield Street, Rochester (603-332-0107; info@governorsinn.com; www.governorsinn.com); $78–168 per night. A popular site for weddings, the historic Governor's Inn offers 20 upscale, individually decorated guest rooms with private baths, air-conditioning, cable TV, luxurious furnishings, an on-site restaurant, and daily continental breakfasts. Several rooms are set aside for pet owners.

Salisbury

Horse Haven Bed & Breakfast, 462 Raccoon Hill Road, Salisbury (603-648-2101; horsehavenbb@ mail.tds.net; www.bbonline.com/ nh/horsehaven); $65–75 per night. It's hard enough finding a place that welcomes your dog; imagine doing the same with your horse. At Horse Haven B&B you can bring both; animal lover and innkeeper Velma Emery welcomes equines to her stables and canines to her comfortable farmhouse. Amenities include daily breakfasts, an outdoor deck, and a dog-agility area. Riding and walking trails, cross-country skiing, snowmobiling, and boating are all available nearby. Dog owners pay an extra $10 per stay; horse owners pay an extra $15 per night.

Dexter's Inn and Tennis Club, 258 Stagecoach Road, Sunapee (603-763-5571; 1-800-232-5571; dexters@tds.net; www.bbhost. com/dextersinn); $130–195 per night. Pets are allowed in some of the 19 guest rooms at Dexter's, an 1800s restored farmhouse with noted gardens, tennis courts, a library, fireplaces, TVs with VCRs, a piano, a swimming pool, mountain views, a screened-in porch, and gathering rooms. Full country breakfasts are served each morning.

ONE OF THE GUEST ROOMS AT THE HORSE HAVEN BED & BREAKFAST IN SALISBURY

Tamworth

Tamworth Inn, 15 Cleveland Hill Road, Tamworth (603-323-7721; 1-800-642-7352; tamworthinn@ firstbridge.net; www.tamworth. com); $115–290 per night. Dagny, the resident St. Bernard, is the four-legged welcoming committee at the Tamworth Inn, a historic accommodation with antiques, private baths, down comforters, a swimming pool, and daily country breakfasts. Well-behaved pets are welcome for an additional $10 per day, provided they are not left unattended in the rooms at any time.

Weirs Beach

Channel Waterfront Cottages, 1192 Weirs Boulevard (Route 3), Weirs Beach (603-366-4673; www.channelcottages.com); $59–179 per night. These housekeeping cottages overlook a channel leading to Lake Winnipesaukee. The units vary in size and style: Each has cable TV, fans, and telephones; some have kitchenettes, screened-in porches, and futon beds. Pets are welcome with advance notice and a $100 refundable fee, provided they are quiet, leashed, and well behaved.

Cottages and Motel at the Highlands, Route 3, Weirs Beach (603-366-5500; info1@thehighlandmotel.com; www.thehighlandmotel.com); motel, $79–94 per night; cottages, $49–84 per night. The motel rooms and cottage units at Highlands can accommodate one to four people; some have kitchenettes (rates for Motorcycle Week are slightly higher). Shopping, restaurants, water slides, and boat rentals are all within walking distance, and you can order take-out from the on-site restaurant. Pets are welcome with a $100 security deposit.

West Lebanon

A Fireside Inn and Suites, 25 Airport Road, West Lebanon (603-298-5906; 1-800-962-3198; info@afiresideinn.com; www.afiresideinn.com); $109–159 per night. Amenities at this full-service hotel include a restaurant, 126 guest rooms, a swimming pool and hot tub, a fitness center, laundry facilities, premium movie channels, free airport shuttles and morning newspapers, alarm clocks, and in-room coffeemakers. Pets are allowed for an extra $10 per night, provided they are not left unattended at any time.

Wolfeboro

Lucas-Nowell House, 166 North Main Street, Wolfeboro (603-569-6187); call for rate information. A historic farmhouse with hilltop views, the Lucas-Nowell House

has four guest rooms with private baths, cable TV, and telephones (some have fireplaces and lake views as well). A continental breakfast is served each morning, and tea is served each afternoon. Children and pets are welcome with prior approval.

Wolfeboro Falls

Berry Motel and Cottages, Center Street, Wolfeboro Falls (603-569-5666); $60 per night. Pets are welcome without extra fees at this affordable family accommodation with six motel rooms, and six cottage units with kitchenettes and screened-in porches. All units have heat and private bathrooms and are within walking distance of shopping and restaurants. Pet owners are asked to clean up after their animals.

Campgrounds

Ashland

Ames Brook Campground, 104 Winona Road, Ashland (603-968-7998; amesbrook@amesbrook.com; www.amesbrook.com); $24–30 per night. This family campground has sites for tents and RVs, rest rooms with showers, a camp store, laundry facilities, a swimming pool, a game room, a playground, and a basketball court. Hiking and biking trails are nearby. Two well-behaved, friendly pets per site are welcome.

Gilford

Gunstock Camping, Route 11A, Gilford (603-293-4341; 1-800-GUNSTOCK; camping@gunstock.com; www.gunstock.com); $24–30 per night. Campers at

Gunstock enjoy a camp store, rest rooms with showers, swimming pools, movie nights and other scheduled activities, a propane filling station, and playgrounds. Guests can also take advantage of activities and events throughout the Gunstock ski resort property. Leashed pets are welcome if owners can show proof of vaccination.

Hampton
Twin Tamarack Family Camping and RV Resort, 101 Campground Road, New Hampton (603-279-4387; twin-tamarack@prodigy.net; www.ucampnh.com/twintamarack); $30–34 per night. Located on the shores of Lake Pemigewasset, this campground offers lots of scheduled activities, a boat launch and boat rentals, sites for tents and RVs, a beach, rest rooms with showers, a recreation hall, a swimming pool, and laundry facilities. Quiet, leashed pets

are allowed but should not be left unattended at any time.

Newport
Crow's Nest Campground, 529 South Main Street, Newport (603-863-6170; www.crowsnest-campground.com); $21–28 per night. Set along the Sugar River, Crow's Nest has 95 shady and sunny sites with picnic tables, a swimming pool, a miniature golf course, a playground, a fishing pond, a camp store, a recreation hall, laundry facilities, and rest rooms with showers. Leashed, well-behaved pets are welcome at campsites but not in rental cabins.

Orford
The Pastures, Route 10, Orford (603-353-4579; camp@thepastures.com; www.thepastures.com); $15–20 per night. Leashed pets are always welcome at The Pastures, as long as their owners clean up after them. The campground's amenities include 40- to

A DOWNTOWN PARK IN WOLFEBORO OVERLOOKING LAKE WINNIPESAUKEE

50-foot-wide sites with picnic tables, a swimming pool, rest rooms with showers, boat rentals, volleyball courts, a putting green, and table tennis. Pets are also welcome at all on-site music concerts and festivals.

Washington
Pillsbury State Park Campground, Route 31, Washington (603-863-2860; 603-271-3628); $13 per night. Some of the sites at this rustic campground are available for walk-ins; others are offered by reservation only. Open seasonally, the campground has primitive sites, pit toilets, canoe rentals, and a playground. One large site is reserved for group youth reservations. For more information on the park, see "Out and About."

West Ossipee
Whit's End Campground, 140 Newman Drew Road, West Ossipee (603-539-6060; whits endllc@aol.com); $22–26 per night. Whit's End has 130 RV and tent sites spread across 50 acres; camp facilities include canoe and kayak rentals, a swimming pool, five beaches, a playground, a recreation hall, laundry facilities, rest rooms with showers, a dumping station, and a camp store. Pets are welcome with proof of vaccination.

Homes, Cottages, and Cabins for Rent

Claremont
Dartmouth–Sunapee Farmhouse, Claremont (413-665-2449; rjdecker3@aol.com); $650–800 per weekend or $800–950 per week. This five-bedroom home can accommodate up to 12 people and has three bathrooms, a brick oven, hardwood floors, a fireplace, cable TV, a barbecue grill, a pond, more than 50 acres of hills and woods, and views of the Connecticut River. Rental rates and pet fees vary according to the number of occupants; call for more information.

Croydon
Lakeside Cottage, Croydon (215-379-0484; 215-379-1676; kasherwin1@aol.com); $550 per week. Compact and rustic, this one-floor cottage can accommodate up to six people and has two bedrooms, one bathroom, a fireplace and woodstove, a barbecue grill, a kitchen, a TV/VCR, and a CD player. A private dock juts out into the 70-acre pond. "Small" pets (call to see if yours qualifies) are welcome.

Groton
Lakes Region Log Cabin, Newfound Lake, Groton (781-826-8274; shoptons@aol.com); $400–500 per weekend or $1,000–1,250 per week. This secluded, charming rental has great views, three bedrooms, one bathroom, a fireplace and woodstove, a barbecue grill, games and puzzles, sleds, table tennis, a kitchen, and a TV/VCR. "We have a crate at the house which anyone is welcome to use," says homeowner Jeanine Adams. "The house is isolated and safe for animals."

Lake Winnisquam
Lakefront House, Lake Winnisquam, Laconia (603-528-2252;

941-389-6756; paulmcmann @attbi.com); $1,500–2,000 per week. Quiet, friendly animals are welcome with prior approval at this three-bedroom rental home on the northern end of Lake Winnisquam. The home has a fireplace, a lawn and beach area, a deck, a boat dock, and cable TV. Pet owners pay $100 per animal, per week, and an additional $200 security deposit.

Waterfront Cabin, Lake Winnisquam (609-896-4999; maryhullllc@yahoo.com); $900 per week. This cozy, unheated cabin is available for rent during the spring, summer, and fall. Located directly on the lake, the cabin has a screened-in porch, a large deck, a fully equipped kitchen, a living room, two bedrooms, a canoe, a swim platform, and an air conditioner. Pets are allowed on a case-by-case basis with a $100 security deposit.

New Durham
Shaw Pond Vacation Home, New Durham (941-485-5373; barbobrien@webtv.net); $1,800–2,000 for two weeks. There's a two-week minimum at this eight-room house rental located directly on the shores of Shaw Pond—about a five-minute drive from downtown Wolfeboro. "It's a great summer camp for dogs," says owner Barbara O'Brien. "We have 4 acres, good fishing, a beach, and a canoe and paddleboat, which we offer to our guests." The home has three bedrooms, a washer and dryer, a kitchen, a dock, and a beach.

OUT AND ABOUT

Cardigan State Park, Route 118, Orange (603-924-5976). Most visitors come to this 5,500-acre park to scale the 3,121-foot peak of mighty Mount Cardigan. Of course, you don't have to go all the way to the top: Picnic areas and shorter (but still scenic) hiking trails make this park a popular day-trip destination.

Downtown Wolfeboro. In addition to having several restaurants with outdoor and eating and take-out ice cream windows, the downtown area also offers a well-landscaped waterfront park with grassy areas, benches, and peaceful views.

The Fells: John Hay National Wildlife Refuge, Route 103A, Newbury (603-763-4789; fells@ tds.net). Though dogs are not allowed in the gardens at this estate and wildlife preserve, they are welcome to join their owners across the street at **The Fells' Sunset Hill** and **Beech Brook Trails.** The 4 miles of walking paths take you to the top of the scenic hill and through woodlands. You can get a map at the visitors center.

Gardner Memorial Wayside Area, Route 4A, Wilmont (603-924-5976). This large picnic area is part of the 6,600-acre **Gile State Forest.** Open in the spring, summer, and fall, the site has a babbling brook and remnants of a 19th-century mill that once stood on the grounds. Dogs are welcome on a leash.

Laconia Motorcycle Week, Laconia. Suit up your Chihuahua with his best Harley-Davidson bandanna and head to the Laconia area in early June for the longest-running annual bike-rally event in America. Hotels and motels fill up well in advance, so do your planning early.

Lakes Region Humane Society (LRHS) Yard Sale, Tuftonboro. Every Labor Day weekend, the staff and volunteers at this non-profit animal welfare organization holds a fund-raising yard sale to help the homeless pets in their care. The society also holds other special events, like sunset cruises and obedience classes, throughout the year. For updated schedules, call LRHS at 603-569-3549, visit www.lrhs.net, or stop by the shelter at 14 Winner's Circle Farm in Tuftonboro.

Madison Boulder Natural Area, Route 113, Madison (603-323-2087). This 17-acre area is named for the on-site granite boulder that is an impressive 83 feet long and 23 feet high, and weighs more than 5,000 tons (yes, tons). Thought to have been deposited here from northern New Hampshire by the movement of the glaciers, it is one of the largest such stones, called erratics, in the world. Take in the sight and then relax for a while in the picnic area. Dogs must be leashed.

Meriden Bird Sanctuary, Main Street, Meriden. This relatively small 30-acre sanctuary is a popular dog-walking spot with locals. The trails wind through wooded and open areas; dogs are welcome on a leash.

New Hampshire Humane Society (NHHS) Events, Laconia. Pancake breakfasts, triathlons, and ice cream socials are just some of the special events scheduled each year by the NHHS. If you're going to be in the area, feel free to stop by or lend a hand. For more information on upcoming events, call 603-524-3252, stop by the society's headquarters at 1305 Meredith Center Road in Laconia, or visit www.nhhumane.org.

Pillsbury State Park, Route 31, Washington (603-863-2860). Hiking, biking, camping (see "Accommodations—Campgrounds"), canoeing, and wildlife-watching are the main visitor activities at this 2,500-acre state park, where it's not uncommon to see loons, moose, and other native species. In addition to its many local trails, Pillsbury is also home to a stretch of the **Monadnock–Sunapee Greenway,** a 51-mile-long trail that runs between Mount Monadnock and Mount Sunapee.

Rollins State Park, Route 103, Warner (603-456-3808). Feeling lazy? You can drive to the scenic upper slopes and picnic area of the park's **Mount Kearsarge** via a 3.5-mile-long road starting at the park entrance. After an energizing picnic, you and Fluffy can hike a half mile to the summit. Either way, the views are impressive.

Scenic Drives. The roads around

Lake Winnipesaukee are all fun to drive, including **Route 109, Route 11, Route 3** between Laconia and Holderness, and **Route 25.** Running past New-found Lake, Route 3 also has pretty views. Toward the west, take a spin on **Route 12A** along the river between Claremont and Lyme, or on **Route 4** between Boscawen and Danbury. Aside from I-89, there's no fast way to get anywhere in these parts, which is usually a good thing.

Sculptured Rocks Natural Area, between Route 3A and Route 188, Groton (603-547-3373). Situated on 200 acres along the Cockermouth River, this popular swimming and day-trip spot features interesting geological formations; its rocks have been molded into curves, dips, and odd angles by running water. You can walk through, view the sights from a park bridge, or settle in for a picnic. Use caution when swimming—the water is very cold, and the uneven edges can be dangerous for young children.

Sled Dog Races. Fast dogs heat up the lakes region every January and February. The most popular events are the **Sandwich Notch Sled Dog Race** in Center Sandwich (603-929-3508); the **Tamworth Sprint Race** in Tamworth (603-353-4601); the **Meredith Sprint Race in Meredith** (603-353-4601); and the **Lakes Region Sled Dog Races** in Laconia (603-524-3064).

Summer Concert Series, Tilton Island Park, Main Street (Route 3), Tilton. Bluegrass, swing, rock 'n' roll, barbershop, Dixieland: The musical styles run the gamut at these weekly free concerts, held every Sunday night in July and August. The park is located on a small island in the middle of the lake, accessed by a footbridge. Bring chairs or blankets. For more information, call 603-286-3232 or e-mail tradeandevents@aol.com.

Winnipesaukee Kayak Company, 17 Bay Street, Wolfeboro (603-569-9926; info@winnikayak.com; www.winnikayak.com). This self-described "pet-friendly organization" allows companion animals to join their owners in any of the rental boats, which vary in size and style. The company's guides also lead half-day, full-day, and multiday tours of area waterways.

Winslow State Park, Route 11, Wilmot (603-526-6168). Located on the opposite side of **Mt. Kearsarge** from **Rollins State Park** (see above listing), Winslow offers the same opportunities for hiking, mountain biking, picnicking, and taking in the views from the mountain's 1,800-foot plateau. The park is named for the Winslow House Hotel, which once stood on the property and was destroyed in a fire.

QUICK BITES

Boathouse Grill, Routes 3 and 104, Meredith (603-279-2253). This waterfront restaurant serves sandwiches, seafood, soups and chowders, steaks, and chicken dishes; diners can eat inside or out on the deck, or order their meals to go; at lunchtime, you can call or fax in your order so it will be ready when you arrive.

Clay's Chocolate Shop, 11 Pemi Drive, Plymouth (603-536-5857). Sure, this decadent shop offers chocolate-covered cherries, almond bark, brownie bites, and peanut-raisin clusters for you. But they also stock gourmet and diet doggie biscuits in regular and peanut flavor for your pooch—dipped in white chocolate, if Spot prefers.

Gilford House of Pizza, 9 Old Lakeshore Road, Gilford (603-528-7788). Visitors to the Gunstock Mountain area can call this local pizza favorite for free delivery. Other menu choices include calzones, hot and cold subs and sandwiches, salads, and pasta dinners.

Jack's Coffee, 180 Main Street, New London (603-526-8003). Panini sandwiches, salads, soups, and of course hot java are all available at Jack's Coffee. The New London location has a front lawn for impromptu picnics; the company will soon be opening its new **Lake Sunapee location,** overlooking the harbor and offering indoor and outdoor seating (call the New London location for updated information).

Maddie's On the Bay, 11 Dockside Street, Wolfeboro (603-569-8888). Maddie's offers grilled sandwiches, fried seafood, and other lunch and dinner choices; order your meal as take-out and relax at the restaurant's waterfront outdoor seating area.

Molly's Restaurant, 43 South Main Street, Hanover (603-643-2570). This popular downtown restaurant has indoor and outdoor seating, and serves wood-fired pizza, burgers, and other traditional lunch and dinner fare to Dartmouth College students and visitors.

North End Pub, New London Shopping Center, New London (603-526-2875). The take-out menu at North End includes pizza, subs, burgers, calzones, salads, pasta, chicken wings, nachos, and express lunch items.

Shibley's Drive-In, Route 11, The Pier, Alton Bay (603-875-3636). This is a walk-up-to-the-window kind of place, offering fast-food treats and, of course, ice cream. There are a few picnic tables in the parking lot, or you can walk across the street to eat on a bench at the waterfront park.

Yum Yum Shop, 16 North Main Street, Wolfeboro (603-569-1919). Order your sandwiches, soup, coffee, cookies, and pastries inside and enjoy your goodies with Rover at the outdoor sidewalk seating.

HOT SPOTS FOR SPOT

Abercrombie and Bridge Pet Supplies and Grooming, Newport Road, New London (603-526-2088; www.abercrombieandbridge.com). This grooming and pet-supply store uses organic shampoos and other care products, including brands like Ark Naturals and Natural Animal. Nutritional supplements and environmentally friendly dog toys and supplies are also available.

Always Better Care, West Lebanon (603-298-9751). Those looking for an alternative to a kennel can give Amy Gamache a call at her home-based doggie day-care and boarding business; house-trained, friendly, well-behaved dogs can play freely together, *sans* cages, during overnight boarding stays ($25) or day care ($15). Appointments are necessary.

Ebony Boarding Kennel, 661 Mayhew Turnpike, Plymouth (603-536-4219; www.ebonykennel.com). Ebony provides traditional overnight boarding services ($6–10 per night) with indoor/outdoor runs, heating and air-conditioning, and separate cat quarters. You can also choose special packages, such as Pamper Your Pet ($33), Dogs Day at the Spa ($21), and Inspired Health ($35). In addition, the kennel is home to **Country Dogs Pet Bakery,** which bakes up fresh gourmet doggie treats daily.

Jeffrey Kropp Pet Care, Canaan (603-523-7875; jeffrey.r.kropp@valley.net). "I'm a one-person operation, but I try to accommodate people's needs, running the gamut from dog walking to staying overnight at someone's otherwise unoccupied home," explains Jeffrey Kropp, who serves pet owners living in and visiting **Canaan, Lebanon, Hanover,** and neighboring towns. Rates vary according to the services requested.

Plymouth Pet and Aquarium, Tenney Mountain Highway, Plymouth (603-536-3299). In addition to stocking food and supplies for cats, dogs, reptiles, birds, small animals, and fish, this store also recently expanded to include the Pet Palace Dog and Cat Grooming Area. The stocked pet-food brands include Nutro, Precise, and One Earth.

West Lebanon Supply, 12 Railroad Avenue, West Lebanon (603-298-8600). This feed store offers food and supplies for farm and companion animals, including ID tags, toys, and dog- and cat-food brands such as Iams, Blue Seal, Pro Plan, and Science Diet. If you're too busy to stop by, they'll deliver to neighboring towns.

Windy Hill Kennels, Route 107, Gilmanton (603-267-6896; www.whkennelcollege.com). Doggie day care, overnight boarding, grooming, and basic and advanced obedience training are all available at Windy Hill, which is also serves as a vocational trade school training students for careers in pet care. The boarding area has indoor/outdoor runs, and each animal receives playtime and basic obedience training each day.

IN CASE OF EMERGENCY

Claremont Animal Hospital,
Charlestown Road, Claremont (603-543-0117).

Kindness Animal Hospital,
5 Water Village Road, Ossipee (603-539-2272).

Lakes Region Veterinary Hospital,
1266 Union Avenue, Laconia (603-524-8387).

Pleasant Lake Veterinary Hospital,
95 Elkins Road, Elkins (603-526-6976).

Plymouth Animal Hospital,
42 Smith Bridge Road, Plymouth (603-536-1213).

Upper Valley Veterinary Services,
7 Slayton Street, Lebanon (603-448-3534).

Northern New Hampshire

The White Mountain region of the Granite State is especially popular with families, and with good reason: Attractions like Story Land, the Alpine Slide, the Mount Washington Cog Railway, the Fort Splash Waterpark, and Santa's Village, not to mention ski resorts like Attitash, Loon Mountain, and Bretton Woods, provide more than enough diversions for kids and adults alike. The bad news is, pets aren't allowed at most of these man-made attractions. The good news is, you won't have to look far to find fun and interesting nature-made alternatives.

In the Great North Woods, the state parks alone are worth the trip. If you're into camping, hiking, sight-seeing, or wildlife-watching, you won't be disappointed in this rustic northern tip of the state. Dramatic gorges, moose-viewing sites, cross-country skiing trails, remote campsites, boat launches, and swimming holes are plentiful. Best of all, almost every North Woods state park welcome pets, unlike those in many other New Hampshire locations. But you don't have to be outdoorsy to take in the region's beauty; visitors looking for maximum benefit with minimal exertion will find plenty of quick rewards on the Mount Washington Auto Road and historical walking tours, and at roadside waterfalls.

ACCOMMODATIONS

Hotels, Motels, Inns, and Bed & Breakfasts

Bartlett

Attitash Marketplace Motel, Route 302, Bartlett (603-374-2300; 1-800-862-1600; stay@attitashmtvillage.com; www.attitashmarketplace.com); $49–169 per night. Pets are welcome in certain rooms at this motel for an additional $25 per night. Guests can take advantage of cable TV, coffeemakers, studios and suites, an indoor swimming pool, a hot tub, tennis courts, a fitness center, playgrounds, a game room, and trails for hiking, mountain biking, and cross-country skiing.

Bartlett Inn, Route 302, Bartlett (603-374-2353; 1-800-292-2353; stay@bartlettinn.com; www.bartlettinn.com); $79–175 per night. Pets are welcome without extra fees in the Bartlett Inn's cottage rooms, provided they are not left unattended. Choose from one-room studios, larger cottages with one or two double beds, and fireplace cottages with kitchenettes. Guests can also enjoy country breakfasts, porch rocking chairs, a gathering

room, and nearby hiking and skiing trails.

Villager Motel, Route 302, Bartlett (603-374-2742; 1-800-334-6988; www.villagermotel.com); $59–189 per night. Accommodations options at the Villager include standard motel units with queen- or king-sized beds, efficiency units, chalets, and apartments. Guests can take advantage of a swimming pool, barbecue grills and picnic tables, a playground, and walking trails. Well-behaved, leashed pets are welcome with prior approval for an extra $8 per night.

Bethlehem

Wayside Inn, 3738 Main Street (Route 302), Bethlehem (603-869-3364; 1-800-448-9557; info@thewaysideinn.com; www.thewaysideinn.com); $88–108 per night. Pets are welcome in designated motel rooms at Wayside, an 1800s homestead with cross-country skiing and snowmobiling trails, basketball and bocce courts, a beach, river views, a restaurant, and a lounge. All rooms have air-conditioning, cable TV, refrigerators, and balconies. Companion animals cannot be left unattended at any time.

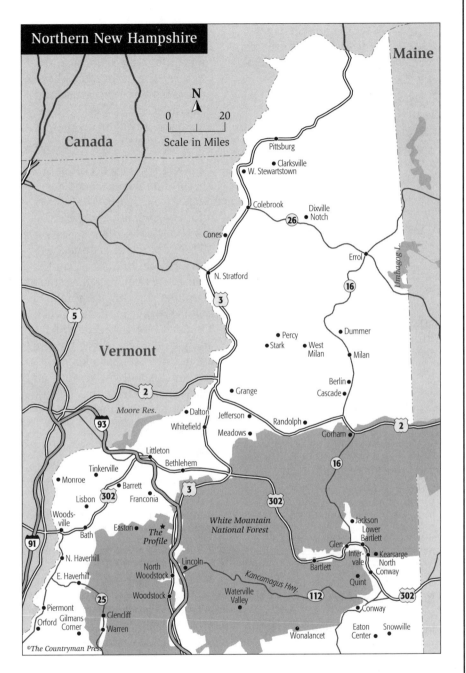

Northern New Hampshire

Maine

Canada

Vermont

N

0   20

Scale in Miles

Pittsburg

Clarksville
W. Stewartstown

Colebrook

26

Dixville
Notch

Cones

Errol

16

N. Stratford

3

Percy

Dummer

Stark   West
Milan

Milan

Grange

Berlin
Cascade

Moore Res.

Dalton   Jefferson   Randolph

93   Whitefield   Meadows   Gorham

2

Littleton   Bethlehem

16

Tinkerville

Monroe   Barrett

Lisbon   302   Franconia

3

Woods-
ville

Easton

White Mountain
National Forest

302

Jackson
Lower
Bartlett

Bath   The
Profile

Glen

Intervale   Kearsarge
North
Conway

N. Haverhill

Lincoln

Bartlett

Quint

302

E. Haverhill

North
Woodstock

Kancamagus Hwy.

112

Piermont   25   Woodstock   Waterville
Valley   Conway

Orford   Gilmans
Corner   Glencliff   Eaton
Center   Snowville

91   Warren   Wonalancet

©*The Countryman Press*

Campton Village
Campton Inn Bed & Breakfast,
383 Owl Street, Campton Village
(603-726-4449; 1-888-511-0790;
camptoninn@aol.com); $75–90
per night. This restored 1830s
farmhouse offers five guest
rooms with private and shared
baths, antique furnishings, a
screened-in porch, full country
breakfasts, and a location that's
close to hiking and biking trails,

ski resorts, and a renowned golf course. Well-behaved pets are welcome for an additional charge of $10 per stay (not per night).

Conway

Sunny Brook Cottages, Route 16, Conway (603-447-3922; info@sunnybrookcottages.com; www.sunnybrookcottages.com); $39–114 per night. The nine cozy cottages at Sunny Brook have fireplaces, cable TV, linens, kitchens, coffeemakers, covered porches, barbecue grills, and patio furniture. Guests can also swim and fish in the on-site Swift Brook, play at the playground, and hike nearby trails. Leashed pets are welcome for an extra $10, as long as owners clean up after them and don't leave them alone in the cabins.

Franconia

Gale River Motel and Cottages, 1 Main Street (Route 18), Franconia (603-823-5655; 1-800-255-7989; www.galerivermotel.com; $65–95 per night). Gale River offers motel rooms with two double beds, cable TV, and air-conditioning, along with two housekeeping cottages that can accommodate five to six people. Most dog breeds are welcome for an extra $10 per night. (At the time of this writing, the owners were considering changing their pet policy; check before making reservations.)

Lovetts Inn, Route 18, Franconia (603-823-7761; 1-800-356-3802; info@lovettsinn.com; www. lovettsinn.com); $125–235 per night. Pets are welcome in some rooms at Lovetts Inn, a c. 1794 restored home that's listed on the National Register of Historic Places. Accommodations include rooms in the main house and cottages. The guest rooms have private baths, sitting areas, and nice views; the cottages feature fireplaces, private baths, porches, and coffeemakers.

Westwind Vacation Cottages, 1614 Profile Road, Franconia (603-823-5532; 1-877-835-3455; info@westwindcottages.com; www.westwindcottages.com); $50–90 per night. With names like Cascade, Bridal Veil, and Flume, each cottage at Westwind is unique and can accommodate two to six people. Each has cable TV and VCRs, barbecue grills, and picnic tables. Some have full kitchens; others have kitchenettes or small refrigerators and microwaves. There are no extra fees for pets, but they must be leashed when outside.

Gorham

Colonial Comfort Inn, 370 Main Street, Gorham (603-466-2732; 1-800-470-4224; paradise@ncia. net; www.hikersparadise.com); $39–125 per night. "We certainly are pet-friendly," says Colonial Comfort proprietor Mary Ann Janicki. "In fact, we believe that people cause more problems than pets do." The motel's rooms have cable TV, heat, and air-conditioning; some have refrigerators and whirlpool bathtubs. Guests can also enjoy a swimming pool, a restaurant, and laundry facilities.

Royalty Inn, 130 Main Street, Gorham (603-466-3312; 1-800-43-RELAX; innkeeper@royaltyinn. com; www.royaltyinn.com);

$47–99 per night. Some of the amenities at the Royalty include indoor and outdoor swimming pools; a hot tub and sauna; a fitness center with stairclimbers, treadmills, a basketball court, and two racquetball courts; a game room; and an on-site restaurant and lounge. Quiet pets are allowed in smoking rooms only for an extra $5 per night.

Top Notch Inn, 265 Main Street, Gorham (603-466-5496; 1-800-228-5496; reservations@top-notchinn.com; www.topnotch-inn.com); $39–142 per night. Pets are allowed in the motel-style rooms (not the country inn-style rooms) at Top Notch, which offers a swimming pool, a hot tub, and flower gardens. The shops and restaurants of downtown Gorham are within walking distance.

Intervale

Swiss Chalets Village Inn, Old Route 16A, Intervale (603-356-2232; 1-800-831-2727; info@ swisschaletsvillage.com; www. swisschaletsvillage.com); $39–239 per night. This very pet-friendly inn welcomes your animal friends for an additional fee of $15 per pet, per night, and the staff encourages guests to exercise their pets on the 13-acre property. Choose from double, queen, and king rooms and suites with fireplaces and hot tubs. All of the rooms have been recently renovated. Guests can also relax in the swimming pool.

Jackson

Mountainside Farm Bed & Breakfast, Carter Notch Road, Jackson (603-383-6531; 1-800-

A GUEST ROOM WITH KITCHENETTE AT THE VILLAGE HOUSE IN JACKSON

782-4270); $45–55 per person, per night. Visiting horses and dogs are welcome at Mountain-side Farm, a B&B surrounded by miles of hiking, biking, horse-back riding, and cross-country skiing trails. The home's Garden Suite and Valley View Suites have private baths, picture windows, and gardens views; other attractions include all-you-can-eat breakfasts and a working farm with animals.

Village House, Route 16A, Jackson (603-383-8966; www. yellowsnowdoggear.com/village house); $60–80 per night. It's no surprise that canines are welcome guests at the Village House, a guest lodging that also serves as the headquarters of Yellow Snow Dog Gear leash and collar manufacturers. Accommodations are available in the main house as well as a backyard annex. Some rooms have kitchenettes, hot tubs, and balconies, and all share access to a swimming pool and hot tub. The inn also has horses, a laid-back atmosphere—you check yourself in and out—and a great location in scenic downtown Jackson.

Jefferson

Applebrook Bed & Breakfast, Route 115A, Jefferson (603-586-7713; 1-800-545-6504; vacation @applebrook.com; www.applebrook.com); $60–100 per night. Perched on a hill overlooking 35 private acres, Applebrook B&B offers White Mountain views, full country breakfasts, and 14 guest rooms with shared and private baths, and many of these can be combined to form suites for larger groups. Pets are welcome for an extra $10 per night; half of that fee is donated to the local humane society's animal shelter.

Josselyn's Getaway Cabins, 306 North Road, Jefferson (1-800-586-9850); $75–125 per night. These nine handcrafted log cabins vary in size and style, and each has a theme—from Appalachian to Christmas, Logger's, Workshop, Rainbow, and Moose. Some have air-conditioning, decks, sleeping lofts, separate bedrooms and living areas, and private yards. Dogs are welcome but must be leashed when outside.

Lincoln

Parker's Motel, Route 3, Lincoln (603-745-8341; 1-800-766-6835; info@parkersmotel.com; www.parkersmotel.com); $39–89 per night. Parker's Motel offers guests a swimming pool, a hot tub and

sauna, a game room, standard motel rooms and larger family rooms, two- and three-bedroom cottages (some with kitchenettes, fireplaces, air-conditioning, and cable TV). Pets are allowed in designated rooms and cottages for an additional $5 per night.

Littleton

Continental Travellers Inn, 516 Meadow Street, Littleton (603-444-5466; 1-800-544-9366; info@continental93.com; www.continental93.com); $40–69 per night. Well-behaved pets are welcome at Continental for an additional $10 per night. Amenities include complimentary breakfasts, air-conditioning, cable TV with premium movie channels, kitchenettes, an indoor swimming pool and sauna, a hot tub, views of the Presidential Mountains, and a pond for fishing and canoeing.

North Conway

Mount Washington Valley Motor Lodge, 1567 White Mountain Highway, North Conway (603-356-5486; 1-800-634-2383; info@motorlodge.com; www.motorlodge.com); $59–149 per night. The MWV Motor Lodge offers standard guest rooms, family rooms, corporate-class rooms with king-sized beds, and two-room suites. Other features include an indoor swimming pool, a hot tub, an on-site restaurant, and a game room. Pets weighing less than 40 pounds are allowed in certain rooms with a $50 refundable security deposit.

North Conway Mountain Inn,

Main Street, North Conway (603-356-2803; 1-800-319-4405); $69–159 per night. Pets are allowed at the North Conway Mountain Inn, a two-story motel-style accommodation with exterior corridors, mountain views, cable TV, balconies, heat and air-conditioning, and daily maid service.

Oxen Yoke Inn and Motel, Kearsarge Street, North Conway (603-356-3177; 1-800-862-1600; www.theoxenyoke.com); $39–149 per night. For an additional $25 per night, your well-behaved pet is welcome in designated rooms at the Oxen Yoke. Accommodations include B&B-style rooms at the inn, motel units, and cottages. Amenities include cable TV, coffeemakers, microwaves, private baths, and a swimming pool. Restaurants, shops, and cafés are within walking distance.

Pittsburg
Timberland Lodge & Cabins, First Connecticut Lake, Varney Road, Pittsburg (603-538-6613; 1-800-545-6613; www.timberlandlodge.com); $45–81 per adult, per night. Guests choose from six furnished cabins at this quiet lakefront resort. All cabins come equipped with woodstoves, kitchens, and linens; some have wraparound decks, living rooms, lake views, cathedral ceilings, and color TVs. Pets are always welcome for an additional $15 per night.

Randolph
Jefferson Notch Motel and Cabins, Route 2, Randolph (603-466-3833; www.jeffnotchmotel-

cabins.com); $56–122 per night. Choose from standard motel units or one-room cabins with kitchenettes at Jefferson Notch, which offers air-conditioning, satellite TV, a swimming pool, two hot tubs, and barbecue grills. Housebroken, well-behaved pets are welcome, provided owners clean up after them, keep them off the furniture, and don't leave them alone in the rooms.

Shelburne
Town and Country Motor Inn, Route 2, Shelburne (603-466-3315; 1-800-325-4386; labnon@ncia.net; www.townandcountryinn.com); $52–74 per night. Town and Country is a pet-friendly motor inn offering 160 guest rooms, an indoor swimming pool, a sauna and hot tub, a fitness center, a video arcade, and a steam room. Live entertainment is provided on Saturday nights, and the staff can also arrange golf vacation packages.

Sugar Hill
Hilltop Inn, 1348 Main Street, Sugar Hill (603-823-5695; 1-800-770-5695; info@hilltopinn.com; www.hilltopinn.com); $45–98 per person. Cross-country skiers will enjoy their stay at this historic B&B; you don't even have to leave the grounds to access 20 acres of winding trails. Amenities include guest rooms and suites, antique furnishings, handmade quilts, ceiling fans, flannel sheets, and electric blankets. The two resident pooches, Beemer and Bogie, will show your canine the way to the walking trails and the large fenced-in play area for dogs.

Homestead Inn, 10 Sunset Hill Road, Sugar Hill (603-823-5564; www.thehomestead1802.com); $60–150 per night. The Homestead just celebrated an impressive milestone: its 200th year of continuous operation in the same family. Innkeeper Paul Hayward is the seventh-generation family proprietor of this inn, which offers full country breakfasts each morning, guest rooms in the main building, and a family cottage. Quiet, housebroken, well-behaved pets are welcome in certain rooms for an extra $10 per night.

Thornton
Gilcrest Cottages and Motel, Route 3, Thornton (603-726-3330; 1-888-741-0129; www.gilcrestcottages.com); $65–105 per night. Pets are allowed in two of Gilcrest's cottages, which can each accommodate two people with a queen-sized bed, a refrigerator, and a microwave. Dogs (sorry, no cats) are welcome as long as they are leashed, well behaved, and not left unattended. Guests also have access to an outdoor swimming pool.

Twin Mountain
Fieldstone Country Inn, Rosebrook Road, Twin Mountain (603-846-5646; fieldstonectry inn@worldsurfer.net); $75–95 per night. Children and pets are welcome guests at Fieldstone, a B&B with great mountain views, seven guest rooms, shared and private baths, a gathering room, a porch, and a dining room where full country breakfasts are served each morning. In the winter, guests can also enjoy an out-door skating rink; skate rentals are available.

Whitefield
DunRoamin' Inn, Route 3, Whitefield (603-837-3010; 1-877-837-3010); $39–119 per night. Standard, king, and deluxe rooms are available at this North Country motel; the facilities also include a hot tub, cable TV and VCRs, free coffee and bottled water, a barbecue grill, laundry facilities, and a game room. Some rooms also have kitchenettes. Pets are welcome for a small fee; call for details.

Spalding Inn, 199 Mountain View Road, Whitefield (603-837-2572; 1-800-368-8439); $129–225 per night. Innkeepers Diane and Michael Flinder welcome companion animals in the Spalding Inn's cottages for an extra $10 per night. Located on 200 acres of lawns, gardens, and orchards, the inn's cottages have fireplaces, kitchens, living rooms, and separate bedrooms. Rates include a full breakfast each morning; dinner plans are also available.

Woodsville
All Seasons Motel, 36 Smith Street, Woodsville (603-747-2157; 1-800-660-0644); $46–70 per night. Owned by Dave and Maryanne Robinson, the same couple who run the nearby **Nootka Lodge** (see listing below), the All Seasons Motel welcomes pets in some rooms. Guests can choose from standard rooms or efficiencies and enjoy a swimming pool, air-conditioning, a playground, and cable TV.

Nootka Lodge, Routes 10 and

302, Woodsville (603-747-2418; 1-800-626-9105; manager_nootka-lodge@hotmail.com; www.nootka-lodge.com); $45–120 per night. This unusual motel has a log cabin design: Rooms on the second floor have cathedral ceilings and balconies; first-floor rooms have interior log walls. Other guest amenities include a swimming pool, a hot tub, a fitness room, and a game room. Pets are welcome in about half of the rooms. (The owners of Nootka Lodge also own the **All Seasons Motel** in Woodsville; see above listing.)

Campgrounds

Bath
Twin River Campground and Cottages, Routes 302 and 112, Bath (603-747-3640; 1-800-811-1040; twinriver@mailhost.ncia. net; www.ucampnh.com/twin-river); campsites, $18–26 per night; cottages, $65–80 per night. Twin River offers campsites for tents and RVs, cottage rentals, rest rooms with showers, a swimming pool, gold panning, hiking trails, a camp store, laundry facilities, a recreation hall, and a playground. Most dog breeds (call for details) are allowed for an additional $5 per night, as long as owners clean up after them.

Cambridge
Umbagog Lake Sate Park Campground, Route 26, Cambridge (603-482-7795); $13–16 per night. One of New Hampshire's newest state parks, Umbagog's camping area contains 68 sites: 30 in the remote wilder-

ness and 38 at a base camp with hookups; canoe, kayak, and rowboat rentals; rest rooms with showers; a camp store; and laundry facilities. The remote sites can be accessed by boat only. Well-behaved pets are welcome.

Campton
Goose Hollow Camp and RV Park, Route 49, Campton (603-726-2000); $25 per night or $149 per week. Pets on a leash are welcome guests at Goose Hollow, a campground with 200 sunny and open sites, picnic tables and fire pits, a camp store, a game room, a swimming pool, 200 feet of river frontage, a playground, bingo and bonfire nights, walking trails, laundry facilities, and rest rooms with showers. Owners are asked to clean up after their animals.

Errol
Mollidgewock State Park Campground, Route 16, Errol (603-482-3373); $13–16 per night. Tucked inside the Thirteen Mile Woods Scenic Area, this campground has 47 primitive tent sites, most available by reservation only. Water and pit toilets are available. The park is popular with canoeists, kayakers, moose-watchers, and fishermen. Pets are allowed.

Gorham
Moose Brook State Park Campground, Jimtown Road (Route 2), Gorham (603-466-3860; 603-271-3628); $13–16 per night. The 62 sunny and shady sites at Moose Brook vary in size and location, and are available for tents, pop-up campers, and RVs (no hookups). Some are set

aside for youth groups, and most are available by reservation only. Leashed pets are welcome. (For more information on the park, see "Out and About.")

Harts Location
Dry River Campground,
Crawford Notch State Park, Route 302, Harts Location (603-374-2272; 603-271-3628); $13–16 per night. Dry River is open seasonally, from May through December. Though not allowed in the park itself, leashed pets are welcome in this campground and the Willey House area. The campground has 31 sites (most available only by reservation) and rest rooms with showers.

Littleton
Crazy Horse Campground,
788 Hilltop Road, Littleton (1-800-639-4107; chores@worldpath.net; www.ucampnh.com/crazyhorse); $20–25 per night. Pets are allowed at all campsites at Crazy Horse, a family campground located on 88 acres beside a lake. The facilities include a swimming pool, rest rooms with showers, laundry facilities, a playground, and separate areas for tents and RVs. Scheduled activities include bonfires, make-your-own sundae nights, and musical entertainment.

North Conway
Saco River Camping Area,
Route 16, North Conway (603-356-3360; www.sacorivercampingarea.com); $20–28 per night. Campers at Saco River can enjoy 40-by-40-foot waterfront and wooded campsites, a swimming pool, laundry facilities, rest rooms with showers, boat rentals, and playgrounds. Most dog breeds are welcome (call to see if yours qualifies), except at the beach, pool, and playground areas; there is a limit of two dogs per site.

Pittsburg
Deer Mountain Campground,
Route 3, Pittsburg (603-538-6965; 603-271-3628); $13–16 per night. This state-run campground offers 24 rustic sites with picnic tables and fire pits, and is located along the Connecticut River and the Canadian–American border. Most sites are available by reservation only, though a few are left open for walk-ins. Youth groups are encouraged to make reservations. Well-behaved pets are always welcome.

Lake Francis State Park Campground, Route 3, Pittsburg (603-538-6965); $13–16 per night. The park is open seasonally, from May through December. Fishermen frequent this quiet campground, which offers sites (some waterfront) for tents and RVs, limited hookups, tent platforms, a boat launch, and a day-use area. Pets are welcome.

Lopstick Lodge and Cabins,
First Connecticut Lake, Pittsburg (1-800-538-6659; vacation@lopstick.com; www.lopstick.com); $80–140 per night. For an extra $10 per night, well-behaved, quiet pets are welcome in most of the housekeeping cabins at Lopstick. The lodge offers hunting and fishing guide services,

and cabins of varying sizes and styles; all have porches, full kitchens, and linens and towels; some have hot tubs, fireplaces, and lake and pond views.

Tall Timber Lodge, 231 Beach Road, Pittsburg (1-800-83-LODGE; vacation@talltimber.com; www.talltimber.com); $70–315 per night. The Tall Timber sport camp welcomes pets in most of its cabins for an additional $120 per night. The cottages are classified as either "rustic" or "luxury," and have fireplaces, kitchens, barbecue grills, and porches or decks (some have hot tubs). Most guests come for fishing or bird and big-game hunting.

Stewartstown
Coleman State Park Campground, Route 16, Stewartstown (603-538-6965); $13–16 per night. Located at Little Diamond Pond, this campground offers a roughing-it experience with limited facilities. The 30 sites can accommodate tents and RVs, though there are no hookups. A boat launch and plentiful trout make this a popular spot with fishermen; other activities include hiking, mountain biking, cross-country skiing, and snowmobiling.

Warren
Scenic View Campground, 193A South Main Street, Warren (603-764-9380; theclarks@surfglobal.net; www.usastar.com/scenicview); $22–32 per night. Animal lovers will appreciate Scenic View's newest service,

called Pup Tent, in which staffers walk, feed, and play with your pet (for a fee) while you're out and about. The campground also offers scheduled family activities, a swimming pool, a recreation hall, three playgrounds, hiking trails, rest rooms with showers, and a camp store.

Woodstock
Broken Branch KOA, Route 175, Woodstock (603-745-8008; 1-800-KOA-9736); $26 per night. This animal-friendly campground has plenty of activities to keep families busy, including a miniature golf course, a playground, hiking trails, a swimming pool, hayrides, a camp store, laundry facilities, and rest rooms with showers. Guests can also swim and fish in the nearby river. Pets must be leashed and cannot be left alone; kennel space is available upon request.

Homes, Cottages, and Cabins for Rent

Bethlehem
Mountain House, Bethlehem (781-223-1364; 781-648-9227; jackisue@aol.com); $700–850 per week or $300–450 per weekend. "I've found that dog people really enjoy the locale and the house," say Jacki Katzman, the owner of this two-bedroom, cedar-shingle home situated on 10 acres of woods and fields. You can see the sunset from the backyard deck, and pets can swim in the Ammonoosuc River, which

is about a 1-mile walk from the house.

Campton
Waterville Valley Chalet,
Waterville Estates, Campton (617-524-6807; 617-983-0084; gj.bradish@verizon.net; www. centerground.org/waterville); $350–1,395 per week or $275–495 per weekend. The owners of this vacation home have a Portuguese water dog and welcome other pets to the rental. Guests will find three bedrooms, two bathrooms, a ski locker and mudroom, a sleeping loft, a kitchen, a swimming pool, a hot tub and sauna, a washer and dryer, a barbecue grill, and cable TV. Hiking trails, rivers, and tennis courts are nearby.

Franconia
Franconia Village Homes,
Franconia (603-823-8409; jkennard@ncia.net); $500–800 per week. Homeowner Jean Kennard offers two Franconia houses for rent. The first, a stately Victorian, can accommodate up to 10 people and has four bedrooms, two bathrooms, a large front porch, and a fireplace. The second, a restored farmhouse, has four bedrooms, 12 acres, and satellite TV. "There's no extra charge for pets, but I just ask people to pick up after their dogs and to not leave them in the house unattended," she says.

Glen
Glen Ledge Station, Glen (207-934-9025; 207-229-4059; jwells@loa.com); $2,995 per week or $1,695 per weekend. Up

to 20 people can comfortably stay at this contemporary eight-bedroom house with four bathrooms and two sleeping lofts. The home also has an atrium/sunporch, a fireplace, a deck, a sauna, cable TV and a VCR, a fully equipped kitchen, and a wet bar. Pets are welcome (first floor only, please) for an additional $25 per week.

Lincoln
Loon Mountain House, Lincoln (603-867-7718; deannechrystal @yahoo.com); $700–850 per week or $350–450 per weekend. Located about five minutes from Loon Mountain, this two-story house is located in downtown Lincoln and is equipped to handle babies as well as dogs: It has gates, a crib, a high chair, a playpen, and dog bowls. The home has three bedrooms, two bathrooms, a full kitchen, a barbecue grill, and cable TV. It can accommodate up to 12 people.

Thornton
White Mountain Log Home,
Thornton (508-748-6624; 603-726-7172); $500 per weekend or $1,200–1,600 per week. This private log home has mountain views, three bedrooms, two bathrooms, a fireplace, and a TV/VCR. It is located about 15 minutes from the Loon Mountain and Waterville Valley ski areas. "My wife and I welcome all pets," says homeowner Jay Houck: He just asks that they be house-trained and well behaved, and that owners clean up after them.

OUT AND ABOUT

Appalachian Mountain Club (AMC) Visitor Center, Route 16, Pinkham Notch. The AMC has been instrumental in establishing, protecting, and maintaining many of New Hampshire's best hiking trails; the organization's Pinkham Notch Visitor Center, also known as the Trading Post, is a popular starting point for many Mount Washington–area hikes, including the **Tuckerman Ravine Trail** (often used by hardy spring skiers) and the northern New Hampshire section of the **Appalachian Trail.** The center offers food, public rest rooms, and a supply and gift shop with maps and souvenirs.

Bark in the Park, North Conway. One of New England's largest animal expos, this fund-raiser for the **Conway Area Humane Society** (CAHS) includes obstacle courses, agility demonstrations, pet-supply vendors, costume contests, and more. The event is typically held at North Conway's Schouler Park in September. For more information on this or any of the CAHS's other events, visit www.conway-shelter.org, e-mail info@conway-shelter.org, call 603-447-3477, or stop by the shelter at 223 East Main Street in Conway.

Bedell Bridge State Park, Route 10, Haverhill (603-323-2087). Frequented by fishermen, this state historic site has about 40 acres with walking trails, a picnic area, and a boat launch. It is the former home of the Burrtuss Bridge, a two-span covered bridge that was destroyed by high winds in 1979. Leashed pets are welcome.

Bethlehem Walking Tours and **Mystery Lantern Tours,** Bethlehem. These self-guided walking tours take you through Bethlehem's historic and notable areas; maps are available at the visitors center at 2182 Main Street (Route 302). The Mystery Lantern Tours are guided walks during which local experts share the true stories and tall tales of the town's colorful past. For more information on both, call the Bethlehem Heritage Society at 1-888-845-1957 or e-mail info@bethlehemwhitemtns.com.

Glen Ellis Falls, Pinkham Notch. With a well-marked parking area on Route 16 in Pinkham Notch, these impressive 65-foot-high falls are easy to find. A walking path and stairs takes you bottom to top and back. The site has a scenic observation area and tall rock walls.

Great North Woods State Parks. As host to more than 10 large, pet-friendly parks and natural areas, the northernmost region of New Hampshire is an ideal spot for animal-loving outdoorsy types. Try these highlights: **Androscoggin Wayside Park** (Route 16 in Errol) has a trail and picnic area overlooking river rapids; **Beaver Brook Falls Wayside** Park (Route 145 in Colebrook) offers a scenic waterfall and picnic areas; **Dixville Notch State Park** (Route 26 in Dixville) is a popular area with a

5-mile-long trail, a gorge, and waterfalls; **Milan Hill State Park** (Route 16 in Milan) has an auto road to the Milan Hill summit; and **Nansen Wayside Park** (Route 16 in Berlin) attracts boaters, fishermen, and day-trippers. For more information on campgrounds, see "Accommodations—Campgrounds." For maps, directions, and details about these or other state parks, contact the New Hampshire Division of Parks and Recreation at 603-271-3254; or visit www.nhparks.state.nh.us.

Kancamagus Highway. Stretching from Lincoln to Conway, this 34-mile scenic byway passes through mountains, gorges, ponds and rivers. You'll find ample opportunities to stop along the way for picnics, hikes and overlooks. On a summer or fall afternoon with the top down, it can't be beat.

Moose Brook State Park, Jimtown Road (Route 2), Gorham (603-466-3860). Companion animals are welcome at Moose Brook, often used as a starting point for hikes into the Presidential and Crescent mountain ranges. Visitors can fish in the Peabody and Moose Rivers, swim in Moose Brook, camp (see "Accommodations— Campgrounds"), or picnic by the water's edge. Pets must be leashed and well behaved.

Mount Washington Auto Road, Route 16, Pinkham Notch (603-466-3988). Sometimes called the first man-made tourist attraction in the United States, this 8-mile-long road leads drivers 6,288 feet up to the top of New England's highest mountain. the THIS CAR CLIMBED MOUNT WASHINGTON bumper sticker is free, but you'll have to pay $15 per vehicle for the privilege of earning it. Some hardy souls also choose to hike, bike, cross-country ski, or snowshoe their way to the top.

North Conway Sidewalk Sales, North Conway. Finally, shopping with Spot! Held each Memorial Day weekend at Settler's Green, this sidewalk sale brings the merchandise from 50 big-name outlet stores outdoors. Browse the clothes, shoes, and accessories, and enjoy the demonstrations and entertainment.

Old Man of the Mountain, I-93, Franconia Notch State Park. Also known as The Profile, this geographical oddity graces the cover of many a New Hampshire guidebook—not to mention the state's newly minted quarters. When you look at it from just the right angle, you'll see a pointy-nosed, bearded man in the red granite formation. You can see it from the road (I-93 in Franconia Notch State Park), but all the neck craning can get dangerous on this fast-moving highway; you're better off stopping at one of the well-marked viewing areas.

Rocks Estate, Route 302, Bethlehem (603-444-6228; info@ therocks.org). The estate is located about a half mile from Exit 40 off I-93. Your dog must be on a leash in the parking and picnic areas, but other than that, Rover is welcome to join you leash-free on the trails at this Christmas tree farm and wildlife sanctuary managed by the **Society for the Protection of New Hampshire Forests.** It's a great, easy walk, complete with history lessons (thanks to descriptive signs along the way), beaver dams, open fields, and shady woodlands.

Wildcat Mountain, Pinkham Notch (1-800-255-6439; www. skiwildcat.com). "The philosophy here is that while pets are not welcome in so many other places, here they need not stay in the car while you're out hav-ing all the fun," says Irene Donnell, communications director for the Wildcat Mountain Ski Area. "Your pet can ride along with you in the gondola and enjoy the bird's-eye scenery too!" Animals are not allowed in the lodge, and owners are asked to clean up after their animals and keep an eye on them. Try the **Way of the Wildcat Trail,** a self-guided walk with explanatory signs about local history and ecology that leads to **Thompson Brook Falls** and its swimming hole.

YOU AND ROVER CAN ENJOY TRAILS, PONDS, AND BEAVER DAMS AT THE ROCKS ESTATE IN BETHLEHEM.

QUICK BITES

Blueberry Muffin, 1769 White Mountain Highway (Route 16), Conway (603-356-5736). Outdoor patio seating is available seasonally at the Blueberry Muffin, a casual restaurant serving pancakes, sandwiches, soups, blueberry muffins (of course), and other breakfast and lunch items.

Chinook Café, Main Street, Conway (603-447-6300). Outdoor seating and a full take-out menu are available at Chinook, which features casual fare such as sandwiches, salads, burritos, bagels, baked treats, vegetarian meals, coffee, teas, and cold drinks.

Cold Mountain Café, 2015 Main Street, Bethlehem (603-869-2500). Treat yourself to a freshly made sandwich, baked goodie, or hot or cold drink at this laid-back coffeehouse.

KimberLee's Deli, Depot Plaza, Lincoln (603-745-DELI). Specializing in "to-go" orders, this deli serves sandwiches, bagels, coffee, and boxed lunches for hikers and travelers. While you're passing through, you can also pick up fully cooked, complete meals and heat them up later.

Thompson House Eatery, Route 16A, Jackson (603-383-9341). The Thompson House serves gourmet food (the chef's recipes have been featured in several magazines) in an upscale atmosphere. Outdoor dining is available seasonally on one of two decks.

Trail's End Ice Cream, Route 302, Bartlett (603-374-2288). In addition to its homemade ice cream, frozen yogurt, toppings, coffee, and cold drinks, Trail's End also offers a playground and an outdoor seating area with picnic tables and great views of the White Mountains.

Willey House Snack Bar, Crawford Notch State Park, Route 302, Harts Location (603-374-2272). Located at the beautiful Crawford Notch State Park, this roadside snack bar offers picnic-table seating for enjoying your quick treats. The Willey House is famous for being the only surviving building in the aftermath of an 1828 landslide.

HOT SPOTS FOR SPOT

Four Your Paws Only, Main Street, North Conway (1-800-327-5957; shop@fouryourpawsonly.com; www.fouryourpawsonly.com). This fun, well-stocked shop carries all the basics in addition to gourmet treats (choose yours at the "doggie deli" counter), pet-related decor for house and garden, and breed-specific clothing and hats. The staff also hosts regular special events, like the Saturday Morning Puppy Hour; call or check out the web site for updated information.

Karla's Grooming and Village Kennels, 590 East Main Street, Center Conway (603-447-3435). In addition to providing all-pet and all-breed grooming, Karla's also offers day care and overnight boarding for dogs and cats. The kennel's small size (20 runs) ensures that each pet gets lots of individual attention. Rates are $13 per day for day care and $12 per night for boarding.

KC's Meadow Kennel, 224 Martin Meadow Pond Road, Lancaster (603-788-2637; info@kckennel. com; www.kcsmeadowkennel. com). Specializing in overnight boarding and grooming, KC's offers heated and air-conditioned indoor/outdoor runs and four individual exercise sessions each day for dogs; there are also limited facilities for cats. All pets must have proof of vaccination.

Brushing, washing, nail clipping, and ear cleaning are part of the standard grooming services.

Littleton Pet Center and Kennel, 1985 St. Johnsbury Road, Littleton (603-444-6285; www.littletonpet-centerandkennel.com). This complete pet-care center provides overnight boarding, doggie day care, and all-breed grooming for dogs and cats. You can also stop in to buy premium dog food, leashes, collars, and other supplies. Overnight boarding rates are $13 per night; day-care rates are $40 per week or $10 per day.

North Country Aquarium and Pets, 112 Pleasant Street, Berlin (603-752-7042). In addition to fish and aquarium supplies, this store also stocks dog and cat food, rawhide bones, toys, cat litter, pet shampoos, small-animal supplies, and anything else you might need for your furry, feathered, or scaled companion animal on the road.

IN CASE OF EMERGENCY

Colebrook Veterinary Clinic,
123 Main Street, Colebrook (603-237-8871).

Conway Veterinary Hospital,
407 White Mountain Highway, North Conway (603-447-3449).

Hussey Veterinary Hospital,
236 Main Street, Gorham (603-466-5002).

Lancaster Veterinary Hospital,
329 Main Street, Lancaster (603-788-3351).

Landaff Veterinary Clinic,
460 Mill Brook Road, Lisbon (603-838-6687).

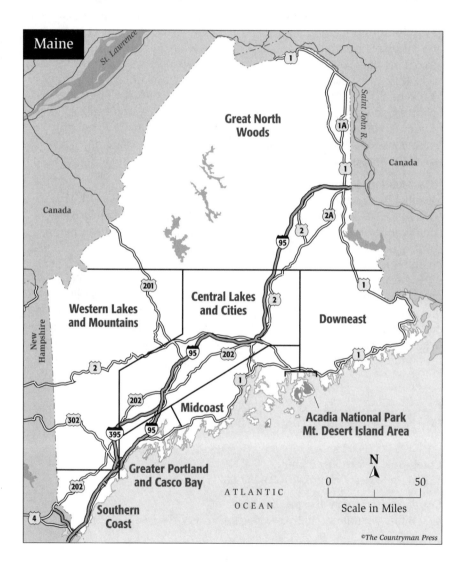

Maine

St. Lawrence

Great North
Woods

Saint John R.

1A

1

Canada

Canada

2A

2

95

201

Central Lakes
and Cities

2

Western Lakes
and Mountains

Downeast

New Hampshire

95

202

1

2

1

202

1

302

Midcoast

Acadia National Park
Mt. Desert Island Area

395

95

N

Greater Portland
and Casco Bay

ATLANTIC
OCEAN

0   50

202

Scale in Miles

4

Southern
Coast

©The Countryman Press

Maine

THE WELLS BREAKWATER AND BOARDWALK REWARDS VISITORS WITH GREAT VIEWS AND SALTWATER SPRAYS.

Southern Maine Coast

PET-FRIENDLY RATING:

In a state known for its rocky coast, the southern tip of Maine offers that most unusual of Vacationland's attractions: vast stretches of smooth, sandy beach. Massachusetts city dwellers and suburbanites have long flocked to this region for summer adventures; it is second only to Acadia National Park in visitation in the state. The south coast is a singularly beautiful and welcoming area for almost any type of traveler, but pet owners should be forewarned that they will face some challenges when vacationing here.

While there are many great reasons to visit this region, let's face it— most people come for the beaches. From the famed, lively stretch at Old Orchard to Ogunquit and York's lower-key shores, the beach umbrellas go up in June and stay up until the fall. Sadly, however, pets are not invited to the party; in recent years, towns along the coast have implemented a "no dogs on the beach" policy from 8 AM to 5 or 6 PM throughout the entire high season. In addition, many of the locals seem less than enthusiastic about accommodating out-of-town animals. One York innkeeper mentioned that her town was actively trying to discourage visitors from bringing their pets, and at the Old Orchard Beach board-walk and pier (the town's *other* main attractions), dogs are not allowed, even on a leash, during the high season. And in Ogunquit, forget "pet-friendly"—at times, this town seems downright pet-hostile. Many hotels and B&Bs here skip the usual "sorry, no pets" phrase on their brochure and tell us their policy in a more, shall we say, direct way: "Pets not welcome." "Pets are not invited." "NO PETS!" (We get it, we get it.)

That said, the southern coast does have noteworthy parks and hiking trails, scenic rivers and lakes, picturesque lighthouses, walkable historic districts, wonderful window-shopping, fabulous seafood, and yes, a healthy sprinkling of pet-friendly accommodations, from posh resorts to campgrounds. And if you don't mind waiting until after dinner or before breakfast to hit the beach, you can do that, too. Don't let a few anti-animal types discourage you from exploring this unique slice of New England; it may take a little more planning, but once you're strolling Kennebunkport's quaint shopping areas, gazing at York's Nubble Light, cracking open a lobster, or hiking one of the area's expansive state parks with Spot at your side, you'll be glad you made the effort.

ACCOMMODATIONS

Hotels, Motels, Inns, and Bed & Breakfasts

Cape Neddick
Country View Motel and Guesthouse, 1521 Route 1, Cape Neddick (207-363-7160; 1-800-258-6598; cvmotel@aol.com; www.countryviewmotel.com); $40–195 per night. This pictur-esque guest house is surrounded by perennial gardens in a tucked-away, quiet spot. A continental breakfast is included in the daily rate, and guests can also enjoy the covered porch, heated pool, and wide, lush lawn. The owners provide a special "walking area" for dogs (complete with trash can); they ask that pets be kept on a leash and not be left unat-tended, and that owners pay a $10 per night fee.

Eliot
Farmstead Bed & Breakfast, 379 Goodwin Road, Eliot (207-439-5033; 207-748-3145; farm steadb@aol.com; www.farmstead. qpg.com); $52–72 per night. Dogs, cats, and even cockatoos have stayed at the Farmstead; animals of all stripes are welcome

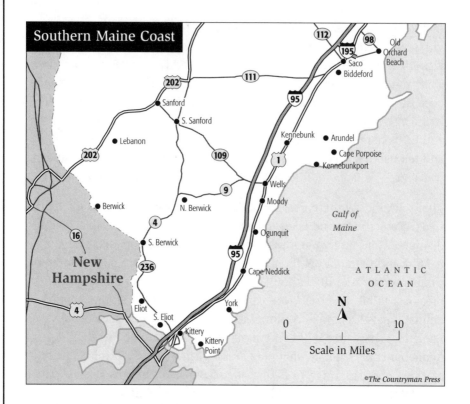

Southern Maine Coast

New Hampshire

Gulf of Maine

ATLANTIC OCEAN

N

0   10

Scale in Miles

©The Countryman Press

as long as they are never left alone in the rooms. (A note to dog owners: There is a resident cat here, so make sure your pooch stays on a leash at all times.) The B&B bills itself as the perfect blending of historic charm with modern conveniences.

Kennebunk
English Robin Guest House,
99 Western Avenue, Kennebunk (207-967-3505); call for rate information. Owner Ann Smith welcomes pets at her family-oriented guest house without any extra fees, though she does restrict her four-legged clientele to adult animals only (no puppies or kittens). Two of the units have private entrances; the third, called The Barn, is a converted carriage house with a family room and full kitchen.

The Kennebunk Inn, 45 Main Street, Kennebunk (207-985-3351; info@thekennebunkinn.com; www.thekennebunkinn.com); $80–160 per night. Step back in time at this 200-year-old inn offering New England charm, tasteful period decor, and modern conveniences. One pet is allowed per room, and a maximum of three pets are allowed at the inn at any one time—so make sure to book early. Your dog is even welcome to join you in front of the fireplace in the public sitting room.

Kennebunkport
The Captain Jefferds Inn,
5 Pearl Street, Kennebunkport (207-967-2311; 1-800-839-6844; captjeff@captainjefferdsinn.com; www.captainjefferdsinn.com); $145–295 per night. This charm-

ing inn has an equally charming history: The 1804 Federal-style home was built by Captain William Jefferds as a wedding gift for his daughter. The current owners refurbished the inn in 1997 and now offer 15 themed guest rooms. The resident canines, Kate and Casey, aren't cat fans, but they do welcome other dogs for a fee of $20 per night.

The Colony Hotel, 140 Ocean Avenue, Kennebunkport (207-967-3331; 1-800-552-2363; reservations@thecolonyhotel.com; www.thecolonyhotel.com); $125–430 per night. The Colony has an impressive facade reminiscent of New England's earliest grand resorts. Expect a luxurious stay: Rooms have period furnishings and verandas that overlook the ocean. Dogs on a leash are allowed on the hotel's private beach and by the pool area, but not in the pool water itself. A "walking area" is provided for pet owners, who pay an extra fee of $25 per night, per pet.

The Green Heron Inn, 126 Ocean Avenue, Kennebunkport (207-967-3315; www.green-heroninn.com); $80–170 per night. With a key location on famed Ocean Avenue and locally renowned hearty breakfasts, the Green Heron Inn is a wonderful stop for any traveler—but it's especially nice for pet owners. Innkeepers Charles and Carol Reid welcome animals in certain rooms with prior notice, as long as they are not left unattended during their stay.

The Lodge at Turbat's Creek, 7 Turbat's Creek Road, Kennebunkport (207-967-8700; info@visitkennebunkport.com; www.visitkennebunkport.com); $79–169 per night. The lodge bills itself as "unpretentious and comfortable," and offers exterior corridors, colorful landscaping, and 26 clean, well-furnished rooms. Guests enjoy continental breakfasts (delivered daily from a local bakery) and a heated outdoor swimming pool. Well-behaved pets are welcome.

The Seaside Motor Inn and Cottages, Kennebunkport (207-967-4461; 1-866-300-6750; www.kennebunkbeach.com); $730–1,470 per week or $2,620–6,995 per month. Though pets aren't allowed in the motor inn, they can stay in eight of the Seaside's well-equipped cottages—and best of all, they can join their owners at the site's private, sandy beach. Seaside charges a fee of $50 per pet, per night, but that will be refunded at the end of your stay providing your animal didn't cause any damages or leave a mess.

Shorelands Guest Resort, Route 9, Kennebunkport (207-985-4460; 1-800-99-BEACH; idlease@cyber-tours.com; www.shorelands.com); $39–175 per night or $245–995 per week. Shorelands offers motel rooms, two-bedroom apartments, and cottages, along with a swimming pool and hot tub, barbecue areas, a playground, laundry facilities, and bicycles for borrowing. Pet owners pay a $20 security deposit and a fee of $10 per night; animals must stay off the furniture, stay on a leash, and stay in the company of their owners.

Wildwood Cottages, 122 Wildes District Road, Kennebunkport (207-967-3377; wildwoodcottages@hotmail.com); $50–80 per night or $300–525 per week. Pets are welcome without extra fees at these cozy, affordable cottages located a few minutes from **Dock Square** (see "Out and About"). Two of the units are chalet-style A-frames with lofts and downstairs living areas; the other two are traditional cottages with separate bedrooms and screened-in porches. All four have cable TV and sleep four to five people.

The Yachtsman Lodge and Marina, Ocean Avenue, Kennebunkport (207-967-2511; innkeeper@yachtsmanlodge.com; www.yachtsmanlodge.com); $129–255 per night. Each room in this luxury hotel, which overlooks the Kennebunk River, features decor intended to mimic the interior of the yachts that cruise along the Maine seacoast: French doors open to a waterfront patio, and down comforters cover the beds. Guests also enjoy the complimentary use of bikes and canoes. Pets that weigh less than 50 pounds are welcome for a fee of $19 per night, per pet.

Kittery
Enchanted Nights Bed & Breakfast, 29 Wentworth Street, Kittery (207-439-1489; www.enchanted-nights-bandb.com); $55–240 per night. The owners of this B&B are serious animal lovers—they serve vegetarian breakfasts, own pets themselves, and donate the pet fee ($15–25 per stay, not per night) to the local animal shelter. You won't have to sacrifice any comfort to get this kind of welcome, however; the rooms have whirlpools, fireplaces, feather beds, and antique furniture.

Litson Villas, 127 State Road, Kittery (207-439-5000; 1-800-8455; info@litsonvillas.com; www.litsonvillas.com); $49.95–115 per night. Dogs are welcome for overnight stays at Litson Villas, a group of 27 affordable and neatly kept cottages located about 1 mile from the Kittery outlet stores. Each cottage has a porch, cable TV, and a full-sized refrigerator, stove, and microwave. There are no extra fees for pet owners.

Ogunquit
West Highland Inn, 14 Shore Road, Ogunquit (207-646-2181; www.westhighlandinn.com); $80–145 per night. White picket fence, gabled roof, quilts, breakfast nook—this place is about as quaint as it gets. The inn's three Westies-in-residence (Ferguson, Clementine, and Eliza Jane) welcome other well-behaved pets to their home with some restrictions: Owners pay a $25–75 one-time pet fee; dogs should not be left unattended; owners are responsible for cleaning up after their animals; and pets are not allowed on the furniture.

Old Orchard Beach
Beau Rivage Motel, 54 East Grand Avenue, Old Orchard Beach (207-934-4668; 1-800-939-4668; brivage@gwi.net; www.beaurivagemotel.com); $45–135 per night. This motel has rooms,

apartments, and suites with air-conditioning, cable TV, and telephones. Guests can take advantage of a swimming pool, hot tub, sauna, and deck, or walk a block to reach the beach. "Small" pets (call to see if yours qualifies) are welcome in certain rooms with a $10 per night charge and a $25 nonrefundable security deposit.

Old Colonial Motel, 61 West Grand Avenue, Old Orchard Beach (207-934-9862; oldcol@gwi.net; www.oldcolonialmotel.com); $60–195 per night. Located directly on the beach, this motel has exterior corridors, an outdoor swimming pool, an exercise room with a hot tub and sauna, a video-rental area with more than 800 movies, a snack counter, and beach chairs, and umbrellas available for rent. Pets that weigh less than 40 pounds are welcome for an additional $5 per night.

Sandpiper Beachfront Motel, 2 Cleaves Street, Old Orchard Beach (207-934-2733; www.sandpiperbeachfrontmotel.com); $55–75 per night. The Sandpiper enjoys a prime location right on Old Orchard Beach. Owners Denis and Daphne Rioux pride themselves on providing "down-home hospitality" and a friendly atmosphere with daily maid service, free coffee, air-conditioning, and kitchenettes. Pets can come along for the fun for an extra $10 per night.

Sea View Motel, 65 West Grand Avenue, P.O. Box 677, Old Orchard Beach (207-934-4180;

1-800-541-8439; www.seaview-getaway.com); $50–250 per night. Choose from rooms, suites, and studios at this three-story beachfront accommodation with a swimming pool. One pet weighing less than 60 pounds is allowed per room with a $100 cash deposit. Owner Kim Verreault has set aside a special "pet relief" area on the property and asks that animals not be left alone in rooms.

Waves Oceanfront Resort, 87 West Grand Avenue, Old Orchard Beach (207-934-4949; www.wavesoceanfront.com); rooms, $59–154 per night; cottages, $450–1,700 per week. This packed resort sits right on the beach—a mixed blessing for pet owners, because dogs aren't allowed on the beach during most daylight hours in the summer. Still, if you're craving the sights and sounds of the surf, this might be just the place for you. The pier is a short walk away, and the resort's rooms and cottages have air-conditioning, decks, and great views. Pets are welcome in all the cottages and certain resort rooms.

Saco
The Classic Motel, 21 Ocean Park Road, Saco (207-282-5569; 1-800-290-3909; vjay@classic-motel.com; www.classicmotel.com); $50–85 per night. The Classic offers suites with kitchenettes, queen- or full-sized beds, air-conditioning, color TVs, and the standard motel-style setup with exterior corridors. (One suite has a whirlpool tub.) You'll

also find an indoor swimming pool, an outdoor hot tub, and a patio area. Pets are welcome.

The Crown 'N' Anchor Inn, 121 North Street, Saco (207-282-3829; 1-800-561-8865); $75–130 per night. "We've had almost every kind of animal stay here, from parakeets to cats and dogs," says John Barclay, the inn's co-owner. "No horses or cows yet!" Never say never . . . This impressive accommodation (on the state's Historic Register) is reminiscent of mansions in the Deep South. Full country breakfasts include fresh-squeezed juice, and ice cream. Pets are welcome at the Crown 'N' Anchor for an extra fee of $5 per pet, per night

Hampton Inn Saco–Old Orchard Beach, 48 Industrial Park Road, Saco (207-282-7222; info@saco-hamptoninn.com; www.saco-hamptoninn.com); $109–149 per night. This modern chain hotel has in-room coffeemakers, irons, and safe-deposit boxes; an exercise room; a pool; cable TV; and a free airport shuttle. It's located in a commercial area about 2 miles from Old Orchard Beach and about 10 minutes from Portland. Pets are welcome with no extra fees.

Wells

Ne'r Beach Motel, 395 Post Road, Wells (207-646-2636; nerbeach@maine.rr.com; www.nerbeach.com); $39–109 per night. "We find that people who travel with their pets really care about them and take good care of them," says Bill Reid, who owns Ne'r Beach with his wife, Joanne. The motel has a large

grassy area for walking dogs; quiet pets are welcome with prior notice for $10 per night, on the condition that they stay off the furniture and are never left alone in a room.

West Lebanon

Inn the Orchard, 456 West Lebanon Road, West Lebanon (1-888-658-3488; info@inntheorchard.com; www.inntheorchard.com); $75–135 per night. Your pet can join the menagerie at Inn the Orchard: Three cats, a bird, and a dog already live on-site—along with the resident veterinarian. Pet owners pay a $10 per night charge on their first visit, though future visits are fee-free (assuming your pet has shown he won't dismantle the place). The inn is away from the hustle-and-bustle of the coastline but close enough (20 miles to Wells beach) to the action if you're in the mood for a crowd.

Campgrounds

Kennebunk

Yankeeland Campground, P.O. Box 829, Kennebunk (207-985-7576); $18–20 per night. Yankeeland is primarily set up to accommodate visitors with pop-up campers and RVs. Full-hookup and drive-through sites are available, along with laundry facilities, a swimming pool, showers, a basketball court, a playground, and a camp store selling ice cream, firewood, groceries, and other sundries. The campground is located about 10 miles from Kennebunkport. Quiet, nonbarking dogs are welcome.

Kennebunkport

Salty Acres Campground,
277 Mills Road (Route 9),
Kennebunkport (207-967-8623;
207-967-2483; beachwood-
motel@adelphia.net; www.beach-
woodmotel.com); $20–28 per
night. Located just outside
Kennebunkport near Goose Rocks
Beach, Salty Acres is home to 300
sunny and wooded sites, an adult
pool and a "kiddie" pool, full
hookups, a camp store, laundry
facilities, hot showers, and flush
toilets. Pets must stay on a leash
and not disturb other guests.

Wells

Elmere Campground, 525 Post
Road, Route 1, Wells (207-646-
5538); $14–20 per night. Located
1 mile from the ocean and
halfway between Wells and
Ogunquit, this family-friendly
campground is an affordable
home base for exploring the
region. Each site has a fire pit
and picnic table; campers also
have access to full hookups, hot
showers, and flush toilets. Dogs
are welcome on a leash at no
extra fee.

Gregoire's Campground, Route
109, Wells (207-646-3711; 1-800-
639-2442, ext.620); call for rate
information. Tents, campers, and
trailers will all find a spot to rest
at Gregoire's, a 30-acre family-
owned campground located just
off the Maine Turnpike. A recreation hall, convenience store,
and outdoor play equipment are
available on-site, and the Wells
trolley stops by regularly. Each
campsite has a fireplace and
picnic table. Dogs must stay on
a leash.

**Ocean View Cottages and
Campground,** 84 Harbor Road,
Wells (207-646-3308); campsites,
$21–30 per night; cottages,
$340–660 per week. Ocean View
has plain-and-simple tent sites,
RV hookup sites, and housekeeping cottages. Some of the larger
cottages feature full-sized
kitchens, cable TV, wall-to-wall
carpets, and air-conditioning.
Campers also have use of a
swimming pool, tennis courts,
a playground, a recreation hall,
and a game room. Quiet dogs are
welcome, as long as they are not
left unattended and are kept on
a leash.

Pinederosa, 128 North Village
Road, Wells (207-646-2492;
info@pinederosa.com; www.
pinederosa.com); $19.50–24.50
per night. Tent campers and RV
owners can choose from sites
surrounded by trees or set in
sunny, open fields (a swimming
pool is also on-site). Dogs on a
leash are welcome as long as
they're quiet and have owners
who will clean up after them:
"We're pet owners ourselves and
know that pets are a big part of
many camping families," say
owners Greg and Dawn.

Sea-Vu Campground, Route 1,
Wells (207-646-7732; www.sea-
vucampground.com); $22–43 per
night. Sea-Vu sits beside the harbor and open ocean; in addition
to the views, parents and their
kids will also appreciate the on-
site 18-hole mini-golf course,
swimming pool, video game
room, basketball and volleyball
courts, playground, lending
library, aerobics classes, and

camp store. Well-behaved pets on a leash are welcome at no additional fee.

York Harbor

Libby's Oceanside Campground, Route 1A, York Harbor (207-363-4171; www.libbysoceancamping.com); $37–47 per night. Pull your RV right up to the beach and watch the waves roll in. With a setting like this, the view is the primary attraction (and the higher-than-average nightly rates show we're willing to pay for it). Sites have water, sewer, and electricity hookups. Pets are welcome but must be leashed and can't be left alone at the campground.

Homes, Cottages, and Cabins for Rent

Kennebunkport

Batson's River Cottages, Goose Rocks Beach, Kennebunkport (207-985-4397; brc@cybertours.com; www.batsonsrivercottages.com); $115 per night or $850 per week. These four fully equipped cottages sit in a secluded location along a scenic tidal pool. All have a deck or a porch, two bedrooms and a pullout couch, showers, picnic tables, barbecue grills, and plenty of room for kids and dogs to play. Owners John and Faith Lush welcome well-behaved pets with prior notice.

Cabot Cove Cottages, P.O. Box 1082, Kennebunkport (207-967-5424; 1-800-962-5424; jcodman @cabotcovecottages.com; www.cabotcovecottages.com); $85–175 per night or $600–1,135 per week. "We make a big deal out of pets here as a general rule," says animal lover and Cabot Cove owner John Codman "We've got plenty of space for them to run around in, and there's a saltwater tidal cove for them to enjoy." (Certain breeds are not allowed.) The cottages have color TVs, pine-board walls, kitchenettes, and stocked linen closets with sheets and towels, including special "doggie towels."

Gail's House, 69 Western Avenue, Kennebunkport (207-967-4321; gdy@gailyork.com); $1,200 per week. This recently renovated home sleeps six in three bedrooms and also features a deck, barbecue grill, TV and VCR, and large living room. Children are welcome, and pets are considered on a case-by-case basis; insurance restrictions prevent the owner from allowing certain breeds on the property. Pet owners pay an additional $100 fee.

The Munson Cottage, 58 South Maine Street, Kennebunkport (207-967-3731; 20south@cstone.net); $2,500 per week. This "cottage" is really a large house with six bedrooms, a big yard, a screened-in porch, and a wooded location about 2 miles from **Dock Square** (see "Out and About"); the breakwater is a five-minute walk away. House-trained dogs—no puppies, please—are welcome with preapproval from the owners. All linens, towels, and kitchenware are provided.

New Harbor View Cottages, 1061 Post Road, Wells (207-646-3356; 1-877-281-9609; cottages@newharborview.com; www.newharborview.com); $55–80 per night or $315–525 per week. These warmly decorated, fully furnished cottages with pine-board interior walls sit together in a row and share a large lawn. Choose from one or two bedrooms: All have screened-in porches, full-sized kitchens and bathrooms, ceiling fans; linens and towels are provided. Pets are welcome with prior approval for an extra fee of $5 per night.

Over the River . . . And Through the Woods, 101 Goose Rocks Road, Kennebunkport (207-967-2105; bobloulipkin@cybertours.com; www.goose-rockspottery.com); "Over the River," $135 per night, $900 per week, or $3,400 per month; "And Through the Woods," $1,100 per week or $4,200 per month. These two cleverly named rentals offer two very different vacation experiences: "Over the River," a Kennebunkport studio apartment, is just two blocks from **Dock Square** (see "Out and About") and has great water views and enough room for four people. "And Through the Woods" is an expansive, tucked-away cottage on 15 secluded acres; it has a bedroom with balcony, a Japanese soaking tub, a screen house, and on-site hiking trails. Pets are welcome at both with a $100 refundable security deposit.

Old Orchard Beach

Scrub Pine Cottages, Seacliff Avenue, Old Orchard Beach (207-934-3731; 1-800-203-2034; edge-lamb@janelle.com; www.janelle.com); $425–775 per week. Just around the corner from the beach, these cute cottages are have been professionally decorated with bright, primary colors and are surrounded by white picket fences. They are equipped with air-conditioning, full baths with showers, and kitchenettes. Each two-bedroom cottage sleeps four on one double and two twin beds. Pets are welcome.

Rental Agencies

Rivers By the Sea, 79 Ocean Avenue Extension, York (207-363-3213; info@riversbythesea.com; www.riversbythesea.com). This 20-year-old agency helps clients find permanent homes as well as vacation rentals. Of their current 250 listed rental properties, some do allow pets, but the owners generally charge an additional refundable pet deposit (anywhere from $150 to $500). Some also charge a nonrefundable fee. The agency asks that pet owners clean up after their animals and not leave them alone "for too long" in any of the properties.

OUT AND ABOUT

Animal Welfare Society (AWS), Old Holland Road, West Kennebunk (207-985-3244; awsedr@cybertours.com; www.animal-welfaresociety.org). Steven Jacobsen, executive director of this animal shelter and welfare society, invites out-of-towners to visit AWS's headquarters, where more than 2 miles of walking paths are available for ambles through the woods and fields. The society also hosts events and gatherings throughout the year, including the annual **Strut Your Mutt Dog Walk** (held the third Sunday in September on Kennebunk Beach) and the **AWS Craft Show** (held the Saturday prior to Labor Day weekend on the Kennebunkport village green).

Architectural Walking Tours, Brick Store Museum, 117 Main Street, Kennebunk (207-985-4802; info@brickstoremuseum.com; www.brickstoremuseum.com); $5 per person. Take an informative stroll through **Kennebunk's Summer Street district,** which is on the National Register of Historic Places. Rich in architectural history, the district includes examples of Colonial, Greek Revival, Queen Anne, Italianate, and Federal-style buildings, mostly homes that once belonged to the area's wealthy ship captains and merchants. The tour is led by staffers and volunteers from the Brick Store Museum.

Cape Porpoise, Kennebunkport. After you've visited the region's gift shops and tourist traps, make a point to stop by this working fishing village located about 3 miles east of Dock Square (see listing below). Renowned (obviously) for its seafood, this is a quiet, picturesque place where locals still work at the trades that Maine is famous for.

Captain Satch and Sons, 793 Morrills Mill Road, North Berwick (207-324-9655; 207-337-0716; satch@cybertours.com; www.captainsatch.com); $55–75 per person or $330–450 per charter. The Captain Satch boats depart twice daily from Wells Harbor for bass fishing charters. They can accommodate six people per trip and do allow pets as long as no human passengers are uncomfortable with the arrangement. "I enjoy letting guests take their pets along, as I have always had dogs myself and still have many other pets at home, including cats, a horse, and a parrot," says Captain Satch McMahon.

Dock Square, downtown Kennebunkport. A maze of art galleries, gift shops, restaurants, and boutiques, Dock Square is the one place every visitor to Kennebunkport wanders through at least once or twice. Traffic can be terrible (and parking even worse), but the place has a charm and lure that few tourists can resist. With a dog in tow, you may have to limit yourself to window-shopping, but you'll nonetheless enjoy meandering through the tree-lined streets and gaping at the former estates (now mostly B&Bs) that watch over the area.

Ferry Beach State Park, 95 Bayview Road, Saco (207-283-0067; 207-624-6080). With all of the region's beaches and attractions competing for attention, it might be easy to miss this 100-acre, diverse park—but don't. The sweeping terrain includes wetlands, open beaches, dunes, and woods; trails are color-coded and easy to follow. You're likely to see piping plovers, rare black tupelo trees, goldenrod, highbush blueberry bushes, and, unfortunately, poison ivy. Pet owners are expected to clean up after their animals.

Finestkind Scenic Cruises, Perkins Cove, Ogunquit (207-646-5227; info@finestkindcruises. com; www.finestkindcruises. com); $7–14 per person. Well-behaved pets are welcome to join their owners at Finestkind for a breakfast cruise, a Nubble Lighthouse cruise, a lobstering trip, or an evening cocktail cruise. (The company does reserve the right to deny access to a pet if one of the passengers is allergic to or afraid of animals.) Finestkind's three traditional wooden boats are docked at Perkins Cove and operate from May 1 through mid-October.

Fort McClary State Historic Site, Kittery Point Road (Route 103), Kittery (207-384-5160). Kittery is called the Gateway to Maine, and Fort McClary protected that gateway from intruders for nearly 300 years during the Revolutionary War, the War of 1812, the Civil War, the Spanish-American War, and World War I. Open during the warmer months, the site includes historic structures such as the Blockhouse, the Rifleman's House, and the remains of a barracks building. Dogs must be on a leash.

Ghostly Tours of York, 250 York Street, York Village (207-363-0000); $7 per person. The town of York is made up of three distinct communities, which the locals call "the Yorks": York Beach, York Harbor, and York Village. In the village, the local historical society maintains a complex of seven historic buildings that highlight the town's past. Ghostly Tours' candlelit nighttime walking trips are narrated to give visitors a glimpse at the spookier side of Old York's folklore—and to raise the hairs on the back of your neck.

Harris Farm, 280 Buzzell Road, Dayton (207-499-2678; dixie-harris@yahoo.com; www.harris-farm.com). This cross-country ski center allows pets on its trails during the week but not on crowded weekends. In warmer weather, visitors often bring their leashed pets for a walk around the farm, and an old-fashioned shopping trip for vegetables, milk in glass bottles, and churned butter.

Lower Village, downtown Kennebunk. This tourist mecca sits across the river from its larger cousin, **Dock Square** (see above listing). Formerly a bustling hub for sea merchants, today the area is lined with shops and eateries. Boats still travel in and out, though now they're likely to be seeking pleasure, not business.

McDougal Orchards, 201 Hanson's Ridge Road, Springvale (207-324-5054; www.mcdougalorchards.com). In the fall, your leashed dog is welcome to help you pick your own apples at this expansive orchard; in the winter, it doubles as a cross-country ski area. Well-behaved dogs under voice control can join skiers on the trail on weekdays (but not weekends). Weekday ski rates are $8 per adult and $5 for students; children six and under are free.

Memorial Park, Heath Street, Old Orchard Beach. They may not be allowed on Main Street, the beach, or the pier from May through Labor Day, but dogs are welcome to romp leash-free at an exercise area in a corner of this pretty park.

Nubble Light, The Nubble. One of the most photographed sights on the south coast, the 1879 Nubble Light sits with its keeper's Victorian-style cottage on an offshore island but can be viewed from the tip of the Cape Neddick peninsula (Route 1A to Nubble Road).

Ocean Avenue, Kennebunkport. Hop in the car and cruise along this breathtaking strip of road beside the Atlantic. You'll find places to pull off and enjoy the many views, including that of former president George Bush's summer estate, located on its own jetty known as **Walker Point.** Don't worry about missing it—even if the home itself were hard to see (which it's not), the crowds of pointing tourists would inevitably lead your eyes in the right direction.

Rachel Carson National Wildlife Refuge, 321 Port Road, Wells 04090 (207-646-9226). Rachel Carson is the author of *Silent Spring,* a 1962 book that many credit with single-handedly starting the environmental movement in the United States. Today her

name lives on at this 7,600-acre refuge spread throughout York and Cumberland Counties. Start at the Route 9 headquarters to get maps and orient yourself before setting off to explore the coastal wilderness. Dogs must be on a leash.

***Second Chance* Scenic Lobster Cruises,** 4 Western Avenue, Lower Village, Kennebunk (207-967-5507; 1-800-767-BOAT; www.firstchancewhalewatch.com); $7.50–15. When trips aren't full, the owners of the *Second Chance* allow pet owners to bring their furry friends aboard to take in views of **Walker Point** (see **Ocean Avenue** above), **Bumpkin Island** (which houses a colony of harbor seals), **Goat Island Light,** and **Cape Porpoise Harbor.** In addition to day trips at 11 AM and 1, 3, and 5 PM daily, the company also offers a sunset cruise at 7 PM. Reservations are recommended.

Vaughan Woods State Park, 28 Oldsfields Road, South Berwick (207-384-5160; 207-624-6080). To find the park, take Route 236 to the intersection of Vine Street and Oldsfields Road and watch for the signs. If you're only in southern Maine for a vacation, you probably won't have enough time to explore all 250 acres of this vast, heavily forested park that lies along the Salmon Falls River. The trails wind through seemingly endless tracts of old-growth forest; if you're looking for solitude, this is the place. Dogs must be on a leash.

Wells Breakwater, Wells. Feeling adventurous? Walk all the way

THE "WIGGLY BRIDGE" IS THE SMALLEST SUSPENSION BRIDGE IN THE UNITED STATES.

out to the end of the rocks at this somewhat hard-to-find jetty and small wildlife preserve. (From Post Road, turn onto Mile Road and drive past the marsh and Billy's Chowder House. Take the next available left and drive to the end of the peninsula until you reach an unmarked parking area.) Dogs on a leash are welcome as long as owners clean up after them; pooper-scooper bags and trash cans are provided.

Wells Harbor Saturday Night Concerts, Wells Harbor Park, Wells. Surfer tunes, piano recitals, Elvis impersonators, country crooners—you name it, you'll probably find it one Saturday night at Wells's weekly free summer concert series. (Check out www.harborconcerts.org for the latest lineups before your visit, or call the Wells Chamber of Commerce at 207-646-8104.) Pets are welcome to groove along with the music but must be leashed and nondisruptive.

Wells Recreational Area, Route 9A, Wells. Dogs on a leash are welcome at this 70-acre site complete with a pond, a picnic area, a baseball diamond, a soccer field, and tennis and basketball courts. It's a great spot for flying a kite or just relaxing away from the tourist crowds. Owners must pick up after their animals.

Whaleback Light, Kittery. Although it sits in Maine waters and is operated by the town of Kittery, the townspeople of nearby Portsmouth, New Hampshire, also claim this well-known lighthouse as a source of local pride. You can catch a glimpse of the historic structure from Fort Foster and other spots along the shoreline, though you'll get your best view from on board a boat sailing in or out of Portsmouth Harbor.

Wiggly Bridge, Old Mill Road, York. The name is silly, but accurate: The country's smallest suspension bridge really does shimmy and shake when you walk across. Park on the street and walk down the raised path, across the bridge, and into **Sherman Woods,** a small preserve. It's a fun stop for getting your feet wet, walking, and exploring.

York Harbor Shore Path, York. This mile-long scenic walking path is where you'll find the area's famous "wiggly bridge" (see above listing), a favorite with kids. The trail starts at Lindsay Road and goes, well, over the river and through the woods. It's an easy and fun way to explore York's shoreline.

QUICK BITES

Amore Breakfast, 178 Shore Road, Ogunquit (207-646-6661; lmcusimano@loa.com). This tiny, nostalgic restaurant serves eggs Benedict, French toast, hash browns, bacon, and other traditional specialties. "We have four tables outside and a patio for take-out, and well-behaved pets are more than welcome," says owner Leanne Cusimano.

Barnacle Billy's, Perkins Cove, Ogunquit (207-646-5575; www.barnbilly.com). Barnacle Billy's is actually two restaurants sitting side by side at Perkins Cove. "Both have a very informal outside dining area," says Billy himself. "We have many customers who bring their pets to dine outside with them." Diners choose from a varied menu that includes items like lobster, burgers, barbecue chicken, and Billy's famous rum punch.

Bob's Clam Hut, 315 Route 1, Kittery (207-439-4233; www.bobsclamhut.com). They call themselves a "corny little clam hut by the side of the road," and that's just about right. Upscale it may not be, but Bob's has been keeping 'em coming to its take-out window and heated indoor restaurant since 1956. Deep-frying, as you might expect, is a specialty, as are "baskets" with fries and 'slaw.

Capt'n Hook's, Route 1, Wells (207-646-6646; www.kennebunkport.org/lobsterbakes). This fish market and seafood take-out restaurant has a picnic area where you can enjoy traditional lobster dinners as well as sandwiches, lobster rolls, and all kinds of fried seafood.

The Clam Shack, Dock Street (at the bridge), Kennebunkport (207-967-2560). You'll smell the delicious deep-fried odor of this always crowded take-out stand while you're waiting in traffic to get into Dock Square (see "Out and About"). Seafood and more seafood is on the menu.

David's Café, 21–23 Shore Road, Ogunquit (207-646-5206). Open April through October, this casual café has plenty of outdoor seating and serves soup and chowder, lobster bisque, salads, seafood sandwiches and rolls, pasta, chicken, vegetarian entrées, and a rotating list of daily specials.

Enrico's Delicatessen, 659 Main Street, Ogunquit (207-646-9238; www.enricosdeli.com). Stop into this small sub shop to grab a sandwich, then enjoy it on the deck out front. No one would accuse this place of being roomy, but it offers a good selection and makes a convenient quick stop for lunch (or for packing up the picnic basket).

Fancy That, Main Street (corner of Beach Street and Route 1), Ogunquit (207-646-4118). This corner spot specializes in serving coffee, pastries and pies, sandwiches, chowders, and bagels during the summer season. Outdoor, streetside tables are covered with cheery green umbrellas.

Rooftop Café, 237 Main Street, Ogunquit (207-646-6655; www.clubogunquit.com/rooftop). Cooks here prepare the sandwiches, fried foods, and salads at an outdoor food bar—while you're waiting, enjoy the views and sip one of the café's famous martinis (the other half of the business is a martini bar). Dogs are welcome to sit on the grassy area next to outdoor tables but must be on a leash.

Scoop Deck, Eldredge Road (at Route 1), Wells (207-646-5150). Pet owners will appreciate the take-out window at this roadside stop serving steamed hot dogs, ice cream and frozen yogurt, cold drinks, and other summer staples. Nothin' fancy, but oh so good.

Seafare Market, Route 1, Moody (207-646-5460). Located next to the Moody Post Office, this market has an extensive take-out selection with items such as lobster bisque, chowders, and crab and lobster rolls. You can also get live lobster packed to travel. During the high season, they're open seven days a week.

HOT SPOTS FOR SPOT

Cool Dogs, Crazy Cats and Chocolate Moose, 17 Perkins Cove Road, Ogunquit (207-646-9040; cooldogs@aol.com). Located near the entrance to Perkins Cove, this eclectic shop specializes in pet gifts and sundries, including gourmet bakery treats, animal apparel, collars and leashes, aromatherapy products, and animal-themed housewares and clothing. "Pets, of course, are always welcome in the store!" says owner Elysa Cooper.

Kennel Shop and Animal Care Center, 4 Scammon Street, No. 18, Saco (207-282-2850). This pet-supply store, located in the Saco Valley Shopping Center, is a good quick stop for refills on treats, toys, food, and other basic needs for all furry, feathered, or scaled travelers.

Keoke Kennels, 5 Hodgman Avenue, Saco (207-282-6574; dplumme5@maine.rr.com). For more than 27 years, Mary Plummer has run this overnight

boarding facility located about a mile from Old Orchard Beach. Dogs have indoor/outdoor pens with roofs, and cats have large indoor pens. Animals are welcome for long-term boarding or for just one night; grooming is also available. "In the summertime, about 70 percent of the dogs we have here are with their owners on vacation," Plummer says.

Lebel Dog Grooming, 1501 Post Road, Wells (207-641-2027; www. lebeldoggrooming.8k.com.) If your pooch gets socked by a skunk on vacation, never fear: Janette Lebel, owner of this cozy grooming salon, will take care of that smelly problem. She can also do a flea bath, cut, shampoo, earwax flushing, and soothing hot-oil skin treatments. Lebel's shop also carries a variety of pet health-care products like bowls, leashes, collars, and coats.

Meadow Winds Farm, 331 Route 103, York (207-439-7800; mwfarm@aol.com).

Chuck and Peggy d'Entremont run this updated facility with their daughter, Katie. Twenty 4-by-13-foot indoor pens provide overnight boarding for dogs, which get out four times a day to romp with the other dogs in an outdoor run or indoor playroom. Cats have a separate area with windows and litter boxes. All the animals get attention throughout their stay. "We treat them the same way we would want our pets to be treated," says Chuck. Rates are generally $18.50 per day.

Paw-zn-Around, 8 New County Road, Saco (207-283-6642; pawznaround@cybertours.com). At this doggie day-care facility, animals interact with each other in play groups and romp in kiddie pools in the summertime. Dogs are welcome for half-day ($14) or full-day ($22) stays; owners can also take advantage of obedience training, handling classes, and grooming. Owner Jeanne Labonte asks only that your dog be up-to-date on standard vaccinations and nonaggressive toward people and other dogs.

Pet Dreams Pet Sitting, 50 Park Avenue, Old Orchard Beach (207-934-7387; dfranco@gwi.net). For more than 10 years, Barbara Sykes has cared for pets in the Old Orchard Beach area with dog- and cat-sitting house calls.

She charges $8 for dogs and $7 for cats for each 45-minute visit (each additional pet is $1 or $2 extra). Sykes also takes care of vacationing pets while their owners are at dinner or are otherwise occupied.

Sweets Pet Supply, 112 York Street (Route 1 South), Kennebunk (207-985-3734). This pet shop specializes in canine treats, according to owner John Kelley. "It's like a candy store for dogs in here," he says. Sweets also sells holistic food and medications, along with supplies for cats, birds, and other small animals. Kelley also does grooming by appointment.

Town 'N' Country Grooming, 1532 Post Road, Wells (207-646-1533). "I love my job!" says groomer and owner Kathy Levesque, which might explain why she's still at it after 20-plus years. In addition to washing and clipping all breeds of dogs, she also works with quite a few cats, especially the state's famous Maine Coons.

York Country Kennels, 915 Route 1, York (207-363-7950). This indoor kennel in a country setting has room for about 50 dogs in its large air-conditioned and heated pens and runs. Cats have "town houses" in separate quarters. Pets are welcome for day care or for overnight short- or long-term stays.

IN CASE OF EMERGENCY

Animal Medical Associates,
838 Portland Road, Saco (207-282-5151).

Kennebunk Veterinary Hospital,
149 Fletcher Street, Kennebunk (207-985-4277).

Kittery Animal Hospital,
195 State Road, Kittery (207-439-4158; 207-439-6674).

Scarborough Animal Hospital,
29 First Street, Scarborough (207-883-4412).

Wells Veterinary Hospital,
418 Sanford Road, Wells (207-646-8323).

Greater Portland and Casco Bay

PET-FRIENDLY RATING: 🦴 🦴 🦴 🦴 🦴

From city streets to country lanes, mountain peaks to rushing rivers, and deep woods to open ocean, the Greater Portland region at times seems like 10 vacation spots all rolled up into one convenient package. One day you might find yourself browsing shops and galleries in the highbrow corners of Old Port; the next, you're outlet hopping in Freeport or hiking a trail on the way back to your waterfront campsite.

And then, of course, there are the islands: So many dot sparkling Casco Bay that they have been termed the Calendar Islands—one for each day of the year. There might not be *quite* that many, but there are certainly more inlets, estuaries, tiny downtowns, and rocky picnic spots than you could ever explore in just a week or two. Fortunately, the local ferry service (see Casco Bay Lines under "Out and About") allows pets on board for visits to many of the isles, and Orrs Island and Bailey Island are connected to the mainland via roadway.

For the most part, animal owners will find this region to be an accommodating place. Pet shops and doggie day cares are plentiful, and the region's many state parks allow ample opportunity for four-legged explorations. Greater Portland attracts and welcomes tourists but is not defined by its tourism—perhaps that's what makes it so appealing. Grab the leash and enjoy.

ACCOMMODATIONS

Hotels, Motels, Inns, and Bed & Breakfasts

Bath
Inn at Bath, 969 Washington Street, Bath (207-443-4294; 1-800-423-0964; innkeeper@innatbath.com; www.innatbath.com); $135–185 per night. Located in Bath's picturesque historic district, the Inn at Bath offers upscale rooms and suites. (Innkeeper Nick Bayard also gives free overnight stays to patients undergoing chemotherapy at the nearby Bath Cancer Treatment Center.) Pets are permitted, but owners must sign a pet-policy form that details the inn's animal-related regulations.

Brunswick
Viking Motor Inn, 287 Bath Road, Brunswick (1-800-429-6661; vikingin@gwi.net; www.vikingmotorinn.com); $79–119 per night. "We have a nicely wooded area for walking pets in the back of the property," says Viking owner and animal lover Sue Kelly. "As long as people are considerate about picking up after their pets, we welcome them." All 28 rooms have parking spaces in front of the door, refrigerators, and microwaves. For larger families or groups, there are also deluxe efficiencies. The inn also has an outdoor heated pool and picnic area.

Cape Elizabeth
Inn by the Sea, 40 Bowery Beach Road, Cape Elizabeth (207-799-3134; 1-800-888-4287; info@innbythesea.com; www.innbythesea.com); $139–489 per night. This luxury resort is somewhat renowned among traveling animal owners. The management strives to provide four-footed guests with "the same level of service and excellence that our human guests have come to know and love." Pet-friendly suites have "special dog amenities," and the room-service pet menu (yes, you read that right) includes items such as Doggie Tapas, turkey dinners, and Gourmet Doggie Bon Bons.

Falmouth
Quaker Tavern Bed & Breakfast, 377 Gray Road (Route 26 North), Falmouth (207-797-5540; quakerbb@aol.com); $75–100 per night. Thirteen acres surround this historic B&B; the

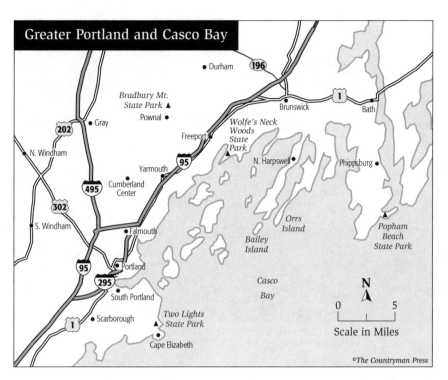

Greater Portland and Casco Bay

Durham · (196)

Bradbury Mt.
State Park ▲
Pownal ·

Brunswick · (1) · Bath

Gray · (202)

Wolfe's Neck
Woods
State
Park ▲

Freeport ·

N. Windham ·

Yarmouth ·

N. Harpswell ·

Phippsburg ·

(95)

(495) Cumberland
Center

Orrs
Island

Popham
Beach
State Park ▲

(302)

S. Windham · Falmouth ·

Bailey
Island

(95) · Portland

(295)

South Portland ·

Casco
Bay

N

(1) · Scarborough

Two Lights
▲ State Park

0 —— 5

Cape Elizabeth

Scale in Miles

©The Countryman Press

innkeeper, Donna Little, prefers to walk through them barefoot, and so asks pet owners to always clean up after their animals! Each of the four guest rooms in the building (c. 1780) has a fireplace, feather bed, and private parlor. There are no extra fees for animals, but owners are asked bring along a pet bed.

Freeport

Freeport Inn and Café, Route 1, Freeport (207-865-3106; 1-800-99-VALUE; info@freeportinn.com; www.freeportinn.com); $60–140 per night. Your dog will have no trouble finding trouble at this pet-friendly inn; with 25 acres of lawns, a tidal river, and a "pet exercise area," there's plenty of room to get out and about. Some of the 80 rooms have water views, and all have cable TV, air-conditioning, and free HBO. Pets are

allowed in designated rooms; doggie cleanup bags are provided.

Isaac Randall House Bed & Breakfast, 10 Independence Drive, Freeport (207-865-9295; 1-800-865-9295; ikesspot@aol.com; www.isaacrandall.com); $65–150 per night. The Violet Room, Sampler Room, Quilt Room, and all other rooms at this historic B&B can accommodate pets for no extra fees, on the condition that animals are not left alone in the room at any time. All rooms have king- or queen-sized beds, private bathrooms, and air-conditioning; some have extra twin-sized beds, fireplaces, and TVs with VCRs.

Maine Idyll Motor Court, 1411 Route 1, Freeport (207-865-4201; www.freeportusa.com/maineidyll); $46–90 per night.

A VIEW FROM THE DOG EXERCISE AREA AT THE PET-FRIENDLY FREEPORT INN

The 20 recently renovated cottages at this complex have one to three bedrooms, refrigerators, linens, and electric or gas heat; some have fireplaces and kitchenettes. You'll also find two playgrounds, picnic tables, and hiking trails on the 20-acre property. Dogs are always welcome.

Maple Hill Bed & Breakfast,
18 Maple Avenue, Freeport (207-865-3730; 1-800-867-0478); $85–175 per night. Riptide, a golden retriever, will greet you when you arrive at this cozy three-room B&B. "Our goal is to be family-friendly, which means welcoming babies, grandparents, parents—and pets," explains Lloyd Lawrence, who runs Maple Hill with his wife, Susie. Pet owners pay an extra fee of $10 per night, per pet, and are asked to keep the animal in a crate if they leave the room.

(They have crates available if you forget yours.)

3 Sisters Bed & Breakfast,
8 Independence Drive, Freeport (207-865-4405; 1-877-865-4405; www.3sistersbb.com); call for rate information. This nonsmoking inn, located close to the downtown area on 1½ acres, is designed in a Cape Cod style and offers antiques, quilts, and modern conveniences. "We love pets!" says owner Connie Blackmer. "It's a sunshiny day when we have animals around." All rooms have a king-sized bed, a private bath, air-conditioning, and cable TV.

White Cedar Inn, 178 Main Street, Freeport (207-865-9099; jgs@whitecedarinn.com; www.whitecedarinn.com); $120–140 per night. Dogs (sorry, no cats) are allowed in the Oak Suite of this Victorian home, within walking distance of downtown

Freeport. The suite has a private entrance, a fireplace, two queen-sized beds, and an outside patio. The resident Lab, Allie, will help keep your pup company; pet owners are asked not to leave their dog alone in the room and to clean up after walks.

Orrs Island
Tower Hill Bed & Breakfast, 1565 Harpswell Islands Road, Orrs Island (207-833-2311; 1-888-833-2311; www.towerhillb-b.com); $125–15 per night. With brass beds, quilts, private baths, and sitting rooms, the three suites at Tower Hill are warm and welcoming. Harpswell Sound, a forest, and a wildlife-filled marsh are all just a few minutes' walk away. The innkeepers welcome one neutered, small- to medium-sized pet per room with prior approval for an extra $10 per night.

Phippsburg
Edgewater Farm Bed & Breakfast, 71 Small Point Road, Phippsburg (207-389-1322; www.ewfbb.com); $85–160 per night. Organic perennial gardens encircle the lawns at this charming B&B located on a Casco Bay peninsula. "We're very dog-friendly here, and I find that most people's dogs are well behaved and not a problem," says Carol Emerson, who runs Edgewater Farm with her husband, Bill. All six of the guest rooms have private baths, and guests can also take a dip in the indoor heated pool or outdoor hot tub. Pet owners pay an extra $25 per stay.

Hidden Mountain Cottages, 1659 Main Road, Phippsburg (207-389-1457; lucrecia@hidden-mtn.com; www.hiddenmtn.com); $60–80 per night or $350–600 per week. These small yellow cottages vary in size and have showers, double beds, refrigerators, and TVs; linens and towels are provided. Pets are welcome without additional fees. An on-site gift shop sells T-shirts, kids' book and activity sets, clothing, jewelry, and handmade crafts.

Small Point Bed and Breakfast, 312 Small Point Road, Phippsburg (207-389-1716); $110–140. Pet owners can stay at Small Point's 1890s carriage house; the renovated structure can comfortably accommodate a couple or small family with a queen-sized bed, sitting area, and loft. A Vermont Castings propane stove keeps things cozy, and guests also have a refrigerator and microwave. Dogs (sorry, no cats) are welcome.

Portland
Andrews on Auburn, 417 Auburn Street, Portland (207-797-9157; dandrew2@main.rr.com; www.andrewsonauburn.com); $99–175 per night. Located about 10 minutes from **Old Port** (see "Out and About"), this historic B&B inn (c. 1780) is open year-round with three rooms and three suites, a resident veterinarian, and dog treats at the front desk. Pets are welcome for an extra $10 per night fee, as long as owners don't leave them alone in the room for longer than two hours.

Best Western Merry Manor Inn, 700 Main Street, South Portland

(207-774-6151; lafayettehotels@ cybertours.com; www.bestwestern.com/merrymanorinn); $79–159 per night. This hotel is set on 5 acres of woods with hiking trails. There are no extra fees for pets, though owners are asked to keep their furry friends quiet and not leave them alone in the rooms. The Merry Manor also has facilities for conferences and banquets, and is a few minutes away from the **Old Port** district (see "Out and About").

Eastland Park Hotel, 157 High Street, Portland (1-888-671-8008; info@eastlandparkhotel.com; www.eastlandparkhotel.com); $79–129 per night. This is the kind of place you'd expect *not* to accept pets—amenities like valet parking, fine dining (with an executive chef), luxurious suites with leather furniture, a rooftop lounge, and a grand ballroom usually don't come with a PETS WELCOME sign. The Eastland Park isn't like most hotels, however, and your pet of any size or species is welcome with no restrictions or extra fees.

Holiday Inn Portland West, 81 Riverside Street, Portland (207-774-5601; www.portland-holidayinn.com); $69–149 per night. This chain hotel has a garden courtyard, country-style rooms, and a location that's close to the airport and the highway. There are no extra fees for pets, but guests traveling with animals are welcome only in the designated smoking rooms.

Howard Johnson Plaza Hotel, 155 Riverside Street, Portland (207-774-5861; info@hojoportland.

com; www.hojoportland.com); $69–119 per night. Pets are welcome at the HoJo Plaza with advance notice and a $50 refundable deposit. Amenities include an indoor swimming pool, a hot tub, a free airport shuttle, two on-site restaurants, and an exercise room. Some rooms have Jacuzzis; all have coffeemakers, irons and ironing boards, and hair dryers.

Inn at St. John, 939 Congress Street, Portland (207-756-7629; 1-800-636-9127; info@innatstjohn.com; www.innatstjohn.com); $34–174. The Inn at St. John has a European, upscale look that complements the cobblestone streets, chic boutiques, and artistic community that surround it. The hotel also offers air-conditioning, free continental breakfasts, bicycle storage, airport pickups, and nonsmoking rooms. Pets are welcome for an extra $10 per night.

Motel 6 Portland, 1 Riverside Street, Portland (207-775-0111); $42.99–63.99 per night. You can expect the standard chain-motel accommodations at this Motel 6, which, like all of the company's locations throughout the country, accepts one "small" pet per room (call to see if yours qualifies). Use the web site (www.motel6.com) to easily make reservations online.

Scarborough
Pride Motel and Cottages, 677 Route 1, Scarborough (207-883-4816; 1-800-424-3350; pjor@prodigy.net; www.holiday-junction.com); $40–105 per night. For an extra $5 per night, pet owners are welcome in any of Pride's seven motel rooms or

10 red-and-white-painted cottages. All have free HBO and air-conditioning; some motel rooms have kitchenettes, and all of the cottages have a full-sized kitchen. Other amenities include an outdoor swimming pool, volleyball court, and recreation room.

Campgrounds

Freeport
Cedar Haven Campground, 39 Baker Road, Freeport (207-865-6254; 1-800-454-3403; campcedarhaven@yahoo.com; www.campmaine.com/cedar-haven); $18–45 per night or $125–180 per week. Most of Cedar Haven's 58 campsites are wooded; 10 are reserved for tents, and the rest have hookups for RVs. Amenities include a swimming pond, a game room, a camp store, hot showers, and laundry facilities. Small camping cabins are also available for rent. Pets are welcome but must stay on a leash and off the beach and recreation field.

Desert Dunes of Maine Campground, 95 Desert Road, Freeport (207-865-6962; info@desertofmaine.com; www.desert-ofmaine.com); $20–32 per night. Located next to the unusual geographical area known as the Desert of Maine, this family campground has trails, open and shaded sites for tents and RVs, hot showers, picnic tables, volleyball and basketball courts, horseshoe pits, and laundry facilities. Pets must be quiet, on a leash, and accompanied by their owners at all times.

Winslow Memorial Park and Campground, Staples Point Road, Freeport (207-865-4198; www.freeportmaine.com/winslow-park); $17–19 per night. Managed by the town of Freeport, this park and campground is set on a Casco Bay peninsula with 100 campsites, a large picnic area, hiking trails, ocean views, a playground, and a boat launch. Dogs are welcome on a leash for a fee of $1 per night, though they are not allowed on the beach, playground, or volleyball court.

Orrs Island
Orr's Island Campground, 44 Bond Point, Orrs Island (207-833-5595; camping@orrsisland.com; www.orrsisland.com); $22–33 per night or $140–217 per week. Situated on 42 acres in Casco Bay, this family campground has a half-mile-long beach, 70 wooded sites for tents and trailers, a camp store, canoe rentals, laundry facilities, and a recreational field. Dogs are allowed at the beach but must stay on a leash. Owners are asked to accompany their animals at all times; there are no extra fees for pets.

Phippsburg
Meadowbrook Camping Area, 33 Meadowbrook Road, Phippsburg (207-386-0335; 1-800-370-CAMP; mbcamp@meadow-brookme.com; www.meadow-brookme.com); $20–30 per night. Choose from tent and RV sites at this 42-acre campground, where dogs on a leash are welcome as long as their owners clean up after them. "We have a mile-long

nature trail that winds its way through the woods to a 25-acre beaver pond where your pet can swim and exercise," says Meadowbrook's Chris Mixon. "It's a Lab's heaven." Aside from the scenery, amenities include a heated pool, bathrooms, and a recreation hall with a kitchen.

Pownal

Blueberry Pond Campground, 218 Poland Range Road, Pownal (207-688-4421; 1-877-290-1381; fun@blueberrycampground.com; www.blueberrycampground.com); $18–24 per night. This campground is located in a quiet inland area, away from the coastline crowds. Tenters and RVers can choose from private, wooded sites or sunny spots. On-site, you'll also find hiking trails, swing sets, hot showers, fire pits and barbecue grills, picnic tables, and a camp store. Dogs must be on a leash and can't be left alone.

Bradbury Mountain State Park Campground, 528 Hallowell Road, Pownal (207-287-3824; 1-800-332-1501); $9 per night Maine residents; $11 per night out-of-state residents. The camping accommodations at this scenic park (see "Out and About") are mainly designed to accommodate tents and small campers, though there are a few large and extra-large sites for campers up to 35 feet in length. The campground has a play area, a picnic area, handicapped-accessible toilets, showers, hiking trails, and a boat launch.

Scarborough

Bayley's Camping Resort, 275 Pine Point Road, Scarborough (207-883-6043; tbayley@gwi.net; www.bayleys-camping.com); $34–47 per night. There's no extra fee for pets at Bayley's, though dogs must be on a leash at all times, can't be left unattended, and are prohibited from certain areas, including the playground, ponds, and pool. Tent campers can set up at Bayley's Acres, an area separate from the RV sites with no hookups, and families can take advantage of an on-site restaurant, a game room, a general store, basketball courts, fishing ponds, and activity fields.

Wassamki Springs, 56 Saco Street, Scarborough (207-839-4276; wassamkisprings@aol.com; www.wassamkisprings.com); $17–31 per night or $95–192 per week. With a 1-mile-long stretch of beach, a trout-stocked fishing pond, boat rentals, scavenger hunts, spooky storytelling, and hayrides, there's plenty for families to do at this busy campground. Dogs must be leashed and should accompany their owners at all times. Wassamki allows most breeds of dogs; call to see if yours qualifies.

Homes, Cottages, and Cabins for Rent

Brunswick

Holland House Cottage, Brunswick (207-729-0709; info@hollandhousecottage; www.hollandhousecottage.com); $115–125 per night or $575 per week. This cute, well-kept cottage has an ocean view, a master bedroom, and a fully equipped kitchen. Breakfast-in-a-basket (usually fresh muffins, fruit, and juice) is included in the rental fee and delivered to your door each morning. "Views are lovely, and it's quiet and secluded," explains owner Pam Holland. "Our dog, Tipton, is across the lane, and he's always very interested in our canine guests!" Pets are always welcome.

Orrs Island

The Nubbin, Lowell Cove, Orrs Island (207-833-6155; msumner@ gwi.net); $695 per week. Owner Philip E. Sumner, M.D., offers this waterfront cabin for rent on Lowell Cove. The recently renovated "pied-à-terre *romantique*" can accommodate two people and one pet, and features a 340-square-foot deck, a private beach, an outdoor grill, a double bed, a kitchenette, and a secluded location. There are no extra fees for pet owners.

West Point

Fish House Cove Properties, various locations, West Point (978-283-3065; info@fhcrentals. com; www.fhcrentals.com). Owner Scott Michaels offers five houses for rent in the village of West Point, just south of Bath on Casco Bay. The **Scott House** is a new, contemporary-style home that sleeps 12 ($899–1,690 per week); the seven-bedroom **Sou'Wester** duplex has two units that can accommodate 6 to 8 people each ($1,580–2,090 per week); **Syb's Place** is a three-story contemporary with four bedrooms and three bathrooms ($1,890–2,090 per week); **Gilliam Village House** sleeps eight in four bedrooms ($800–

1,190 per week); and **Cordelia Cottage** has two bedrooms and one bath ($800–1,290 per week). All accommodations are ocean-front, and dogs (sorry, no cats or puppies) are welcome at each for an extra fee of $100 per week.

Rental Agencies

Ashmore Realty Island Rentals, 20 Welch Street, Peaks Island (207-766-5702; rentals@ashmore-realty.com; www.ashmorerealty. com). Ashmore is full of pet-loving rental agents (Wilbur the dog often hangs out at the office). Pets are allowed at many of the agency's listed rental properties, though owners usually have to pay a $100 security deposit. Available units range from small summer cottages to full-sized, year-round homes, ranging in price from about $500 to $1,500 per week. All are located on Peaks Island in Casco Bay.

Casco Bay Properties, P.O. Box 335, Freeport (207-865-2092; laney@cascobayproperties.com; www.cascobayproperties.com). "We are very pet-friendly and do our best to accommodate renters with pets," says Laney Pitt, president of this company that specializes in finding short-term accommodations for vacations and corporate stays. Choices range from studio apartments to four-bedroom luxury homes, all fully furnished and equipped. Many rentals are located directly on the ocean.

Coldwell Banker Harnden Beecher, 778 Roosevelt Terrace, Windham (207-892-0629; www.

coldwellbankerhb.com). According to rental manager Mary Jo York, the agency does manage some pet-friendly rental properties in the area that are available for short-term stays. Home-owners typically ask for a $250 to $350 security deposit, and some deposits are fully refundable. The available rentals vary each season; call for the latest listings.

OUT AND ABOUT

Baxter Woods, Portland. Dogs can run off-leash at this 30-acre park at Forest and Stevens Avenues in Portland. Pets must be under voice control but are otherwise welcome to roam the trails and woods alongside their owners.

Books Etc., 38 Exchange Street, Portland. Mutts of all shapes and sizes are welcome to browse with their owners at this friendly bookshop; you can usually find the resident border collie, Fly, napping among the stacks, and a few doggie biscuits on hand at the register.

Bradbury Mountain State Park, 528 Hallowell Road, Pownal. This inland park comprises about 590 acres of forest, crisscrossed with trails designed for hikers, bikers, snowshoers, cross-country skiers, and, we like to think, dog walkers. (The park also allows horseback riders, so make sure your pooch isn't afraid of his larger animal friends.) Take in the view from the summit, or enjoy the on-site picnic tables, playground, and baseball field.

Casco Bay Lines, Franklin Street, Portland (207-774-7871; info@ cascobaylines.com; www.casco-baylines.com); passengers, $3– 9.25; cars, $45–65. Sometimes described as a lifeline for the residents of the Casco Bay islands, this ferry service (the oldest in America) is the chief mode of transport to and from the mainland and **Peaks Island, Little Diamond Island, Great Diamond Island, Diamond Cove, Long Island, Chebeague Island**, and **Cliff Island.** The company also provides scenic cruises and trips (prices vary). Leashed dogs and other pets are welcome on board all Casco Bay vessels for a $3 round-trip charge.

Chase Charters, Falmouth (207-767-5611; info@cruisemaine.com; www.cruisemaine.com); $450 per day; $2,500–2,250 per week. This charter company has two sailboats (36 and 40 feet) and one 26-foot powerboat; the skippers can take you to a particular destination or design a trip that will take you past the Maine coast's most spectacular sights. Popular destinations include the **Harraseeket River, Richmond Island, Hog's Island**, and **Boothbay Harbor.** Owner Pete Stoops says he's never had a dog on board, but pets are welcome as long as owners clean the boat carefully after use.

Crescent Beach State Park, 66 Two Lights Road, Cape Elizabeth. Pets are not allowed on the beach for which this 243-acre park was named, but they are allowed (on a leash) in the picnic area, playground, coves, and wooded areas, and on the rock ledges and trails. The park is closed to vehicles during the off-season, but visitors are welcome to hike or cross-country ski their way in to enjoy the sights.

Deering Oaks Park, Portland. Located between Deering and Forest Avenues, this is Portland's largest park. An amble through the 53 acres will take you past rose gardens, basketball and tennis courts, hiking trails, and a pond (ice-skating is allowed). Dogs are welcome on a leash.

Eastern Promenade, Portland. This 4.2-mile-long paved trail runs from India Street to Tukey's Bridge in Portland. It's extremely popular with dog walkers, in-line skaters, and joggers. The views of Casco Bay are great, and the trail is mostly flat, making for a relaxing and scenic outing.

Logan's Marina, Dolphin Lane, Bailey Island (207-833-2810; marina@logansmarina.com). Drew and Diana Logan, who run this busy marina, encourage people to take their pets with them out on the rental boats. "I believe a cat or two has even ventured out onto Casco Bay from our dock," says Drew. "On occasion we have dog-sat when the dog proved to be unseaworthy." He recommends the flat-bottom boats for those traveling with animals (or any other potentially seasick passenger), as they tend to be kinder to the stomach than round-bottom version.

Old Port, Portland. Spend a day wandering through this old-meets-new shopping and arts district in Portland. Stretching from the harbor on up, Old Port is an intriguing mix of bustling docks, umpteen restaurants, gift shops, microbreweries, antiques stores, art galleries, and condominiums. Cars can traverse the cobbled streets, but this place is really made for walking—slowly. Take your time and let it all sink in.

Palawan Sailing, Long Wharf, Portland (207-773-2163; palawan-@nlis.net; www.sailpalawan. com); $20–40. Take to the sea for a two- to three-hour sail aboard a vintage 58-foot sailboat, racing past the **Calendar Islands** of Casco Bay and up to seven lighthouses. Captain Tom Woodruff welcomes pets but forewarns owners that their pet should be the hardy, seafaring type, as the boat can heel up to 15 degrees.

Portland Head Light, 1000 Shore Road, Cape Elizabeth. As one of Maine's more famous lighthouses, Portland Head attracts more than its share of shutterbugs. The 1791 beauty is located in **Fort Williams Park** (Route 207 to Route 77 to Shore Road). There's a large parking lot on-site; expect to run into tour buses full of admirers. Dogs must be on a leash.

Two Lights State Park, 66 Two Lights Road, Cape Elizabeth. You won't find a much better spot for a picnic overlooking Casco Bay than Two Lights, named for (you guessed it) two nearby lighthouses—they were the first "twin" lights in the state, both built in 1828. Picnic tables sit on a cliff over the ocean, and the park's 40 acres also include charcoal grills, shoreline trails, and unbeatable views. Dogs must be on a leash.

Window-Shopping in Freeport. When you ask local B&Bs and hotels where they're located, most start by telling you how far they are from L. L. Bean—that might give you some idea of how important shopping is to the residents and visitors of Freeport. There are small boutiques and walkable historic districts here, too, but the big draw is the outlets: more than 125 big-name stores offering bargains, bargains, bargains.

Wolfe's Neck Woods State Park, 425 Wolfe's Neck Road, Freeport. Interpretive signs guide you along more than 5 miles of trails of this 233-acre park; along the way, you'll pass by quiet wooded areas, estuaries, and the shoreline of the Harraseeket River and Casco Bay. Wolfe's Neck's most famous animal inhabitants are the ospreys that mate and nest nearby. Dogs must be on a leash.

Yarmouth Clam Festival, Yarmouth. This annual carnival, crafts fair, and seafood extravaganza starts each year on the third Friday in July and lasts for three days. The competition is stiff during the clam shucking contest, road races, bike races, and canoe and kayak races, and the parade and fireworks always draw a crowd. This is definitely the place to be seen for Yarmouth residents and visitors. Dogs must be on a leash.

QUICK BITES

Bill's Pizza, 177 Commercial Street, Portland (207-774-6166). The picnic tables go out and the umbrellas go up in the springtime at Bill's. Dogs on a leash can join their owners for pizza, subs, soups, chili, and salads.

Coffee By Design. This Portland-area chain has three shops in the downtown area: 620 **Congress Street** (207-772-5533); 24 **Monument Square** (207-761-2424); and 67 **India Street** (207-879-2233). All three locations have outdoor seating and are pet-friendly. Choose from baked

goods and freshly roasted signature coffees, including Tuxedo Mochas, Caramel Cream Lattes, and Peanut Butter Mochas.

Cole Farms, 64 Lewiston Road, Gray (207-657-4714; info@cole farms.com). This restaurant and gift shop also has a picnic area, playground, and take-out window serving informal favorites such as burgers and fries, chowder, chicken, baked beans, seafood, sandwiches, and ice cream.

Federal Spice, 225 Federal Street, Portland (207-774-6404). In the summertime, pets can sit beside their owners at Federal Spice's outdoor seating area to enjoy multi-ethnic food specialties, including wraps and quesadillas.

The Lobster Shack Restaurant, 225 Two Lights Road, Cape Elizabeth (207-799-1677). Enjoy your lobster, chowder, stew, fisherman's plate, crabcakes, or other seafood meal at one of the many picnic tables overlooking Portland Harbor and the Atlantic Ocean. The only thing between you and the water is a dramatic, rocky ledge.

Snow Squall Restaurant, 18 Ocean Street, South Portland (207-799-2232; 1-800-568-3260; chef@snowsquall.com; www. snowsquall.com). This Portland Waterfront Market restaurant is known for its seafood, but you'll also find ample offerings of meat, chicken, and vegetarian dishes. Dogs are welcome to join their owners out on the patio for lunch or dinner dishes such as clam chowder, Jamaican jerk chicken, club sandwiches, fried calamari, and Thai salmon.

Thailand, 29 Wharf Street, Portland (207-775-7141). This Thai restaurant has a small streetside seating area (four to five tables) where dogs are welcome to join their owners. There are lots of options here for vegetarians and vegans: Menu items include spring rolls, spicy salads, pad Thai, and stir-fry dishes.

HOT SPOTS FOR SPOT

Another Dog Day, 156 Pleasant Hill Road #3, Scarborough (207-883-1445). Dying to go whitewater rafting? Or skiing? When your pooch can't come along, this doggie day-care spot will be happy to lend a hand. According to owner Lisa Sands, Another Dog Day has an indoor play area and outdoor fenced-in area to keep the animals active and busy during their stay. They also offer grooming and hope to expand soon to include a "doggie motel" and "doggie gym."

Brickyard Kennels, 14 Snowhook Trail, North Yarmouth (207-829-5661; www.brickyardkennels.com). This kennel specializes in spoiling: Dogs can cuddle up to heated ceramic floors and lambskin bedding, and have all the treats they can eat; cats hang out in three-story kitty condos and scratch to their hearts' content on rope-covered posts. Doggie day care ($15) is available, along with overnight lodging ($25 per dog, $13 per cat). Dogs that stay three nights or longer get a complimentary bath, and all animals get plenty of personalized attention.

The Doggie Cottage, 35 Bull Run Road, Gray (207-657-7311; www.doggiecottage.com). The Doggie Cottage is actually a "pet resort" specializing in doggie day care and overnight stays. The resort is designed to mimic a home environment to make the pets more comfortable—there's a living room, a recreation room, six outdoor play areas, and 10 private theme rooms with wallpaper, furniture, and tile floors. "It's fun here," says Sean Kelley, who designed the canine resort with his wife, Jill. "It's more like a dog park than a kennel." The Kelleys charge $15 for day care and $25 for overnight stays. Their "turn-down service" includes a cookie on the pillow and a hug before bed.

Fetch, 102 Congress Street, Portland (207-773-5450; www.fetchorama.com). Fetch's owner, Kathy Palmer, welcomes your canine or feline into her well-stocked pet store: "If you're a regular and you come *without* your dog, we usually ask, 'Didn't you forget something?'" Palmer says. In addition to running the shop, she's also working on a project, called Welcome Mutt, designed to make her city more pet-friendly and to encourage businesses to allow pets onto their property. So far, she's succeeded in getting video rental stores, banks, bookstores, florists, and others involved. Each participant gets a WELCOME MUTT sticker for the store window, and unlimited doggie treats to hand out.

Pampered Pets, 52 Pine Street, Portland (207-761-1666; pampered petsme@aol.com). Here's a great solution to your dining-out-with-the-dog problem: Pampered Pets owner Lori Sanford is not allowed to serve food in her store because she also allows pets inside. But nothing says she can't let you eat your *own* food inside her store. To that end, this pet boutique offers the Pooch Café, with plenty of seating for humans, and gourmet doggie treats for their best friends. Grab a pizza or sandwich next door and eat it at the café with your mutt. The store also sells upscale animal-related items such as Casa Fina dog dishes, Sandicast sculptures, and Harmony Kingdom treasure boxes.

Pet Pantry, 140 Main Street, Freeport (207-865-6484; 1-888-772-9392; info@petpantry.com). Half of this 4,000-square-foot store is stocked with supplies for pets—the other half is filled with animal-related items for their owners. Most are breed-specific gifts and sundries, including T-shirts, mugs, jewelry, notepads, and bags.

Pet Quarters, 147 Bath Road, Brunswick (207-725-1818). This store is part of a locally owned chain of eight shops. According to the manager, much of Pet Quarters's summer business comes from out-of-town visitors traveling with their animals. You'll find a decent selection of food, supplies, and treats for dogs, cats, and small animals.

IN CASE OF EMERGENCY

Bath–Brunswick Veterinary Association,
257 Bath Road, Brunswick (207-729-4164).

Cape Veterinary Clinic,
391 Cottage Road, South Portland (207-799-2188).

Cat Doctor,
183 Brighton Avenue, Portland (207-874-2287).

Falmouth Veterinary Hospital,
174 Route 1, Falmouth (207-781-4028).

Forest Avenue Veterinary Hospital,
973 Forest Avenue, Portland (207-797-4840).

Portland Veterinary Specialists,
2255 Congress Street, Portland (207-780-0271).

Veterinary Centre,
207 Ocean House Road, Cape Elizabeth (207-799-6952).

Midcoast Maine

Purists say this is where the real Maine coast begins: From Boothbay Harbor all the way up to the Blue Hill peninsula, you'll find small fishing villages, gracious former ship captains' estates, historic transportation museums, spectacular oceanfront parks, and tiny, inspirational islands. Many Vacationland visitors simply speed through the midcoast area on their way to Acadia. But if you stop to catch your breath, you'll find Searsport, Rockland, Monhegan Island, Castine, and other midcoast spots are more than satisfying destinations in and of themselves.

This is a diverse region in both geography and personality. Throughout the area, simple pleasures combine seamlessly with luxury: clam shacks and fine dining, state parks and manicured lawns, ramshackle thrift shops and upscale art galleries. There are hundreds of midcoast inns, motels, and B&Bs, but only a sprinkling allows pets; luckily, the innkeepers listed here are friendly and welcoming enough to make up the difference.

ACCOMMODATIONS

Hotels, Motels, Inns, and Bed & Breakfasts

Belfast

Belfast Harbor Inn, 91 Searsport Avenue, Belfast (207-338-2740; 1-800-545-8576; stay@belfast-harborinn.com; www.belfast-harborinn.com); $49–129 per night. Choose from pool-view or ocean-view rooms at this scenic inn situated on 6 acres beside Penobscot Bay. All rooms have either king- or queen-sized beds with updated furnishings, and guests can take advantage of a heated outdoor pool. Pet owners pay an extra fee of $10 per pet, per night.

Belhaven Inn Bed & Breakfast, 14 John Street, Belfast (207-338-5435; stay@belhaveninn.com; www.belhaveninn.com); $105 per night. Pets are welcome in the efficiency suite of this 16-room Victorian home; the suite has a queen-sized bed, daybed sitting area, bathroom with skylight, sundeck, and private entrance. "The entrance opens to a side lawn and wooded area, perfect for walks," explains innkeeper Anne Bartels. "We have pet bowls for those who forget them, and doggie biscuits for welcoming." Pets cannot be left alone in the suite.

Comfort Inn Ocean's Edge, Route 1, Belfast (207-338-2090; 1-800-303-5098; comfort@agate. net); $79–275 per night. True to its name, this hotel overlooks Penobscot Bay, and each room has its own deck or patio to take in the view. Amenities include a heated pool and sauna, a lounge, laundry machines, and a game room; suites and nonsmoking rooms are also available. Pets are allowed in certain rooms for a fee of $10 per night.

Seascape Motel and Cottages, 202 Searsport Avenue, Belfast (207-338-2130; 1-800-477-0786; info@seascapemotel.com); $39–105 per night. Enjoy a view of Penobscot Bay from these simple, recently remodeled accommodations. All units have cable TV and queen-sized beds. Pets are allowed (for a onetime fee of $10) during May, June, September, and October. "There's a large area behind the cottages for walking, and scooping is always appreciated," says manager Chris Signorino.

Blue Hill

Auberge Tenney Hill, 1 Mines Road, Blue Hill (207-374-5710; raguay@hypernet.com; www. inn-guide.com/tenneyhill); $45–95 per night. At this historic B&B, built in 1869, guests enjoy fresh pastries from a local *patisserie* every morning on the sunporch, where the hosts also serve tea each afternoon. Daylilies surround the outdoor patio, and the rooms are decorated with antiques in a Victorian style. Pets are permitted with prior approval from the innkeepers.

Boothbay

White Anchor Inn, Route 27, Boothbay (207-633-3788; stay@

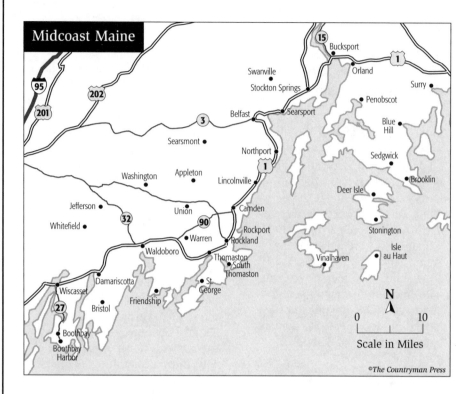

Midcoast Maine

Bucksport · 15
Orland ·
Surry ·
Swanville ·
Stockton Springs ·
Penobscot ·
Belfast · Searsport ·
Blue Hill ·
Searsmont ·
Northport ·
Sedgwick ·
Washington · Appleton ·
Lincolnville ·
Brooklin ·
Deer Isle ·
Jefferson · Union ·
Camden ·
Whitefield ·
Rockport ·
Stonington ·
Warren ·
Waldoboro · Rockland ·
Isle au Haut ·
Thomaston ·
South Thomaston ·
Vinalhaven ·
Damariscotta · St. George ·
Wiscasset ·
Friendship ·
Bristol ·
Boothbay ·
Boothbay Harbor ·

N

0   10

Scale in Miles

©*The Countryman Press*

whiteanchorinn.com; www.white-anchorinn.com); $45–79 per night. The 23 units at the White Anchor have color TVs, heat, and air-conditioning. Animals are welcome in designated pet rooms for an extra $5 per night, as long as they remain on a leash while on the property and are not left alone in the rooms. Pet rooms are located on the ground floor, making walks on the 6-acre grounds more convenient.

Boothbay Harbor

Flagship Inn, 200 Townsend Avenue, Boothbay Harbor (207-633-5094; 1-800-660-5094; flag-ship@boothbaylodging.com; www.seene.com/flagshipbooth bay); $49–95 per night. This clean, friendly place is located next to Pier 1, Boothbay's activi-ties hub. The inn offers large, air-conditioned, motel-style rooms with exterior corridors, a heated outdoor swimming pool, and free coffee each morning in the lobby. One animal is allowed in each designated pet room for an extra $10 per night.

Pond House, 7 Bay Street, Boothbay Harbor (207-633-5842; 7bayst@gwi.net; www.gwi.net/~ 7bayst); $65–85 per night. Once owned by the founder of the Cross Art School, the Pond House caters to artists and others looking for solitude and relax-ation. The current owner, Mary Huntington, allows one pet at a time in the inn in one of the five guest rooms; visitors can also explore their creative side in a converted-barn studio space. Animals should be quiet and not left unattended.

Camden

High Tide Inn, Route 1, Camden
(207-236-3724; 1-800-778-7068;
info@hightideinn.com; www.
hightideinn.com); $50–175 per
night. Pets are allowed in certain
designated rooms at this oceanfront accommodation that
includes an inn, cottages, and a
motel. High Tide's best feature is
its location: The only thing
between guests and the ocean is
a vast expanse of lawn. You'll
also find a private beach, library,
and large porch where breakfast
is served each day.

Castine

Castine Harbor Lodge,
147 Perkins Street, P.O. Box 215,
Castine (207-326-4335; chl@
acadia.net; www.castinemaine.
com); $85–225 per night. The
innkeepers at this large oceanfront 1893 lodge have one yellow
Lab and cats; they welcome your
pet, as well, with a fee of $10 per
night. All 16 guest rooms have
water views and country-cottage
furnishings, including Oriental
rugs, four-poster beds, and
patchwork quilts. Other amenities include a 350-foot porch and
a private dock.

Manor Inn, Battle Avenue,
Castine (207-326-4861; info@
manor-inn.com; www.manor-
inn.com); $95–205 per night. An
impressive, historic home overlooking a large lawn and the
open ocean beyond, the Manor
Inn offers 14 rooms individually
decorated with period furniture
and bright touches. The innkeepers charge a pet fee (call for
details) but otherwise welcome

animals to explore the home and
grounds with their owners.

Deer Isle

Pilgrim's Inn, Main Street, Deer
Isle (207-348-6615; innkeeper@
pilgrimsinn.com; www.pilgrims-
inn.com); $165–215 per night.
Pets are allowed in any of the
three on-site cottages at
Pilgrim's: The two **Ginny's
Cottages** have living rooms,
kitchenettes, and separate bedrooms with queen-sized beds.
Rugosa Rose Cottage has two
floors, a private deck, a queen
bed, and a full bath. Innkeepers
Dan and Michele Brown welcome animals and provide doggie
cleanup bags for their guests.

Edgecomb

Cod Cove Inn and Cottages,
Edgecomb (207-882-9586; 1-800-
882-9586; www.codcoveinn.
com); $55–105 per night. These
1930s-era cottages are located
high on a bluff over Sheepscot
Bay. Each has a deck, skylights,
and cable TV; the larger two-
room units can accommodate
four to five people. Guests can
also take advantage of a swimming pool and free coffee and tea
in the morning. Pet owners pay a
onetime fee of $10.

Sheepscot River Inn, 306 Eddy
Road, Edgecomb (207-882-6343;
1-800-437-5503; innkeeper@
sheepscotriverinn.com); $79–139
per night. Located on the water
next to the village of Wiscasset,
the Sheepscot's accommodations
include the inn itself, a lodge, and
15 cottages. "Pets are always welcome!" say the innkeepers, and
they don't just mean dogs—they

SHORELINE CABINS FOR RENT AT THE SHEEPSCOT RIVER INN IN EDGECOMB

once had an annual hedgehog visitor. Animal owners pay a fee of $10 per night and might just find doggie biscuits at check-in.

North Brooklin

Lookout Bed & Breakfast, HC 64, Flye Point, North Brooklin (207-359-2188; lookout@juno.com; www.acadia.net/lookout); $840– 1,300 per week. This country inn, located on the tip of the Blue Hill peninsula, offers great views of Blue Hill Bay and Herrick's Bay, a meadow, an organic vegetable garden, and a flower garden. Pets are welcome in any of the seven on-site cottages for an extra $40 per week; the one- to four-bedroom cottages all have ocean views, kitchens, and small decks.

Penobscot

Brass Fox Bed & Breakfast, Southern Bay Road, Penobscot (207-326-0575; brassfox@netscape.net; www.brassfox.com); $75–95 per night. Pets are allowed pending prior approval

at the Brass Fox, but only during the off-season (mid-October through mid-May). The B&B is located in an 1830s farmhouse that has been recently remodeled with antiques and tin ceilings: Each guest room has a private bathroom and access to the wraparound deck.

Rockland

Navigator Motor Inn, 520 Main Street, Rockland (207-594-2131; 1-800-545-8026; navigator@hotmail.com; www.navigator-inn.com); $60–129 per night. Located across the street from the Maine State Ferry Terminal, the Navigator has 81 rooms and five suites, all with refrigerators. There's also a restaurant on-site. No pets are allowed in the suites, but they are welcome in any room on the condition that they're not left alone at any time.

Trade Winds Motor Inn, 2 Park Drive, Rockland (207-596-6661; 1-800-834-3130; twmi@midcoast.

com; www.tradewindsmaine. com); $55–139 per night. Pets are welcome in any of the Trade Winds' 138 rooms; many have balconies and views of the Rockland Breakwater Lighthouse and Rockland Harbor. The in-town location is within walking distance of shops, restaurants, and museums. Animals must be accompanied by their owners at all times.

Rockport

Oakland Seashore Cottages and Motel, 50 Dearborn Lane, Rockport (207-594-8104); $45–95 per night or $266–630 per week. The small cabins and motel at Oakland Seashore are surrounded by a 75-acre forest and front a private beach. Accommodations are simple and clean with full bathrooms and maid service; some have kitchenettes. In an effort to maintain the "peace and quiet," no telephones or TVs are provided. Quiet, well-behaved pets are welcome.

Searsport

Homeport Inn, 121 East Main Street, Searsport (207-548-2259; hportinn@acadia.net); $700–850 per week. Though not allowed in the historic inn building, pets are welcome in Homeport's Victorian Cottages. Each has two bedrooms with full and twin beds, a kitchen, heat, and supplied linens; they share access to the property's large lawns, gardens, and ocean views. The cottages rent by the week only.

Inn Brittania, 132 West Main Street, Searsport (207-548-2007; 1-866-INN-BRIT; info@innbritannia. com; www.innbritannia.com);

$100–150 per night. This historic inn underwent a complete renovation in 2002; well-behaved dogs that weigh less than 50 pounds are allowed in the London Room, which has a private entrance and can accommodate up to three people. Guests enjoy ocean views, afternoon tea, and walks on the property's 5 acres.

Sedgwick

Seaside Bed & Breakfast, RR 1, Sedgwick (207-359-2792; seasidebb@yahoo.com; www. hypernet.com/seaside); $85–170 per night. Pets are welcome with prior approval in the Garden Apartment of this B&B; the apartment has a canopied double bed, one twin bed, a kitchen, and an ocean view. The public boat landing at Benjamin River is a short walk away. Breakfasts at the round family table typically include items such as blueberry pancakes, fruit, juice, and coffee.

Spruce Head

Craignair Inn, Clark Island, Spruce Head (207-594-7644; 1-800-320-9997; innkeeper@craig-nair.com; www.craignair.com); $52–125 per night. This 1928 restored home offers 13 guest rooms (6 with private baths) decorated with antique furniture and quilts; many have ocean views. Downstairs, guests relax in the parlor, library, and dining room. "Small and medium-sized" pets (call to see if yours qualifies) are allowed in about half of the rooms for a fee of $10 per night.

Stonington

Boyce's Motel, Main Street, Stonington (207-367-2421; 1-800-224-2421); $49–110 per night.

This motel has a great location overlooking Stonington Harbor and is a short walk from the shops and restaurants of the village. Pets are welcome in the standard rooms or larger apartments and efficiencies but should not be left alone on-site. The apartments have sundecks, and all rooms have heat, cable TV, and in-room coffeemakers.

Penny's Bed & Breakfast, Stonington (207-367-5933); call for rate information. This cozy, three-room B&B is located at the outermost reaches of Deer Isle in Penobscot Bay. In keeping with the home's Victorian architecture, the furnishings and decor have a classic feel, and guests also have ocean views. The house is located within walking distance of town.

Tenants Harbor

East Wind Inn, Mechanic Street, Tenants Harbor (207-372-6366; 1-800-241-VIEW; info@eastwind-inn.com; www.eastwindinn.com); rooms and suites, $79–299 per night. Gent, the resident black Lab, enjoys having canine guests with prior notice at the East Wind for a fee of $15 per visit; innkeeper Tim Watts just asks that your dog be well socialized and friendly. All of the inn's buildings offer sweeping views and antique furnishings. The inn also has a wharf restaurant with outdoor seating, where dogs are allowed (see **Chandlery Grill** under "Quick Bites"). All in all, a very pet-friendly place.

West Boothbay Harbor

Lakeview Inn, 48 Lakeview Road, West Boothbay Harbor (207-633-0353; 1-866-851-0450; comehome@thelakeviewinn.com; www.thelakeviewinn.com); $59–129 per night. Animals are welcome guests at the Lakeview, a waterfront inn with a large dock, a swimming pool, a beach, canoes, air-conditioning, cable TV, and balcony suites. The on-site restaurant serves breakfast, lunch, and dinner. Shops, nature trails, and the **Boothbay Railway Village** (see "Out and About") are a short drive away.

Lawnmeer Inn, West Boothbay Harbor (207-633-2544; 1-800-633-7645; www.lawnmeerinn.com); $68–195 per night. Perennial and herb gardens dot the grounds of this quiet waterfront inn, which offers water-view and forest-view rooms, cottages, and apartments, along with a restaurant serving breakfast and dinner. "Small" pets (call to see if yours qualifies) are welcome for an extra pet fee of $10 per night.

Campgrounds

Camden

Camden Hills State Park Campground, 280 Belfast Road (Route 1), Camden (207-236-3109; 207-236-0849); $13 per night Maine residents; $17 per night out-of-state residents. This fairly remote and scenic campground offers 112 sites, flush toilets, hot showers, and a picnic area in an expansive state park (see "Out and About"). It's an ideal spot for tenters looking for a "true Maine," somewhat wilderness-like experience, yet it is still close to the shops, restaurants, and activities of downtown Camden.

Damariscotta
Lake Pemaquid Camping,
Biscay Road, Box 967, Damariscotta (207-563-5202); $22–40 per night or $145–250 per week. Your dog or cat will be greeted by free pet treats at the camp store at this family-friendly, lakefront campground. Some of the 200 sites are waterfront; all have a fire pit and picnic table and can accommodate a tent, trailer, or RV. Facilities include a large snack bar, a swimming pool, tennis courts, and a beach. Pets must be on a leash.

Georgetown
Sagadahoc Bay Campground,
Georgetown (207-371-2014; kosalka@midmaine.com; www. sagbaycamping.com); $22–27 per night or $147–165 per week. Many of the 38 RV and tent sites at this cozy campground are at the water's edge; all tent sites are secluded in the woods, and most RV sites have hookups for water and septic. When the tide goes out, there are miles of packed sand for your dog to run along. The resident poodle, Kampa, will show your mutt the ropes. There are no extra pet fees.

Lincolnville
Warren Island State Park
Campground, Lincolnville (207-236-3109; 207-236-0849); $12 per night Maine residents or $16 per night out-of-state residents. Talk about seclusion: There's only one way to access this site, and unless you enjoy long swims, you'd better have a boat. Warren Island sits off the coast of Lincolnville in Penobscot Bay. There are no phones, no ferry, and just 10 campsites. Fresh drinking water is provided, along with mooring facilities. Pets are allowed on a leash.

Rockport
Camden Hills RV Resort, Route
90, Rockport (207-236-2498; 1-888-842-0592; www.camden-hillsrv.com); $20–34 per night or $600–650 per month. This recently renovated campground can accommodate any size RV and offers full hookups and cable TV connections. The site also has a swimming pool and hot tub, along with a camp store, laundry facilities, and rest rooms. Two pets are allowed per site as long as their owners pick up after them and keep them on a leash.

Megunticook Campground By
the Sea, Route 1, Rockport (207-594-2428; 1-800-884-2428; camp@camdencamping.com; www.campgroundbythesea.com); $20–36 per night. The woods meet the sea at Megunticook, a campground for RVers and tenters with a heated swimming pool, a bathhouse, laundry facilities, a camp store, lobster bakes, free coffee, a playground, and waterfront gardens. Pets must be on a leash and accompanied by their owners (with cleanup bags) at all times.

Searsport
Searsport Shores Camping
Resort, 216 West Main Street, Searsport (207-548-6059; camping@ime.net; www.camp ocean.com); $23–65 per night. Oden, a Newfoundland, is the

unofficial greeter at Searsport. Other pets are welcome to join him on the campground's trails and beach as long as they are leashed and quiet, and owners must clean up after them. Guests enjoy planned activities, a private beach, a canoe and kayak launch, hot showers, a playground, and a video arcade.

South Thomaston
Lobster Buoy Campsites, 280 Waterman Beach Road, South Thomaston (207-594-7546); $15–25 per night. You'll want to bring your fishing gear along to this campground on the water, featuring a 400-foot beach, hot showers, and flush toilets (no sewer hookups). All of the 40 sites are located within 150 yards of the ocean; 12 are reserved for tents, and the rest have water and electric hookups. One quiet, leashed dog is allowed per site.

Stonington
Old Quarry Ocean Adventures, Settlement Quarry Road, Stonington (207-367-8977; 1-877-479-8977; oquarry@prexar.com; www.oldquarry.com); $20 per night. Water-loving dogs and their companions will get more than just their feet wet at this campground, located on the shore of Webb Cove, which offers 10 tent sites along with a kayak and boating center. Its owners strive to maintain a peaceful, private, and all-natural camping experience—no RVs allowed. Hiking trails connect to the 9-acre site.

Homes, Cottages, and Cabins for Rent

Brooksville
Bryn Teg Cottage, Town Landing Road, Brooksville (207-843-7935); $750–900 per week. This weather-shingle cottage is set high on a hill over looking Smith Cove—its name means "beautiful hillside" in Welch. Inside you'll find two bedrooms, two bathrooms, a kitchen, a living room, a stone fireplace, and a large deck with a barbecue grill. "There are plenty of opportunities to walk pets nearby, including a wildlife sanctuary across the cove" says owner Lew Payne. Pet owners pay an extra $80 cleaning fee.

Liberty
Lake St. George Cottage, Liberty (410-836-2794; ducktape@mindspring.com). Greg and Paula Smith offer a waterfront cottage for rent in the town of Liberty; it has a private dock, a canoe and rowboat, a washer and dryer, a screened-in porch, and two bedrooms to accommodate up to four people. One housebroken dog is allowed. Rate information is available upon request.

Lincolnville Beach
Beach House Suites, Lincolnville Beach (207-789-5200; whalepub@tidewater.net; www.tidewater.net/~whalepub); $800 per week. These two waterfront suites—one upper, one lower—offer views of Penobscot Bay and are a short walk from the town pier, shops, and eateries. Both units have a full kitchen, cable TV, a washer and dryer, linens and towels, and two bedrooms. One pet is allowed

per unit, provided he is quiet, housebroken, and not left alone.

Rockland

Rockland House, 30 State Street, Rockland (207-363-5773; annpa@aol.com); $750 per week. Located about one block from Harbor Park, this Cape Cod–style home has four bedrooms, a full kitchen, cable TV, a bathroom with tub, supplied linens and towels, a barbecue grill, and a backyard. "Responsible pet owners are welcome," says owner Ann Pardoe.

Stonington

Yellow House on Pink Street, Pink Street, Stonington (207-367-8827; chiz@hypernet.com; www.hypernet.com/yellowhouse); $125 per night or $700 per week. This cute, *very* yellow house has a cheery, updated interior with one bedroom, a bathroom, sitting room, full kitchen, dining area, futon, and TV/VCR. Parking is available on-site. The house is located 100 yards from Penobscot Bay and within walking distance of downtown shops and restaurants. Pets are welcome.

Woolwich

Whitney's Wilderness Cabins, 141 Old Stage Road, Woolwich (207-442-7676; awhitney@gwi.net); $30–35 per night or $175–200 per week. Think rustic: If you're looking for a secluded, "roughing it" experience, these small, simple cabins can provide it. Cabin 1 has a double bed and bunk beds; Cabin 2 has two twin beds. Both have a gas stove, TV, and "portable potty." A nearby well provides water, and a shower is located on the grounds. The Kennebec River is nearby.

Rental Agencies

Camden Accommodations, 43 Elm Street, Camden (207-236-6090; 1-800-344-4830; info@camdenac.com; www.camdenac.com). According to manager Jenni Seidel, this midcoast agency handles about 100 cottages, camps, houses, apartments, and estates available for vacation rental. Some allow pets, usually with a nonrefundable pet fee. Most owners rent by the week during the high season.

OUT AND ABOUT

Birch Point State Park, Owls Head. This is a scenic, oceanfront parcel of land that overlooks Penobscot Bay and offers a rare, northern Maine sand beach. Dogs are not specifically prohibited from the beach, as they are at many other waterfront parks, though they must be on a leash and owners must clean up after them. Finding the park can be a little tricky: It's located just south of Ash Point along the Mussel Ridge Channel. From Route 73 take North Shore Drive, turn right onto Ash Point Drive, continue past the airport, turn right onto Dublin Road, then turn left onto Ballyhoc Road and look for the STATE PARK sign less than a mile in on the left. The park is also signposted from Route 73 in Owls Head.

Boothbay Railway Village, Route 27, Boothbay (207-633-4727; railvill@lincoln.midcoast.com; www.railwayvillage.com); $7 adults, $3 children. This is a great stop for history buffs: The 30-acre museum has 60 antique cars and farm vehicles and a nostalgic steam-train ride. In addition, an on-site outdoor village features historic structures, including the 1847 Town Hall, the 1923 Spruce Point Chapel, and a one-room schoolhouse, along with live demonstrations and a village green. Pets on a leash are permitted as long as their owners pick up after them.

Boothbay Region Land Trust. Headquarters: 1 Oak Street, Boothbay Harbor (207-633-4818). The 16 miles of hiking trails that comprise the trust are spread throughout Boothbay, Boothbay Harbor, Edgecomb, and Southport. The trust manages seven properties, including the 12-acre **Colby Wildlife Preserve** at Salt Marsh Cove; the 94-acre **Linekin Preserve** along the Damariscotta River; the 46-acre **Lobster Cove Meadow,** which stretches from the Damariscotta River to Linekin Bay; and the 19-acre **Porter Preserve** on Barters Island in Boothbay. Trail maps are available at the trust's Boothbay Harbor headquarters. Dogs are welcome on a leash as long as their owners pick up after them.

Camden Hills State Park, 280 Belfast Road (Route 1),

Camden. Get a bird's-eye view of the midcoast region from atop **Mount Battie,** located within the park (the summit is accessible by auto road or by foot). There are few places to better enjoy the dramatic fall foliage and year-round vistas. Within the 5,000-acre park you'll find 30 miles of trails, more than a few remote spots, the renowned 800-foot **Maiden Cliff,** and a campground (see "Accommodations—Campgrounds").

Damariscotta Lake State Park, 8 State Park Road, Jefferson. With plenty of opportunities for swimming, fishing, and sunbathing, this 17-acre shoreline spot is especially popular in the summer. Indeed, the park is only open between Memorial Day and Labor Day, and parking can be a challenge. Picnic areas with grills, a playground, and flush toilets are also available on-site. Owners must clean up after their leashed pets.

Dodge Point, River Road, Newcastle. This impressive 500-acre preserve is located along the Damariscotta River. Keep your eye out for beaver dams and other coastal wildlife. The wooded and waterfront trails are popular in the summer for hiking and in the winter for cross-country skiing. Dogs must be on a leash.

Goddess of the Sea **Cruises,** Mechanic Street, Tenants Harbor (207-877-7824; capfrank@mint.net; www.goddesscruise.com); $100–450 per person. Captain Frank P. Grande (a dog owner himself) welcomes pets on board his sailboat for private, custom-designed trips: "They're part of the family!" he says. Choices include an eight-hour day sail, an overnight trip, or a two-day getaway or three-day adventure. Lobster and steak dinners are included on the longer trips.

Heritage Park, end of Main Street, Belfast. Pull up a seat at a picnic table and watch the boats go by at this popular grassy area. In addition to the great views, the area also has historic architecture, interesting shops, and a turn-of-the-20th-century feel. Dogs must be on a leash.

Humane Society of Knox County Events, 55 Dexter Street Extension, Thomaston (207-594-2200; www.humanesocietyof-knoxcounty.org). The society offers visitors and their furry companions plenty of chances to join in at animal-friendly activities and fund-raisers. Among the society's most popular events are: the **Fur 'n' Foliage Pet Walk,** usually held on a Sunday early in October at Beauchamp Point in Rockport; the **Art for Animals** silent auction, held the second Sunday in August at Sparrow Framing in Rockland; and the **Blessing of the Animals,** held with the help of a local pastor on the third Saturday of September at the society's shelter facility.

Monhegan Boat Line, Port Clyde (207-372-8848; barstow@monheganboat.com). Call for fares. Monhegan is one of Maine's best-known and most visited islands. Tiny and dramatic, it's especially popular

among artists—in the summer, you'll trip over an easel no matter where you wander. The Monhegan Boat Line can get you there, and welcomes pets on a leash for an extra $2 fee. One note of caution: Company representative Karen McGonagle says that the deer tick, Lyme disease problem is growing on Monhegan Island and recommends that owners inspect their pets carefully after a visit.

Northeast/Logical Choice Boat Rentals, 14 Alden Street, Camden (207-236-6886; www.logical-choice.cjb.net). "We're very pet-friendly," says company owner Don Symington, who offers a fleet of 10 powerboats for rent by the half day, full day, week, or month. Most rentals start out from docks in Camden or Lincolnville Beach Harbors, though the company will deliver anywhere in New England. Prices vary, but you can expect to pay about $150 per day and $750 per week.

Owls Head Light, Owls Head State Park, West Penobscot Bay, Owls Head. The well-known lighthouse is only 30 feet high—a tiny stature for a Maine light—but the structure sits on a hill that nonetheless leaves it towering nearly 100 feet above the water. The much-painted building stands guard at the entrance to Rockland Harbor.

Reid State Park, Seguinland Road, Georgetown. Sand dunes and beach grass mark this seashore park, where visitors can enjoy picnic areas with grills and a snack bar. The site also has flush toilets. The natural wonders here include tidal pools, wild roses, and long stretches of beach (keep watch for poison ivy). Because this is an active bird-nesting area, dogs should be kept under close control and on a leash at all times.

Seasonal Therapy Cruises, 750 Cape Newagen Road, Newagen (207-633-0555; 207-633-5496; captain@seasonaltherapy.com; www.seasonaltherapy.com); $15 per person, per hour. Set off from Carousel Marina in Boothbay Harbor on one of Seasonal Thera-py's custom-designed cruises to see Maine wildlife (including seals, eagles, and porpoises), lighthouses, and islands. Up to six people can fit on board the Albin 27 power cruiser. "Pets are welcome," says Captain Jonathan Rutenberg. "We've hosted many varieties of dogs, cats, and even some birds."

Wiscasset, Waterville and Farmington Railway Museum, Sheepscot Station, Alna (207-882-4193; webmaster@wwfry.org; www.wwfry.org). Vintage-railroad buffs will appreciate this slice of transportation history. The WW&F, a 2-foot gauge common carrier, stopped operations in 1933; today, a railway museum stands at the site of the original Sheepscot station. Admission is free, and leashed pets are permitted on the grounds but not on the train itself.

QUICK BITES

Bayview Lobster, Bayview Landing, Camden (207-236-2005; jdh@midcoast.com). Most of the seats at this cozy seafood restaurant are located outside; the pet-friendly owners offer water bowls and even have a Frosty Paws ice cream dessert for their four-footed patrons. Choose from lobsters, sandwiches, burgers, chowder, and more.

Boothbay Region Lobstermen's Co-Op, 97 Atlantic Avenue, Boothbay Harbor (207-633-4900; 1-800-966-1741). Members of the co-op ship lobster "anywhere, anytime," and also serve up their best catches at this casual lobster pound. Sit outside and dine on seafood dinners and baskets, sandwiches, and snacks like fried zucchini, macaroni salad, chowder, and pie.

Cappy's Chowder, Main Street, Camden (207-236-2254; good eats@cappyschowder.com). "We love pets and have doggie water out all the time," says owner Johanna at Cappy's Chowder, a reasonably priced, well-known local eatery with take-out and outdoor seating. The menu offers seafood, nachos, salads, sandwiches, and bakery treats.

Captain's Fresh Idea, Route 1, Waldoboro (207-832-7054). Captain's has "wicked good" seafood, lobster rolls, fried clams, and burgers, along with a take-out window, outside tables, and a large yard—perfect for walking Fido after lunch or dinner.

Chandlery Grill, East Wind Inn, Mechanic Street, Tenants Harbor (207-372-6366). Located at the **East Wind Inn** (see "Accommodations—Hotels, Inns, and Bed & Breakfasts"), the Chandlery serves casual lunches and dinners on the wharf; picnic tables and lots of flat, large rocks provide seating. Dogs often accompany their owners here for boiled lobster, seafood rolls, or sandwiches.

Cook's Crossing Ice Cream Shop, 237 East Main Street, Searsport (207-548-2005). For a fun stop on a hot afternoon, grab a cone at this restored-railroad-station-turned-ice-cream-shop. There's also a gift store on-site and a small deck for lounging.

Robinson's Wharf, West Boothbay Harbor (207-633-3830). Robinson's has a large outdoor seating area with picnic tables overlooking the harbor. It's the perfect atmosphere in which to enjoy lobster dinners (served with a roll and corn-on-the-cob), fried seafood plates, salads, stews, and chowders.

Scarlet Begonias, 212 Maine Street, Brunswick (207-721-0403; www.scarletbegonias.org). There's no outdoor seating here, but you can order garlic bread, salads, sandwiches, pasta, and personal pizzas as take-out. "We're located

just across the street from Brunswick's lovely town green, and it's not unusual for folks to 'order out' and eat on a park bench or the gazebo steps," says owner Doug Lavallee.

Second Read Books and Coffee, 328 Main Street, Rockland (207-594-4123). Choose a secondhand book from the shelves; grab a coffee, tea, soup, salad, or pastry; and relax in the sidewalk seating area. "Polite" dogs are welcome to pass the time outside with their owners.

Sweet Sensations, 315 Commercial Street (Route 1), Rockport (207-230-0955). Steve Watts, a.k.a. the Macaroon Man, is a pastry chef, dog lover, and the owner of this bakery specializing in (you guessed it) macaroons, along with a host of other tasty treats. "We have an outside deck, and many people bring their dogs in the summer," Steve says. "We're known for our dog biscuits, which we make from scratch."

Young's Lobster Pound, 4 Mitchell Avenue, Belfast; ray-young@mint.net). With outdoor seating and a separate picnic area, this seafood eatery is an oasis in the desert for hungry pet owners. The friendly staffers serve up lobsters (choose your own), clams, crabmeat, mussels, king crab legs, haddock, halibut, sole, cod, and other delights in a casual setting.

HOT SPOTS FOR SPOT

Canine Country Club, 387 Atlantic Highway (Route 1), Northport (207-338-8300; dunns@ime.net). This state-of-the-art kennel has 54 runs in a 12,000-square-foot facility; floors have radiant heat, and there's even a doggie septic system to control odors. Most dogs stay overnight, though day care is available upon request if space permits. Grooming and training are also available, and staff play with the dogs throughout the day. Rates are $15 per day for one pet, $23 per day for two pets in the same kennel.

Critter Outfitter, 474 Main Street, Rockland (207-594-5269; www.critteroutfitter.biz). Owner Skip Nelson says his store has "provisions for pets, essentials for pet lovers." He specializes in holistic remedies and nutritional supplements, and also carries a line of pet-traveling supplies, including tote bags and folding bowls, from Outward Hound and other manufacturers.

Family Pet Center, RR 1, Box 5007, Belfast (207-338-4480). Located in Reny's Plaza on the corner of Routes 1 and 3, this store stocks Eukanuba, Nutro, Science Diet, and most other popular pet-food brands. You'll also find a full line of leads, collars, doggie sweaters and coats, natural bones, rawhide treats, and toys for all types of pets.

Hollydachs Pet Center, 246 Main Street, Rockland (207-594-2653). This family-owned pet shop houses reptiles, fish, guinea pigs, hamsters, and all other small animals, and sells supplies for cats, dogs, and other pets. In addition to leashes, bowls, and other paraphernalia, you'll also find food brands such as Science Diet, Precise, Triumph, and California Natural.

Louis Doe Pet Center, 93 Mills Road, Newcastle (207-563-3234). This crowded and homey store sells supplies and food for small animals, birds, cats, dogs, and fish. You'll find all the premium brands of dog and cat foods, along with horse feeds, bowls, leashes, and toys.

IN CASE OF EMERGENCY

All Creatures Veterinary Hospital, 881 West Street (Route 90), Rockport (207-594-5039).

Belfast Veterinary Hospital, 193 Northport Avenue, Belfast (207-338-3260).

Boothbay Animal Hospital, 1033 Wiscasset Road, Boothbay (207-633-3447).

Maine Coast Veterinary Hospital, 163 South Street, Blue Hill (207-374-2385).

Searsport Veterinary Hospital, 322 West Main Street, Searsport (207-548-2924).

Union Veterinary Clinic, Route 17, Union (207-785-4709).

A WALK AROUND JORDAN POND PROVIDES TYPICALLY BEAUTIFUL ACADIA VIEWS.

Acadia National Park and Mount Desert Island

PET-FRIENDLY RATING: ☑ ☑ ☑ ☑ ☑

It's hard to imagine a more dramatically scenic spot than Mount Desert Island. Home to Acadia National Park, the region offers an unusual mix of beaches, mountains, lakes, quaint downtowns, and—perhaps its most famous feature—mile upon mile of rugged, rocky coastline. Pet owners will feel welcome here; dogs are a common sight on park trails and city streets alike, and shopkeepers, passersby, and even the occasional traffic cop often make a point of stopping to scratch your pooch's ears. Whether you and your pet prefer challenging hikes, leisurely strolls, or lazy waterfront lounging, you'll find what you're looking for in this popular Downeast spot. (Tourist tip: The locals pronounce their island's name, true to its French roots, as *Dessert*.)

Bar Harbor is the most populous and bustling town in the region, serving as willing host to the thousands of tourists who want to be as close as possible to Acadia's main entrance. Despite the annual influx of summer crowds, the town manages, for the most part, to maintain a dignified and unharried ambience. Those looking for a more isolated vacation experience should opt for lodging on the Quiet Side of the island in sleepy, lost-in-time towns such as Southwest Harbor, Bass Harbor, Seal Cove, and Somesville. Here you'll find restaurants and shops (though not nearly as many as in Bar Harbor) as well as solitude—even during the high season. The only catch: Acadia's main entrance is a 15- to 35-minute drive away, though many alternate access points and trails are scattered throughout the island's Quiet Side as well. Across the bridge on the mainland, Trenton, Ellsworth, and neighboring towns offer more affordable lodging options and a more commercial atmosphere; mini-golf courses, strip malls, outlets, RV parks, and motels line Route 3, the main road heading into the island.

Bar Harbor and its neighboring towns all have leash laws, and local officials ask pet owners to follow the rules of doggie etiquette and to carry pooper-scooper bags at all times.

ACCOMMODATIONS

Hotels, Motels, Inns, and Bed & Breakfasts

Bar Harbor

Balance Rock Inn, 21 Albert Meadow, Bar Harbor (1-800-753-0494; barharborinns@aol.com; www.barharborvacations.com); $95–595 per night. With impressive views of Frenchman's Bay, antique furnishings, perennial gardens, and in-room hot tubs, this luxury inn is among Bar Harbor's most elegant. A limited number of pets are allowed as guests at any one time for a $15 per night fee; pet owners are asked to keep their animals off the furniture and not to leave them alone in rooms.

Bar Harbor Inn, Newport Drive, Bar Harbor (207-288-3351; 1-800-248-3351); $85–299 per night. This full-service resort includes the **Main Inn,** the **Oceanfront Lodge,** and the **Newport Motel.** The New England–style inn, home to the historic **Reading Room Restaurant,** is the most elegant option. Rooms in the lodge each have private balconies with water views, while the motel rooms overlook landscaped grounds. Outdoor seating is available at the restaurant, and pets are welcome in certain rooms for a fee of $25 per pet, per night.

Eden Village Cottages and Motel, Route 3, Bar Harbor (207-288-4670; edenvillage@acadia.

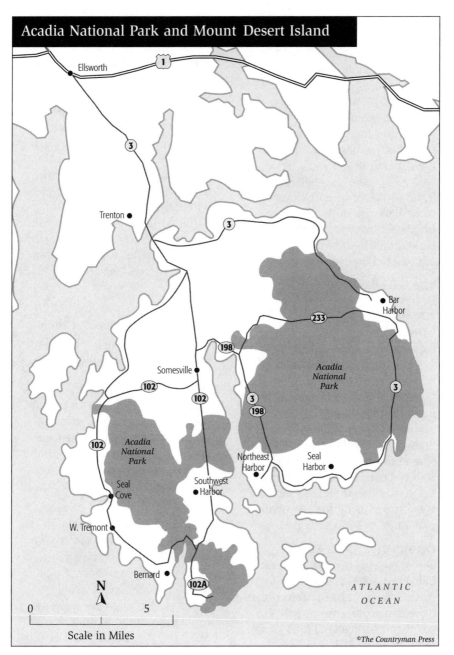

Acadia National Park and Mount Desert Island

Ellsworth

Trenton

Somesville

Acadia National Park

Bar Harbor

Northeast Harbor

Seal Harbor

Seal Cove

Southwest Harbor

W. Tremont

Bernard

Acadia National Park

N

0   5

Scale in Miles

ATLANTIC OCEAN

©The Countryman Press

net; www.edenvillage.com); motel, $39–79 per night; cottages, $250–569 per week. Eden Village's 25 acres include a pond, a playground, and a picnic area with grills. Each housekeeping cottage is equipped with a kitch-enette, a fireplace, and a screened-in porch. Dog owners (sorry, no cats) must clean up messes, keep dogs off the furniture, keep barking to a minimum, and pay a $5–10 cleaning fee and a $100 refundable deposit.

Hutchins Mountain View Cottages and Motel, Bar Harbor (207-288-4833; 1-800-775-4833; hutchins@acadia.net; www.hutchinscottages.com); $40–138 per night. This family-owned and -operated motel is just a few miles from the park and downtown Bar Harbor. The cottages are situated in a 20-acre field well away from the road. Each has a screened-in porch, and some have a living room and fireplace. Rover is welcome to make himself comfortable without extra charges.

The Ledgelawn Inn, 66 Mount Desert Street, Bar Harbor (207-288-4596; 1-800-274-5334; barharborinns@aol.com; www.barharborvacations.com); $75–275 per night. Built in 1904, this stately mansion-turned-inn features period furniture (including four-poster beds in many rooms) and a dignified Colonial ambience. Thirty-four rooms are spread throughout the inn and its restored carriage house. Animals cannot be left alone and must stay off the furniture. Pet owners pay an extra $15 per night.

Ocean Drive Motor Court, 400 Main Street, Bar Harbor (207-288-3361; 1-800-754-9909; info@oceandrivecourt.com; www.oceandrivecourt.com); motel, $84–115 per night; cottages, $125–145 per night or $625–875 per week. Guests choose from motel rooms, cabins, or an apartment-style suite at Ocean Drive, which is located within a short walking distance of Compass Harbor and enjoys mountain views. The facility also has a heated pool and

cable TV. Pet owners pay a one-time fee of $15.

Rose Eden Cottages, Bar Harbor (207-288-3038; roseeden@prexar.com; www.roseeden.com); $38–77 per night or $255–516 per week. Located 4 miles from the main park entrance, Rose Eden (a self-described "pet-friendly establishment") offers 10 clean housekeeping cottages complete with cable TV, electric heat, baths with showers, coffeemakers, and refrigerators. The owners recommend a wooded area behind the cottages for dog walking.

Ellsworth

Colonial Travelodge, 321 High Street, Ellsworth (207-667-5548; 1-800-578-7878; colonial@acadia.net); $68–159 per night. The Travelodge, a motel-style inn with exterior corridors, has an indoor pool and hot tub, free continental breakfasts, free movie channels, and a 24-hour front desk. You'll have to travel about 20 minutes to reach Acadia, but there are no extra fees for pet owners.

Comfort Inn, 130 High Street, Ellsworth (207-667-1345; 1-800-228-5150; moa131@downeast.net); $54–139 per night. Children under 12 stay free at this Comfort Inn; dogs are welcome as well for an additional charge of $5 per pet, per night. The inn has a standard chain-hotel ambience with cable TV, free local calls, 24-hour wake-up calls, and an exercise room.

Jasper's Motel, High Street, Ellsworth (207-667-5318; info@jaspersmaine.com); $39–

69 per night. With an attached restaurant, clean rooms, and reasonable rates, this motel appeals to visitors looking for a hassle-free vacation. Jasper's is located about 23 miles from Acadia and features single, double, and cottage-style rooms, some of which are smoke-free. Those traveling with animals pay an extra fee of $15 per night, per pet.

Twilite Motel, Routes 1 and 3, Ellsworth (207-667-8165; 1-800-395-5097; twilite@downeast. net; www.twilitemotel.com); $54–74 per night. Though technically classified as a motel, Twilite has many of the homey touches you'd expect to find at an inn or B&B. Pets are welcome in certain rooms with a fee of $7 per night, per pet. The motel is about 18 miles from Acadia and offers free continental breakfasts, nonsmoking and smoking rooms, a gift shop, and cable TV.

White Birches Motel, Route 1, Ellsworth (207-667-3621; 1-800-435-1287); $49–199 per night. Efficiencies and standard rooms are available at this motel, along with a few Presidential Suites that feature whirlpool tubs, wet bars, couches, and 35-inch TVs. The accommodations sit next to the White Birches Golf Course, and there's also a restaurant on-site. Pets are welcome without extra fees.

Southwest Harbor
Harbor View Motel and Cottages, 11 Ocean Way, Southwest Harbor (207-244-5031;

1-800-538-6463; motel, $75–125 per night or $480–795 per week; cottages, $500–625 per week. This aptly named motel and cottage complex overlooks bustling Southwest Harbor; if you like the music of clanging boats, this is the spot for you. The seven housekeeping cottages all have picture windows; pets are allowed in all of the cottages and some of the motel rooms for an extra $5 per night or $30 per week.

Trenton
Isleview Motel and Cottages, Bar Harbor Road (Route 3), Trenton (207-667-5661); $30–105 per night. For an extra $3 per night, pets are allowed in the cottages only at this affordable Trenton spot. Rustically decorated, they have ceiling fans, electric heat, and cable TV; some also have kitchens and/or refrigerators. If you stay seven nights or more, you'll receive a 10 percent discount and a reduced pet fee of $5 per week.

Sunrise Motel, 952 Bass Harbor Road, Trenton (207-667-8452; 1-800-419-2473; sunrise@ downeast.net; www.sunrisemotorinn.com); $30–80 per night. The owners of this animal-friendly motor inn offer a large grassy area behind the building for walks and romps; the two-story motel itself has simple, clean accommodations, cable TV, air-conditioning, and some efficiencies. Dogs aren't allowed in the pool area or on the beds. There are no extra fees for pet owners.

Campgrounds

Acadia National Park

Acadia National Park Campgrounds (www.acadia.national-park.com.). The park has two campgrounds: **Blackwoods** ($14–18 per night), located 5 miles south of Bar Harbor; and **Seawall** ($12–18 per night), 4 miles south of Southwest Harbor. Dogs are allowed at both but must be kept on a leash and can't be left alone. Campers can make reservations in advance at Blackwoods (1-800-365-2267), but Seawall operates on a first-come, first-served basis—making it a risky proposition during the busy season from July through September. At both campgrounds, sites are located within a 10-minute walk of the ocean and within a half-mile walk of showers and a camp store. From spring to fall, campers can also make use of rest rooms, cold running water, picnic tables, and a dumping station. Utility hookups, however, are not provided.

Bar Harbor

Hadley's Point Campground, Hadley's Point Road, Bar Harbor (207-288-4808; www.hadleys-point.com); $18–26 per night. Leashed pets are welcome at Hadley's Point without any extra fees—though owners are expected to clean up after their animals and not leave them unattended. Each RV and tent site has a fireplace and picnic table; campers can also take advantage of a heated pool, laundry facilities, shuffleboard courts, and other diversions.

Mount Desert Narrows Camping Resort, Bar Harbor Road, Bar Harbor (207-288-4782; camp@narrowscamping.com; www.narrowscamping.com); $22–65 per night. Campers can settle in for a fun stay at this oceanfront resort featuring nightly live entertainment in the summer (including magicians, comedians, sing-alongs, and line dancing), 25 acres of tenting, complete hookups for RVs, a heated pool, canoe rentals, a camp store, and a playground. Dogs must be on a leash and attended at all times.

Bass Harbor

Bass Harbor Campground, Route 102A, Bass Harbor (207-244-5857; 1-800-327-5857; info@bassharbor.com); campsites, $23–34 per night; cabins, $435–625 per week. Kids and dogs alike will find plenty to do at this bustling campground featuring 130 sites, a heated pool and hot tub, full hookups, separate tenting areas, hot showers, laundry facilities, a playground, and a gift shop. Owner Mike Clayton has just one request of pet lovers: "You know the jerk who ruins it for everyone else by not taking care of his pets? Well don't bring him!"

Quietside Campground, Route 102, Bass Harbor (207-244-5992; quietside@acadia.net; www.quietsidecampground.com); campsites, $14–20 per night; cabins, $35–50 per night. While Quietside does have a few large RV sites, they mainly cater to visitors with pop-up campers and smaller RVs; the campground also has tent sites and cabins for rent.

Pets are welcome for an extra fee of $1 per pet, per night, but must be quiet and well behaved, and owners are expected to clean up after their animals.

Ellsworth

Patten Pond Camping Resort, 1470 Bucksport Road (Route 3), Ellsworth (207-667-7600; 1-877-667-7376; www.pattenpond. com); $17–37 per night. With boat rentals, playgrounds, basketball and volleyball courts, a game room, and a camp store, this waterfront resort caters to families. Acadia National Park is about 20 minutes away, and Route 3 is lined with other activities to keep the kids busy. Dogs must be on a leash at all times, and pet owners are required to clean up after their animals.

Mount Desert

Mount Desert Campground, Route 198, Mount Desert (207-244-3710; mdcg@midmaine. com); $24–35 per night. This quiet waterfront campground primarily caters to tenters but does have a few sites available for RVs. Visitors enjoy a view overlooking the northern end of Somes Sound, a boat-launching ramp and canoe rentals, a camp store, and lots of blueberry bushes. Dogs are allowed only during the spring and fall.

Somes Sound View Campground, 86 Hall Quarry Road, Mount Desert (207-244-3890); $15–21 per night. At this campground you can perch your tent or RV right at the pink granite water's edge. Each site has a fire pit and picnic tables; campers share rest rooms, a dumping station, ice and soda machines, and firewood. Take advantage of the nearby water with canoe rentals and a fishing dock. Pets must be vaccinated and remain on a leash throughout your stay.

Southwest Harbor

Smuggler's Den Campground, 28 Main Street, Southwest Harbor (207-244-3944); $25–33 per night. Tucked into the trees on the Quiet Side of Mount Desert Island, Smuggler's Den has a heated pool, a recreation field, and forested and sunny sites to accommodate tenters and RV owners alike. Acadia's Echo Lake is a 20-minute walk away, and many of the park's carriage roads and trails are a short car ride away. One pet per site is welcome.

Trenton

Narrows Too Camping Resort, Bar Harbor Road, Trenton (207-667-4300; camp@narrowstoo. com; www.narrowstoo.com); $20–55 per night. Owned by the same family that runs the nearby Mount Desert Narrows campground (see above listing), this resort offers a waterfront location, a heated pool, basketball and volleyball courts, and an onsite mini-golf course. No need to rough it—you'll also find hot showers, a camp store, and laundry facilities. Dogs must be on a leash and shouldn't be left alone.

Homes, Cottages, and Cabins for Rent

Bar Harbor

Chickadee's Nest, 2 Devon Road, Bar Harbor (207-288-2538; chickadee@acadia.net; www.chickadeesnest.com); $1,000–1,200 per week. Parking can be tricky in downtown Bar Harbor—when you stay at this rental home, you can leave your car in the driveway and walk a mile to reach the hub of the action. Located in a residential neighborhood, the house has three bedrooms, a fully equipped kitchen, and a large living room. Pets are welcome as long as they are not left alone.

"Eight Great Places,"

127 Lookout Point Road, Bar Harbor; pauld@acadia.net; www.barharborrentals.cc); $495–995 per week. Paul DeVore and Karen Kenney own and rent eight properties on and around Mount Desert Island, each categorized by its intended use: "romantic," "family," or "reunion." They call themselves "pet negotiable," meaning they like to talk to pet owners to match them up with a property that best suits their needs. "For example, multiple pets might be okay in one of the larger houses but inappropriate for the honeymoon suites," Paul says.

Stone Haven, Eagle Lake Road, Bar Harbor (207-666-5623; stonehaven@nqi.net; www.stonehavencottages.com); $470–890 per week. Pets are allowed at Stone Haven, a cluster of small houses on a mountaintop overlooking Acadia National Park, but only during the off-season (spring and fall). Pet owners pay a $50 per week, per dog, fee and a $100 refundable security deposit. The homes feature cathedral ceilings, kitchens, and dining rooms that open onto decks.

Summertime, 1 Bloomfield Road, Bar Harbor (207-288-2893; summertime@acadia.net); $850–1,650 per week. "We are a *very* pet-friendly place and have many repeat canine guests," say owners Sam and Sonja Callahan. "Pooper-scooper duty" is the only requirement for dog owners, although a clause in the Callahans' insurance policy prevents them from allowing certain breeds on the property. Located one block from the ocean, Summertime offers three cottages with updated, tasteful furnishings, decks, and plenty of room for families.

Gouldsboro

Eagle Cove Cottage, Eagle View Lane, Gouldsboro (860-645-1032; chrisglenny@home.com; www.eaglecoverentals.com); $1,000–1,400 per week. This enormous private home with decks and picture windows overlooks Frenchman's Bay and Acadia. Six to eight people can sleep comfortably in three bedrooms, a kids' bunk room, and a loft, and the eat-in kitchen is fully equipped. Dogs must stay off the furniture, but otherwise can have the run of this secluded property.

Manset

The Mansell House, Shore Road, Manset (207-244-5625; mansell@downeast.net; www.mooringsinn.com); $95–150 per night. This house has three accommodations for visitors: two efficiency apartments (each with one double bed) and one penthouse apartment. All have decks and great views of Manset and the Acadia mountain skyline. The penthouse can sleep four. There is no extra fee for pet owners, though animals are not allowed to be left alone in the apartments.

Mount Desert

Acadia Pines Chalets, Mount Desert (207-244-9251; epat@ acadia.net); $595–995 per week. Owner E. Pat Foster offers four chalet-style properties for rent in the Somes Sound area. Spread out on 9 acres near Echo Lake, the cottages are roomy enough for eight people and also have living areas with cathedral ceilings, fully equipped kitchens, private decks, and fireplaces. Pets are considered on a case-by-case basis.

Southwest Harbor

Anny's Treetop Apartment, Route 102, Southwest Harbor (207-244-7323; 207-244-9484; hotflashanny@acadia.net); $125–150 per night or $700–850 per week \. Well-behaved dogs are welcome at this second-floor apartment located near downtown Southwest Harbor. (Your pooch might even enjoy frolicking with the resident Bouvier pup, Boomer.) Amenities include spacious rooms, a washer and dryer, and plenty of privacy in a tucked-away setting. Owners Wendell and Anny Seavey require that you take your dog along with you on all island adventures.

Seawall Point, 490 Seawall Road, Southwest Harbor (207-244-3980; knorberg99@hotmail.com); $400–475 per week. "We welcome pets because we've never had any problems," say the owners of this cozy cottage near

Acadia's seawall and Wonderland Trail. "Pet owners are always considerate." Set on a lawn and surrounded by apple and evergreen trees, the secluded cottage features a screened-in porch, simple country furnishings, one double and one twin bed, a kitchen and dining area, and a barbecue grill.

West Tremont

Parsons' Oceanfront Cottages, HCR 33, West Tremont (207-244-5673; 941-426-9612); $425–750 per week. The three Parsons rentals share access to a private pebble beach and have wonderful water views. An extra fee of $5 per night, per pet, will give your dog access to the cottages as well, though the smallest, the First Mate's Cabin, is a bit too snug to accommodate you along with your furry friends. The Captain's Cottage is closest to the water, and the Guest House is the largest of the three. No matter which one you choose, the Parsons—who live on-site—will make sure you feel at home.

Rental Agencies

LS Robinson Co. Real Estate, 337 Main Street, Southwest Harbor (207-244-5563; info@ lsrobinson.com). LS Robinson, which also handles vacation rentals for the Lynam Real Estate Agency in Bar Harbor, helps visitors find homes for rent in every corner of the island. You can search the company's web site (www.acadia.net/guest/lsrobinson) by category, including one that highlights rentals where dogs are considered welcome guests. The agency charges a commission on the lease amount.

Maine Island Properties, 1281 Main Street, Mount Desert (207-244-4348; info@maineislandproperties.com; www.maineislandproperties.com). This vacation rental agency handles every type of accommodation, from rustic cabins to luxurious oceanfront homes. A limited number of property owners listed with the agency do allow pets but often charge a "pet fee" of $50–100 per week.

OUT AND ABOUT

Acadia National Park. Few national parks allow pet owners to bring their best friends along for the ride (or hike, as the case may be). Luckily for us, Acadia is the exception. Start your adventure at the **Hull's Cove Visitor Center** to pick up maps and guidebooks, then get oriented with a trip around the famed **Park Loop Road** (the visitors center sells an excellent point-by-point "Motorist Guide to Park Loop Road" for $1.25). With plenty of turnoff and parking areas, the 27-mile-long road winds its way past Acadia's most prized mountain and ocean views and historic sites.

Once you're ready to leave the car behind, the options for hiking, biking, and gaping are almost limitless. You can scale cliffs on iron rungs and ladders if you want, but hikers with pets in tow tend to stick to shorter, less strenuous byways. Some of the best include: **Ocean Trail** (stretching from Otter Point to Sand Beach; the views from this smooth, narrow dirt path will literally take your breath away); **Jordan Pond Nature Trail** (mostly flat with some rocky areas; smaller dogs may have to be carried in certain spots); and **Wonderland Trail** (bring a picnic lunch—even during the most crowded season, you'll find a rocky ledge or pebble beach all to yourself). You'll also want to stop by **Thunder Hole,** where trapped waves and air in the rocks sometimes make a thundering sound and an impressive display, as well as **Bubble Pond** and **Bubble Pond Bridge.** A 44-mile-long web of historic stone roads, known as the **Carriage Roads,** is especially popular among bicyclists. And few visitors leave Acadia without watching at least one sunset from the top of **Cadillac Mountain:** Hardy souls make the hike, but you can also take the easy way out with a beautiful drive up a paved road. Expect a crowd.

All dogs must be on a leash no longer than 6 feet, and pet owners are required to clean up after their animals. Pets are not allowed on Sand Beach, Echo Lake Beach, Isle au Haut Campground, or on any ranger-led activities.

Bar Harbor Whale Watch,
1 West Street, Bar Harbor (207-288-3322; 1-800-WHALES-4); $8–43 per person, depending on age and type of trip. Board one of the company's four vessels (*Friendship V, Acadian, Helen H., and Katherine*) for three-hour whale-watch tours, whale- and puffin-watch tours, two-hour nature and lighthouse sight-seeing trips, and lobster- and seal-watch trips. Pets are not allowed on the deck, but on-board kennels are provided at no extra charge.

Bar Island Crossing, Bar Harbor. From downtown Bar Harbor, follow West Street to Bridge Street and you'll stumble across this sandbar that connects the town to a tiny, forested section of Acadia known as Bar Island. The island is beautiful (and has great views), but the real fun here is the crossing itself. Like a long beach with water on both sides, it harbors hundreds of tide pools perfect for two- and four-footed explorers. Time your visit carefully, however: If you're out on the island once high tide rolls in, you'll find yourself stranded.

The Bay Ferries' Cat, 121 Eden Street, Bar Harbor (207-288-3395; 1-888-249-7245; comments@ canadaferry.com); passengers, $45–50 one way; vehicles, $85–500 one way (depending on size); day cruises, $40–55. Who says you have to restrict your Acadia vacation to the U.S. shore? The Cat is a high-speed catamaran—the fastest in North America—that takes up to 900 passengers and 240 vehicles to and from Yarmouth, Nova Scotia, for day trips or overnight stays.

Pets are not permitted on passenger decks, but kennels are provided for temporary boarding until you reach your destination.

Canoeing. You'll find canoe-rental stands alongside main roads throughout the island; rent for a few hours or a few days and explore the inlets and outlets of Long Pond, Somes Sound, or Eagle Lake; as always seems to happen on this island, the view around every corner seems more spectacular than the last.

Downeast Windjammer Cruises, Bar Harbor Inn Pier, 27 Main Street, Bar Harbor (207-288-4585; 207-546-2927; decruise@mid-maine.com; www.downeastwindjammer.com); $14–38 per person. Captain Steven F. Pagels welcomes pets and their owners on board Windjammer's vessels for 1½- to 2-hour cruises, 4-hour deep-sea fishing expeditions, and 1-hour ferry trips from Bar Harbor to Winter Harbor and back. Dogs must be leashed and well behaved, but otherwise are free to enjoy the sea air in their fur.

Hadley Point Beach, Route 3, Bar Harbor. Pooches may not be allowed at Acadia's beaches, but this town-owned property allows dogs on the condition that their owners adhere to local leash laws and have pooper-scooper bags handy. The scenic saltwater beach, complete with picnic area, sits along Frenchman's and Thomas Bays and is prized by local sailborders for its strong north wind. After you enjoy a picnic with Spot in the midafternoon sun, you'll probably add this gorgeous spot to your top-10 list, too.

Independence Day Parade, downtown Bar Harbor. Break out the red, white, and blue: This town gets seriously patriotic on the Fourth of July, and nearly everyone—including pets of all shapes and sizes—shows up for the extravaganza. Volunteers from several local animal rescue organizations march in the parade (along with the dogs in their care that need homes), and so many canines attend with their owners that children on floats often throw candy *and* dog biscuits to the crowd.

***Lulu* Lobster Boat Rides,** 55 West Street, Bar Harbor (207-963-2341; luluinc@prexar.com; www.lulu-lobsterboat.com); $15–25 per person. Hop on a traditional wooden lobster boat for a slow, scenic tour of Frenchman's Bay. Captain John L. Nicolai is an animal lover and does allow pets on board with a few restrictions: Because the vessel holds a maximum of six passengers, each passenger must be comfortable with the idea of traveling with a pet on board. Also, dog owners are responsible for keeping their pet on a leash and repairing any animal-caused damage.

M.A.M.A. Thrift Store, Route 1, Hancock (207-422-2353). You can save money *and* help animals at this eclectic shop, where all profits go to benefit the local M.A.M.A. (Mature Animals for Mature Adults) low-cost spay and neuter clinic. Choose from clothing, jewelry, toys, housewares, books, and more; store hours are 10 AM to 4 PM, Monday through Sunday.

***Sea Princess* Nature Cruises,** Town Marina, Southwest Harbor (207-276-5352; rliebow@acadia. net); $8–16 per person. The *Sea Princess* sets out for morning, afternoon, and sunset cruises each day to take in the wildlife and scenery of Acadia National Park, Somes Sound, Little Cranberry Island, and Bear Island Lighthouse. Children under age four ride for free, and pets can join the fun as long as they're on a leash and friendly to other passengers.

Shore Path, Bar Harbor. This footpath starts near the Bar Harbor Inn and continues for a mile or so along the water, allowing an unusual view of Frenchman's Bay on one side and Bar Harbor's most impressive waterfront homes on the other. It's a perfect spot for a jog, but most prefer to take it a bit slower and soak in all the scenery.

Window-Shopping in Bar Harbor. You can spend the good part of day perusing the hundreds of in-town shops selling clothing, candy, ice cream, art, sunglasses, maps, Maine blueberry jam, pottery, and nearly every other type of product imaginable. (At **Ben and Bill's** on Main Street, you can even get a "doggie ice cream" with a biscuit on top.) A small, picturesque park in the center of it all provides shade, and the waterfront is never more than a few blocks away. All in all, it's a fun and relaxing destination when you need a break from all that hiking.

QUICK BITES

Beal's Lobster Pound, Clark Point Road, Southwest Harbor (207-244-7178). Dogs are welcome on a leash at this ultra-casual, outdoor restaurant. Plan to get down and dirty cracking your lobster, munching corn-on-the-cob with melted butter, and digging into Captain's Galley menu items like fried foods and burgers.

Chef Marc and **Eat-A-Pita,** 326 Main Street, Southwest Harbor (207-244-4344). These two restaurants sit side by side in downtown Southwest Harbor; at Chef Marc, diners can choose from a variety of upscale lamb, seafood, pasta, and vegetarian dishes. Eat-A-Pita's casual menu is best known for blueberry pancakes and generously stuffed pita sandwiches and salads. Both offer outdoor seating next to the sidewalk.

Ellsworth Giant Sub and **Blueberry Hill Dairy Bar,** Route 3, Ellsworth (207-667-5585). These next-door neighbors are a great stop for lunch and dessert: Choose from 60 eat-in or take-out varieties of subs and then walk up to the window for an ice cream at Blueberry Hill. A grassy area with picnic tables is available for relaxing and eating in the sunshine.

Jordan Pond House, Bar Harbor (207-276-3316). Located within the park, this historic restaurant has outdoor tables sitting high atop a hill overlooking Jordan Pond. (A hiking trail encircles the pond and makes for a great walk before or after your meal; see **Jordan Pond Nature Trail** in **Acadia National Park** under "Out and About.") The menu includes soups, sandwiches, and entrées, but most people come for the famous popovers, served with butter and strawberry jam. The wait staff have been known to bring water bowls to thirsty four-legged patrons, as well. Be prepared for a long wait for a table.

Maine-ly Delights, Grandville Road, Bass Harbor (207-244-3656). Overlooking the bustling waterfront of Bass Harbor, this take-out spot offers lobster, burgers, hot dogs, and the house specialty: doughboys with ice cream and fresh fruit. Place your order at the take-out window and settle into the outdoor seating area.

Rupununi, 119 Main Street, Bar Harbor (207-288-2886). This popular restaurant sits in the heart of the downtown action. If you can get a table on the patio next to the street, you can park your pooch next to you, curbside, while you enjoy burgers, steaks, gumbo, chowders, and soups.

The Seafood Ketch, McMullin Avenue, Bass Harbor (207-244-7463). This welcoming, casual restaurant allows leashed dogs on its deck and lawn seating areas, which overlook Bass Harbor. A full-service bar offers wine, beer, and cordials, and the menu includes fresh seafood (of course) and homemade breads and desserts.

HOT SPOTS FOR SPOT

Acadia Woods Kennel,
31 Greta's Lane, Bar Harbor (207-288-9766; applegate@acadia.net). This kennel prides itself on providing plenty of personal attention to each of its four-legged visitors, including twice-daily walks for dogs. You can leave your pet overnight (each dog has a heated sleeping area and a private, covered outdoor run; cats have two-story "condos"), or drop him off just for the day. For dogs, you'll have to prove he's received rabies, distemper, and parvovirus vaccinations. Cat owners must show proof of rabies and distemper protection.

Bark Harbor, 202 Main Street, Bar Harbor (207-288-0404). Four-footed customers are more than welcome inside this fun, crowded store designed with them in mind. Your dog can drool at the home-baked animal treats in the glass-front bakery case while you browse a wide selection of leashes, doggie bandannas, pet-care books, picture frames, T-shirts, knickknacks, and other canine and feline items of interest. If you're in the downtown area, this is a can't-miss shop.

Cat Nap Inn, Branch Pond Road, Ellsworth (207-667-5012). This tucked-away spot offers "fine feline lodging" for $8.50 per night. Each cat gets his or her own kennel with piped-in classical music, floor-to-ceiling windows, and, not coincidentally, views of the yard's many bird feeders. Pets are welcome on a per night basis or for extended stays.

Cats 'n' Dogs, Ellsworth (207-667-8048; kathawk@prexar.com). Native Downeaster Kathy Hawkes specializes in short-term pet day care for year-round residents as well as Ellsworth-area vacationers. For $15, she'll come to your house, cottage, hotel room, or even RV (sorry, no tents) to spend an hour walking, feeding, or playing with your furry, scaled, or feathered travel companions. For visits farther than 15 miles away, she charges $1 per mile, one way, and she'll stay longer than the standard one-hour visit for $10 per extra hour.

MDI Pet Sitting, Bar Harbor (207-288-5053; 207-266-5454). For $15 per half hour or $20 for two or more animals, local resident Jenny Buzzell will visit your home (or home-away-from-home) to keep your pet company with playtime, a walk, or whatever else Fluffy might need. She'll even give shots or medication to pets with medical conditions.

IN CASE OF EMERGENCY

Acadia Veterinary Hospital,
21 Federal Street, Bar Harbor (207-288-5733).

Southwest Harbor Veterinary,
Seal Cove Road, Southwest Harbor (207-244-3336).

Small Animal Clinic,
9 Toothaker Lane, Ellsworth (207-667-8087).

Downeast Maine

PET-FRIENDLY RATING: 🦴 🦴 🦴 🦴

Most coastal Maine visitors never make it past Acadia. If you're among the hardy few who keep driving north, you'll be more than rewarded for your efforts when you enter this pristine and wild corner of the state. The region has many nicknames: Downeast, so called because ships sail downwind from Boston and New York to get here; the Bold Coast, a name that refers, perhaps, to the grit of the locals; and the Sunrise Coast, because the sun touches these shores before any other spot in the country.

Downeast towns are small and genuine—when asked for her street number, one Cherryfield resident reacted with surprise: "We don't have street numbers!" she explained. More than 85 percent of the nation's blueberries are grown here, and many of the locals are involved with that, well, fruitful industry. You'll see the full beauty of the blue splendor if you arrive in late summer (see Blueberry Barrens under "Out and About").

There are fewer accommodations here than there are farther south, along with fewer restaurants and touristy businesses—a blessing for those looking to escape the crowded hotels and T-shirt shops of other vacation areas. For the most part, your pets can romp with you as you explore rocky beaches, wildlife refuges, and lively festivals. You may want to stock up on food and supplies beforehand, however: Compared to other, more populated regions, pet shops are in short supply here.

ACCOMMODATIONS

Hotels, Motels, Inns, and Bed & Breakfasts

Dennysville

Robinson's Cottages, Route 86, Box 323, Dennysville (207-726-3901); $305–350 per week. These seven rustic cottages, ranging in size from one to four bedrooms, sit beside the Denny's River. Most have a screened-in porch; all have a kitchenette, outdoor grills, and picnic tables. Linens, towels, and blankets are also provided, and guests can use the canoes and rowboats free of charge. Pets are welcome.

Eastport

Motel East, 23A Water Street, Eastport (207-853-4747; moteleastport@acadia.net); $80–95 per night. Rooms at this oceanfront motel have views of Passamaquoddy Bay and Campobello Island; most have private balconies, and all have a queen-sized bed and full bath (suites and nonsmoking rooms are also available upon request). Pets are welcome for an extra $25 fee.

Southmeadow Cottages, Perry, Boyden Lake; contact Meg McGarvey, 2A Pleasant Street, Eastport (207-726-4259; 207-853-2318; megmcgarvey@hotmail.com); $450 per week. Located in the town of Perry of Boyden Lake, these six housekeeping cottages are spread out on about a half mile of shorefront. Each cottage has a unique architecture and decor, from an A-frame to a two-story with a fireplace. Each has either a deck or screened-in porch, full bathroom, kitchen, and telephone. "We've had all kinds of dogs and cats visit over the years, and we welcome them all as long as they're well behaved," says Southmeadow owner Meg McGarvey.

Todd House Bed & Breakfast, Todd's Head, Eastport (207-853-2328); $50–90 per night. Pet owners (or any visitor, for that matter) will feel welcome at Todd House, a waterfront B&B. The five guest rooms are adorned with quilts, wooden chests, and Shaker-style furniture; some have private entrances to the large

Downeast Maine

Princeton

Canada

Grand Lake
Stream

Woodland

Calais

Moosehorn
Wildlife
Refuge

Robbinston

Ayers

Perry

Wesley

Cooper

Quoddy
Eastport

Dennysville

Marion

N. Lubec

Northfield

Moosehorn
Wildlife
Refuge

Lubec

Beddington

Machias

S. Trescott

Whiting

Quoddy
Head
State
Park

Deblois

Centerville

E. Machias

Waltham

Columbia
Falls

Jonesboro

N. Cutler

Eastbrook

Cherryfield

Addison

Cutler

Franklin

Indian
River

Sullivan

Millbridge

Ashville

Steuben

South
Addison

Jonesport

Sorrento

Prospect
Harbor

Winter
Harbor

Acadia National Park
Schoodic Point

Frenchman's
Bay

N

0   20

Scale in Miles

©The Countryman Press

yard out back, ideal for canine romping. "I welcome all pets," says innkeeper Ruth McInnis. "I've had everything from owls to tarantulas stay here. I loved the owls!"

Grand Lake Stream

Canal Side Cabins, Grand Lake Stream (1-888-796-2796; canal side@nemaine.com; www.canal-sidecabins.com); $28–30 per night or $360–450 per week. These informal cabins were designed with families and sportsmen in mind. Each is heated with a furnace or fireplace and has a living room, dining area, kitchen, and full bathroom. The smallest cabins accommodate two people; the largest sleeps six. Well-behaved

pets are welcome with no extra charge.

Hancock Point

Crocker House Country Inn, Point Road, Hancock Point (1-877-715-6017); $90–150 per night. Tucked away on a quiet peninsula, this 1884 inn is located at the midpoint between Acadia National Park's Cadillac Mountain and Schoodic Point. Pets are not allowed in the dining room, but they are welcome in the 11 guest rooms, each of which has a private bathroom and a unique decor.

Harrington

Ocean Spray Cottages, RR 1, P.O. Box 38, Harrington (207-483-2780; www.oceanspray-cottages.com); $75–90 per night or $500–600 per week. These two-bedroom heated cottages are available for rental year-round. Each can accommodate four people and offers a living room, a kitchenette, and window bird feeders. "We have three dogs and love to meet our customers' pets," says owner Cathy Strout. "Our experience has been that anyone who travels with their pets takes really good care of them."

Machiasport

Micmac Farm Guest Houses and Gardner House, Route 92, Machiasport (207-255-3008; www.micmacfarm.com); $55–70 per night. Animals are allowed inside the guest cabins at this cozy, secluded farm. The three cabins and farmhouse are surrounded by 50 acres of forest and meadow; each cabin has two double beds, a full bathroom, knotty-pine walls, a dining area with a kitchenette, and electric heat. The decks have sliding doors and views of the Machias River.

Sorrento

Bass Cove Farm Bed & Breakfast, 312 East Side Road, Sorrento (207-422-3564; bass-cove@downeast.net; www.bass-covefarm.com); $75–90 per night. This B&B is secluded enough to offer repose but close enough to the sights to be convenient. "We've enjoyed the company of dogs, cats, a rabbit, and a bird," says Bass Cove innkeeper Mary Ann Solet. She asks that pets not be left alone in the rooms for long periods of time; there are no extra pet fees.

Campgrounds

Alexander

Pleasant Lake Camping Area, 371 Davis Road, Alexander (207-454-7467; pllake@nemaine.com); call for rate information. Just off Route 9 you'll find this family camping area with 120 tent and RV sites (some waterfront), full hookups, picnic tables, and fire rings. There's plenty here to keep the family busy, including basketball and tennis courts, hiking trails, a boat ramp, horseshoe pits, a playground, and a camp store. Quiet, well-behaved pets are welcome on a leash.

Danforth

Greenland Cove Campground, East Grand Lake, Danforth (207-448-2863; 207-532-6593); $22 per night. Pets on a leash are welcome at this lakeside, rural campground that caters to fishermen and families. On-site, you'll find wooded trails, a sandy beach, waterfront and wooded campsites, water and electric hookups for RVs, boat rentals, a camp store, a heated pool, a game room, and a playground.

Dennysville

Cobscook Bay State Park Campground, RR 1, Box 127, Dennysville (207-726-4412); $12 per night Maine residents; $16 per night out-of-state residents. The 100 campsites at this state park (see "Out and About") are fairly secluded to provide a rustic camping experience: Some are located right on the water. Amenities include hot showers, shelters, and a picnic area. Cobscook Bay surrounds the park on three sides. Owners are expected to clean up after their pets and keep them on a leash.

Eastport
Seaview Campground, 16 Norwood Road, Eastport (207-853-4471; info@eastport.com; www.eastportmaine.com); $13–34 per night or $475–918 per month. This oceanfront campground juts out into Passamaquoddy Bay. Tenters and RV owners can enjoy the beach, dock, boat launch, recreation hall, laundry facilities, showers, and flush toilets, along with a host of planned activities including barbecues, fish frys, and pig roasts. Quiet, leashed pets are welcome but cannot be left alone at a campsite.

Steuben
Mainayr Campground, 321 Village Road, Steuben (207-546-3780; info@mainayr.com; www.mainayr.com); $18 per night. Located on 25 acres at the edge of a tidal cove, Mainayr is a quiet campground with 35 sites for tents, campers, and RVs. Families can enjoy a playground, a small beach, laundry facilities, and a camp store; a saltwater tank houses fresh lobsters for campers to cook at their fire pits, located at each site. Pets are welcome on a leash.

Sport Camps

Grand Lake Stream
Grand Lake Lodge, West Grand Lake, Grand Lake Stream (207-796-5584; lakelodge@nemaine. com; www.nemaine.com/grand-lakelodge); $29–39 per night or

$325–550 per week. These housekeeping cabins sleep two to six people along the shores of West Grand Lake, where fishermen know they can count on finding landlocked salmon and lake trout. The small log cabins are popular with deer and bear hunters as well. Well-behaved pets are welcome as long as owners clean up after them and don't leave them alone in the cabins.

Indian Rock Camps, Grand Lake Stream (207-796-2822; 1-800-498-2822; indianrockcamp@nemaine. com); $70–82 per night on the American plan. Guests here can take advantage of some of the best fishing spots in Grand Lake Stream and Big Lake, on their own or with a guide. Facilities at the camp include a beach, basketball and tennis courts, miniature golf, housekeeping log cabins with screened-in porches, and the **Indian Rock Lodge** for dining. Pets are welcome.

Leen's Lodge, Route 1, Grand Lake Stream (1-800-99-LEENS; www.leenslodge.com); $90–125 per person per day on the American plan. This lodge bills itself as the Waldorf of the Wilderness, offering 10 fully furnished cabins on West Grand Lake, a dining lodge, a lounge area, a deck house, a sundeck, and boat docks. Activities here revolve around fishing and bird hunting; guides are available for hire. Dogs are welcome on a leash.

Weatherby's: The Fisherman's Resort, off Route 1, Grand Lake Stream (207-796-5558; weather@

somtel.com; www.weatherbys.
com); $108 per day for adults;
$55 per day for children. This
sportman's haven has a main
lodge and 15 rustic cabins for
rent, and also offers fishing
opportunities and lessons in
Grand Lake and Grand Lake
Stream. Weatherby's owners,
Charlene and Ken Sassi, are willing to allow one dog per room
for an extra $18 per day, pro-
vided that the animal is crated
when left alone.

Princeton

Long Lake Camps, West Street,
Princeton (207-796-2051; longlake
@nemaine.com; www.longlake-
camps.com); $80 per person, per
night on the American plan;
$55–80 per person, per night on
the housekeeping plan. Fishing is
the focus at this family-friendly
camp. The 14 cabins available
for rent sit on the water's edge;
each has a full bathroom, hot
and cold water, and electricity.
Pets are welcome for an additional $5 per day. "We're located
on a peninsula, so it's easy to
keep track of pets," says owner
Sandra Smith. "Also, we have a
2-mile-long dirt road system that
works well for walks."

Homes, Cottages, and Cabins for Rent

Beals

Frost Farm, Box 265, Beals (207-
497-3055; frostfarm@maineline.
net); $500–1,000 per week. Frost
Farm, a four-bedroom 1870s
home with an ocean view and
7-acre pasture, is located near
Hannah's Cove on Beals Island.

The house also has 1½ bathrooms, a kitchen, a TV/VCR,
dishes and utensils, huge windows, and a washing machine.
Pets are negotiable.

Hancock

Virtue's Sea Cottages, Hancock
Point, Hancock; dhvirtue@mint.
net; www.virtue.to/cottages);
$539 per week. These blue-
shingle cottages sit on the edge
of Frenchman's Bay and share a
private beach; each can accommodate up to five people with
one double bed, one twin bunk
bed, and one daybed, along with
a kitchenette, bathroom, and
woodstove. For park lovers, the
cottages are close to Mount
Desert Island and the Schoodic
section of Acadia.

Lubec

Lubec Vacation Rental, Johnson
Bay, Lubec (207-733-5501);
$400–700 per week. This three-
bedroom home, located near
Campobello Island on 10 acres,
can accommodate up to eight
people. The property has a private rocky beach, and the home
offers a washer and dryer, linens
and towels, a full kitchen, and a
deck overlooking the water. Dogs
(sorry, no cats) are welcome.

Quoddy House, Lubec (207-255-
8584; 207-255-4861; joancart@
ptc-me.net); $650–850 per week.
This oceanfront, weathered-shingle farmhouse dates from the
1830s. Located next to Quoddy
State Park, it has sweeping views,
fields, a large lawn, and plenty of
privacy. Inside, there's a fireplace,
kitchen, TV/VCR, and stereo.
Dogs (sorry, no cats) are permitted for a onetime fee of $50.

Silverman Farmhouse, Lubec coast (202-292-0646; 301-891-0600); $950–1,200 per week. This enormous, modernized farmhouse sits right on the water, about 4 miles from Quoddy Head State Park, and has 10 acres and its own private beach. Inside, renters will find a fireplace, washer and dryer, dishwasher, full kitchen, TV/VCR, and stereo/CD player. All dishes and utensils are provided. Dogs are free to romp and roam off-leash.

West Quoddy Rental, RR 2, Box 1470, Lubec (207-733-4404; 207-733-2197; rental@westquoddy gifts.com); $550–650 per week. Pets are welcome for an extra $25 per week at this three-bedroom home located within a mile of West Quoddy Head Lighthouse. The home has a view of the Lubec Channel, private shore access, a living room, a full kitchen, and satellite TV with 50-plus channels. Linens are provided for the queen-, full-, and twin-sized beds along with a daybed.

Pembroke
Yellow Birch Farm, 272 Young's Cove Road, Pembroke (207-726-5807; yellowbirchfarm@acadia.net); $380 per week. Dogs can join the fun at the Yellow Birch's weathered-shingle cottage, where the farm's resident golden retriever, Cross, will undoubtedly serve as tour guide. "We love to meet other people's dogs," says owner Gretchen Gordon. "And there are lots of super places here for a dog to run: around the farm, at the shore, or on our dirt road." The cottage has one dou-

ble and two twin beds, a barbecue grill, a toaster, and a coffeemaker.

Sorrento
Downeast Coastal Cottage, near Route 1, Sorrento (1-800-572-7921; ruthnski@aol.com); $65 per night or $400 per week. This cozy one-room guest house is big enough for two and is located on a private 10-acre farm. Gardeners, take note: The farm's owners raise vegetables for sale, and are willing to offer reduced rates in the summer to guests who want to help out with planting, harvesting, and weeding. Flea-free and well-behaved pets are welcome.

South Princeton
Hideaway on Pocomoonshine Lake, 29 The Hideaway Lane, South Princeton (207-427-6183); $100 per night or $600 per week. Dogs, cats, and even birds have stayed at these waterfront housekeeping cottages located at the headwaters of the East Machias River. Each rental has a "great room" (living, dining, and kitchen area) along with a full bathroom, one or two bedrooms, a charcoal grill, a dock, and a rowboat. There are no extra fees for pets.

Whiting
Summer Cottage, c/o Puffin Pines Country Gift Store, Whiting (207-733-9782; patsue1046@aol.com); $500–600 per week. Owner Pat McCabe has been renting this cottage and welcoming pets for more than five years. Located about 100 feet from Lubec Channel, the cottage

accommodates up to four people with two bedrooms, one bathroom, a combined kitchen/living room area, a TV/VCR, and a barbecue grill. Animal owners pay an extra $25 per week.

Rental Agencies

Due East Real Estate and Property Management, Whiting (207-733-5511; barbara@dueeast.com; www.dueeast.com). Due East handles home, apartment, farm, cottage, and cabin rentals throughout the Downeast and Washington County region. Some of the units allow well-behaved animals for an additional fee; call or e-mail for up-to-date listings and availability.

Hearts of Maine Seaside Rental Properties, 260 Cape Split Road, Addison (207-255-4210; 207-557-6611; eoafish@nemaine.com; www.boldcoast.com/maine-cottages). This rental agency is extremely pet-friendly: More than 75 percent of the listed properties allow animals. "We have very few problems with pets at our rentals, and we know that pets are an important part of people's families," says Greg Burr, who owns the agency with his wife, Sue. The homes and apartments are located in Castine, Lubec, and everywhere in between—animals must be flea-free and quiet, and owners must pick up after them.

OUT AND ABOUT

Acadia National Park, Schoodic Section. Spread throughout the towns of Gouldsboro and Winter Harbor, this is the only section of Acadia National Park located on the mainland. Much like the Loop Road in the Mount Desert Island section of the park, Acadia's Schoodic region also offers a one-way, scenic "loop" around the peninsula with impressive views of the rocky coastline and wild terrain. This section of the park is relatively small (2,194 acres compared with Mount Desert Island's 30,300 acres), but the crowds are smaller, too—a bonus in these popular parts.

Blueberry Barrens. Washington County produces the majority of the United States' blueberries. Starting in August, the region's barrens are ready for harvest, and the entire landscape in these parts turns, well, blue. To get the best views of this unusual sight, follow **Route 193** from Cherryfield toward Deblois, **Route 1** heading north from Harrington or Jonesboro, or **Route 9** in Wesley.

Blueberry Festival, Centre Street Congregational Church, Centre Street, Machias. Usually held during one of the last weekends in August, this Friday-through-Sunday annual fair celebrates the region's blueberry harvest with musical performances, fish frys, parades, more than 100 crafters and artists, and of course blueberry pancake breakfasts.

Bold Coast Trail, SR-191, Cutler. As the largest stretch of undeveloped coastline in the state of Maine, this 4½-mile-long trail holds special appeal for residents and visitors alike. Along the way, you'll pass cliffs, beaches, forests, and sea arches; out at sea, whales, songbirds, and herring may be passing by. Primitive camping is allowed off the main trail. To find the trailhead, drive 1–2 miles north of Cutler along SR-191 until you reach the small entrance.

Calais Waterfront Walkway. This wonderful, winding pathway is worth a visit. Part of the former train line of the Calais Railway, it hugs the St. Croix River from the library to Todd Street and South Street, with benches and picnic tables along the way. The 1-mile-long walkway passes right by the **International Bridge.**

Cherryfield Historic District, Cherryfield–Narraguagus Historical Society, Cherryfield (207-546-7979). A quiet walk through this quaint old section of town will take you past impressive examples of Second Empire, Federal, Greek Revival, Italianate, and Queen Anne architecture—in taverns, shops, and homes. The local historical society publishes a guide that starts a self-guiding tour at the corner of Main Street and Route 1.

Cobscook Bay State Park, RR 1, Box 127, Dennysville (207-726-4412). Bald eagles, wildflowers,

and more than 200 species of birds make their home in this 888-acre park, whose name comes from the Passamaquoddy word for "boiling tides." The trails are especially popular among hikers and cross-country skiers. The park entrance is located about 4 miles south of Dennysville along Route 1. There is also an extensive campground on-site (see "Accommodations—Campgrounds").

Deer Island Ferry, Water Street Terminal, Eastport (506-747-2159; www.eastcoastferries.nb.ca); passengers, $2; car and driver, $13. East Coast Ferries Ltd. operates this service to take travelers to and from Eastport, Maine, and Deer Island, New Brunswick. The tiny island makes for a great day trip, with galleries, shops, villages, lobster pounds, beaches, and whale-watching trips. Restrained pets are welcome on the ferry, provided their owners clean up after them.

International Festival, Calais. The town of Calais hosts this festival every August with its Canadian friends across the border in St. Stephen, New Brunswick. The weeklong festivities typically include parades, horse shows, fireworks, beer and food tents, and crafts fairs. For up-to-date festival information and locations, call the Calais Regional Chamber of Commerce at 207-454-2308.

Moosehorn National Wildlife Refuge, Charlotte Road, Baring. Moose, wood ducks, eagles, blue herons, barred owls, ruffed grouse—this is wild Maine at its finest. The park has nearly 60 miles of road and trails available for hiking, bird-watching, and cross-country skiing. Beavers build dams in the 50 lakes and marshes, and the woodcock perform their astounding aerial mating dances each spring. This is a big place with big wildlife (black bears are often seen foraging through the blueberry patches in late summer), so exercise extreme caution with your pets.

Petit Manan National Wildlife Refuge, Pigeon Hill Road, Steuben. Among the more famous residents of this 3,000-acre preserve are endangered peregrine falcons. You might also spot kestrels, goshawks, puffins, and sandpipers in marshes, peat bogs, and forests that make up Petit Manan. Much of the park's island property is accessible only by boat, but you can get to Petit Manan Point by car. Two trails—Birch and Shore—leave from the parking area on Pigeon Hill Road.

Robertson Sea Tours, Milbridge Marina, Milbridge (207-546-3883; robertsonseatours@yahoo.com; www.awa-web.com/seatours); tours, $20–45 per person; charters, $300 per day. Captain James Robertson welcomes pets aboard his boat for Petit Manan Puffin Cruises, Scenic Island Tours, Island Lobster Cruises, and personalized, private charters. (A seaworthy golden retriever was a guest on a recent voyage.) While at sea, don't be surprised to spot seals, porpoises, blue herons, ospreys, and bald eagles.

Rocky Lake Public Reserve, SR-191, East Machias. More than 11,000 acres of coastline, forests, coves, inlets, and primitive camping sites await visitors to this pristine reserve. Fishermen gather at the **East Machias River, Meadow Brook, Northern Inlet, Rocky Lake, Second Lake**, and other fishing and swimming holes throughout the area, and bird-watchers, hikers, and boaters will find plenty to do here as well. As with all northern Maine and wilderness areas, use caution during hunting season.

West Quoddy Head Light, Quoddy Head State Park, Lubec (207-733-0911; 207-941-4014). This barberpole of a lighthouse has graced innumerable calendars and coffee-table books. Located in Quoddy Head State Park, its 49-foot, red-and-white-striped tower watches over the Bay of Fundy and the town of Lubec. There are other, equally beautiful lighthouses in the Quoddy Loop area, but this is by far the most famous. The 532-acre park is located about 4 miles off Route 189 in Lubec.

QUICK BITES

Crossroads Restaurant, Route 1, Pembroke (207-726-5053). Area residents like to linger at this family-style seafood restaurant, attached to a motel of the same name. But there are also plenty of menu items available for take-out, if you want to take some lunch along with you when you go to see the sights.

Downeast Deli, Routes 186 and 195, Prospect Harbor (207-963-7021). You can relax on Downeast Deli's lawn or pack up your picnic basket with New York–style hoagies, soups and chowders, seafood sandwiches, and even pizza.

Frank's Pizzeria and Deli, 34 Water Street, Eastport (207-853-2709). Call ahead and order pizza, sandwiches, subs, calzones, salads, chicken dishes, pasta, and more at this primarily take-out restaurant.

Lobster Crate, Route 190, Perry (207-853-6611). This casual seafood restaurant, recommended by the locals, has plenty of picnic tables as well as a take-out window.

Polar Treat, Route 1, Perry. Help yourself to lunch, frozen yogurt, or ice cream (including three flavors of soft-serve) at this A-frame take-out spot. For Rover, the staff serves up "doggie dishes" of ice cream with a dog bone on top.

Rosie's Hot Dogs, Town Wharf, Eastport. The dogs at this famously popular take-out stand are served with locally ground mustard. (You can also order onion rings, french fries, and chili.) Bun in hand, you can eat at the picnic tables overlooking the harbor.

Schoodic Snacks, Main Street (Route 186), Winter Harbor (207-963-2296). Oven-baked fries, hamburgers, hot dogs, crab rolls, steamers, and lobster are available at this casual take-out place with picnic tables.

HOT SPOTS FOR SPOT

Amittai Grooming, Hilltop Lane (Route 93), Cherryfield (207-546-7425). Cynthia Huntington has been a dog groomer for more than 30 years—at one time on the show circuit, and now in homey Cherryfield. Much of her business comes from Downeast visitors and vacationers. She charges about $25 for most visits, and can do shampooing, skin treatments, clipping, and more.

C.P.L. Kennels, 6 Kendall Head Road, Eastport (207-853-4484). Animal lover Carolyn Lowe boards cats and dogs at her small facility (there are 10 runs available for dogs). She also provides day care for the pets of locals and vacationers. "In a lot of cases, I take care of dogs while their owners are out whale-watching or sight-seeing," Lowe explains. She charges $7 per day for dogs and $4 for cats.

Dogs by Dawn, Route 1, Box 2280, East Machias (207-255-3994; www.dogsbyd.com). Boarding, grooming, and doggie day care (for $1 an hour) are all available at this full-service facility that also sells pet food and supplies. Grooming services include shampoos and breed-specific clipping, and the building has 17 kennels and seven indoor/outdoor runs.

Pet Pantry, 24 High Street, Milbridge (207-546-7941). This well-stocked shop offers dog and cat food, bird supplies, treats, toys, shampoos, and other necessities. The owners also run obedience-training classes in an adjoining room.

IN CASE OF EMERGENCY

Calais Veterinarian Clinic,
234 North Street, Calais (207-454-8522).

Four Corners Veterinary Clinic,
Stagecoach Road, Columbia Falls (207-483-4727).

Perry Animal Clinic,
Route 1, Perry (207-853-0671).

Sunrise County Veterinary Clinic,
Stagecoach Road, East Machias (207-255-8538).

Great North Woods

PET-FRIENDLY RATING: 🦴 🦴 🦴 🦴

This is Maine's true wilderness: From vast tracts of forest to majestic lakes and mountains, the Aroostook and northern Katahdin region is not for the faint of heart—or the tourist in search of indoor luxuries. In other parts of the state you hear about moose; here you see them, provided you know where and when to look. The friendly, laid-back local innkeepers and shop owners will be more than happy to share that information, along with anything else you might need to know about their neck of these woods.

This area has many leisure possibilities, including hiking, boating, and leaf peeping, but most people, it seems, come to northern Maine to hunt. Moose, bear, deer, and birds are the primary trophies. The vast majority of the accommodations here, including many sport camps, are set up to provide a home base for hunters and fishermen. Snowmobilers, as well, have discovered the region's charms and are becoming a growing force behind the local tourism industry. Much of the land and many of the roads of the North Woods are owned by timber and paper companies; be prepared to pay fees as you drive along.

Another important fact to note before you pack your bags is that dogs are not allowed in Baxter State Park, the 200,000-acre reserve that is the region's jewel and best-known attraction. But if you don't mind missing out on Baxter, numerous other parks, reserved lands, and campgrounds do welcome dogs. Beautiful Moosehead Lake, wildlife-viewing "safaris," and other adventure-filled spots also exist for you and your four-legged friends to explore together.

ACCOMMODATIONS

Hotels, Motels, Inns, and Bed & Breakfasts

Caribou
Caribou Inn and Convention Center, 19 Main Street, Caribou (207-498-3733; 1-800-235-0466; www.caribouinn.com); $45–106 per night. This long-standing Caribou favorite has 73 rooms and three executive suites, along with a restaurant serving breakfast, lunch, and dinner; a fitness center; an indoor pool, a sauna and whirlpool; and a lounge with pool tables, TVs, and Friday-night comedy shows. Pets are enthusiastically welcomed.

Russell's Motel, 357 Main Street, Caribou (207-498-2567); $34–40 per night. This small, simple, and clean motel offers an affordable night's stay in Caribou, and its location beside an established, groomed trail makes it popular with snowmobilers. "We do offer lodging to people with dogs and cats," says owner Donna Murchison. "All I ask is that the pets not bother other people and that the owners clean up after their animals."

Crouseville
Rum Rapids Inn Bed & Breakfast, Route 164, Crouseville (207-455-8096; rumrapids2@ainop.com; www.mainerec.com/rmrapids); $78 per night. This is the only B&B in the Presque Isle area; lucky for us, innkeeper Judy Boudman allows pets in one of the quaint rooms. "There is ample room on the grounds for exercising a pet, including nature trails and river walks," Judy explains. She also runs a gourmet food shop on-site and serves a full Scottish breakfast each morning.

Fort Kent
Northern Door Inn, 91 West Main Street, Fort Kent (207-834-3133; northerndoorinn@fkglobal.com; www.northerndoorinn.com);

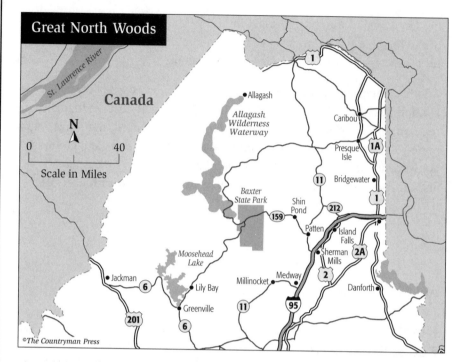

Great North Woods

Canada

St. Lawrence River

N

0   40

Scale in Miles

Allagash
Allagash
Wilderness
Waterway

Caribou

Presque
Isle

1A

Baxter
State Park

Shin
Pond

159

Bridgewater

11

212

Patten

Island
Falls

Sherman
Mills

2A

Moosehead
Lake

Jackman

6

Lily Bay

Greenville

201

6

Millinocket

Medway

Danforth

2

11

95

©The Countryman Press

$50–71 per night. This one-story hotel (also called **La Porte Du Nord**) was recently remodeled; most rooms have two double beds and standard hotel-style furnishings. Staff are knowledgeable about all of the local events and festivals, and the inn frequently hosts family reunions and other gatherings on-site. Pets are welcome to stay with no extra fees.

Greenville

The Black Frog, Main Street, Greenville (207-695-1100; info@theblackfrog.com; www. theblackfrog.com); $85–110 per night. This informal lodging and restaurant is located at the southernmost tip of Moosehead Lake. The two available suites have views of East Cove and are within walking distance of the busy village. "Our only restrictions for pets are that they be housebroken, not eat the furniture, and not keep us up all night," explains owner Leigh Turner. "And if they'd like to play with our 100-pound Doberman pinscher, all the better."

Kineo View Motor Lodge, Route 15, Greenville (207-695-4470; the view@moosehead.net; www. kineoview.com); $55–79 per night. This three-story motor lodge is located on 55 private acres, and each room overlooks the Moosehead Lake region. The rooms have a large balcony, color TV, and full bath. Restaurants and shops are nearby, along with skiing at Squaw Mountain and prime leaf-peeping opportunities in fall. Animals are welcome in designated pet rooms for an extra $5 per night, but they cannot be left unattended at any time.

Lakeview House Bed & Breakfast, 358 Lily Bay Road, Greenville (207-695-2229; info@lakeviewhouse.com; www.lakeviewhouse.com); $125–160 per night. Pets are welcome in the Moosehead Family Suite of this cozy B&B. The suite has cherry furniture, one queen-sized and two four-poster twin beds, picture windows, a separate living room area with a TV/VCR, and a private entrance that opens out onto a large lawn. Snow-mobiling, skiing, boating, and biking are some of the more popular nearby activities.

Leisure Life Resort, Greenville (207-695-3737; www.leisurelife-resort.com); $55–76 per night. Animals are welcome for an extra $5 per night at this 36-acre hotel with 17 rooms and efficiencies. Located on the ITS 86 snowmobile trail, the hotel also offers a swimming pool, an on-site driving range, room service, a restaurant and lounge, volleyball and basketball courts, horseshoe pits, and a catch-and-release trout pond.

Greenville Junction
Chalet Moosehead Lakefront Motel, Route 15, Greenville Junction (207-695-2950; 1-800-290-3645; www.moosehead-lodging.com); $65–85 per night. Every unit in this motel has a picture window and a view of the lake, as well as daily maid service, cable TV with HBO, and a full bathroom. The larger efficiencies have a separate bedroom, a living room, and a kitchenette. With advance notice,

dogs (sorry, no cats) are welcome in some rooms for an extra $10 per night, provided they aren't left alone in the room at any time.

Island Falls
Sewall House Retreat, 1027 Crystal Road, Island Falls (207-463-3428; 1-888-235-2395; info@sewallhouse.com; www.sewallhouse.com); $88–111 per day. This is one of most unusual accommodations in northern Maine—a B&B with an emphasis on Kundalini yoga and meditation, set beside deep woods and Mattawamkeag Lake. The daily schedule includes a morning and afternoon yoga class; free time for bicycling, journaling, swimming, hiking, and other activities; and breakfast, lunch, and dinner. Pets are welcome; there is a cat already in residence.

Jackman
John's Four Seasons Accommodations, SR-64, Jackman (1-888-668-0098; www.maineguide.com/jackman/johns4); $20–101 per night. John's offers a wide variety of options when it comes to finding a place to bunk for the night. Guests can choose from a motel, a lodge, a campground, a wilderness park, and a mobile home park. Canoes, campers, motorboats, lobster pots, and party tents are also available for rent. Pets are welcome with a $50 refundable deposit.

Patten
Mt. Chase Lodge, Route 159, Upper Shin Pond, Patten (207-528-2183; mtchaselodge@ainop.

com; www.maineguide.com/ patten/mtchase); $69–79 per day; $475–550 per week. For an extra $5 per night (and preapproval from innkeepers Rick and Sara Hill), guests can bring pets along for a stay in one of the lodge's cabins, which can accommodate two to eight people. Cabin guests can cook for themselves or choose a plan that allows them to enjoy family-style meals in the lodge dining room.

Presque Isle
Northern Lights Motel,
72 Houlton Road, Presque Isle (207-764-4441; motel@northern-lightsmotel.com; www.northern-lightsmotel.com); $36.95–60.95 per night. Each of the 12 units in this comfortable motel is individually decorated with pine-board walls, bright bedspreads, wood furniture, and mini-refrigerators. Guests will find swings and a gas barbecue grill out on the lawn, and free Internet access and coffee in the lobby. Pets are always welcome.

Presque Isle Inn and Convention Center, 116 Main Street, Presque Isle (207-764-3321; 1-800-533-3971; www.presqueisleinn.com); $45–106 per night. Recently acquired by the owners of the Caribou Inn, this very pet-friendly hotel has 151 newly renovated rooms, indoor corridors, an on-site tavern with wide-screen TV, a pool and sauna, an attached restaurant, meeting rooms, and live entertainment on weekends. There are no extra fees for pets.

Rockwood
Abnaki Cottages, P.O. Box 6, Rockwood (207-534-7318; abnaki@ abnakicottages.com; www.

abnakicottages.com); $63–95 per night or $378–570 per week. Sitting alongside Moosehead Lake, these five housekeeping cottages sleep four to six people and have separate bedrooms, bathrooms, controllable heat, and color TVs. One has hickory paneling; another has a screened-in porch. Children and pets are welcome to run and play on the surrounding lawn area.

Birches Resort, P.O. Box 41, Rockwood (1-800-825-WILD; wwld@aol.com; www.birches. com); cabins, $100–250 per night; cabin tents and yurts, $22–55 per night. Pets on a leash are welcome in the cabins, cabin tents, and yurts (but not in the lodge) for an extra fee of $7–8 per pet, per day. Dogs are also allowed on the on-site cross-country ski trail. The resort serves as a base for **Wilderness Expeditions,** an adventure tour company that escorts guests on biking, kayaking, floatplane, whitewater rafting, ice-fishing, and moose-viewing trips.

Sherman Mills
Katahdin Valley Motel, P.O. Box 412, Sherman Mills (207-365-4554; 1-888-500-2418; kvm@ ainop.com; www.mainerec.com/ kvmotel); $35–75 per night. Just off the highway (Exit 58 off I-95), this motel is neat, affordable, and convenient. Choose from standard rooms and larger apartments with washers/dryers and kitchenettes. Snowmobilers especially appreciate Katahdin Valley's location, right beside the ITS 83 groomed trail. Pets are welcome for an extra fee of $4 per night.

Silver Lake

Dunloggin' Bed & Breakfast,
Silver Lake, Lee (207-738-5014;
dunlogbb@linc-net.net; www.
dunlogginbnb.com); $50–70 per
night. A large, log cabin–style
home on the shore of Silver
Lake, this B&B offers feather
beds, home-cooked breakfasts
(included in basic rate), lunches,
and dinners (upon request), paddleboats, canoes, bicycles, a boat
dock, and a large deck. Pets are
welcome. "We're on a lake with
lots of woods, so dogs can be
walked without worrying too
much about bothering anyone,"
says innkeeper Gail Rae.

Campgrounds

Abbott Village

Balsam Woods Campground,
112 Pond Road, Abbott Village
(207-876-2731; info@balsam-
woods.com; www.balsamwoods.
com); $21–43 per night or
$126–258 per week. Campsites
and cabins are available at
Balsam Woods, which also offers
a snack bar (with burgers, fries,
and other treats), a lobster pound,
a camp store, laundry facilities,
and firewood, gas, and propane.
"We have always welcomed pets,"
says owner Jay Eberhard. "We
just ask that pets not be left alone
to bark or disturb other campers,
and owners are required to clean
up after their pets." Animals are
not allowed in the buildings or
pool area.

Greenville

**Lily Bay State Park
Campground,** HC 76, Lily Bay
Road, Greenville (207-695-2700;

207-941-4014); $12 per night
Maine residents; $16 per night
out-of-state residents. Two separate Lily Bay campgrounds have
91 sites, some of which are right
on Moosehead Lake. Campers
can enjoy a boat launch, swimming area, beach, and hiking
trail along the water. This is a
great way to see the lake and its
famous Mount Kineo. Dogs are
welcome as long as their owners
pick up after them.

**Moosehead Family
Campground,** Route 15,
Greenville (207-695-2210;
www.mooseheadcampground.
com); $17–22 per night. Pets on
a leash are welcome at this
campground, where you'll find
shaded and sunny sites for RVs
and tents, along with a playground, a game room, a camp
store, picnic tables, and free coffee and tea—all within a mile of
Moosehead Lake. Animals cannot
be left alone at campsites, and
owners must pick up after them.

Jackman

Loon Echo Family Campground,
Route 201, Jackman (207-668-
4829; loonecho@webtv.net;
www.campmaine.com/loon-
echo); $16–30 per night. Loon
Echo's owners, Bill and Holly
Erven, are true animal lovers—
they even raise and train service
dogs to help the handicapped.
Pets are welcome at their campground as long as they stay on a
leash and aren't left alone at a
site. Campers here will find lots
of fly-fishing opportunities, a
recreation area, vegetable gardens, abundant wildlife, boat
docking, and sites for tents and

RVs; waterfront camping cabins are also available.

Moose River Campground, off Pleasant Street, Jackman (207-668-3341; mooservr@ctel.net); $14–20 per night. Moose River Campground is located on the shores of Attean Lake, about a half mile from the river for which it is named. Campers here enjoy fishing, swimming, boating, and hiking. There are sites for tenters and RVers, along with rest rooms, a solar-heated swimming pool, laundry facilities, boat rentals, and a dining room. Pets are welcome.

Medway

Katahdin Shadows Campground and Cabins, Route 157, Medway (207-746-9349; 1-800-794-5267; katshadcamp@midmaine.com; www.katahdinshadows.com); campsites, $18–23 per night; cabins, $23–69 per night. This is an exceptionally pet-friendly campground; the owners offer pet-sitting for $10 per day and also sell "leash-mates," leash attachments with pooper-scooper bags, for $5. The cabins are old-fashioned log-style (all are heated and some include kitchenettes), and the campground offers boat rentals, a pool, athletic fields, a function hall, a camp store, and free morning coffee.

Pine Grove Campground and Cottages, Route 11, Medway (207-746-5172; pgcac@mid maine.com); $28–65 per night. Trailer and tent sites at this campground are located in the woods and along the shores of the Penobscot River. The cottages

sleep three to five people and offer bathrooms, kitchenettes, and small living room areas. On-site, you'll also find a recreation hall, a horseshoe pit, a swimming hole, a camp store, and laundry facilities. All kinds of pets are welcome.

Millinocket

Hidden Springs Campground, 224 Central Street, Millinocket (1-888-685-4488; tentrus@mid-maine.com; www.hiddenspring.com); $15–21 per night. "As pet owners, we know how hard it is to leave the baby home," says Hidden Springs owner Gail Seile. Dogs must be on a leash and not left alone at tent sites, and owners must clean up after them. The campground has miles of bike trails and facilities for tenters and RVers, and is close to shops, restaurants, and grocery stores.

Mount Chase

Shin Pond Village, 1489 Shin Pond Road, Mount Chase (207-528-2900; www.shinpond.com); $16–22 per night, $99–139 per week, or $299–399 per month. A family- and pet-friendly campground, Shin Pond offers tent sites with picnic tables and fire pits, and RV sites with hookups. Lakes, mountains, and forests are close by. The campground also has housekeeping cottages for rent, and a gift shop and country store. Pets are welcome for an additional fee of $5 per day.

Presque Isle

Arndt's Aroostook River Lodge and Campground, 95 Parkhurst Siding Road, Presque Isle (207-764-8677); $14–22 per night,

$108–132 per week, or $400–490 per month. Though not permitted in the lodge, pets can join their owners in the campground section of this Presque Isle riverfront facility. Secluded and private, Arndt's is also close to shopping, restaurants, a golf course, and bike trails; on-site, campers make use of a recreation hall, laundry facilities, bike rental shop, and a shower/bathhouse.

Aroostook State Park Camp-|ground, 87 State Park Road, Presque Isle (207-768-8341); $10 per night Maine residents; $12 per night out-of-state residents. With 28 well-spaced sites, this campground can accommodate tents, pop-up campers, and a few RVs. You can launch a boat or catch some rays at Echo Lake. Toilets, shelters, picnic areas, and water spigots are also provided. (See "Out and About" for more park information.)

Fieldstone Cabins and RV Park, 24 North Street, Presque Isle (1-800-764-0324; 1-888-734-1476; kward@mainerr.com; www. mainerec.com/rainbowcove); $65–85 per night or $400–550 per week. Fieldstone's 100-year-old log cabins are homey, clean, and full of country touches like lofts, wooden ladders, front porches, and rustic interiors. Each is equipped with a kitchen, gas grill, full bathroom, two bedrooms, two double beds, and a twin bed. At the time of this writing, the RV section of the campground was under construction; call for updated information.

Rockwood

Seboomook Wilderness Campground, HC 85, Rockwood (207-280-0555; seboomook@ starband.net); $14–16 per night. Animals are welcome at the Adirondack shelters, tent sites, and RV sites with hookups at Seboomook, which is located at the upper end of Moosehead Lake. The site offers a sandy beach, activity/lawn area, and camp store. Fishermen and hunters are frequent guests, as are families and cross-country skiers. There are no extra fees for pets.

Sinclair

Waters Edge R.V. Resort Campground, Route 162, Lot 334, Sinclair (207-543-5189; 941-793-6280; rvresort@ncil.net; www. watersedgeresort.net); call for rate information. With a motto like "No Rig Too Big," owners Doran and Patsy Bouchard make it clear that they aim to cater to RV owners and vacationers. Full hookups are available, as are regularly scheduled events and activities, a dining room, a grocery and souvenir store, a recreation hall, rest rooms, and laundry facilities. "Our park is pet-friendly," Patsy says.

Sport Camps

Brownville

Beech Ridge Camps, 60 Beech Ridge Road, Brownville (1-800-965-8819; brcamps@kynd.com); $400–1,300 per week. The emphasis here is on bear, moose, deer, and bird hunting; the camp's owners, Wayne and

Marie McSwine, are registered Maine guides. All cabins are modernized with bathrooms, kitchens, heat, utensils, and barbecue grills; the camp is open year-round and also features a community dining room. Housebroken pets are welcome.

Danforth

Rideout's Lakeside Lodge, RR 1, Box 64, East Grand Lake, Danforth (1-800-594-5391; info@ rideouts.com; www.rideouts. com). Choose from the American plan ($75–85 per person, per day), the weekly housekeeping cabins ($265–465 per week), or the daily housekeeping cabins ($60 for two people) at this waterfront sporting resort. On-site, you'll find a dining room with lake views, a sandy beach, canoe and kayak rentals, and numerous spots to catch landlocked salmon and smallmouth bass. Well-behaved pets are welcome.

Greenville

Beaver Cove Camps, Greenville (207-695-3717; info@beaver-covecamps.com; www.beaver-covecamps.com); $75 per night for two people. From fishing season in the spring to hunting season in the fall and winter, Beaver Cove is always full of activity and bustling with visitors. The heated cabins, located on the eastern shore of Moosehead Lake, have kitchens and full baths; all linens are provided. Pet owners must pay an extra fee of $3 per night, clean up after their animals, and use a crate when leaving pets alone in the cabins.

Wilson Pond Camps, Lower Wilson Road, Greenville (207-872-8692; 207-695-2860; info@wilson-pondcamps.com; www.wilson-pondcamps.com); $550 per week. Animals are allowed at the camp's Top Secret Lodge, a secluded cabin located on Upper Wilson Pond. The cabin is accessible by boat from the main camp area, or by floatplane; it has an outhouse, refrigerator, gas lights, and a small stove. Fishermen frequent the 7-mile-long pond and neighboring streams in search of trout and salmon.

Millinocket

Katahdin Lake Wilderness Camps, Box 398, Millinocket (207-723-4050; 207-723-9867; www.katahdinlakecamps.com); $60–125 per person, per day. The name WILDERNESS CAMPS is more than accurate in this case: At Katahdin Lake, you'll find no electricity, telephones, or stores— just lots of peace and quiet. The camp caters to hunters and fishermen, along with hikers and cross-country skiers. Dogs are welcome on a leash for $10 per day, but pet owners will have to fly in to the secluded camps because dogs are not allowed on the surrounding Baxter State Park land. Owners Al and Sue Cooper offer a floatplane service.

Millinocket Lake

Libby Camps, Township 8, Range 9, Millinocket Lake (207-435-8274; matt@libbycamps. com; www.libbycamps.com); $130–260 per person, per day. Guests here stay at log cabins on Millinocket Lake, complete with home-cooked meals, daily maid service, and access to motorboats and canoes. Some packages also include seaplane flights to more remote locations. Hunting and fishing are the focus at Libby; registered Maine guides are available on-site. Dogs are welcome for an extra $10 per day.

Rockwood

Gray Ghost Camps, Route 15, Rockwood (207-534-7362; grayghostcamps@acadia.net; www.grayghostcamps.com); $75–155 per night or $450–795 per week. Guests at Gray Ghost can take full advantage of Moosehead Lake by renting a variety of boats and docking them right in front of their cabins. Though the camp was originally designed for fishermen, it has become increasingly popular with families and sight-seers. Well-behaved pets are welcome as long as their owners clean up after them.

Homes, Cottages, and Cabins for Rent

Eagle Lake

Picture Perfect Cottages, Eagle Lake (207-444-6358; 207-834-4510; briant@sjv.net; www.mainerec.com/pictureperfect cottages); $230–450 per week. Each of these three lakefront homes has a screened-in porch and access to about 100 feet of water frontage. Though they vary slightly in size, the Brown Log Cottage, Kamp Kumfort, Ash Brown Camp, and White Cottage all have two bedrooms and a bathroom, along with hot-air heating. Bedding and linens can be provided for an extra charge. Pets are welcome.

Greenville

Moosehead Hills Cabins, Lily Bay Road, Greenville (207-695-2514; info@mooseheadhills.com; www.mooseheadhills.com); $125–160 per night or $750–1,500 per week. These large log cabins have two to three bedrooms, sunset views over Moosehead Lake, decks or porches, and full baths (two with whirlpools). "We love animals and we welcome them at our cabins," says owner Sally Johnson, who is also happy to arrange skiing and snowmobiling trips, boating and fishing expeditions, and moose-viewing "safaris." Pet owners pay an additional fee of $5 per pet, per day.

Millinocket

Great Northern Cabins, 1024 Central Street, Millinocket (207-723-2105; 1-877-6-CABINS; gncabins@gnpaper.com; www.greatnorthernpaper.com); $82 per night. New and rustic, these log cabins are owned and operated by the Maine Timberlands Company on the company's Millinocket land. Each cabin accommodates six people in bunk beds, and has an outhouse, propane gas, and drainage sink. (You'll need to bring your own bedding, including a foam pad, as well as water, pots, and pans—this is essentially camping with a roof.) All pets are welcome.

Moosehead Lake

Moosehead Lake Vacation Home, Moosehead Lake (207-695-8953; outfitter@moosehead.net; www.maineoutfitter.com/house-rental); $600–900 per week. The owners of this rental are animal owners and lovers, and welcome pets at their two-bedroom, 1½-bath waterfront home. Greenville is about 15 minutes away, and a marina is within short walking distance. Renters also share a private beach and can walk to a nearby hiking trail.

Orient

Paradise Cabins, Orient (207-448-2078; copo427@hotmail.com; www.paradisecabins.net); $55 per night, $350 per week, or $1,200 per month. These two cabins are located on the Mattawamkeag River in Bancroft, an area renowned for its prime bass and trout fishing. Each nonsmoking cabin has a full kitchen, linens, stereo, and phone, and is designed to accommodate four adults. Pets are welcome at no extra charge.

Rockwood

Maine Escapes Cabin, Rockwood (207-691-1101; info@maineescapes.com); $135–165 per night. This company manages rentals throughout Maine; their Moosehead-area rental is a cabin in Rockwood that can accommodate up to six people. Dogs are welcome for an additional fee of $5 per day, provided that renters clean up after their pet inside as well as outside the cabin. Renters will also be charged for any animal-related damage to the property.

Sundown Cabins, Routes 6 and 15, Rockwood (207-534-7357; sundown@acadia.net; www.maineguide.com/moosehead/sundown); $65–115 per night or $425–675 per week. These cheery, sunny rentals, which

vary in size and style, sit along the edge of Moosehead Lake. Popular with sportsmen as well as families, the cabins accommodate two to eight-plus people and offer heat, kitchens, picture windows, cable TV, outdoor gas grills, and linens. Pets are welcome in each cottage.

Weston

First Settler's Lodge, Route 1, Weston (207-448-3000; info@firstsettlerslodge.com; www.first-settlerslodge.com); cabin and cottages, $65–75 per night or $375–475 per week. Although animals are not allowed in the lodge itself, they are permitted at three lodge-owned private rentals—one cabin and two cottages—located near the Baskahegan and Mattawamkeag Rivers. (For the most part, these are used by game hunters in the fall.) The lodge can arrange guides and trips for hunting, fishing, snowmobiling, and boating.

Rental Agencies

Mooers Realty, 69 North Street, Houlton (207-532-6573; mooersrealty@mooersrealty.com; www.mooersrealty.com). Though Mooers primarily deals in sales, the agents can also help you find short-term rental housing (usually for a month or more). Some of the homes do allow pets; you can check out the web site for the latest vacancies. The Realtor typically charges a $100 finder's fee.

Northwoods Camp Rentals, Main Street, Greenville (207-695-4623; bporter@midmaine.com; www

.mooseheadrentals.com). This agency oversees the rental of about 50 homes in the Moosehead Lake area, from basic, rustic cabins to more luxurious accommodations. Many are waterfront, and some of the owners do allow pets. The rental period is typically Saturday to Saturday, though some exceptions can be made for long weekends.

Ross Realty, Greenville Junction (207-695-2289; rossrlty@aol.com). This Realtor handles North Woods–area sales and rentals; each rental property (some on the water, some inland) differs in its pet policies, but owner-broker Avis Canders says that a few do allow animals. A security deposit is required for all accommodations at the time of reservation.

OUT AND ABOUT

Allagash Wilderness Waterway. This 92-mile-long protected area stretches along lakes, rivers, and ponds from the town of Allagash all the way down to the top of Baxter State Park. It is extremely popular with ice fishermen, hikers, and canoe campers (motorboats and personal watercraft are prohibited). The Bureau of Parks and Lands does not recommend the waterway for casual or first-time campers; facilities are primitive and remote, access to roads is limited, and visitors must be fully self-sufficient and prepared to handle emergencies on their own.

Aroostook State Park, 87 State Park Road, Presque Isle (207-768-8341). This 600-acre park was Maine's first, though it began with only 100 acres and gradually expanded to its current size. Located on the U.S. border with Canada, Aroostook's **Quaggy Jo Mountain** and **Echo Lake** are popular with Canadians and Americans alike. Visitors also take advantage of groomed cross-country and snowmobiling trails, various marked hiking trails, and bird-watching opportunities. Camping is also available (see "Accommodations—Campgrounds"). Dogs must be on a leash.

Central Aroostook Humane Society Walk-a-Thon, Presque Isle. Locals and visitors alike are welcome at this annual fundraising event, usually held in early May. Pets and their owners take a 2-mile trek to benefit the humane society, which shelters and adopts out homeless animals. For more information, write or visit the society at P.O. Box 1115, Cross Street, Presque Isle, ME 04769, or call 207-764-3441.

Eagle Lake Public Reserved Land, Eagle Lake (207-827-5936). This is a great access point for fishing, boating, or exploring 23,000 acres of the Eagle and Square Lakes area. For access, launch your boat in the town of Eagle Lake or take Route 11 to Sly Brook Road.

Fort Kent State Historic Site,
off Route 1, Fort Kent. This site's
blockhouse stands as evidence of
a 1800s conflict between Maine
and New Brunswick, Canada. The
lumbermen of each area felt enti-
tled to the valuable forests that
surrounded the St. John River, and
often invaded the other's lands to
illegally harvest trees. The border
dispute continued even after the
fort was built in 1839 as a base for
protecting and monitoring Maine
forestland. Today you can get a
peek at the blockhouse, along
with equipment and artifacts from
the volatile era.

Gero Island. More than 3,800
acres of public reserve land are
available for exploration at this
Piscataquis County island and
nearby **Chesuncook Village.** The
island is located in the middle of
Chesuncook Lake and is frequented by canoeists, fishermen,
and campers.

Island Falls Summerfest, Island
Falls. Typically held in late July
and early August, this weeklong
celebration of summer includes
fireworks, concerts, boat races,
road races, dance competitions, a
crafts fair, a parade, an auction,
antique-car shows, and more. For
the latest information, call 207-
463-3628.

Lily Bay State Park, HC 76, Lily
Bay Road, Greenville (207-695-
2700; 207-941-4014). About 9
miles north of Greenville, you'll
find this 924-acre park on the
eastern shore of **Moosehead
Lake.** Fishing, hiking, snowmobiling, boating, and cross-country
skiing are among the common

activities; camping is also available (see "Accommodations—
Campgrounds"). Moose, bear,
deer, and many species of birds
all live nearby. The cliffs of
Mount Kineo rise 800 feet over
the lake. Pet owners must clean
up after their animals.

Maine Potato Blossom Festival,
Fort Fairfield. This annual celebration is held during the third week
in July, when the local potato
fields come into bloom. Activities
typically include a parade, pag-
eants, arts and crafts, fireworks,
and (believe it or not) mashed-
potato wrestling contests.

Market Square, Houlton. This is
a cute downtown area with
shops, eateries, banks, and tree-
lined sidewalks. For tourists looking for a break from the wilderness, Houlton is a wonderfully
civilized place to wander for a
morning or afternoon. Dogs must
be on a leash, and owners must
pick up after them.

Moose Viewing. The **Greenville
area** is rumored to have the
largest population of moose in
the United States. Get some
advice from locals and set out on
your own, or ask your innkeeper
or campground manager to help
you set up a viewing "safari"
with local guides. Though hunting has traditionally been the
moose-related activity of choice
in these parts, shooting these
majestic animals with nothing
but a camera is quickly growing
in popularity.

Patten Lumbermen's Museum,
Shin Pond Road, Patten (207-528-
2650; www.lumbermensmuseum.

com). Open seasonally, this non-profit organization preserves the history of Maine's logging industry with artifacts, equipment, documented personal tales, and other exhibits. The annual **Bean Hole Day** event is held each August, featuring traditional lumbermen's fare like bean-hole beans (baked overnight in the ground), reflector-oven biscuits, and campfire coffee. Well-behaved, leashed dogs are welcome at the museum and its events.

Presque Isle Bike Path, Presque Isle. Stretching for 4 miles along the former C.R. Railroad track bed, this path starts at North Main Street and ends at Riverside Drive. Bikes, of course, are every-where, but you'll also find joggers, walkers, and parents pushing baby strollers, all out to enjoy the fresh northern Maine air.

Scraggly Lake Public Reserved Land, Scraggly Lake Road, Penobscot. Pets on a leash are welcome at this 10,000-acre tract of forest located just north of Baxter State Park. With trails, ponds, bogs, lakeshore, marshes, wetlands, and a boat launch, you won't run out of things to do. Due to its remote location, visitors are advised to arrive prepared for first-aid emergencies and to bring plenty of water and food. To access the park, take the Route 159 extension out of Shin Pond to American Thread Road.

QUICK BITES

Auntie M's, 13 Lily Bay Road, Greenville (207-695-2238). Pets are allowed to join their owners at the outdoor seating area of this family restaurant as long as they don't disturb other diners. Breakfast, lunch, and dinner are served each day, with menu items ranging from homemade soups and desserts to burgers and dogs, and daily specials are offered in addition to the regular menu.

Bishop's Store, 461 Main Street, Jackman (207-668-3231). On your way to the trail or the lake? Stop here first for take-out pizza, sandwiches made with fresh bread, other small grocery items, and a lunch counter with a full menu.

Coffin's General Store, Route 11, Portage Lake (207-435-2811). Popular with local sportsmen, this quick-stop store offers pizza and sandwiches, groceries, souvenirs, hunting and fishing licenses, and snowmobile registrations.

Kelly's Landing, Route 15, Greenville Junction (207-695-4438). Located next to the wharf, this popular restaurant has an outdoor deck and dinner-time meals such as pasta, steaks, and veal. You can order anything on the menu as take-out, including lunch sandwiches like a fish fillet, lobster roll, prime rib, grilled cheese, Reuben, and pastrami.

Mai Tai Restaurant, 449 Main Street, Presque Isle (207-764-4426). After a day of exploring, stop by Mai Tai for fresh Chinese take-out. You'll find all your favorites, including lo mein, fried rice, sesame chicken, vegetarian specialties, chow mein, dumplings, and shrimp with snow peas.

Reno's, 117 Sweden Street, Caribou (207-496-5331). You can take out anything on the menu at this family restaurant, including specialty pizzas, ham steaks, fresh seafood dinners, Italian sandwiches, lasagna, BLTs, liver and onions, salad, burgers, and fries—they even offer breakfast to go.

Rod-n-Reel Café, Pritham Avenue, Greenville (207-695-0388). With permission, well-behaved dogs are allowed on the Rod-n-Reel's outdoor deck or the lawn seating area. The restaurant, located across from Moosehead Lake, offers Ray's Famous Prime Rib dinners, burgers, baked and fried seafood, a variety of sandwiches, and a bar. The atmosphere is casual and cozy.

Village Restaurant of Fort Fairfield, 202 Main Street, Fort Fairfield (207-472-5223). This sit-down casual restaurant also does a booming take-out business, especially at lunchtime. They'll wrap anything on the menu to go, including seafood, steaks, chicken, sandwiches, chowder, fish-and-chips, lobster stew, and burgers and pizza.

York's Dairy Bar, North Road, Houlton (207-532-6079). Open seasonally, York's serves cool ice cream treats, along with burgers, fries, onion rings, and other quick meals, from its take-out window. You can relax at the outdoor tables and even walk the dog at a nearby grassy area.

HOT SPOTS FOR SPOT

Black Hill Kennel, 6 Richards Road, Caribou (207-496-3751). Cats and dogs will get TLC (and free baths) at this kennel with heated floors, 18 indoor/outdoor runs, and a separate area for felines. In addition to overnight boarding, Black Hill also recently started a doggie day care. The cost for all services is $9 a day for dogs and $5.50 a day for cats.

Home Farm Kennels, 186 Old Washburn Road, Caribou (207-498-8803). This overnight boarding facility, which started 26 years ago with the slogan "The Inn for Precious Pets," is popular with local animal owners and visitors—especially snowmobilers who are anxious to hit the trail. There are 28 indoor/outdoor runs. Fees are $8.50 per day for dogs and $5 per day for cats.

Morrills' New Directions, 5 Court Street, Houlton (1-800-368-5057). Morrills' is a natural pet-supply store offering supplements, homeopathic remedies, herbal products, and pet foods made with organic vegetables, fruits, nuts, and grains. You can order online or stop by their Court Street showroom for a look around.

Natalie Voisine Pet Sitting, 322 Katahdin Avenue, Millinocket (207-723-5722). "A lot of people are surprised to learn when they show up that dogs aren't allowed in the park," says pet-sitter Natalie Voisine, who often jumps in to save the day. For $20 per day, she'll keep an eye on your pooch in her home while you explore Baxter. "There's no time limit; people can stay out as long as they want," Natalie explains. "I just like dogs, and like to have them around." Her only restriction: She likes to talk with owners beforehand to learn about the dog's breed and temperament.

IN CASE OF EMERGENCY

Animal Hospital of Houlton, 48 Court Street, Houlton (207-532-4800).

Caribou Veterinary Clinic, 31 Herschel Street, Caribou (207-498-3873).

Greenville Veterinary Clinic, Pritham Avenue, Greenville (207-695-4408).

North Woods Animal Clinic, 153 Main Street, East Millinocket (207-746-9052).

Presque Isle Animal Hospital, 79 Mapleton Road, Presque Isle (207-764-6392)

THE HOLT POND NATURE AREA IN BRIDGTON IS A SECLUDED SPOT WITH BOARDWALKS, WOODS, AND WETLANDS.

Western Lakes and Mountains

PET-FRIENDLY RATING: 🦴 🦴 🦴 🦴

Naples, Paris, Mexico, Denmark, Peru, Sweden: The internationally named towns of the Western Lakes and Mountains region hint at its diverse travel offerings, from majestic peaks to cool river valleys. The area's lakes, ski trails, and spectacular foliage keep the tourists coming—and the innkeepers hopping—year-round. For many skiers, Sunday River is *the* downhill resort of the Northeast, and the nearby village of Bethel is its perfect companion. (The region is also home to the Sugarloaf, Saddleback, and Mount Abram resorts.) The southern Sebago Lake region, long popular with families, is full of campgrounds, activities, and lazy-day fun to keep the kids busy. And as for fishermen, they'll flock to just about any spot in this waterlogged section of the state.

With so much of the focus on the outdoors, dog owners will find plenty to see and do here with their animals. Unfortunately, despite the numerous lodging options in western Maine, dog owners have fewer accommodation choices here than in many other parts of the state. Still, the inns, motels, campgrounds, and vacation homes that do allow animals are exceptionally friendly and enthusiastic about welcoming you and your pet. They'll give your vacation a good start, and Mother Nature will deliver the rest.

ACCOMMODATIONS

Hotels, Motels, Inns, and Bed & Breakfasts

Andover

Andover Guest House, 28 South Main Street, Andover (207-392-1209; info@andoverguesthouse.com; www.andoverguesthouse); $40–55 per night. Located in a quaint historic village, the Andover Guest House is a restored 18th-century Colonial with seven guest rooms and a bunk room that can accommodate up to 10 people ($15 per person, per night). Guests can feel free to lounge in the living room, relax on the porch, or use the kitchen 24 hours a day to prepare and eat meals. Pets are welcome.

Bethel

Bethel Inn and Country Club, on the common, Bethel (207-824-2175; www.bethelinn.com); $99–209 per night. With a renowned golf course and a location right down the road from the Sunday River ski area, this hotel attracts visitors throughout the year (the prices above include greens fees). Guests can also enjoy an outdoor swimming pool, dining room and tavern, game rooms for the kids, and cross-country ski clinics. Dogs— sorry, no cats or other pets—are allowed in some rooms for an additional $10 per night.

Briar Lea Inn and Restaurant, 150 Mayville Road, Bethel (207-824-4717; 1-877-311-1299; www. briarleainnrestaurant.com); $69–132 per night. Situated just outside the village, this 150-year-old Bethel farmhouse is only a few minutes from Sunday River. The six guest rooms are decorated with antiques. "We've had really good experiences with pets here," says innkeeper Gary Brearley. "For the most part, I find that people who travel with pets take really good care of them." Animals are welcome for an extra $10 per night but cannot be left alone in the rooms.

Chapman Inn Bed & Breakfast, Bethel common, Bethel (207-824-2657; info@chapmaninn. com; www.chapmaninn.com); $55–125 per night. This antiques-filled inn is one of the oldest buildings in Bethel;

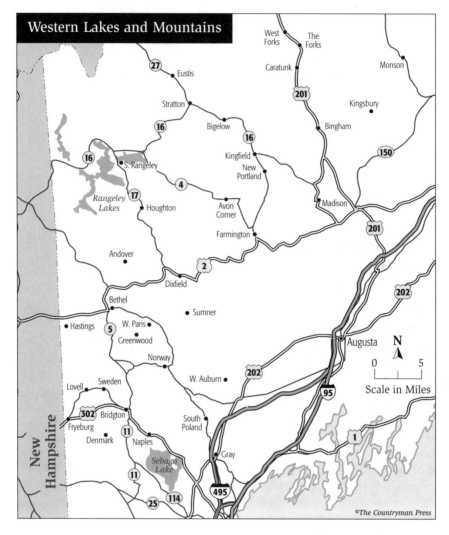

Western Lakes and Mountains

West Forks
The Forks
Caratunk
Monson
201
Kingsbury
27
Eustis
Stratton
Bingham
16
Bigelow
16
150
16
Kingfield
New Portland
S. Rangeley
16
4
Rangeley Lakes
17
Houghton
Avon Corner
Madison
Farmington
201
Andover
2
Dixfield
202
Bethel
Sumner
Hastings
5
W. Paris
Greenwood
Augusta
Norway
N
W. Auburn
202
0   5
Lovell
Sweden
Scale in Miles
Bridgton
302
95
Fryeburg
11
South Poland
Denmark
Naples
Gray
1
New Hampshire
Sebago Lake
11
495
25
114

©*The Countryman Press*

inside, you'll find sleigh beds, quilts, two saunas, and a business center. Those seeking a bargain will appreciate the on-site dorm, which offers a semi-private bunkhouse and recreation hall. Pets are welcome for an extra $10 per day, though they must be crated when left alone in the rooms.

L'Auberge Country Inn and Bistro, Mill Hill Road, Bethel (207-824-2772; 1-800-760-2774; inn@laubergecountryinn.com; www.laubergecountryinn.com); $69–139 per night. All types of pets are welcome for an extra $10 per night at L'Auberge, an 1800s inn and American-French restaurant. The resident pooch, Moses, will show your dog the ropes; the front-desk staff can help you arrange dog-walking services or even off-site horse boarding. The inn is popular with skiers looking for a little off-slope luxury.

Sudbury Inn, Main Street, Bethel (207-824-2174; 1-800-395-7837; sudbury2@thesudburyinn.com; www.thesudburyinn.com); $79–109 per night. Relax on the front porch, nap beneath your canopy bed, dine in the restaurant, or hang out in the pub at The Sudbury, as the locals call it. The inn's Main Street location is within walking distance of shops, restaurants, and a small movie theater. Pets are welcome in the carriage-house annex during the spring, summer, and fall for an extra $10 per night.

Casco
Maplewood Inn and Motel, 549 Roosevelt Trail (Route 302), Casco (207-655-5131; info@shindamen.com; www.shindamen.com); $44–63 per night. Pets are allowed in the motel section of Maplewood for an extra $10 per night for "big" dogs; the owners often cut the fee in half for smaller animals. The recently renovated rooms are simple and clean, with wall-mounted TVs and air-conditioning. The motel units look out over the outdoor swimming pool.

Farmington
Mount Blue Motel, 454 Wilton Road (Route 2), Farmington (207-778-6004); $36–65. Open year-round, this motel offers affordable accommodations near snowmobile trails and **Mount Blue State Park** (see "Out and About"). The smoking and nonsmoking rooms have air-conditioning, cable TV, and phones. Picnic tables are outside. Pets are welcome for an additional $7 per stay.

Naples
Augustus Bove House Bed & Breakfast, RR 1, Naples (207-693-6365; augbovehouse@pivot.net; www.naplesmaine.com); $59–175 per night. A dog and a cat already live at Augustus Bove, and they'll be happy to welcome your well-behaved pet to this B&B located within walking distance of shops and restaurants. Homemade breakfasts typically include pancakes, French toast, apple-walnut syrup, and other goodies; each room is individually decorated. Pets are restricted to certain rooms, so advance notice is required.

Rangeley
Terraces Housekeeping Cottages, Route 4, Rangeley (207-864-3771; 207-864-5451); $425–625 per week. These six waterfront cottages each have views of Rangeley Lake and can accommodate two to eight people (they're popular with families and fishing parties). Amenities include picnic tables with umbrellas, barbecue grills, fireplaces, boat rentals, a dock, and full kitchenettes. Pets are welcome for an additional $5 per pet, per day.

Wilhelm Reich Museum Cabins, Dodge Pond Road, Rangeley (207-864-3443; wreich@rangeley.org; www.rangeleyme.com/wilhelmreich); $400–550 per week. Two housekeeping cabins, Bunchberry and Tamarack, are available for rent at this museum and nature center commemorating the life and work of scientist Wilhelm Reich. Located on Dodge Pond, the rentals have full kitchens and bathrooms, fireplaces, living rooms, and accommodations for five to eight people. Pets are welcome.

Raymond
Crescent Lake Cottages,
7 Cottage Lane, Raymond (207-655-3393; murmgmt@maine.rr.com; www.crescentlakecottages.com); $395–495 per week. These 10 cottages sit on 8 lakefront acres; each has two bedrooms, a full bath and shower, a living room with a pullout couch, cable TV, and a screened-in porch. Guests also share a recreation hall, a beach, tennis and volleyball courts, canoes, and sailboats. Well-behaved pets are welcome with advance notice.

Northern Pines Bed & Breakfast, 31 Big Pine Road, Raymond (207-935-7579; norpines@pivot.net; www.maine.com/norpines); $95–130 per night. "We're always happy to have dogs as guests," says Northern Pines innkeeper Marlee Turner. "We charge $5 per dog, and they're free to roam the property and swim in the lake." Guests can enjoy a variety of spa services, including massage, herbal facials, and body wraps (for $60 per service), in addition to more traditional Maine vacation pursuits such as swimming, hiking, and boating.

Wind in Pines on Sebago Lake, Route 302 to Fire Lane 175, Raymond (207-655-4642; wind-in-pines@juno.com; www.wind-in-pines.com); $425–1,100 per week. This "family vacation colony" includes 11 housekeeping cottages on Sebago Lake that can accommodate two to eight people. Each cottage is unique: Many feature fireplaces, and some have screened-in porches and full kitchens. Dogs are permitted for an extra $50 per week; they must be leashed and are not allowed on the beach.

Rumford
Madison Inn, Route 2, Rumford (207-364-7973; 1-800-258-6234; innkeeper@madisoninn.com; www.madisoninn.com); $79–150 per night. This motor inn, which bills itself as Fido-Friendly, is open year-round with 60 rooms; all have air-conditioning and cable TV, and some have a full kitchen and living room/dining room area. Guests can also use the fitness center, outdoor swimming pool, restaurant and lounge, hiking trails, sauna, and game room. There's also a campground next door (see **Madison's Riverside Wilderness Campground** under "Campgrounds").

Waterford
Waterford Inne, Chadbourne Road, Waterford (207-583-4037); $90–135 per night. Set on 25 wooded acres, this historic farmhouse offers peace and quiet, flower and vegetable gardens, daily country breakfasts, and four-course dinners. Pewter, antiques, and Americana decorate the guest rooms and main living areas. Well-behaved pets are welcome for an additional $15 per night.

West Paris
Snow Falls Cabins, c/o River Restaurant, Route 96 at Snow Falls, West Paris (207-674-3800;

www.riverrestaurant.com); $45–75 per night. These seasonal cabins on the Little Androscoggin River, managed by the owners of the nearby **River Restaurant** (see "Quick Bites"), can accommodate two to four people. Each has a shower, at least one full-sized bed, and a kitchenette. Well-behaved pets on a leash are welcome; there's also an 8-by-12-foot kennel on-site for guests' use.

Wilton

Whispering Pines Motel and Gift Shop, 183 Lake Road, Wilton (207-645-3721; 1-800-626-7463; whpmotel@exploremaine.com; www.thewhisperingpines-motel.com); $60–78 per night. Pets are allowed in smoking rooms at this lakefront motel for an extra $3 per night, provided owners keep their animals off the furniture. (They'll charge a $100 cleaning fee if pet hair is found in or on the bed.) Some of the units have kitchenettes, and all guests can enjoy the playground, large backyard, and free use of canoes and rowboats.

Campgrounds

Bethel

Bethel Outdoor Adventure and Campground, 121 Mayville Road (Route 2), Bethel (207-824-4224; 1-800-533-3607; info@betheloutdooradventure.com; www.betheloutdooradventure); $14–18 per night. Located on the Androscoggin River, this campground is popular with families and pet owners who like to take canoe trips. "We can tell them about all the islands to stop at on the

way," says owner Pattie Parsons. Pets on a leash are welcome as long as their owners clean up after them; in addition, Pattie's son has started a doggie day-care business on-site (see "Hot Spots for Spot").

Brownfield

River Run Camping and Canoe Rental, Route 160, Brownfield (207-452-2500; www.riverrun-canoe.com); $5 per person, per night. This secluded 100-acre campground caters to tenters with wooded and waterfront sites as well as private beaches. River Run also specializes in canoe rentals for day trips ($21–28 per day) and provides a shuttle service to Swan's Falls, Lovewell Pond, Walker's Bridge, and other locales. Quiet dogs are welcome at no extra charge.

Shannon's Saco River Sanctuary, Route 160, Brownfield (207-452-2274; shannonscamping@hotmail.com); $22–26 per night. This waterfront campground has sites for tents and RVs alike; full hookups are available. The facilities include a camp store, a playground, a dock for fishing and boating, a recreation hall, and bathrooms with showers. Quiet, leashed dogs are welcome for an extra $5 per stay (not per night).

Woodland Acres Campground, Route 160, RFD 1, Brownfield (207-935-2529; campcanu@nxi.com; www.woodlandacres.com); $22–34 per night. For an extra $5 per day, leashed dogs are welcome to join the fun at Woodland Acres, a Saco River campground and canoe-rental service. Campers can choose from wooded or riverfront sites for tents and RVs, and take advantage of the camp store, honeywagon service, and rest rooms with hot showers. Pets cannot be left unattended.

Naples
Loon's Haven Family Campground, Route 114, Naples (207-693-6881; loonshaven@ yahoo.com; www.loonshaven. com); $24–29 per day. With three beaches on Trickey Pond and campsites for tents and RVs, Loon's Haven is especially popular with young families. You can rent rowboats and canoes at the boat ramp; fish for trout, bass, and salmon; hang out on the volleyball and basketball courts; frolic at the playground; or take part in movie nights, dances, bingo games, and other planned activities. Pets are welcome.

North Bridgton
Lakeside Pines Campground, Route 117, North Bridgton (207-647-3935; www.lakeside-pinescamping.com); $25–41 per night or $175–231 per week. This campground has 185 sites; some are set in the middle of the action and others are secluded. The shorefront is 3,500 feet long with a beach, two swimming areas, and canoe rentals. Quiet, leashed pets are welcome "for now," though they are not allowed on the beach and must be with their owners at all times.

Peru
Honey Run Beach and Campground, 456 East Shore Road, Peru (207-562-4913;

drjeff@mindspring.com); $15–25 per night. Relax on Honey Run's private beach on Worthley Pond, or explore the rest of the campground's 93 acres. The facilities include tent and RV sites, a camp store, boat rentals, rest rooms with hot showers, telephones, and laundry facilities. Pets must be vaccinated and on a leash.

Rangeley
Rangeley Lake State Park Campground, HC 32, Route 17 or Route 4, Rangeley (207-864-3858; 207-624-6080); $13 per night Maine residents; $17 per night out-of-state residents. With just 50 sites, this camping retreat located in the midst of **Rangeley Lake State Park** (see "Out and About") offers a remote outdoor experience. Still, you won't be totally on your own: The campground also has a playground, picnic area, boat launch, and bathrooms with hot showers. Leashed dogs are welcome as long as owners pick up after them.

Rumford
Madison's Riverside Wilderness Campground, Route 2, Rumford (207-364-7973; 1-800-258-6234; innkeeper@madisoninn.com; www.madisoninn.com); $15–30 per night. This campground sits on the Androscoggin River next to the **Madison Inn** (see "Hotels, Motels, Inns, and Bed & Breakfasts") and can accommodate tents, campers, and RVs. Each site has a picnic table and fire pit, and campers can also enjoy free use of canoes as well as the fitness center, pool, restaurant, and lounge at the inn. Pets on a leash are welcome.

Steep Falls
Acres of Wildlife Campground, Route 113, Steep Falls (207-675-2267; office@acresofwildlife.com; www.acresofwildlife.com); $18–36 per night. For an extra $5 per night, dogs are permitted at campsites but not in rental units or in the inn at Acres of Wildlife, a large private campground located just south of Sebago Lake. Amenities include two eateries, a country store, scheduled family activities throughout the season, boat rentals, minigolf, and a playground. Dogs must be on a leash, and owners must clean up after them. Your pooch is allowed to swim in the on-site pond but not in the lake.

Waterford
Papoose Pond, 700 Norway Road (Route 118), Waterford (207-583-4470; thepond@papoosepond-resort.com; www.papoosepond-resort.com); $34–68 per night. "We consider our facility very pet-friendly, and many of our guests return each year because of our pet policies," explains General Manager A. R. "Rocky" Cameron. Animals are allowed in many of the campsites and some of the cabins at this waterfront campground, which features a half-mile-long beach, regularly scheduled family activities and entertainment, a café, a recreation hall, and tennis and basketball courts. Pets must be on a leash and are not allowed on the beach.

Weld
Mount Blue State Park Campground, 299 Center Hill Road, Weld (207-287-3824; 1-800-332-1501); $13 per night Maine residents; $17 per night out-of-state residents. The campground at this 5,000-acre park (see "Out and About") includes 136 sites for tents and trailers, a playground, picnic tables and fire pits, a nature center, bathrooms, showers, and a boat launch. Although your pet isn't allowed on Webb Beach, he is free to wander the trails and other areas of this park as long as he's on a leash.

Sport Camps

Eustis
King and Bartlett Fish and Game Club, Route 27, Eustis (207-243-2956; info@kingand-bartlett.com; www.kingand-bartlett.com); $160–210 per person, per night or $940–1,090 per person, per week. The rates include three meals a day, a rental cabin, and use of boats and canoes. The facility includes 34,000 acres with 14 ponds and lakes, which makes it popular with fishermen and hunters (guided trips and fly-fishing instruction can also be arranged for an extra charge). Well-behaved pets are welcome as long as owners keep an eye on them.

Tim Pond Camps, Eustis (207-243-2947; 207-897-4056; info@timpondcamps.com; www.timpondcamps.com); $120 per person, per night. In addition to lodging, Tim Pond offers a fly-fishing school and guided hunting trips. The waterfront site has cabins, mountain biking and hiking trails, floatplane rides, and wildlife-watching opportunities. Three home-cooked meals per day are included in the rate. Pets are welcome.

Homes, Cottages, and Cabins for Rent

Bryant Pond

Bryant Pond Station, Bryant Pond (207-229-4059; jwellis@ loa.com); $2,995 per week. Popular with wedding parties, this large lakefront home can accommodate up to 25 people with six bedrooms and 2½ baths. It's located on Lake Christopher, about 20 minutes from Sunday River and 10 minutes from Mount Abrams. The owners charge a $25 per pet fee.

Embden

Lakeside Cottage, Embden Lake (352-481-2671; rjordan41@msn. com); $492–795 per week. A half hour's drive from Sugarloaf, this waterfront, recently renovated cottage has three bedrooms, a Jacuzzi, a barbecue grill, a kitchen, cable TV, a swimming platform and dock, and a kayak available for use. There's also a dog run in the yard; all renters, including, pet owners, pay a $200 refundable security deposit.

Greenwood

Greenwood Ski Home, Greenwood (802-384-4904; 802-773-6280; tkkc@mindspring. com); $1,000–3,500 per week. With 3,000 square feet, vaulted ceilings, flower gardens, and water views, this home offers a secluded getaway just a short drive from Sunday River and downtown Bethel. In the summer, there's also a dock, swimming, fishing, and boating to enjoy. Pets

are welcome, provided they stay out of the flower beds.

Luxury Ski Home, Greenwood (508-785-0558; 508-560-0558; lisalanser@aol.com); $900–2,300 per week. This three-story contemporary near Sunday River boasts an added extra: It's fully "baby-equipped," including a full-sized crib, changing table, baby swing, high chair, and playpen. The home also features vaulted ceilings, hardwood and tile floors, accommodations for nine people, and a private beach and dock. Dogs are welcome; there's even a dog run available for renters' use.

Norway

Secluded Lake Cabin, Norway (207-774-4950; mabrown6@juno. com); $1,000–1,200 per week. Pets are welcome at this log cabin with a large deck and frontage on a pond. (Because of the steep drop-off to the water, the owners generally don't recommend the rental to families with young children.) Inside, you'll find vaulted ceilings, knotty-pine walls, and accommodations for up to eight people. Sunday River is located about 30 minutes away. Pets are welcome as long as their owners keep an eye on them.

Oquossoc

Moose Lodge, Oquossoc (207-864-5661; mtnhse@tdstelme.net; www.etravelmaine.com/moose-lodge); $125 per night or $800–900 per week. Well-behaved animals are welcome at this waterfront cottage on Rangeley Lake. The house has cathedral ceilings, picture windows, two bedrooms and a pullout couch, a wood-stove, a TV/VCR, and a barbecue grill. The property has access to snowmobile and cross-country ski trails, and the lawn opens up to a cove for swimming and boating.

Mountain House, Oquossoc (207-864-5661; mtnhse@tdstelme. net; www.etravelmaine.com/ mountainhouse); $150 per night or $995–1,100 per week. This large three-bedroom home sits on 84 acres near Rangeley Lake. Inside, you'll find all the modern finishes; outside, the property has a large deck, trails for cross-country skiing or hiking, an Adirondack shelter with lake views, and 14-foot motorboats available for guests' use. Pets are welcome.

Peru

Brackett Properties, Worthley Pond, Peru (207-364-6035; 207-369-8084); call for rate information. Donna Brackett manages the rental of three Worthley Pond–area homes: the "cozy camp," a year-round lakefront cottage located about a half hour from three ski areas; the "waterfront home," which can accommodate up to 10 people; and the "English Tudor home," a spacious, newly built house with a fenced-in backyard. Pets are welcome in all.

Farm at Worthley Pond, Worthley Pond, Peru (1-888-367-4940; www.agate.net/~paulb/ski/ farm); $950–2,500 per week. Located in a valley and surrounded by 5 acres, this 17-room private retreat has a huge lawn, an outdoor tub and sauna, a washer and dryer, a private beach with a dock, and two full kitchens. It's a good choice for family reunions or other large gatherings: The farm can accommodate up to 23 people. Pets are welcome at no extra charge.

Phillips

Elcourt North, c/o Elcourt Bed & Breakfast, Phillips (207-639-2741; elcourt@tdstelme.net); $100 per night. This pond-front log cabin is located in Phillips, about 15 minutes from Rangeley. "Well-behaved, house-trained pets are most definitely welcome," says owner Elsie Dill, who also operates the nearby Elcourt B&B with her husband, Courtland. The cabin has a new bathroom, a living room with a TV/VCR, two bedrooms, a loft, and a full kitchen. Kayaks, canoes, and a rowboat are in the yard.

Rangeley

Hunter Cove Cabins, Hunter Cove Road, Rangeley (207-864-3383; norway@rangeley.com; www.huntercove.com); $130–190 per night or $850–1,000 per week. Located directly on Rangeley Lake, these large cabins have extras like rocking chairs, knotty-pine walls and ceilings, woodstoves, and sleeping lofts for the kids. Each cabin also has a living room/dining room area, full kitchen, screened-in porch, picnic table, and barbecue grill. Pets are welcome for an extra $10 per day, per pet.

Rangeley Lake

Rangeley Lakefront House, Rangeley Lake (207-594-5708; 207-864-3898; rwcurley@webtv. net); $850–1,100 per week. The owners of this newly built home have a golden retriever and welcome other animals to their wooded retreat for an additional $15 per pet, per night. The house accommodates four people and has air-conditioning, satellite TV, a deck, a dock and beach area, a kitchen, and a barbecue grill.

Rental Agencies

Russell's Lakeside Rentals, Main Street, Rangeley (207-864-0935; crussell@megalink.net; www.rlrentals.com). Agency owner Connie Russell manages the rental of vacation homes throughout the Rangeley Lakes area. Rates range from $450 to $1,800 per week, and many of the owners do permit animals. "I've seen an increase in requests to bring pets," Connie explains. "I have posted pet rules, and I find that telling renters what is expected eliminates 90 percent of potential problems." Check out the web site for up-to-date property listings.

Sunrise Vacation Rentals, Route 302 and Mountain Road, Bridgton (207-647-2591; 1-888-STAY-SUN; rentals@megalink. net; www.maineholiday.com). Sunrise specializes in helping visitors find short- and long-term rentals in the Shawnee Peak area. You can look at each currently available rental on the web site. At any given time, about 15 of them allow pets—sometimes more, according to agent Jennifer Regan. Rates range $875–3,500 per week, along with a refundable pet deposit of $200.

OUT AND ABOUT

Appalachian Trail. This world-famous trail begins (or ends, depending on how you look at it) in Maine, at Baxter State Park, and continues all the way down to Georgia. Dogs are allowed on the trail, except in a few designated areas like Baxter itself. Many hikers say that the Maine stretch is the most difficult; it's usually not recommended for beginners. In the western lakes and mountains region, the most popular sections are the **Bigelow Mountain Range** and, right below it, **Saddleback Mountain** to Route 4. The Appalachian Trail Conference, a nonprofit organization that founded and manages the trail, recommends that dogs be on leashes at all times.

Bald Mountain Reserve, Bald Mountain Road, Oquossoc (207-778-8231). You can boat, fish, hunt, camp, and swim at this 22,000-acre park in the Rangeley region, but by far the most popular activity is hiking. Start with the 1-mile-long summit trail, which affords fantastic views. The reserve also has miles of shoreline on ponds and lakes, and a primitive camping area (call 207-364-5155 for more information).

Bigelow Preserve, Route 27 or Long Falls Dam Road, Stratton (207-778-8231). From mayflies to moose, if it lives in Maine, you can find it at Bigelow. This expansive and remote 36,000-acre preserve encompasses 30 miles of the **Appalachian Trail** (see above listing), 20 miles of designated snowmobile trails, and the entire Bigelow mountain range, including the peaks of **Avery, Cranberry, Little Bigelow, The Horns,** and **West Peak.** Primitive camping sites are available free of charge; no reservations are necessary.

Farmington Historic District, Farmington. This area, which includes Academy, Anson, Grove, and High Streets, features many structures dating from the 1700s and makes for a nice walking

tour. It's also a stop on the 14-mile-long Jay to Farmington Trail.

Five Fields Farm, Route 107, Bridgton (207-647-2425; www. fivefieldsfarmx-cski.com); $10 all-day trail pass. Leashed pets are welcome at this 70-acre apple orchard and cross-country ski center. In the winter, you can stay on the groomed trails and logging roads or venture with snowshoes into the more deeply packed areas. In the summer, bring Fido for a day of apple picking. As a bonus, the 450-acre **Loon Echo Land Trust** sits right next door.

Grafton Notch State Park, 1941 Bear River Road, Newry (207-824-2912; 207-624-6080). Whether you're looking for a pretty picnic spot or a challenging daylong hike, Grafton Notch can

ENJOY A PICNIC, TAKE A SWIM, AND EXPLORE AT THE HEMLOCK BRIDGE IN FRYEBURG.

deliver. The site's **Screw Auger Falls** and **Mother Walker Falls** are impressive, the **Appalachian Trail** (see above listing) and the ITS 82 snowmobile trail both cross through the park. Other attractions include **Moose Cave** and **Old Speck Mountain**. Pets must be on a leash.

Hemlock Bridge, Hemlock Bridge Road, Fryeburg. This quaint covered bridge is worth a stop, especially if you're passing between northern New Hampshire and western Maine. You can walk or drive over the bridge, located in a solitary spot down a long, bumpy road off Route 302, then enjoy some privacy while you swim or picnic. (Tip: Use patience once you reach the rustic road—it's a slow 3-mile ride, but worth the effort.)

Holt Pond Nature Area, Grist Mill Road, Bridgton (207-647-8580). If you can brave the mosquitoes, this tucked-away spot is a real find. (Follow Route 107 to Fosterville Road, then watch for Grist Mill Road. The parking area is about 1 mile down on the right.) Boardwalks and trails wind through quiet wetland and forest areas, allowing for plenty of solitude and wildlife-watching opportunities.

Mahoosucs Reserve. Vehicle access: East B Hill Road, between Upton and Andover (207-778-8231). First-timers may want to start out at the trailhead on Route 26, where you'll find pit toilets, parking, brochures, and trail maps. The **Appalachian Trail** (see above listing) passes through the higher elevations of this 27,000-acre park, where the most popular attractions are **Mahoosuc Notch** and **Cataracts Gorge.**

Maine Nordic Ski Council, P.O. Box 645, Bethel (1-800-SKI-XCME; www.mnsc.com). Though the ski council happens to be located in Bethel, this organization is a wonderful source of information for cross-country skiers no matter which region you're visiting. They're also savvy about pet-friendly accommodations and trails; check out their web site for the latest updated information.

Mount Blue State Park, 299 Center Hill Road, Weld (207-585-2347; 207-585-2261). This park is a hiker's paradise with three peaks—**Bald, Blueberry,** and **Mount Blue**—and countless trails to choose from. First-timers should check out the 1½-mile-long main trail, which reaches to the summit. Don't be surprised to see other dogs, horses, bikers, and snowmobile riders. Pets are welcome on a leash, though they are not allowed on Webb Beach. (See "Accommodations—Campgrounds" for information about camping at Mount Blue.)

Moxie Falls, The Forks. There isn't a much better spot for a picnic: With a dramatic 60-foot drop, Moxie Falls is the largest single-drop waterfall in New England. To reach the falls, take Route 15 out of Shirley Village for about 12 miles (the road eventually turns to dirt). Turn left at Moxie Lake, then take the first right. You'll see the sign and parking area on the right.

Nine Lives Thrift Shop, Route 302, Fryeburg (207-935-4358; www.harvesthills.org). All proceeds from sales of furniture, clothing, housewares, and antiques at this shop benefit its next-door neighbor, the **Harvest Hills Animal Shelter.** Since opening in 1992, the nonprofit organization has helped more than 9,000 homeless pets find shelter and new homes each year.

Rangeley Lake State Park, HC 32, Route 17 or Route 4, Rangeley (207-864-3858; 207-624-6080). Fishermen flock to Rangeley Lake for the salmon, though even without a rod and reel you can have a good time exploring the 869 acres of this secluded park. Visitors will find a picnic area and boat launch, as well as a snowmobile trail that connects to the groomed ITS 89 trail. Dog owners must use a leash and clean up after their animals; pets are also welcome at the park campground (see "Accommodations—Campgrounds").

Range Pond State Park, Empire Road, Poland Spring (207-998-4104; 207-624-6080). Located off Empire Road, this 750-acre park has a picnic area, a beach, a boat launch, a playground, a baseball field, and miles of hiking trails. The area is popular with boaters, and canoeists, kayakers, and sailborders frequently bob in the lake. As with other state parks, dogs are not allowed on the beach, but they are permitted in other park areas with a leash.

River's Edge Sports, Route 4, Oquossoc (207-864-5582). Say hello to the in-store pup, Dixie, when you stop by here to rent a canoe or kayak (guides are also available if you'd like some help navigating the nearby Rangeley, Cupsuptic, Mooselookmeguntic, and Richardson Lakes). The shop is located right next to a public boat launch.

Sebago Lake State Park, 11 Park Access Road, Casco (207-693-6613; 207-693-6231). The 1,400 acres of this popular waterfront park are spread throughout the towns of Casco and Naples. The big attraction here is the beach, but pet owners will have to enjoy the other diversions because dogs aren't allowed on the sand (or at the on-site campground). Luckily, there are also plenty of wooded trails for hiking, biking, and cross-country skiing.

Sunday River Farm Loop, Cross Country Ski Center, 23 Skiway Road, Newry (207-824-2410). Skiers throughout New England know and love Sunday River, a huge resort that anchors the popular ski town of Bethel. Though pets, as you might expect, are not the focus at Sunday River, the cross-country center does have one trail, the Farm Loop— aka The Poop Loop—where canines can join their owners on a 1-kilometer Nordic trek.

White's Marina, 93 Lake Road (Route 117), Norway (207-743-5586; www.whitesmarina.com). Pets of all kinds are welcome at this marina offering canoes, paddleboats, and other craft for rent, along with a store, gasoline facility, and service department. One caveat: The resident cat, Boris, is not a dog fan, so be sure to give the Whites (marina owners and animal lovers) some advance notice if you plan to bring a canine.

QUICK BITES

Café DiCocoa and **DiCocoa's Marketplace/Bakery,** 119 and 125 Main Street, Bethel (207-824-JAVA; www.cafedicocoa.com). Located next door to each other, these Bethel eateries each offer a delicious break for dog lovers. Pets are welcome at the front-porch seating at the café, which serves up ethnic specialties, salads, desserts, dinners, and weekend brunches. Doggie water bowls are plentiful at the bakery, which also has outdoor seating—it's a relaxing spot to enjoy fruit smoothies, sugary treats, coffee, and espresso.

Center Lovell Market and Deli, Route 5, Center Lovell (207-925-1051). This packed shop has everything you might need for a picnic (indoor or outdoor), including chips, fried chicken, beer, sandwiches, pizza, bottled water, and, of course, dog biscuits.

Java House, Lower Main Street, Bethel (207-824-0562). Pets are welcome at the small outdoor deck at Java House, a café serving breakfast, wraps, soups, chowders, sandwiches, and fresh-roasted coffee in downtown Bethel. They're open seven days a week until midafternoon.

Ken's Kove, Route 302, Bridgton (207-647-3867). The focus here is on seafood, and you can get all of Ken's dinners, plates, and sandwiches to go. The restaurant is open year-round; seasonally, you'll find a few picnic tables out front.

Loon's Nest, West Lovell Road, Lovell (207-925-3000). Located at Kezar Lake Marina, this casual restaurant has two outdoor decks in addition to its indoor dining room. Choose from pizza, lobster, chowder, and other dishes.

Pine Tree Frosty, 55 Main Street, Rangeley (207-864-5894). Grab a cool Gifford's Famous Ice Cream cone or a hot lobster roll, french fries, or fish sandwich and savor your treats overlooking Haley Pond.

Red Onion Restaurant, Center Main Street, Rangeley (207-864-5022). Everything on the menu here is available for take-out, including fresh-dough pizzas, pasta dishes, steaks, soups, chowders, and sandwiches. The Red Onion staff cater to large groups, vegetarians, and kids.

River Restaurant, Route 96 at Snow Falls, West Paris (207-674-3800; www.riverrestaurant.com). Well-behaved pets can join their owners on the deck for lunch or dinner at this waterfront eatery.

Executive Chef Paul Cornish makes all the dishes from scratch, including beef and bean chili, the River Crab Cake Sandwich, scallop fettuccine, and chicken Marsala.

Ruby Food, 78 Main Street, Bridgton (207-647-8890). Take out all your Chinese food favorites at this popular Bridgton stop and bring the hot cartons back to your cabin, hotel room, or RV.

HOT SPOTS FOR SPOT

Bethel Outdoor Adventure and Campground—Pet Care,
121 Mayville Road (Route 2), Bethel (207-824-4224; 1-800-533-3607; info@betheloutdoor-adventure.com; www.bethel-outdooradventure). The Parsons family owns this busy campground (see "Accommodations—Campgrounds"), and their son, Charles, has also started a pet day-care business for visitors who want to attend a conference, canoe, shop, or enjoy a meal in a nice restaurant. He charges $5 per pet, per day.

Bridgton Veterinary Hospital,
Route 117, Bridgton (207-647-8944). Boarding, grooming, and doggie day care are all available at this veterinary office. "The dogs are walked at least twice daily on our grounds," explains staff veterinarian Gary Wheeler, D.V.M. "We have medical rounds three times daily, and we include the boarding animals in our observations."

Companion Creatures Pet Shop, 179 Broadway, Farmington (207-778-6863). You'll find pet food, bowls, leashes, toys, and treats at this animal-focused Farmington

stop, along with harder-to-find items such as dog seat belts, grooming supplies, pet-care books, and travel crates.

Doggy and Kitty Motel,
596 West Bethel Road, West Bethel (207-836-3647). Reservations are required at this popular ski-town kennel that offers overnight accommodations ($13 per night for dogs, $9 per night for cats) as well as day care ($1 per hour). Cats have kitty condos, and dogs have heated/air-conditioned indoor kennels with 15-foot outdoor runs. The owners also match up friendly dogs in a recreation area for a little group playtime.

House of Stillwater Pet Grooming and Styling,
957 Farmington Fall Road (Routes 2/27), Farmington (207-778-3388). Two retired schoolteachers and certified master groomers recently opened this shop specializing in "tailored styling" for all breeds of dogs. They also have boarding facilities and offer a pet taxi service from local B&Bs and hotels. The owners breed Stillwater Dobermans and hope to open a grooming school in the near future.

Kaylish-Kartel Kennels,
107 Libby Road, Mechanic Falls
(207-345-3258; www.brittany-
dog.com). In addition to raising
champion Brittany spaniels,
owner Karen Thorne also runs a
doggy day-care and boarding
facility with 20 heated and air-
conditioned runs. "Lots of people
like to go skiing and leave their
dog, so we usually offer winter
specials," Karen says. "Plus, we
live right here, so it's easy to
keep an eye on them." The daily
rate is $11.

Lazy L Kennel, 188 Scribner Hill
Road, Oxford (207-539-9188). Pets
get lots of individual attention at
this small, family-run facility that
can accommodate dogs and cats
for overnight stays. There are 12
heated and air-conditioned runs,

and a separate cat area, along
with a play area where dogs can
frolic together. The boarding fee is
$11 per night for dogs and $8 per
night for cats.

Little Jungle, 384 Main Street,
Norway (207-743-0356). In addition to the traditional pet-shop
accessories, medicines, and
foods for dogs, cats, reptiles,
fish, and birds, the Little Jungle
also has a cat rescue center and
a doggie deli.

Mexico Pet Shop, 95 Main Street,
Mexico (207-364-8528). This full-
line store carries all the popular
brands of dog food, including
Iams, Eukanuba, Science Diet,
and Agway brands, in addition to
toys, treats, and supplies for all
types of companion animals.

IN CASE OF EMERGENCY

Bethel Animal Hospital,
179 Walkers Mill Road, Bethel (207-824-2212).

Bridgton Veterinary Hospital,
Route 117, Bridgton (207-647-8944).

Countryside Veterinary Hospital,
1035 Route 2, Rumford (207-369-9969).

Farmington Veterinary Clinic,
246 High Street, Farmington (207-778-2061).

Fryeburg Veterinary Hospital,
41 Bridgton Road, Fryeburg (207-935-2244).

Naples Veterinary Clinic,
Route 302 and Lamb Mill Road, Naples (207-693-3135).

THE WALKING TRAILS AT THORNCRAG BIRD SANCTUARY IN LEWISTON WIND THROUGH
OPEN FIELDS AND DEEP WOODS.

Central Lakes and Cities

PET-FRIENDLY RATING:

This region is literally the heart of its state, from the capital city of
Augusta and other busy urban centers to colleges and universities
like Bates, Bowdoin, Colby, the University of Maine, and the University
of Southern Maine. In many ways, it is a more diverse region than the
others around it, attracting a wide variety of business travelers, vacationers, students, culture vultures, and sportsmen.

You'll find a museum around every corner here, along with vast lakes,
snowmobile trails, and cheery public parks. Chain hotels outnumber their
independent brethren, especially in the cities. Still, a decent number of
small campgrounds, motels, and B&Bs welcome guests—and their dogs—
to explore the outer reaches of this somewhat overlooked section of
Vacationland. While other travelers are crowding along Maine's seacoast
or flocking to the western mountains, you and your four-legged friend can
fish the lake by day and check out the cosmopolitan scene by night.

ACCOMMODATIONS

Hotels, Motels, Inns, and Bed & Breakfasts

Augusta
Holiday Inn Augusta—Civic Center, 110 Community Drive, Augusta (207-622-4751; lsearcy@ fine-hotels.com; www.sixcontinen-thotels.com/holiday-inn); $75–125 per night. Located a few minutes from the Augusta State Airport, this two-story Holiday Inn has 102 guest rooms, a restaurant and lounge, air-conditioning, and pho-tocopying and fax services. It's a popular resting place for visitors to the Civic Center, the University of Maine at Augusta, the capitol building, and Maine General Hospital. Pets are welcome with at no extra charge.

Motel 6, 18 Edison Drive, Augusta (207-622-000) $26–49 per night. All Motel 6s allow pets with advance notice; these are simple, convenient lodgings that are pretty much the same at each location. Smoking and nonsmok-ing rooms are available, as are laundry facilities, air-condition-ing, color TVs, and phones.

Travelodge Augusta, 390 Western Avenue, Augusta (207-622-6371; www.travelodge-augusta.com); $69–89 per night. This hotel features an on-site Mexican restaurant, a swimming pool, extended-stay rooms with refrigerators and microwaves, a rental-car desk, free continental breakfasts, laundry facilities, and 128 recently renovated rooms. Pets are welcome, and their own-ers might be especially interested in the property's picnic tables and barbecue grills.

Bangor
Best Inn of Bangor, 570 Main Street, Bangor (207-942-1234; www.bestinn.com); $64–99 per night. Guests with pets get a kick out of a sign hanging in this hotel's lobby: "We've never had a dog who smoked in bed and set fire to the blankets . . . who stole the towels . . . who played the TV too loud . . . So, if your dog can vouch for you, you're welcome, too!" The rooms here are clean and comfortable, with cable TV, alarm clocks, data ports, irons and ironing boards, and free newspapers. There are no extra fees for pets.

Best Western White House Inn, 155 Littlefield Avenue, Bangor (207-862-3737); $49–89 per night. This family-owned hotel sits on 40 acres of fields and woods. Some of the rooms have fireplaces; all have king- or queen-sized beds, TVs with remote controls, in-room hair dryers and ironing boards, and refrigerators. Amenities also include a sauna, laundry facili-ties, free continental breakfasts, and a Hall of Presidents display. Pets are welcome.

Comfort Inn, 750 Hogan Road, Bangor (1-800-338-9966; comfort @midmaine.com; www.placesto-stay.com/bangor-comfortinn); $50–99 per night. For an extra $6 per night, your pet can accom-pany you at this hotel located

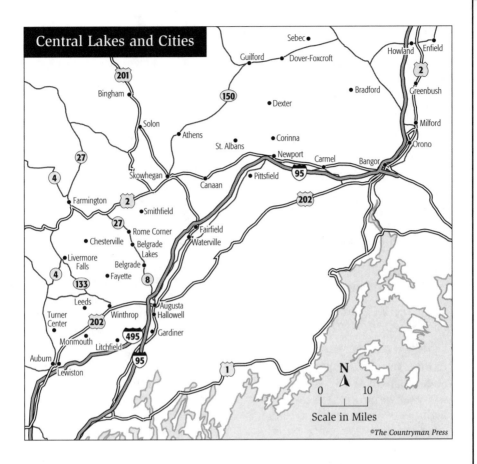

Central Lakes and Cities

©The Countryman Press

just down the road from the Bangor Mall. Guests enjoy free continental breakfasts, a fitness center, an outdoor swimming pool, free daily newspapers, a video arcade, and in-room coffee-makers and hair dryers.

Days Inn Bangor, 250 Odlin Road, Bangor (1-800-835-4667; daysinn@midmaine.com; www. placestostay.com/bangor-days inn); $50–62 per night. An indoor pool and Jacuzzi, a video arcade, cable TV with Nintendo, photocopying and fax services, and free continental breakfasts are some of the amenities at this Days Inn located around the cor-

ner from Bangor International Airport (free shuttles are also available). Pets are welcome for an additional $6 per stay.

Econo Lodge Bangor, 327 Odlin Road, Bangor (1-800-393-0111; econo@midmaine.com; www. placestostay.com/bangor-econo-lodge); $30–80 per night. Guests at this Econo Lodge have access to laundry facilities, cable TV, Nintendo, nonsmoking rooms, free coffee around the clock, and photocopying and fax services. The Bangor Mall is 5 miles away, movie theaters are just across the street, and Blackbeard's Family Fun Park is next door. Pets are welcome.

Holiday Inn Bangor—Civic Center, 500 Main Street, Bangor (207-947-8651; 1-800-799-8651; www.holiday-inn.com/bangor-civic); $49–99 per night. This modern facility welcomes pets, as long as their owners use "common sense" in terms of cleaning up after their animals, not leaving them alone in rooms, and other considerations. "Yes, we once had a guest bring a full-sized show horse into a pool-side suite," says Director of Sales Paul Hilchey-Chandler. The hotel has an on-site restaurant and lounge, laundry facilities, and fitness center.

Motel 6, 1100 Hammond Street, Bangor (207-947-6921). (See listing under Augusta.)

Ranger Inn, 1476 Hammond Street, Bangor (1-888-NITE-NITE; www.rangerinn.com); $25–55 per night. Pets are welcome in about 20 of the inn's 89 rooms: "It is more costly to clean the pet rooms, but we find there are so few places that allow pets that we are providing a much-needed service," explains owner Joel Ranger. All rooms have TVs and phones; smoking and nonsmoking rooms and free coffee and ice are available.

Riverside Inn, 495 State Street, Bangor (207-973-4100; 1-800-252-4044; www.riversidebangor.org); $74–108 per night. This hotel has an interesting history; owned by Eastern Maine Healthcare Systems, it once served as a nurses' residence for the nearby hospital owned by the same company. The building was converted into an inn about 20 years

ago, but it still primarily caters to hospital-related guests during the week and tourists on weekends. Pets are welcome for an extra $5 per night.

Sheraton Four Points, 308 Godfrey Boulevard, Bangor (207-947-6721); $99–139 per night. It doesn't get much more convenient than this: The Four Points is connected to the Bangor International Airport via an enclosed skyway. The full-service hotel offers room service, an on-site restaurant and lounge, a 24-hour front desk, a fitness center, a game room, and an outdoor swimming pool. Pets are welcome for an additional $15 per day.

Travelodge Bangor, 482 Odlin Road, Bangor (207-942-6301; 1-800-214-2152); $69–89 per night. Children under 10 stay free at this Travelodge (formerly known as the **Budget Inn of Bangor**). You can get complimentary coffee 24 hours a day in the lobby, and all the rooms have air-conditioning, cable TV with HBO, coffeemakers, hair dryers, and alarm clocks. Pets are welcome.

Belgrade

Yeaton Farm Inn Bed & Breakfast, 422 West Road, Belgrade (207-495-7766; connie@ maineloons.com; www.maine-loons.com/yeaton); $135 per night. Forty acres surround this vintage B&B with private baths and period furnishings. Innkeeper Connie Parker serves a full country breakfast each day. Pets are welcome with advance notice for an extra $8 per night, and Connie keeps them well fed, too, with

Science Diet and Friskies cat and dog food, dishes of warm milk, and bowls of water.

Bingham

Gateway Recreation and Lodging, Route 201, Bingham (1-800-440-0053; gateway@gwi.net; www.gateway-rec.com); $75–90 per night or $400–500 per week. Each of these seven housekeeping cabins can accommodate six to eight people; four of them have kitchens, and all are located directly on the Kennebec River. Gateway guides can lead guests on hunting, fishing, whitewater rafting, snowmobiling, and canoeing trips. "Well-mannered" pets are welcome.

East Winthrop

Lakeside Motel and Cabins, P.O. Box 236, Route 202, East Winship (1-800-532-6892; lakeside@ctel.net; www.lakeside-lodging.com); $69–89 per night. "We understand that pets are part of the family, and a lot of people wouldn't leave them home any more than they would leave their children," says Sheree Wess, who owns Lakeside with her husband, Andy. The motel and cabins sit next to the Lakeside Marina, where families can rent a variety of boats for fishing or cruising (canoes are free to guests). There are no extra fees for pets.

Leeds

Angell Cove Cottages, Bishop Hill Road, Leeds (207-524-5041; angellcove@ctel.net; www.angellcovecottages.com); $795 per week. Located under towering pine trees on the shores of Androscoggin Lake, each of these recently built housekeeping cottages has a screened-in porch, a kitchen, two bedrooms, a living room with a foldout couch, and water views. Each is individually decorated with its own Maine wildlife theme, and linens are provided. Pets are always welcome.

Lewiston

Motel 6, 516 Pleasant Street, Lewiston (207-782-6558); $26–49 per night (See listing under Augusta.)

Newport

Pray's Motel, Main Street (Route 2), Newport (207-368-5258; 207-368-4636); $34–48 per night. House-trained pets are welcome at this conveniently located motel in Newport, about halfway between Bangor and Waterville and near large Sebasticook Lake. All rental units have a living room, bedroom, full bathroom, and kitchenette, along with cable TV and complimentary coffee. Dogs can enjoy romping in the large backyard.

Orono

Best Western Black Bear Inn, 4 Godfrey Drive, Orono (207-866-7120); $59–85 per night. Convenient to the University of Maine, the Black Bear Inn offers king- and queen-sized beds; free continental breakfasts; cable TV; and in-room hair dryers, ironing boards, and alarm clocks. The hotel's conference space can accommodate up to 300 people. Pets are allowed but cannot be left alone in rooms.

University Inn Academic Suites,

5 College Avenue, Orono (207-866-4921; 1-800-321-4921); $48–69 per night. Formerly known as the **University Motor Inn,** this motel is located on the Stillwater River and right next to University of Maine. The 48 rooms are air-conditioned and have cable TV; outside, you'll find a swimming pool and nearby bike trails. Downtown Orono is within walking distance. Pets are welcome as long as they are not left unattended.

Skowhegan
Kyes Motel and Resort, Route 2, Skowhegan (207-474-3384; 1-800-981-1355; kyesmotel@ skow.net; www.kyesmotel.com); $42–78 per night. Located on 14 acres along the Kennebec River, Kyes Motel offers motel rooms, cottages, and cabins. Guests can enjoy an events pavilion, canoeing, hiking and walking trails, group barbecues, lawn sports, and a swimming pool. "Most" pets are gladly welcomed (call to see if yours qualifies).

South China
Lakes Region Motel, 163 Route 3, South China (207-445-2411); $39–59 per night. The owners of this one-level motel leave part of the back lawn unmowed to provide an exploration spot for canine guests; there are no extra fees for pets. The standard rooms rent on a per night basis, while the efficiencies and one-bedroom apartments typically rent by the month. The motel has a convenient location near the highway.

Waterville
Best Western Waterville Inn, 356 Main Street, Waterville (207-873-3335); $45–89 per night. The 86 rooms at this two-story hotel have cable TV with remote control, alarm clocks, irons and ironing boards, hair dryers, and coffeemakers. An outdoor pool and hot tub are surrounded by lounge chairs, and there's also a family restaurant on-site. All types of pets are welcome.

Budget Host Airport Inn, 400 Kennedy Memorial Drive, Waterville (207-873-3366; 1-800-87-MAINE; budget@mint.net; www.members.mint.net/budget); $38–109 per night. Pets are welcome in the Budget Host's 45 rooms for an extra $10 per stay (not per night). Outside, you'll find a large lawn area with plenty of room to run around; inside, there are typical chain-style hotel rooms; a 24-hour front desk serving complimentary coffee, tea, and hot chocolate; and data ports in each room.

Campgrounds

Dover-Foxcroft
Peaks-Kenny State Park Campground, 500 State Park Road, Dover-Foxcroft (207-564-2003; 207-941-4014); $13 per night Maine residents; $17 per night out-of-state residents. The 56 sites at this park campground are fairly secluded. Campers have access to bathrooms with showers, a picnic area, tele-

phones, scheduled family programs in the amphitheater, and hiking trails. Pets are not allowed at the beach.

Hermon
Pleasant Hill RV Park and Campground, 45 Mansell Road, Hermon (207-848-5127; info@ pleasanthillcampground.com; www.pleasanthillcampground. com); $17–31 per night or $102–186 per week. Located just outside Bangor, Pleasant Hill caters to RVers (though it does have some tent sites) with paved roads, room for even the largest rig, fire pits and picnic tables, a recreation hall, a camp store, two playgrounds, basketball and volleyball courts, and a fishing pond stocked with trout. Leashed pets are welcome for an extra $10 per night.

Pumpkin Patch RV Resort, 149 Billings Road, Hermon (207-848-2231; 1-866-644-2267; rvoffice@pumpkinpatch.com); $22 per night, $132 per week, or $430 per month. This RV camp offers free hot showers, laundry facilities, an events pavilion, picnic tables, ice and fax machines, clean rest rooms, and plenty of room for large rigs. Most pets are welcome on a leash; the first pet is free, and any additional animals are $2 per night. Pit bulls and rottweilers are not allowed.

Mount Vernon
Five Seasons Family Resort, 156 Five Seasons Road, Mount Vernon (207-685-9141; resort@ 5seasonsfamilyresort.com; www. 5seasonsfamilyresort.com); $24–28 per night. Pets are welcome in the campground section of this resort but not at the inn. Campers at the 135 sites (some waterfront) enjoy a private beach, a recreation hall, a camp store, rest rooms, and hot showers.

Newport
Christie's Campground and Cabins, 83 Christie's Camp Road, Newport (207-368-4645; campsites, $14–21 per night; cabins, $300–375 per week. This year-round campground along the shores of Sebasticook Lake has sites for tents and RVs, as well as winterized cabins. Many guests enjoy fishing for perch, pickerel, and smallmouth bass; for the kids, there's also swimming, boating, a playground, basketball and volleyball courts, a video arcade, and potluck suppers. Pets are welcome.

Stetson
Stetson Shores Campground, Route 143, Stetson (207-296-2041; stetson@gwi.net; www. campmaine.com/stetson); $20–25 per day or $120–150 per week. The tent and RV sites at Stetson Shores are located on 32 wooded and lakefront acres. Amenities include laundry facilities; flush toilets; hot showers; a camp store; a boat launch; and canoe, kayak, and paddleboat rentals. Pet owners are welcome to bring their furry friends as long as they keep them on a leash and clean up after them.

Sport Camps

Belgrade

Whisperwood Lodge and Cottages, Taylor Woods Road, Belgrade (207-465-3983; info@ whisperwoodlodge.com; www. whisperwoodlodge.com); $35–80 per person, per day; $238–539 per person, per week. Guests here stay under the American plan (the rates include lodging and three meals a day). Located at the southern tip of Salmon Lake, Whisperwood's focus is on fishing and boating (though the lodge maintains a strict catch-and-release policy due to dwindling populations). Dog owners are asked to keep their pets on a leash and off the furniture.

Smithfield

Sunset Camps, Route 8 and Route 137, North Pond, Smithfield (207-362-2611; sunset-ca@tdstelme.net; www.sunset-camps.com); $350 per week. Pets are allowed in the cabins (but not cottages) at this family-friendly sporting camp located about 15 minutes from Waterville. Docking areas service fishermen heading out onto North Pond, and some of the cabins are heated year-round for hunters, skiers, and snowmobilers. The facility also offers a private beach, snack bar, and game room.

Solon

Breezy Acres Camps and Guide Service, Drury Road, Solon (207-643-2920; breezy1@tdstelme.net; www.breezyacrescamps.com); $25 per person, per day. Yogi the Newfoundland will be on hand to welcome you and your pets to this year-round sport vacation camp. Each cabin sleeps six people and has a full kitchen, a TV and radio, outdoor fire pits, and linens. Guides are available to lead campers on hunting and fishing trips. Animals are welcome, provided they stay off the furniture.

Homes, Cottages, and Cabins for Rent

Kents Hill

Cornerstone Cottage, RR 3, Kents Hill (207-897-5485; eric@megalink.net; www.cornerstonecottage.com); $120 per night. *Cottage* is definitely a misnomer in this case: Cornerstone is a full-sized, luxurious house, complete with country furnishings, knotty-pine walls and bedposts, handmade quilts, three bedrooms and two sleeping lofts, a large deck, a screened-in porch, skylights, and an organic garden with vegetables and fresh eggs. Guests are also free to use the canoe and two kayaks. At the time of this writing, owner Eric Ellis also planned to start renting another nearby home, **Barn Loft Cottage,** for $100 per night.

Orrington

Loon Hollow Getaway Cottages, 22 Loon Hollow, Orrington (207-825-3128; loonhollow@aol.com; www.loonhollow.com); $550–1,450 per week. It's all in the gingerbread details at these lovingly maintained cottages: The Well House, the smallest of the three, has window bays, skylights, a sleeping loft, and a kitchenette; the Victorian Jewel sleeps nine and sits directly on the water; and the Honeymoon Cottage has a separate Ping-Pong room, two bedrooms, a full kitchen, and a sleeping loft. Pets are welcome in the off-season with prior approval from the owners, though they should not be tied up on-site and cannot be left alone in the cottages.

Sebec

Northern Farm, Sebec. Contact Jayne Lello, 651 North Road, Sebec (207-564-7740; jayne-lello@hotmail.com; www.dover-foxcroft.com/vacationrental); $600 per week. An 1800s farmhouse, Northern Farm is surrounded by 200 acres of woods and fields. You won't have to worry about linens, cookware, room to roam, or privacy—all are provided, and then some. The house is close to the Moosehead Lake area as well as Maine's central cities and attractions. Much of the interior has been recently remodeled. Pets are welcome as long as they don't bother the resident deer and other wildlife.

OUT AND ABOUT

Capital Park, Augusta. This picturesque 34-acre plot, located between the State House and the Kennebec River in Augusta, has served many functions in its nearly 200-year history as a public park: It was used as a soldier's camp during the Civil War, leased for farming purposes after that, and once was crisscrossed by a busy railroad track. Today, the park serves as a peaceful place to walk, jog, relax, and admire the State House dome and the river. Dogs must be on a leash.

Fort Halifax, Route 201, Winslow. A reconstructed building now stands in place of the original Fort Halifax, America's oldest blockhouse, which was nearly wiped out during a 1987 flood. The original structure was built in 1754 by Massachusetts and Maine residents who feared attacks from French troops and Native Americans. Despite the flood, parts of the historic blockhouse remain intact. The site is located about 1 mile south of the Winslow–Waterville bridge. Dogs must be on a leash.

French's Mountain and **Blueberry Hill,** Rome. The Belgrade Lakes region has many beautiful mountain trails, but French's Mountain has the best views of scenic **Long Pond.** To reach the trail, follow Route 27 north out of Belgrade Lakes Village. Drive for about 1.2 miles and turn left onto Watson Pond Road. Or, if you'd rather not hike to the views, you can drive there: Blueberry Hill lookout is also on Watson Pond Road, and you won't even have to get out of your car to see vistas of Long Pond and **Great Pond.**

Historic Lewiston. Lewiston's Historic Preservation Board publishes a self-guided tour book designed to help you navigate your way around more than 120 of the city's noteworthy historic places. The guide includes information on buildings such as the **Healy Asylum** (c. 1892), the **Church in the Triangle** (c. 1903), the **Empire Theater** (c. 1903), the **J. L. Hayes Store** (c. 1880), and the **Art Deco Block** (c. 1929), to name just a few. For more information, call 207-784-2951.

Kennebec "Whatever" Family Festival, Augusta. For 18 days in early summer, Augusta bustles with fun and activities for kids and adults, locals and visitors. Events vary from year to year but typically include talent shows, fireworks, barbecues, crafts fairs, puppet-theater shows, sing-alongs, trolley rides, road races, golf tournaments, face painting, hot-air balloon rides, and more. For up-to-date information, call the Kennebec Valley Chamber of Commerce at 207-623-4559 or visit www.augustamaine.com.

Lake George Regional Park, Canaan and Skowhegan (207-474-0708). This 275-acre park is managed by a nonprofit organization and offers a boat launch, forested area, and trails for hiking and cross-country skiing. Pets are allowed from September 15 through May 15 in the park proper, but you can hike the **East Side Trail System** year-round. Take Route 2 for about a mile out of Canaan Village toward Skowhegan; you can park at the second boat launch, where you'll also find the trailhead.

Peaks-Kenny State Park, 500 State Park Road (Route 153), Dover-Foxcroft (207-564-2003; 207-941-4014). This 839-acre park is largely uncrowded (compared to other state parks) and offers miles of hiking trails. Dogs on a leash are welcome everywhere except the beach. There's also a family campground on-site (see "Accommodations—Campgrounds").

Pine Tree State Arboretum, Hospital Street and Piggery Road, Augusta (207-621-0031). This 200-acre preserve is home to hundreds of cultivated trees, shrubs, and other plants. The arboretum is designed to educate the public and advance horticultural science, but it's also just a beautiful place to wander and enjoy in all seasons. Dogs on a leash are welcome, provided that their owners clean up after them.

Thorncrag Bird Sanctuary, Highland Spring Road and Montello Street, Lewiston (207-782-5238). This 310-acre nature preserve has sunny open fields, wooded trails, and plenty of opportunities for bird-watching, cross-country skiing, exploring, picnicking, and hiking. You can use the main entrance or an unmarked entrance and parking area at the end of East Street. Dogs are welcome on a leash.

Two-Cent Bridge, Front Street, Waterville. This free-swinging bridge has earned a spot on the National Register of Historic Places as the last-known toll footbridge in the country. It was built in 1901 to allow pedestrians to travel between Waterville and a paper mill in Winslow.

Window-Shopping in Hallowell. From clothing boutiques to flower, gift, and clock shops, downtown Hallowell has much to offer meanderers on a lazy afternoon. Antiques dealers crowd Water Street, in particular; and Park, Water, and North Streets all have plenty to peer at—and eat. Check out **Dana's Hot Dogs** (under the umbrella) and the unique gifts at **Cushnoc Trader.**

QUICK BITES

Bagel Central, 33 Central Street, Bangor (207-947-1654). With outdoor seating, take-out service, and even a dog tie-out area out front, this sandwich shop is popular with canine lovers. Menu items include bagel and deli sandwiches, pastries, and soups.

Brown Bag of Brewer, 272 State Street, Twin City Plaza, Brewer (207-989-9980). As the name suggests, this convenient eatery offers a big selection of take-out items, including Reubens, roasted turkey sandwiches, egg salad, baked goods, soups and chowders, and breakfast foods.

Butterfield's Ice Cream, 136 West Main Street, Dover-Foxcroft (207-564-2513). Walk up to the window and choose from 31 homemade, creamy, cool flavors in a cone, sundae, or shake. If you're in the mood for something hot, you can also get burgers, hot dogs, fries, and other fast-food items to go.

C&H Country Store, 288 West River Road, Waterville (207-872-2541). This quaint stop has a full deli with lots of take-out sandwiches to choose from. There's also an outdoor deck with a few tables.

Grand Central Café, Railroad Square, Waterville (207-872-9135). In addition to its indoor dining room, this brick-oven pizzeria also has an outside seating area where well-behaved pets are often allowed to sit quietly with their owners. Menu items include gourmet specialty pizzas, brick-oven quesadillas, and hot and cold sandwiches.

Granite City Grinders, 272 Water Street, Hallowell (207-622-4088). From breakfast to dessert, this riverfront eatery offers a lot more than its name implies. You can order a pizza, bagel sandwich, wrap, or grinder to enjoy at the picnic tables overlooking the Kennebec River. Dog owners, keep an eye out: You may just find some doggie treats at the take-out window.

Luiggi's, 63 Sabattus Street, Lewiston (207-782-0701). Everything on the menu at this casual

Italian restaurant is also available for take-out, including pizza, spaghetti, lasagna, sandwiches, french fries, and chicken wings.

Moose Alley Inn, Route 201, Bingham (207-672-2055). Though the main attractions here are indoors (including pool tables, a dance floor, and a bar), Moose Alley also has a small outdoor seating area with umbrellas. The menu includes bar-and-grill fare such as steaks, sandwiches, and burgers.

Old Mill Pub Restaurant, 39 Water Street, Skowhegan (207-474-6627). This cozy eatery is located in a historic mill building beside the Kennebec River. Though dogs aren't allowed on the outdoor deck, you can order any item on the menu as take-out—including lobster rolls, club sandwiches, and pub burgers—and eat at one of the nearby benches along the river.

Sam's Italian Foods, Lewiston and Auburn. You can grab a sandwich or pizza to go at any of Sam's area locations: 268 Main Street, 902 Lisbon Street, and 963 Sabattus Street in **Lewiston;** and 229 Center Street and the Taylor Brook Mall in **Auburn.**

Simones' Hot Dog Stand, 99 Chestnut Street, Lewiston (207-782-8431). In the summer, you can usually find one or two outdoor tables here, or you can order Simones' dogs, chili, burgers, salads, sandwiches, and soups to go.

HOT SPOTS FOR SPOT

Animal Crackers Pet Supply Company, 204 Hammond Street, Bangor (207-990-3232). Pet owners can browse grooming supplies; toys for dogs, cats, birds, and small animals; crates; collars; and premium dog and cat foods at this cozy shop. "We have everything," says owner Joel Gottlieb. "It's a very small store, but it's filled right to the ceiling."

Family Pet Center, 245 Center Street, Auburn (207-783-6061). This family-owned shop offers a full line of pet supplies, including food and accessories for dogs, cats, fresh- and saltwater fish, rodents, reptiles, and birds. If you run out of anything while you're on the road, take heart that you should be able to find it here.

Furry Friends and You Boutique, 1795 Hallowell Road, Litchfield (207-268-7297). Pets are welcome inside this gift shop catering to animal lovers; humans can check out the selection of doormats, hand towels, T-shirts, mugs, and other pet-related merchandise while canines enjoy the store's handmade doggie treats.

Groom N' Board Kennels,
1412 Essex Street, Bangor (207-941-9825). Overnight boarding, grooming, and doggie day care are all available at this Bangor facility. Dogs are walked twice a day, and cats can enjoy a new feline room with a large picture window. Day care is $10 per day; overnight boarding is $12 per night for dogs and $7 per night for cats.

Manchester Pet Care,
1014 Western Avenue, Manchester (207-623-4976). Manager Betsy Barker gives the pets in her charge lots of personal attention at this boarding and doggie day-care facility. "It's really important to me that the animals don't get stressed out while they're here," she says. Dogs and cats alike enjoy aromatherapy, meditation, CDs, and TLC for short- and long-term stays: The rates are $10.50–12.50 per day for dogs, and $9 per day for cats.

Second Home Kennel, Wing Road, Hermon (207-848-2606). Owner Shirley Murden welcomes dogs and cats to this small boarding facility. The 20 dog runs each have a 4-by-6-foot interior and a 4-by-10-foot exterior area; in addition, each dog gets to run around three to four times each day in the 50-by-60-foot fenced-in yard. Cats have their own separate boarding area. Shirley charges $8 per day for dogs and $5 a day for cats.

IN CASE OF EMERGENCY

Animal Emergency Clinic,
37 Strawberry Avenue, Lewiston (207-777-1110).

Auburn Animal Hospital,
864 Center Street, Auburn (207-782-4466).

Penobscot Veterinary Hospital,
411 Davis Road, Bangor (207-947-6783).

Pine Tree Veterinary Hospital,
220 Western Avenue, Augusta (207-622-6181).

Winthrop Veterinary Hospital,
1942 Route 202, Winthrop (207-377-2520).

Index